King Edward III

MICHAEL PACKE

King Edward III

Edited by
L. C. B. SEAMAN

ROUTLEDGE & KEGAN PAUL
London, Boston, Melbourne
and Henley

First published in 1983
by Routledge & Kegan Paul Ltd
39 Store Street, London WC1E 7DD,
9 Park Street, Boston, Mass. 02108, USA,
296 Beaconsfield Parade, Middle Park,
Melbourne, 3206, Australia, and
Broadway House, Newtown Road,
Henley-on-Thames, Oxon RG9 1EN
Set in 10 on 12pt Sabon by
Rowland Phototypesetting Ltd, Bury St Edmunds, Suffolk
and printed in Great Britain by
St Edmundsbury Press, Bury St Edmunds, Suffolk

Library of Congress Cataloging in Publication Data

Packe, Michael St. John.
King Edward III.

Bibliography: p.
Includes index.
1. Edward III, King of England, 1312–1377.
2. Great Britain – History – Edward III, 1327–1377.
3. Great Britain – Kings and rulers – Biography.
I. Seaman, L. C. B. (Lewis Charles Bernard)
II. Title
DA233.P33   1982   942.03'7'0924 [B]   82-13227

ISBN 0-7100-9024-2

CONTENTS

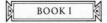

INTRODUCTORY
NOTE

At the time of his death, Michael Packe had completed the typescript of Books I and II and all but the last few pages of Book III. Book IV existed only in the form of a brief synopsis and a collection of notes. My task therefore was to put the final editorial touches to Books I, II and III and, on the basis of Michael Packe's notes, to write Book IV in a way that would, as far as possible, accord with his intentions as I understood them and be in harmony with his general view of his subject. The result, I hope, is a work not unlike that which, had he lived, Michael Packe would himself have completed.

L. C. B. Seaman

PREFACE

King Edward III ruled for fifty years. Under his genial splendour, the fractious wilderness inherited from his murdered father became transformed into an English nation. It was a reign outstandingly rich in dramatic events and sometimes violent in its contrasts. There were spectacular feats of war at Sluys, Crécy and Poitiers, as well as at Nájera beyond the Pyrenees. They made the king and his eldest son, the Black Prince, into figures of legend. Yet the brightly coloured pageantry of the chivalric king and his sons and loyal captains has to be set against the horrors and miseries of the Black Death. Similarly, if less sensationally, the king founded his new Order of the Garter for the benefit of a select group of those whom he and future monarchs might delight to honour just when the humble Commons were repeatedly demanding that he show a quite new respect for their own, less exalted persons and in particular for their pockets. It was an age of indefatigably statesmanlike bishops but of mounting hostility to the church, a time when Wyclif was preaching anti-clerical heresies, and devout laymen, such as the Lollards, putting them into practice more or less independently. And in his own person, Edward, after his years of effulgent glory with the admired Queen Philippa at his side, presented at the last the contrasting spectacle of a once great warrior enfeebled in his mind and dominated by a greedy mistress.

Yet though we know more than we did about Edward's times, we seem still to know little of his strengths and weaknesses as a man. He remains something of a pasteboard figure. Since Victorian days no large-scale personal study has appeared, and the standard work is still that of Dr Joshua Barnes, printed in 1688. Monumental though it is, it is obviously outdated. It is time for a reappraisal. This book seeks to fill the gap for the general reader.

L. C. B. S.

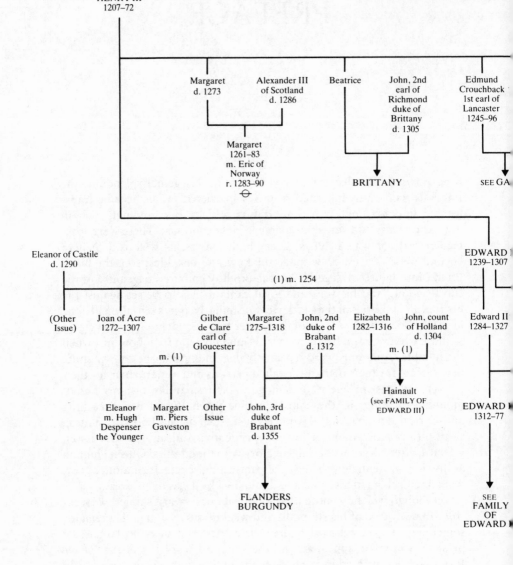

HENRY III
1207–72

Margaret
d. 1273

Alexander III
of Scotland
d. 1286

Beatrice

John, 2nd
earl of
Richmond
duke of
Brittany
d. 1305

Edmund
Crouchback
1st earl of
Lancaster
1245–96

Margaret
1261–83
m. Eric of
Norway
r. 1283–90
⊖

BRITTANY

SEE GA

Eleanor of Castile
d. 1290

EDWARD
1239–1307

(1) m. 1254

(Other
Issue)

Joan of Acre
1272–1307

Gilbert
de Clare
earl of
Gloucester

Margaret
1275–1318

John, 2nd
duke of
Brabant
d. 1312

Elizabeth
1282–1316

John, count
of Holland
d. 1304

Edward II
1284–1327

m. (1)

m. (1)

Eleanor
m. Hugh
Despenser
the Younger

Margaret
m. Piers
Gaveston

Other
Issue

John, 3rd
duke of
Brabant
d. 1355

Hainault
(see FAMILY OF
EDWARD III)

EDWARD
1312–77

FLANDERS
BURGUNDY

SEE
FAMILY
OF
EDWARD

1   Ancestry and family connections of Edward III

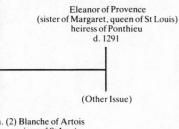

Eleanor of Provence
(sister of Margaret, queen of St Louis)
heiress of Ponthieu
d. 1291

(Other Issue)

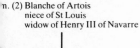

m. (2) Blanche of Artois
niece of St Louis
widow of Henry III of Navarre

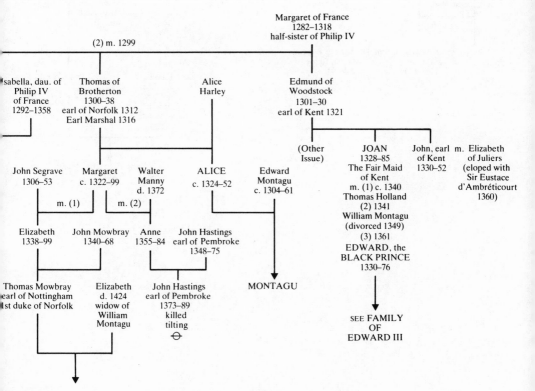

Margaret of France
1282–1318
half-sister of Philip IV

(2) m. 1299

Isabella, dau. of
Philip IV
of France
1292–1358

Thomas of
Brotherton
1300–38
earl of Norfolk 1312
Earl Marshal 1316

Alice
Harley

Edmund of
Woodstock
1301–30
earl of Kent 1321

John Segrave
1306–53

Margaret
c. 1322–99

Walter
Manny
d. 1372

ALICE
c. 1324–52

Edward
Montagu
c. 1304–61

(Other
Issue)

JOAN
1328–85
The Fair Maid
of Kent
m. (1) c. 1340
Thomas Holland
(2) 1341
William Montagu
(divorced 1349)
(3) 1361
EDWARD, the
BLACK PRINCE
1330–76

John, earl
of Kent
1330–52

m. Elizabeth
of Juliers
(eloped with
Sir Eustace
d'Ambréticourt
1360)

m. (1)   m. (2)

Elizabeth
1338–99

John Mowbray
1340–68

Anne
1355–84

John Hastings
earl of Pembroke
1348–75

Thomas Mowbray
earl of Nottingham
1st duke of Norfolk

Elizabeth
d. 1424
widow of
William
Montagu

John Hastings
earl of Pembroke
1373–89
killed
tilting
⊖

MONTAGU

SEE FAMILY
OF
EDWARD III

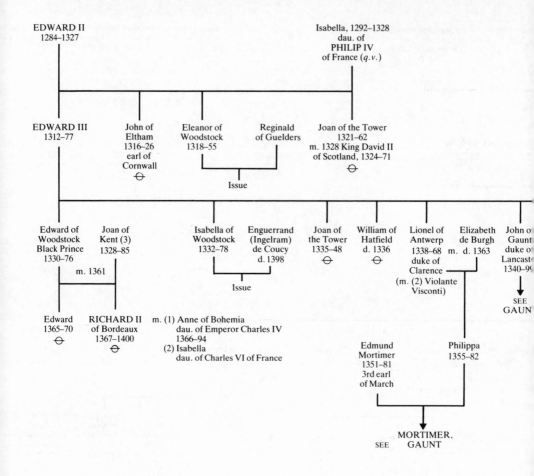

EDWARD II
1284–1327

Isabella, 1292–1328
dau. of
PHILIP IV
of France (*q.v.*)

EDWARD III
1312–77

John of
Eltham
1316–26
earl of
Cornwall
⊖

Eleanor of
Woodstock
1318–55

Reginald
of Guelders

Joan of the Tower
1321–62
m. 1328 King David II
of Scotland, 1324–71
⊖

Issue

Edward of
Woodstock
Black Prince
1330–76

Joan of
Kent (3)
1328–85

m. 1361

Isabella of
Woodstock
1332–78

Enguerrand
(Ingelram)
de Coucy
d. 1398

Joan of
the Tower
1335–48
⊖

William of
Hatfield
d. 1336
⊖

Lionel of
Antwerp
1338–68
duke of
Clarence
(m. (2) Violante
Visconti)

Elizabeth
de Burgh
m. d. 1363

John of
Gaunt
duke of
Lancaster
1340–99

SEE
GAUNT

Issue

Edward
1365–70
⊖

RICHARD II
of Bordeaux
1367–1400
⊖

m. (1) Anne of Bohemia
dau. of Emperor Charles IV
1366–94
(2) Isabella
dau. of Charles VI of France

Edmund
Mortimer
1351–81
3rd earl
of March

Philippa
1355–82

SEE

MORTIMER,
GAUNT

2   Family of Edward III and Philippa of Hainault

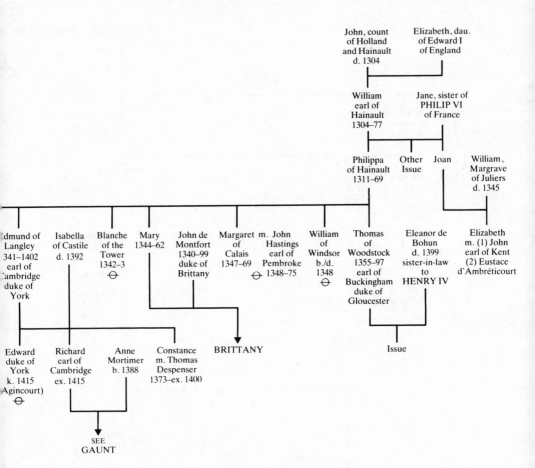

John, count of Holland and Hainault d. 1304 — Elizabeth, dau. of Edward I of England

William earl of Hainault 1304–77 — Jane, sister of PHILIP VI of France

Philippa of Hainault 1311–69 | Other Issue | Joan | William, Margrave of Juliers d. 1345

Edmund of Langley 1341–1402 earl of Cambridge duke of York ⊖

Isabella of Castile d. 1392

Blanche of the Tower 1342–3 ⊖

Mary 1344–62

John de Montfort 1340–99 duke of Brittany

Margaret of Calais 1347–69 ⊖ m. John Hastings earl of Pembroke 1348–75

William of Windsor b./d. 1348 ⊖

Thomas of Woodstock 1355–97 earl of Buckingham duke of Gloucester

Eleanor de Bohun d. 1399 sister-in-law to HENRY IV

Elizabeth m. (1) John earl of Kent (2) Eustace d'Ambréticourt

Edward duke of York k. 1415 (Agincourt) ⊖

Richard earl of Cambridge ex. 1415

Anne Mortimer b. 1388

Constance m. Thomas Despenser 1373–ex. 1400

BRITTANY

Issue

SEE GAUNT

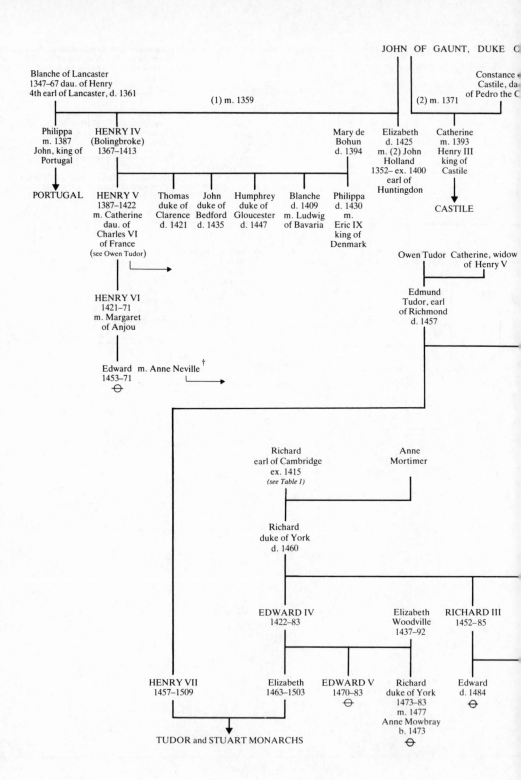

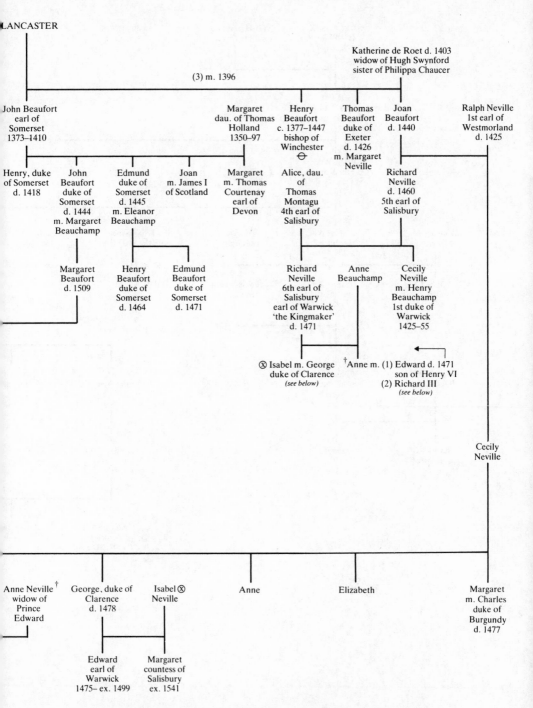

3   Descendants of John of Gaunt, fourth son of Edward III

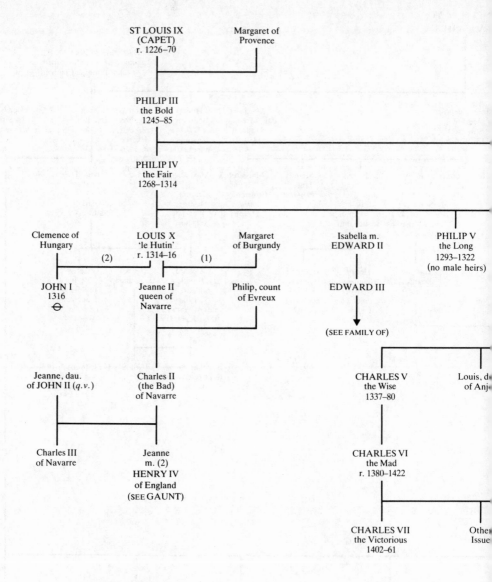

4 Capet and Valois kings of France, 1226–1422

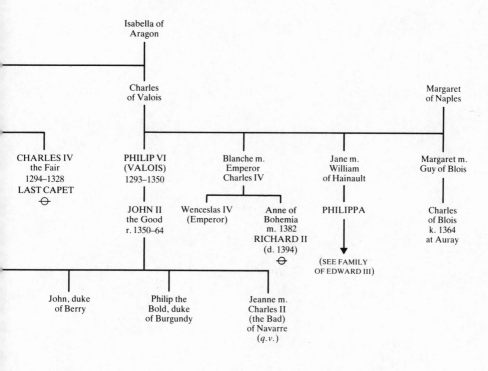

Isabella of
Aragon

Charles
of Valois

Margaret
of Naples

CHARLES IV
the Fair
1294–1328
LAST CAPET
⊖

PHILIP VI
(VALOIS)
1293–1350

Blanche m.
Emperor
Charles IV

Jane m.
William
of Hainault

Margaret m.
Guy of Blois

JOHN II
the Good
r. 1350–64

Wenceslas IV
(Emperor)

Anne of
Bohemia
m. 1382
RICHARD II
(d. 1394)
⊖

PHILIPPA

Charles
of Blois
k. 1364
at Auray

(SEE FAMILY
OF EDWARD III)

John, duke
of Berry

Philip the
Bold, duke
of Burgundy

Jeanne m.
Charles II
(the Bad)
of Navarre
(*q.v.*)

Isabella
of Bavaria

Isabella
m. (1) 1396
RICHARD II
of England
⊖

THE BATTERED HERITAGE

'Do this,' seith he; 'Al redy, sire,' seith she
O blisful ordre of wedlock precious.
The Merchant's Tale, 1346/7

THE BATTERED HERITAGE

Edward of Windsor, the prince who was to become King Edward III, was born in Windsor castle at twenty minutes to six on the morning of Monday, 13 November 1312. It was two days after the feast of Martinmas, when, by custom, the autumn-killed beef was served up in mountainous joints, accompanied by the first wines of the new vintage, just arrived from Gascony, and miraculously fermented by St Martin. St Martin was famous for having divided his cloak with a beggar, and certain charitable rites were observed at the feast, to keep the point in suitable remembrance.

On the Thursday the child was christened, by a papal legate who happened to be in England for the purpose of resolving a bitter quarrel between the new prince's father and his barons, in the chapel of St Edward, built by Henry III. Louis, count of Evreux, half-brother to the king of France and uncle to Queen Isabella, the prince's mother, was one of his eight godfathers. The French contingent requested that he be given the name of Philip, after Philip the Fair, his mother's father and their reigning monarch. But the preponderant English preferred that he should be called Edward, like his father and his grandfather before him.

A few days afterwards, the king his father created his first-born infant earl of Chester. For their service during her lying-in, the queen's valet, John Launge, and his wife, Isabel, were granted a handsome pension of £24 a year out of the farm of London. According to Thomas Walsingham, chronicler of St Albans, the news of the birth was received with great rejoicing by the people.

Thus far, out of regard for astrological influences, the facts were noted with care in the contemporary records. But, that duty done, the spring of information dried, and little more is heard of the royal child for the next thirteen years. His history during that formative period was incorporate with the fortunes of his parents, by whom both he and the condition of the kingdom he would one day rule were fashioned. It was a disastrous interval. They were vivid personalities, and their married life so stormy that they could hardly have avoided an historical tragedy from the pen of

Shakespeare, had they not, by his day, already received it from his predecessor Marlowe.

* * *

The new prince's father, Edward of Caernarvon, misfit son of the formidable Edward I, Longshanks, had become heir to the throne unexpectedly a few months after his birth when the last of his three brothers died. Left motherless when he was six on the death of the Spanish queen Eleanor of Castile, his youth was spent in the seclusion of her country manor of King's Langley. He grew up 'faire of body and grate of strength', the more handsome for having reverted from his father's dark hair to the auburn of the earlier Plantagenets. But he set his lion's strength to unsuitable pursuits. Instead of cultivating the manners and techniques of knighthood, he liked rowing about the quiet waters of the river Gade, and swimming, not then considered a proper exercise for princes. He went digging and thatching on the estate, building walls and hammering at the anvil. He hobnobbed with grooms and ploughmen, and had altogether too much of the common touch.

He had many unruly companions in his household, among them Piers de Gaveston, whom the king had made a royal ward to honour the memory of his father, a trusted Gascon knight. With Gaveston, the prince frequented taverns, wenched, diced and played pitch and toss (his father had always spent his infrequent leisure hours at chess, played elegantly with jasper and crystal chessmen), and borrowed money from the servants to pay his debts. No one could get through money quicker than Edward of Caernarvon. He gave away anything to his friends on impulse, and he dressed not merely grandly, but in *outré* fashions, splashed with gems.

He was a fine horseman, and liked hunting, which was as it should be. His huntsman, William Twici, wrote *Le Art de Vénerie*, the earliest handbook of the chase; his windings of the horn, *Trout, tro ro rot*, and rallying cries of *illoeques! illoloco!* (since shortened to Yoicks!) have come echoing down the centuries. Prince Edward studied form, and breeding. He bought up a famous stud from the earl de Warenne, who was in financial difficulty. He borrowed a stallion from the archbishop of Canterbury, and begged for his sister's bitch to mate with his beautiful white greyhound. He kept a pack, as he himself described them, 'of bandy-legged harriers from Wales who can well catch a hare, if they find it asleep'. But here again, his fondness for animals, in itself no unroyal predilection, could not stop short of excess. He kept a camel in his stables. And when he went on his progresses, he expected to be attended by a cartload of Genoese fiddlers, and a lion on a silver chain.

His intellect was well up to average. Far from ill-read, he is said to have borrowed (and failed to return) lives of St Anselm and St Thomas from the monks of Canterbury. It is thought that he wrote poetry. His unusual pastimes gave him a grasp of sciences such as architecture and ship-building uncommon in a prince. He loved minstrelsy and music. He pioneered a new stringed instrument lately discovered during the wars in Wales, the *crwth*. He raised a private orchestra, asked the abbot of Shrewsbury to lend him his expert fiddler, and dunned 'our very dear clerk', Walter Reynolds, the Keeper of his Wardrobe, for trumpets for his 'little players', and kettledrums for 'Francekin our nakerer'. He dabbled before his time in interludes, or plays, regarded then as a sure sign of perdition.

His flair for theatre was perhaps the key to his personality. Walter Reynolds, the shrewd son of a Windsor tradesman, worked his way up to the archbishopric of Canterbury by flattering this propensity, and not the least of Gaveston's attractions for the prince was his gift for mimicking the nobles. At a great banquet in Westminster Hall, the most magnificent, it is said, since Arthur was crowned at Caerleon, held both to celebrate the knighting of his heir and a huge crowd of his contemporaries, and to speed their departure for the war in Scotland, the king his father condescended to the prince's whims. Among two hundred instrumentalists assembled from many noble households and directed by no fewer than five Kings of Minstrels, his 'little players' were allowed to take their part; while the command performers included stars as famous as the unforgettable Matilda Makejoye, and Pearl in the Egg. Two of the young knights were trampled to death in the excitement.

The old king did his best with his unpromising successor. He presented him in Parliament, and made him write hundreds of official letters. On going abroad he left him, aged only thirteen, as regent to quell a near rebellion of the barons. He took him on campaign. He made him earl of Chester and first prince of newly subdued Wales; and on his coming of age he invested him as duke of Aquitaine.

It was all in vain. Like many sons of illustrious fathers, their physical resemblance apart, the prince seemed to travesty his father's qualities. His father's courage took the form, in him, of mawkish obstinacy; his steadfastness, of passionate loyalty to unworthy friends; his searing anger, of peevishness. For Edward Longshanks had a violent temper, balanced by an even more devastating righteousness. Having quarrelled, for instance, with his daughter Elizabeth over her wilfulness about her marriage, he had felt bound, on cooling off, to make it up with her by paying 'for a great ruby and a great emerald, bought to set in a certain coronet of the Countess of Holland, the King's daughter, in place of two stones which were lost when the King threw the coronet in the fire'.

Clashes with his son were inevitable. One giddy June the prince and Piers Gaveston were caught poaching in the woods of Bishop Walter Langton, the royal Treasurer, and instead of apologizing, rudely insulted him. The pair were separated, the prince's allowance was docked, and for months he had to follow the court as a distant penitent until rescued by his sister Joan, who lent him her seal as a means of raising credit, and by the intervention of his young stepmother, Margaret of France.

Some ten years after the death of Queen Eleanor, whose funeral journey from Nottinghamshire to Westminster King Edward had marked, in his grief, by twelve stone crosses, he had sealed his peace with Philip the Fair of France by marrying Philip's half-sister. Margaret was then seventeen; Edward Longshanks was sixty, but vigorous, and she quickly bore him two more sons, Thomas of Brotherton (1300) and Edmund of Woodstock (1301). If the charming carving of her in Winchelsea church is anything of a likeness, Margaret was a rare ornament of mediaeval royalty. Bountiful, she founded the great church of the Grey Friars north of St Paul's, where later she was buried. Thereafter for two centuries it was the most fashionable church in London, until Henry VIII despoiled it. Forty-three years younger than her lord the king, she was only two years older than the prince her stepson. She was better able to understand his foibles, and her discreet intercession for him was successful.

But not for long. Next year the Scots, still unsubdued after repeated batterings, responded violently to the capture and savage execution of William Wallace. Robert Bruce, whose claim to the throne King Edward, as arbitrator, had set aside in favour of his pensioner John Baliol, produced from its hiding place the royal banner of Scotland and had himself crowned at Scone upon a makeshift throne, since the Stone of Destiny had been carried off to London.

After the feast in Westminster Hall, where vows of Bruce's extirpation had been sworn, the newly knighted Prince of Wales led an army to the North, followed by the old king, in a dull rage, riding in a litter. Worsted, Bruce vanished into the mists and heather, but his brothers were caught, hanged and disembowelled. His half-English wife, who had warned him sadly that they were but King and Queen of the May, was consigned to an English convent. Bruce's sister Mary and his mistress, Isabel, countess of Buchan, who, as a Macduff, had unwisely fulfilled her historic duty by crowning him, were rigged up in latticed cages on the castle walls at Roxburgh and Berwick, and remained there for years for all to see.

At Carlisle, during the winter lull, the prince, thinking himself now fully back in favour, suggested giving his inheritance from his mother, the county of Ponthieu, on the Somme about Abbeville, to Gaveston. His infuriated father seized him by the hair and tore it out in tufts. Gaveston was banished from the land. The offending prince fled southward. When Bruce reappeared like a Jack o' Lantern in the spring of 1307, the king once more climbed painfully into the saddle; but before he could reach the Border, he was dead.

* * *

A king of England in the fourteenth century had to face a constant three-fold threat: the designs of the kings of France upon his remaining French duchy of Aquitaine; the security of his domestic borders, especially against the Scots; and the pretensions of over-mighty vassals who, combined, could field a greater power than his own. A conjunction of any two (and a revival of the 'Auld Alliance' between the French and the Scots was always probable) was dangerous. A conjunction of all three was deadly.

Edward I had abated all three dangers for his lifetime, though they would all recur. Aquitaine was quiet, and relations with France were fair, balanced on an uneasy equipoise of rival royal interests. Wales, and for the time being Scotland, had been subdued. He had stood no nonsense from his barons. He had brought the earldoms under his control by dictated family marriages, regardless of whether the parties inclined to them or not. The rudiments of parliamentary government had become established, he had defined the law of the land, and had governed through an army of administrative clerks overseen by capable if acquisitive churchmen. The harsh old man had inspired more awe than love. Many were ready to welcome his hopeful successor, news of whose eccentricities had not yet leaked out, and who was thought of as well-schooled to his task. All the same, Edward Longshanks, destroyer of de Montfort in the Barons' War, hero of Acre (where, the story goes, Queen Eleanor sucked poison from his wound, though sceptics say she had to be taken fussing from his tent), Hammer of the Scots, the great lawgiver, had left a mighty legend to live up to. Significantly, his son was often improperly styled not, as he should have been, 'King Edward after the Conquest second', but more evocatively, 'Edward, son of King Edward'. His father's shadow dwarfed him still.

If Edward of Caernarvon saw the challenge, he did not attempt to take it up. He did not obey his father's dying command that his boiled bones should be carried at the head of the avenging army into Scotland. Instead, having fortified the unprofitable Border, he carried the august remains south for burial at Westminster, where they were kept in readiness for the auspicious day, now indefinitely postponed, and rewaxed every second year until the end of the Plantagenet dynasty nearly a century later. He sent his father's unobliging Treasurer, Bishop Langton, former cause of his disfavour, to the Tower, and replaced him by the pliant Walter Reynolds. He recalled the banished Gaveston, carved out from the royal estates a new earldom of Cornwall for him, and married him above his station to his niece Margaret, of the great house of Clare. On going abroad he left Gaveston in charge of the realm, to the scandal of all, especially of his powerful cousin Thomas, earl of Lancaster, who saw himself as High Steward of England, and natural chief adviser to the king.

In one field only, that of France, the new king continued his father's policy. When in his settlement with Philip the Fair Edward I had agreed to marry Margaret of France, he had further arranged that, for double assurance, his son should marry the French king's daughter Isabella. Nothing had happened since, because Isabella was too young. Infant betrothals were common enough, but the church would not normally countenance marriage before the age of twelve for girls and fourteen for boys, the latitude in the case of girls being justified, in canonical theory, on the ungallant grounds that 'ill weeds grow apace'. Isabella was now nearly sixteen and marriageable.

The peace, and therefore the marriage, were still to the benefit of both kingdoms. The kings of France, originally no more than counts of Paris, had not yet gained full control over their great feudatories. Of these, the kings of England, lords of their heritage in Aquitaine,[1] and the counts of Flanders at the opposite extremity of the country, now caused the most concern; particularly Flanders, whose burghers, revolting against France's meddling, had recently shattered her mail-clad knights before Courtrai. The two doubtful appanages had strong commercial interests. The cloth-weavers of Flanders depended as much upon English wool as did the king and the people of England upon the sale to them of what was their 'soveraine marchandise'. Philip did not wish to see an alliance between them. Conversely, England was an inconsiderable country compared to France. In view of the troubles in Scotland, and the uncertain temper of his barons, Edward II, who had no aspirations as a warrior, had no desire to provoke his powerful neighbour.

During the Christmas festivities following his accession, Edward went over to claim his French princess. Dutifully, he performed his liege homage to her father for his fiefs of Aquitaine and Ponthieu, a formality much insisted on by the French kings whenever either of the thrones changed hands, in order to keep the idea of vassalage alive, and equally evaded if possible by the kings of England, who preferred to think of their dominion in France as absolute. He married Isabella at Boulogne in the presence of King Philip and her family, and carried her off to England.

It was a solemn moment for young Isabella, as she lay tossed about in the little bark on the wintry sea, though probably it was not too great a wrench, since the two kingdoms did not regard themselves as foreign to each other. They spoke the same language, shared the same culture, observed the same manners, and more or less obeyed the same Vicar of Holy Church. In fact, to the English, the wild Scots were more alien than the French. Twice yearly, wine fleets of Bordeaux braved the Atlantic in and out of English ports. Merchants, pilgrims, priests, embassies, heralds, minstrels, outlaws, students going between Oxford and Paris, plied the waters of the Channel at the set fare of sixpence a head or two shillings for each horseman. Knights would cross the sea merely to attend a tournament. Kings had gone together, and might still go again, on crusade against the Paynim or the Moors in Granada. Royalty was a family connection, and high-born retinues moved freely between the palaces, bringing gifts and gossip and cousinly interest. Isabella had, in her aunt Margaret, still young though now Queen Dowager, a well-accepted ally at the English court. And the boisterous man who was now her husband seemed affable enough, if distant; he behaved as though he had mentally added her to his large list of sisters. At Dover he left her, to inspect the damage the ship had suffered on the voyage, and displayed his shipwright's skill in giving orders for its repair.

Isabella, by nature self-possessed, bore her part composedly in the joint coronation ceremony, when the oath for the first time was taken in French, instead of Latin, perhaps for her benefit, and during the long banquet afterwards. She watched with a cool eye as Gaveston, decked out like a peacock in a suit of royal purple strewn with pearls, paraded the sacred sword and crown before the king, and she heard the disapproving murmurs of the magnates and the people. Whatever she made of it, she was sharp to notice and quick to complain when the wedding presents brought from France were given to the favourite. Her royal uncles, who had come to see her settled in, cut short their stay and indignantly reported to the king her father. To appease them all, Edward gave her the county of Ponthieu as her generous marriage portion, and thereafter she showed no resentment of her catamitic rival.

The barons took to arms over Gaveston, and there followed four years of virtual civil war, wherein Edward was alternately forced to accept or able to elude Ordinances giving control of his government and household, his choice of ministers, his finances, even his own movements, to a commission of Lords Ordainers. Gaveston meanwhile was variously sent by Edward to govern Ireland with a batch of blank charters to cover his expenses; returned secretly; was exiled for life; was stripped of his titles by the Lords; and was restored by Edward's own writs which for extra emphasis the king laid, when sealed, upon his bed, the intimate sanctuary of the royal will.

Forced out of London by the Ordainers, the two friends went north in a vain attempt to raise an army. After bargaining unsuccessfully with the rebel Bruce for shelter for Gaveston in Scotland, they fled down river from Newcastle to Tynemouth, leaving the royal treasure and the now pregnant Isabella to fall to the pursuing Lancaster, though this did not much dismay her, since Lancaster, another uncle on her mother's side, was not unfriendly to her.

In the end Gaveston, separated from the king and trapped in the fastness of Scarborough castle, yielded to the moderate earl of Pembroke on terms of a safe conduct infrangibly sworn to on the Holy Sacraments, only to be waylaid on the journey south and have his head hacked off by agents of Lancaster and Warwick. The deed of sacrilege was a blunder. Pembroke in particular was horrified at the blot upon his house, perhaps not without reason, for as the chronicler Thomas Walsingham points out, from this day forward until the line ended seventy-five years later, no earl of Pembroke ever knew his son, or the son his father, so persistent were their misfortunes. He denounced Lancaster for dishonouring him, and rallied to the king.

Gaveston gone, Lancaster's power flagged. Edward was able to re-enter London and shelve the Ordinances; but not strong enough for the revenge he vowed, he wasted his empty fury digging ditches for weeks on end. When Pembroke, whom he had sent to fetch help from France, brought not an army, but Isabella's diplomatic uncle Louis of Evreux and a bunch of lawyers, followed by papal mediators, they persuaded Lancaster to disgorge the captured treasure and patch up a hollow peace.

At that tactful moment in 1312, Isabella brought her first-born, Edward, into the world, and to his baptism at Windsor.

* * *

In the year 1313, the royal family, now honourably augmented by a son and heir, returned from Windsor to their place of duty in the palace of Westminster, where they received a congratulatory procession of the City Guild of Fishmongers, riding behind a carnival fishing boat, and clad in livery of linen shot with gold whereon were shared the arms of England and of France. Though only meant as a compliment to the new prince's doubly elevated parentage, this quartering of the royal arms was to prove prophetic.

Afterwards, Isabella took her baby off to Eltham, always in her opinion the most healthy of the royal residences near London. In May, she sailed with the king from Dover for the court of France, where her three brothers were to be simultaneously knighted. They spent a carefree two months away from their discordant kingdom, marred only by a fire at Pontoise when they had to escape from the palace in their nightgowns.

In Scotland, Robert Bruce had made good use of the recent ructions across the Border. Castle after castle had fallen to him, and at last his brother Edward laid siege to Stirling, the gateway to the Highlands, where the governor agreed to surrender if not relieved within a year. Such an undertaking, though not uncommon at the time, need never have been given, since the up-to-date fortress on its high escarpment was quite irreducible by the lightly armed Scots. None the less, the difficulty with Bruce had always been in finding him, and in this way he was tied down to open battle. Pembroke advised the king it was too good a chance to miss; it would, besides, offer him fame and glory worthy of his father, and confirm his new-found reconciliation with the barons.

His usual exuberance restored, Edward set about raising, in 1314, the greatest army that had ever marched north. Nothing was overlooked, even down to the napery and gold vessels for his table, and when the gorgeous if rather tinselled host set out, the baggage train alone stretched twenty leagues. At the last moment Lancaster and his associates refused to join the expedition, so that when the scattered remnants of the army came trailing back after its failure at Bannockburn, weary, downhearted and utterly disgraced, he, with his force at Pontefract, was well placed to exploit the king's complete disaster.

For the next few years Lancaster was in full control. He rigidly enforced the Ordinances, replaced Edward's ministers, cut his spending to £10 a day, and claimed the right, as hereditary High Steward of England, to appoint the Steward of the Royal Household, the last custodian of the king's financial independence. In this he was successfully resisted. Disposed to hector, not to help, Lancaster kept mistrustfully away from Westminster, and ruled the Council from the far security of his rival northern empery. He was the more easily deceived.

Moreover, fortune did not favour Lancaster's ascendancy. The summer of 1315 was one of unrelenting rain. Crops rotted where they stood. Disease followed upon the floods, and a murrain among the cattle. There were no oxen to draw the plough, efforts to control prices failed, and famine set in for several years. Horses and dogs were eaten, and, some say, children. Thieves in the jails devoured their fellows. Anarchy ruled. Robber knights and disbanded soldiers ravaged the countryside, ruffians and *roveres* terrorized the city of London. Two cardinal legates were robbed and stripped naked in the North. At Bristol, second port in the land, siege engines had to be brought up to reduce civic rebellion.

In addition, Lancaster had troubles of his own, and the king fanned them spitefully whenever possible. An armed rising in Lancashire, led by Adam Benastre, though bloodily put down by the earl's lieutenant, Sir Robert Holland, claimed to be in the name of the king. Then Lancaster's wife, Alice de Lacy, who on the death of her father had become a considerable heiress, ran away with a squire called Ebulo l'Estrange. Lancaster, who had other consolations, minded not so much the loss of his wife as that of her two earldoms, Lincoln and Salisbury. A private war ensued, and the king led troops to the countess's assistance.

Lancaster was blamed for incompetence, and was suspected of secret dealings with the Scots, whose triumphant maraudings he was powerless to prevent. He lost ground to Pembroke in the Council, and in August 1318 he was persuaded, with Isabella's help, to accept the compromise of Leake with the moderate royalists. He was badly outwitted in the negotiations, and when an expedition to recover Berwick ended in total failure, Bruce cutting round behind the English supply lines and all but capturing Isabella at York, whispers of Lancaster's treachery grew louder, and he retired sulkily to his North Midland stronghold.

If Edward had now let himself be ruled by Pembroke, the best man of his generation, and by Pembroke's assistant, Bartholomew de Badlesmere, the Steward of the Household, all might yet have been well. He did not do so.

Among his new advisers were the two Hugh Despensers, father and son, old friends of his youth, and members of the minor baronage from the Welsh Marches. He turned instead to them.

Hugh the elder, once a trusted retainer of Edward I, had befriended Edward II, when prince, in his troubles with his father, had carried insignia at his coronation, and almost alone of the nobility had stood by him at the time of Gaveston's murder. He was one of the godfathers chosen for the new heir apparent, and had been at the king's side in the flight from Bannockburn. Dismissed by Lancaster, who hated him, he returned to duty on Lancaster's departure, an elderly man of fifty-eight, with Pembroke and the moderates. Though no more selfless than the other magnates of his time, his ruling tenet was one of simple loyalty to his sovereign.

Hugh the younger was more subtle, and a great deal less straightforward. He had grown up as a companion of the prince, and had been knighted with him. He had then sided against Gaveston, and had so impressed the barons with his invention of a constitutional grounding for the Ordinances that they had installed him as their agent in the royal household. But foreseeing advantage in taking the dead favourite's place with the confiding king, he had once more shifted about, and was soon playing the Ordainers false. Lancaster suspected nothing, and Despenser's retention as Chamberlain in the settlement at Leake was accepted without objection on all sides.

The death at Bannockburn of Gilbert de Clare, Edward's nephew and another boyhood friend, had left the earldom of Gloucester in abeyance, and the great Clare estates in the Marches of Wales to be divided equally between his three sisters. These, hoping to create a family bond, Edward had given in marriage; the eldest, Eleanor, to Hugh Despenser; Margaret, Gaveston's widow, to Hugh of Audley; and the third to Roger Damory.

Despenser's share, Glamorgan, was not big enough for his ambitions, and he badgered his brothers-in-law for theirs. He acquired deserted Lundy Island, commanding the Bristol approaches. He persuaded the king that, by a technicality of feudal law, the important Gower lands around Swansea were forfeit to the crown and should be given to him.

Roused out of their differences, the lords of the Marches rose in common cause against Despenser. Edward marched west to his support and agreed that the whole affair should be thrashed out in Parliament. But Gower bordered certain lands of the earl of Lancaster, who saw an opportunity, by converting the local conflict into a national one, to smash Pembroke's party and regain his lost control. He called the disgruntled Marchers to conferences with his Midland vassals, and in the summer of 1321 they set off in arms for London, where they seized the gates and occupied the city, cutting off Edward at Westminster from his base in the Tower, where Isabella had found a safe, if leaky, refuge for the birth of her fourth child, Joan.

In Parliament, the Lords were adamant that the Despensers had to go. Pembroke, his party in ruins, urged the king that the alternative was deposition, and Isabella, weak from childbirth, likewise begged him on her knees. Edward gave way. The elder Despenser accepted his banishment gracefully and went to France. Hugh the younger, with the example of Gaveston before him, remained on close call and took to piracy in the Channel. The Lords, thinking the day was won, dispersed to their estates for the autumn harvest. But they overlooked the fact that Hugh, an able Chamberlain, had left the king unexpectedly well in funds.

In October, Isabella set off on pilgrimage to Canterbury. Passing close to Leeds castle, near Maidstone, she sent in word requiring shelter for the night, as well she might, since it was royal property and its keeper, Badlesmere, was Steward of the Household. Badlesmere was not in residence, but his wife was, and she refused admission to the queen. Perhaps she feared a coup, for her husband had had a hand in the fall of the Despensers, and although he had received a pardon, he was at that moment away in Wales, where, as a de Clare, Lady Badlesmere had interests, picking over with the other rebels the Despenser leavings. High words passed between the ladies, fighting started, six of Isabella's men were killed, and she was forced to spend the night in a Dominican priory before returning to London in a rage.

A letter from Badlesmere defending his wife's action increased Isabella's indignation. In punishing Badlesmere, Edward saw his chance to settle other old scores; Lancaster hated Badlesmere for becoming Steward against his wishes, and so long as Edward appeared to be only after Badlesmere Lancaster would not lift a finger to protect him. The king stormed Leeds castle and hanged the officer in charge. Lady Badlesmere and her children were sent to the Tower. He then drove after Badlesmere to the west, where the Despensers rejoined the king from exile as if by magic.

In the new year, 1322, Edward rounded up the Marcher lords. Some, like the two Roger Mortimers, uncle and nephew, surrendered on terms and were sent to the Tower. Others, like the earl of Hereford, fled northward towards Pontefract to join Lancaster, Edward's real quarry, who was only now preparing belatedly for action. Edward pressed them close. Surprised and out-manoeuvred, Lancaster made off to claim his treasonable sanctuary in Scotland, but at Boroughbridge his way was barred by Sir Andrew Harclay with the northern levies. Trapped before and behind, and left to his fate by his trusted Sir Robert Holland, the defeated Lancaster was brought back to Pontefract where he had lately built a dungeon to imprison, as he boasted, the king before whom he now stood prisoner. Isabella made her customary plea for mercy for her uncle, but he was treated as he had treated Gaveston. Condemned unheard, he was brought out of the castle 'on a lene white Jade without Bridil', pelted with snowballs by a mob of his own people and beheaded.

Badlesmere was caught, and hanged at Canterbury, and other executions followed up and down the country. Opposition to the Despensers had been broken. Lancaster's successor, his brother Henry Wryneck, was a milder man, and two years later it was considered safe to restore him to the earldom of Leicester, part of the escheated Lancaster estates. Hereford had met a horrible death at Boroughbridge, spitted by a spear upthrust from below the bridge. Roger Damory had died of wounds. Audley and many others were in prison. Pembroke's moderating influence had been discarded, and he died soon afterwards in France. The only great lords remaining were securely royalist, such as the king's two young half-brothers, Thomas of Brotherton, now earl of Norfolk, and Edmund of Woodstock, earl of Kent.

The Despensers took pains to appear conciliatory. The parliament they held at York in May 1322 was widely representative and even included delegates from Wales. The heir to the throne, Prince Edward of Windsor, 'our very dear son', now nearly ten years old, was called to take his place as earl of Chester. He had been summoned once before, in 1320, but had been omitted from the acrimonious proceedings of the intervening year. From now on his attendance became regular. No doubt he was edified by the plausible display of orthodox procedure, for Hugh Despenser was an effective showman. Prince Edward was, though, a shrewd lad, and would have noticed that, while Hugh's pretensions to the earldom of Gloucester were tactfully not pressed, his father, Hugh the elder, was dignified as earl of Winchester; and he may have suspected that constitutional rule by king in Parliament was not the real aim of the Despensers.

After one more disastrous Scottish expedition, when Isabella again nearly fell into the hands of Bruce at Byland abbey and had to make a harrowing escape by sea, it became clear that Bruce was unchallengeably king of Scots in deed. Though for propagandist reasons Sir Andrew Harclay, guardian of the North and newly made earl of Carlisle for his bravery at Boroughbridge, was hanged for his premature admission of that fact, a few weeks later the Despensers were forced to accept his logic, and concluded a truce with Bruce for thirteen years.

Released from constant pressure in the North, the Despensers proceeded to consolidate themselves. They had already encompassed a huge principality in the Marcher territories, and had snatched Lancastrian forfeits far and wide. In addition, Hugh the younger was picking up enormous credits with Florentine bankers. Their avarice knew no bounds. At the same time, the king's strength was their only safety, and it paid them to exalt his image. Finance was of first importance, and Hugh the younger exerted his considerable skill to make the machinery of government more fruitful. As Treasurer, Bishop Stapledon of Exeter overhauled the Exchequer, while Robert Baldock, the Chancellor, did the same for the Chancery. As for the king's more private business, such as granting manors to the

Despensers, Hugh kept it ever more tightly in his own hands as Chamberlain.

Yet fiscal efficiency in the government is not always to the taste of the governed. The people loathed the Despensers; the towns and the clerical orders detested their cunning and extortion, the nobility cursed their barefaced presumption. Much of the resentment brushed off on Edward, who pursued unheeding his bizarre amusements. Rumours spread that he was no real king, but a changeling. Knowing explanations were given for his intimacy with the younger Hugh. Of more moment was the increasing cult of Lancaster. Weeping crowds thronged his tomb at Pontefract, where miracles began to happen. In St Paul's, candles by the hundred lit his plaque commemorating the Ordinances; when it was removed by the Despensers the pillar that had borne it was venerated instead. Chroniclers called him a martyr and there were demands that he be sainted. Never was there a less probable saint than Lancaster; but then, the ugly inference ran, never was there a less likely king than Edward.

In the absence of suitable earls, leadership of the growing resistance fell to the bishops. They too had their grievances. John Stratford had been mulcted of £1,000 by Hugh the younger for securing from the pope the see of Winchester for himself instead of for Chancellor Baldock. Bishop Hethe of Rochester had to tip the Chamberlain to release his temporalities. Hotham of Ely lost his treasure and his plate. Droxford of Bath and Wells was in unexplained disfavour. To make matters worse, the usually easygoing archbishop of Canterbury, Walter Reynolds, took umbrage because Melton of York was allowed to carry his cross with him when visiting the South, a point of protocol long at issue between the two leaders of the church.

Two prelates in particular had serious grounds for disaffection. One was Henry Burghersh of Lincoln. Burghersh was a nephew of Badlesmere and, in his time of prosperity as Steward of the Household, it was Badlesmere who had paid the pope to 'provide' Burghersh to the see of Lincoln. When fortune changed, the bishop's brother, Sir Bartholomew Burghersh, had helped Lady Badlesmere to defend Leeds castle against the king, and like her had been sent to the Tower. Later, Badlesmere, just before his execution, was found hiding at the bishop's manor. Henry Burghersh was thus deeply compromised, and although the pope refused to remove him from his bishopric, the king, or Hugh Despenser, impounded his possessions.

The other aggrieved prelate was Adam of Orleton, who, as a youth of ability, had been employed in the Papal Curia at Avignon. To reward him, and despite the king's objections, John XXII had made him bishop of his native Hereford. Locally born, he was a choice congenial to the barons of the Marches, and became especially so to Roger Mortimer, lord of Wigmore to the north of his diocese. For a year or two Orleton served the king usefully in diplomatic missions overseas, but he joined his Marcher friends in their revolt, and during their brief triumph at the London parliament of 1321, he was chosen to extort from the king the dismissal of the Despensers and a pardon for the rebels. In the reaction after Borough-bridge, the Despensers charged him with treason in Parliament, the first prelate ever to be cited in a lay tribunal. He refused to answer, and to his credit Archbishop Reynolds, with the other clerics, took him under their protection. As in the case of Burghersh, the king applied unsuccessfully to the pope for Orleton's dismissal, and confiscated his estates.

The two bishops had known each other at least since 1320, when Orleton had attended Burghersh's consecration at Boulogne. Both were worldly, and shared the tenacity of self-made men. Burghersh was a little more bold, Orleton by a trifle the more adroit. Often abroad, they had access to the pope. At home, it was not easy for the secular power to get at them, and in their consistories they stirred their reverend brethren's discontent, especially Orleton, in the remote depths of Herefordshire. They were both committed to destroy or be destroyed by the Despensers; but in order to act they needed a figurehead among the laity. They found it, surprisingly, in the person of the queen.

* * *

Because of her part in the catastrophe that followed, Isabella has not been handled gently by historians. Though the chroniclers of her own time on the whole treated her with restraint, she has been reviled century after century, and in the 1750s, when France was once again the national enemy, Thomas Gray flung out the devastating couplet that has clung fast to her reputation ever since:

> She-wolf of France, with unrelenting fangs
> That tearest the bowels of thy mangled mate.

Is it possible that she was such a monster, such a black and midnight witch of melodrama? That she had, as Maurice Druon nowadays repeatedly assures us, sharp-pointed little carnivore's teeth?[2] What was she really like?

Jean Froissart, or rather Jean le Bel, from whom he copied the first part of his history, says that she was one of the greatest beauties in the world; but then courtly raconteurs of chivalry were apt to say much the same of almost any lady they admitted to their pages. The Oxenbridge tomb in Winchelsea church does not support their claim, for her face looks plump and greedy, not a patch on the lovely Margaret of France on a neighbour-ing boss. But there again, the stone carvings of the time were of doubtful accuracy, and in any case the fourteenth century evidently admired a fuller female figure than has since become the fashion, to judge from Chaucer's adulatory Duchess:

Ryght faire shuldres and body long
She had, and armes, every lith [limb]
Fattysh, flesshy, not gret therwith;
Ryght white handes, and nayles rede,
Rounde brests; and of good brede
Hyr hippes were, a streight flat bak.

Certainly Isabella's father and her youngest brother were both called 'the Fair', some indication of family good looks in those days of frank soubriquets – the Fat, the Mad, the Bald, the Cruel, and so forth.

She is said to have been extravagant, and of course she was. In the last year of her life, when she was professedly a Poor Clare, and should have been preparing her soul for judgment, she spent £1,400 on jewellery: this at a time when a fat living might be worth £10 annually to the parish priest, less necessary church repairs; when thirteen shillings a year was an excessive wage for hired labour, when bows twanged contentedly at twopence each a day, and knights did their valorous duty in the field for two shillings, dawn to dusk.

No big occasion could pass without Isabella commissioning a chaplet of gold, set with 'balays' (rubies), sapphires, emeralds, diamonds and pearls. For the wedding of her maid-in-waiting, Katherine Brovart, she ordered a girdle of silk studded with silver, three hundred rubies at twenty pence the hundred, eighteen hundred pearls at twopence each, and a circlet of gold – £32 worth in all. She was, after all, the daughter of the king of France; the daughter, too, of Joan, queen of Navarre; sister of three brothers, each in his turn king of France; queen of England. She was royal to her finger-tips; pale economy did not occur to her.

In 1323 Isabella had been married fifteen years, and had borne four children, two boys, two girls, with becoming regularity. She had accompanied her husband dutifully on his inept forays, which so often seemed to end with her either on her knees, trying to retrieve some *sottise* he had created, or else making hair's-breadth escapes from capture by his enemies – and there was no telling what Bruce might have done with her, remembering his own womenfolk in their cages.

She shared her husband's interests. She had a sizeable library, and once laid out fourteen shillings for the making of a book, with a further sum to Richard Painter for azure to illuminate. She was suitably devout, favoured, as did Edward, the Dominicans, and was always riding out on pilgrimage to Canterbury or to Walsingham to venerate Our Lady's milk.

Like Edward she loved minstrelsy. She paid for Walter Hert, one of her 'vigiles' (viol players) to be trained in London during Lent. She scrubbed up a ragged Scottish orphan, cured his disease of the scalp, and sent him to the wife of Jean the Organist for schooling. She was, too, a more accomplished actress than Edward realized. Dr Joshua Barnes, in his life of her great son, speaks stiffly of her 'charming tears', and there is no doubt that on occasion she could shed them to advantage. She encouraged her husband's love of hunting, and a hooded tercel was often on her wrist. No effete princess, on going to France in 1325 she boarded her pack of hounds upon the prior of Canterbury, who soon complained they were eating him out of house and home.

The king, within his lights, showed consideration for her. On the birth of his heir, Prince Edward, he gave her the resources of his lamented Gaveston's earldom of Cornwall, in addition to her dower of Ponthieu. He ferociously avenged her quarrel with the Badlesmeres, and, that Christmas, favoured her with bales of rich cloth to make dresses for her very numerous ladies. In 1316 he had deferred so far to her prayers as to drop his own candidate for the vacant see of Durham in favour of her jovial French cousin Louis de Beaumont, despite justified protests from the Chapter that Louis was illiterate. To overcome that handicap, Louis agreed to take reading lessons. Even so, when the day of the ceremony arrived, he was flummoxed by the Latin. For a time he passed muster by saying, after several stumbles, 'Let it be taken as read.' But, floored finally by *in aenigmata*, he exclaimed, 'By St Louis, the man who wrote that had no courtesy in him.'

Until 1323 Isabella at least pretended to obey her lord. Whatever she made privately of his 'silly swimmers' and his 'little players', she seems to have endured his foibles. Miss McKisack says that Isabella was more than ordinarily acquisitive, a broad indictment in an extraordinarily rapacious age, when even her pious mother-in-law, Queen Eleanor of Castile, had been refused deathbed absolution by Archbishop Pecham until she had first relieved her groaning peasantry. But, indeed, her cupidity was the key to what ensued. The rivals that Isabella noticed were not sexual but financial. Her only grievance against Gaveston had been that he had stolen her jewels. So, with the Despensers, knowing their greed and Edward's susceptibility, she realized that her estate was again in peril. Inevitably a struggle grew between Isabella and Hugh the younger for possession of the wayward king. Despenser was winning, and she was therefore more than half receptive of the approaches made to her by Bishops Burghersh and Adam of Orleton.

On 1 August 1323 Roger Mortimer of Wigmore escaped from the Tower and got away to France. It was only the second escape in the Tower's long history, and had been elaborately prepared. During revels on the night of St Peter ad Vincula, Mortimer climbed through a hole in the wall of his 'lofty and narrow chamber' into the kitchen of the palace. Afterwards, he rewarded the royal cook, though whether for preparing 'sleepy drinks' to anaesthetize the guards, or for permitting him to use the kitchen chimney to get up on to the leads, is not declared. On the bank of the Thames, Bishop Orleton and two prominent citizens, John de Gisors and Richard Bettoyne, both in their turn mayor of London, and both at present, like most of the city, in the king's displeasure, had a boat ready to take him and his accomplice, Gerard Alspaye, under-lieutenant of the Tower, to the Surrey side, and horses to carry them thence to the Channel coast.

It is probable that Isabella was concerned in the affair.[3] After her flight from Byland abbey in 1322 she had returned to London leaving Edward in the North, where he remained until after Mortimer's escape. It may have been then, while living in the White Tower, half palace and half dungeon, that her intimacy with the fascinating prisoner ripened. Mortimer was inexplicably lucky to be still alive. On his first arrest in Wales in early 1322 he had been condemned to death, but rapidly reprieved, although he had despoiled Despenser territories to the enormous value of £60,000. Next year, an armed force seized the castle of Wallingford and set free two other Marcher rebels, involved in a wider plot, which failed, to rescue Mortimer and capture the Tower and Windsor castle. Mortimer was condemned a second time, and a second time pardoned. More remarkable still, his lands were preserved from the Despensers and were administered for the crown by the earl of Arundel. It is hard to see why, in the completeness of the Despenser victory, Mortimer should have been so favoured, unless his friend Bishop Orleton of Hereford spoke for him to Isabella, and unless she, Hugh Despenser notwithstanding, had used her influence with the king.

Mortimer's escape was the overture to a deep and wide conspiracy in northern Europe. It is clear that the king never understood at all what was going on. Despenser, though he did not realize its scope until too late, had an early inkling. Suspecting, rightly, that the queen was intriguing with her French relations, and particularly with her uncle Charles of Valois, on 18 September 1324 he induced Edward to confiscate her county of Cornwall and all her other lands, on pretext of securing them against a possible invasion. Isabella's income was drastically reduced, her household was dismissed, and Despenser's wife, Eleanor de Clare, was set to oversee her. At the same time he started soundings in the Vatican for a dissolution of the royal marriage.

Thus, in Despenser's mind, the last enemy capable of resisting his encroachment of the king, Isabella, had been humiliated and made harmless. Despenser underestimated her furious sense of outrage, the extent of the hatred she would now marshal against him, and the naked power a skilful woman can derive from apparent helplessness.

* * *

Meanwhile, ever since Edward and Isabella had visited Paris for the knighting of her brothers in the spring of 1313, French royalty had been having troubles of its own. The three sons of Philip the Fair had been married to Burgundian princesses, two of them sisters and the third a cousin. In May 1314 it was discovered that for some time past these frisky girls had been enjoying lubricious orgies in the Tour de Nesle in the ramparts on the south bank of the Seine, under the noses of their husbands in the Louvre across the river. There is nothing to support the story that it was Isabella who, though certainly in Paris when the scandal broke, revealed to her father what her sisters-in-law had been getting up to. All three princesses were locked up, the two most flagrant in Château-Gaillard, and the third, a go-between, in the castle of Bourdon.

The abrupt incarceration of so many royal wives had a restricting effect upon the succession to the throne of France, for none of the three princes had as yet acquired a son. The point was emphasized a few months later when Philip the Fair died unexpectedly. His eldest son, Louis X, le Hutin (the Quarrelsome), at once did what he could to restore his prospects from that point of view. His first and errant wife, Margaret, dying suddenly in her prison, he rapidly married Clemence of Hungary. But he was too late. After a short reign of only eighteen months he too was dead before his heir was born, and the infant, when it came (John I), lived only for five days. In strict hereditary right Louis's true successor was his daughter Jeanne, but she was only seven years old and her legitimacy was questionable; in any case the principle of female succession had never been put to any test, since for more than three hundred years the Capetian kings had followed each other in orderly sequence from father to son down to this very moment. So Louis's next brother, Philip the Long, who had already assumed the regency, had himself crowned as Philip V, if not with much enthusiasm, at least without much trouble, and fobbed off his young niece with a promise of her grandmother's title of queen of Navarre, though he kept her county of Champagne for himself.

To regularize his position, Philip induced an assembly of notables to declare that 'a woman cannot succeed to the Kingdom of France', quite contrary to feudal custom whereby a kingdom was regarded as no different from an ordinary inheritance, and was transmissible to women. He then called on his vassals to ratify what had thus been laid down by doing him homage: these included Edward II, not as king of England, but as lord of Ponthieu and duke of Aquitaine. The kings of England were invariably reluctant liegemen, and in the present case it was additionally inconvenient for Edward to leave home because of his domestic difficulties; he was, at that moment, heavily beset both by the Scots and by the Earl of Lancaster. Already, he had avoided the irksome duty once, during the short reign of Louis X; this time he could not escape the summons. To gain time, in May 1319 he sent commissioners, Bishops Orleton of Hereford and William Stapledon of Exeter – a strange assortment as things were to turn out later, for Stapledon, the virtuous founder of Exeter College, Oxford, and rebuilder of his fine cathedral, was, unlike Orleton, a staunch royalist. A year later, in June 1320, Edward and Isabella met her brother Philip at Amiens and did what was required of them.

After reigning for five years, Philip V died in January 1322. He had not remarried after the débâcle of the Tour de Nesle, and left five daughters only. The remaining brother, Charles the Fair, who had loudly criticized Philip for his shabby treatment of their niece Jeanne of Navarre, without hesitation himself passed over all six girls and became king as Charles IV. He made strenuous efforts to preserve the Capetian line. He divorced his flighty Burgundian queen, Blanche; he married again, and later yet again a third time, but still could not get a son. Incredibly, after three centuries, by the death of three kings in eight years, the life of Charles IV alone stood between the Capetians and extinction. It began to be noticed that the fourth member of this usurpatory though short-lived family, Isabella, had just as much right as her brothers to set aside their nieces; and that if, as a woman, she was barred from the throne by Philip's dubious edict, she had a son in England who quite possibly was not.

Alone of the family, Charles IV had a brotherly fondness for Isabella. Accordingly, his demands on his brother-in-law Edward II in the matter of homage for Aquitaine were, to begin with, reasonable. He could, had he wished, have put a short end to the tiresome problem by swiftly adding the duchy to his own domains. Edward, embroiled at home, was in no position to mount a campaign in Gascony, even had he been able to command the sea lanes, swarming with Norman and Breton pirates. Given the advantage of overland internal lines, such a seizure would have been easy, as Philip the Fair had shown in the time of Edward I, a far more redoubtable opponent than his son.

Charles did not take his opportunity. Instead he waited politely until Edward had disposed of the earl of Lancaster, and had made his thirteen-year truce with Scotland. Then, in September 1323, he suggested that the following Easter would be a suitable time for them to meet for the homage ceremony. When Edward demurred, he extended the date until July. But by then Isabella had been driven from her husband's side by the Despensers and had joined Orleton's conspiracy against them. Mortimer had been for a year in France, an active agent. In the interval French policy had undergone a drastic change.

Far below the high-flown royal exchanges over homage, there were many more real causes of friction in Aquitaine itself; these the Treaty of Paris of 1259, seeking to lay down once and for all the relations between the duchy and the king of France, had left unclarified. Local jurisdiction remained an inchoate mass of conflicting rights and duties, a welter of unwritten feudal custom. Territorial boundaries were ill-defined, French officials used jackboot methods to enforce French edicts upon the liegemen of the English king, and ignoring the proper channels of suzerainty, hauled intransigents directly before the Parlement of Paris. They were resisted by the Gascons, who stood by their lackadaisical allegiance to their dukes, since it allowed them virtual independence and guaranteed the all-important English wine trade. Time and again in the last sixty years there had been clashes, and despite commissions appointed by both kings, the animosity had never been resolved. Another such clash now erupted.

Both sides had taken to building *bastides* along the disputed frontiers and these now bristled with rival fortresses. The Agenais, north of the Garonne, was one of these districts, where Edward I had built the castle of La Réole, and Charles IV now countered with another, at Saint-Sardos. In November 1323, the English Seneschal of Gascony burnt it down, and hanged the constable on a gallows contemptuously decorated with the royal arms of France. Edward II disowned his ducal subordinates; Charles commanded them to appear before him as their overlord, and when they failed to do so, ordered the forfeiture of their estates. Edward not only failed to carry out the sentence, but made further evasions about his oath of homage. Charles declared all his French territories confiscated, and in August 1324 sent his uncle Charles of Valois with an army into the Agenais to give effect to the arrest. The temporary distraint, pending obedience, of the possessions of a rebellious vassal was a normal piece of feudal discipline. There was nothing to indicate that Charles meant the seizure to be permanent. But Isabella and her confederates made the most of it, whether or not with his collusion.

The plan was, since the Despensers were unassailable in England, to build up the forces to destroy them overseas, while Orleton and Burghersh, protected by their cloth, kept watch at home. One after another, new adherents – John of Brittany, earl of Richmond, the king's cousin; Henry, Lord Beaumont, the queen's cousin and brother of Louis de Beaumont, the ill-read bishop of Durham – left England. Edward's peacemaking embassies in Paris were riddled with his enemies. Pembroke, the faithful leader of the moderate party, died en route. John Stratford, bishop of Winchester, Airmyn of Norwich, and the archbishop of Dublin – all of these envoys had fallen foul of the Despensers. When trouble started in the Agenais, the king's half-brother Edmund, earl of Kent, because of his hitherto undoubted loyalty, was given the command in Aquitaine. But his mishandling, having made war inevitable, then lost it, so that it is doubtful whether even one so incompetent as he was really doing his best. Advised by Sir Oliver Ingham, normally a capable soldier, who, however, was shortly to emerge as right hand man to Mortimer, Kent shut himself up in La Réole, and tamely surrendered it a month or so later, on 22 September 1324. Edward could not afford the loss of Gascony, with its profitable revenue, as great as that of the whole of England; but neither could he undertake a major war for its recovery. Diplomacy at high level was the only course. It thus came about that the opportunity arose for Isabella to join the rest of her cabal in France.

By roundabout ways a suggestion, started probably by Isabella herself, came from the French court to the papal referees in Paris that King Charles could be moved towards a peaceful settlement by the personal persuasion of his sister. The papal referees passed it on to the English commissioners, and Bishop Stratford strongly commended it to Edward. Edward and the Despensers took the bait. On 9 March 1325 Isabella, with a fine display of patient poverty (it was just six months since her property had been sequestered), bade them an affectionate farewell. Dissemblers both, the felinities that underlay her honeyed parting from Hugh the younger as she went on board escaped the inexpert king.

What passed between Charles and Isabella is not certain. She is thought to have complained that she had been treated churlishly in England, *comme souillon*. At all events her mission was strikingly successful. By the end of May she had obtained a six months' truce, and a promise that Ponthieu and Aquitaine would be returned, reserving the Agenais for arbitration. There was only one stipulation, apparently fair but in the circumstances crippling: Edward must come at once to do his homage. Upon that all the rest depended.

The Great Council advised, since that was the way to peace, that Edward ought to go, and he began to make his preparations. The Despensers strongly objected. They dared not expose him to the rival blandishments of his wife in the climate of her brother's court. And bereft of the royal protection, what would become of them at home? They urged that the opposition was gaining ground. Henry of Lancaster, restive for the return of his brother's earldoms, had adopted Thomas's arms and had erected a cross to his miracle-performing memory at Leicester. He was also known to be in correspondence with Bishop Orleton.

The king, in an agony of indecision, went down to Langdon abbey near Dover. On 21 August he seemed ready to embark. On the 24th he wrote to Charles that he could not do so, having been taken ill upon the road. At his point another neat proposal came from Paris, by way of the pope's intermediaries. Since it was difficult for the king to get away, why did he not invest his eldest son, the twelve-year-old Prince Edward, with Aquitaine and Ponthieu, and send him to do the homage in his place? King Charles was willing to accept such an arrangement; and subject to the payment of a sizeable relief of 60,000 *livres* for damage in the Agenais, he would restore the duchy and the lordship.

The Despensers may or may not have realized how little the scheme would benefit the king of France, except as a means to oblige his sister Isabella, who, on the contrary, had a great deal to gain from it. They evidently reckoned that the loss of the heir apparent would be less dangerous than the loss of the king in person. So 'they gave counsel and prevailed, that the King's son should go'.

On 2 September 1325, at Langdon abbey, King Edward made over the county of Ponthieu to his son, and on the 4th, Charles IV consented to the transfer by letters patent. On the 10th, Aquitaine was similarly conveyed, and on the 12th the prince set sail for France.

Before he left, the king earnestly admonished him about what he should and should not do abroad. He also put him in the charge of the trustworthy Bishop Stapledon, his Treasurer. The prince, slim, straight and grave, listened as boys will do with distant eyes to his father's homily, and made replies that gave appropriate comfort to the fond, anxious, hefty, ineffectual king. The prince did not like the hovering Hugh Despenser. He looked out, speculative, across the mild autumnal sea towards France. He did not know it was the last time he would see his father.

Prince Edward joined the French court at Vincennes, to the east of Paris. Not yet the great walled fortress, the 'Versailles of the Middle Ages', that it was shortly to become, it was a manor reputedly distinguished by St Louis's oak of justice, buried in stately woods ablaze with autumn foliage. Here, on 21 September 1325, the prince duly performed his homage, and King Charles, his uncle, ordered a withdrawal from his newly enfeoffed domains.

The diplomatic crisis being now evidently ended, it may have seemed to the prince that he and his mother should return to England as soon as was politely possible. But his mother seemed much at home in her surroundings; she spent all her time with Roger Mortimer. The little knot of English magnates too, the so-called ambassadors, who had just been joined by the king's half-brother Edmund of Kent from Gascony, were strangely vague in their manner; or so thought Bishop Stapledon, who found the atmosphere so charged that he fled back to England disguised as a pilgrim, and reported to the king.

King Edward sent Bishop Stratford a safe-conduct for Isabella's return, and wrote to her many times, begging her to 'come to Us with all the haste you can, as a wife should to her lord'. Her replies were disingenuous. '*Dame*', he addressed her more sharply, and expressed amazement at her alleged fear of Hugh Despenser, recalling 'so amicable and sweet was your deportment' when they parted. 'And, certes, lady, we know for truth, and so know you, that he has always procured from us all the honour he could for you, nor to you hath either evil or villainy been done since you entered into our companionship; unless, peradventure, as you may yourself remember, once when we had cause to give you secretly some word of reproof for your pride, but without other harshness.'

To his son, sensing the chill of disaster, he wrote urgently:

Trescher Fiutz, although you are carefree and of tender age, remember well what We charged and commanded you when you left Us at Dover, and what you then replied which was most agreeable to Us; and do not trespass or contravene what We then charged you in any point, on any account.

And since your Homage has been received, go to our most dear brother the King of France, your uncle, and take your leave of him; and then come away to Us in the company, the very dear company, of the Queen, your Mother, if she comes so soon.

And if she does not come, come you with all haste, without longer stay, for We have a very great desire to see and speak with you. And thereof fail not by any means, neither for Mother, nor for any other person, as you value our blessing.

It was all to no avail. What Bishop Stapledon feared was true. There was treason in the air. Rumours that might justify an invasion of England were being carefully put about in France. King Edward, it was said, had denounced his wife and son as outlaws, and had forbidden their return. On 15 April 1326 Edward protested formally to the pope that, on the contrary, he had done all in his power to bring them home. 'And as for Our said son, indeed he has not offended Us, nor does his youth allow either that he could do any harm, or that it should be imputed to him. Wherefore it would be inhuman and unnatural to treat them with so much rage and cruelty.' In Paris, Mortimer and Isabella paraded, shamelessly adulterous; and at Whitsun Edward had to take his son to task again for having 'notoriously held companionship, and your mother also, with Mortimer, your traitor and mortal enemy, who, in company with your mother and others, was publicly carried to Paris in your train to the solemnity of the coronation' of Charles IV's third wife, Jeanne of Evreux.

Hugh Despenser began to fortify the Tower, and prudently drew out £2,000 from his bankers. Commissions of array were ordered, and beacons erected to give warning of invasion. Frenchmen in England were arrested. Incoming ships were searched for messages from Isabella's partisans. Mortimer was outlawed, and his mother shut up in a convent.

The alarms were premature. Charles the Fair had no mind to back his sister beyond the contemporary limits of propriety. It is true that when Edward reclaimed Aquitaine from his son as from a contumacious vassal, Charles maintained his nephew's rights by force of arms. But manoeuvres over Edward's fiefs in France were one thing; to abet Isabella in rebellion against her king and husband was another. The pope was much against it; nor did Charles, remembering his Blanche's similar lapse, approve of Isabella's gross affair with Mortimer, a commoner. There was also the question of Charles's own successor. He made it plain that Isabella's suggestive lingering with her son in Paris was an embarrassment.

By the summer of 1326 Isabella's purse was running low. It was time for new, more bold horizons. Among her many cousins by marriage was William II, count of Hainault, Holland and Zeeland. His scattered provinces, unlike their neighbour Flanders, owed no allegiance to the king of France, but had the same vital interest in English wool. In 1319, Bishop

Stapledon, when over in France to arrange Edward II's homage to Philip V, had been sent on to Valenciennes to sound out a possible match between one of Count William's daughters and the young English heir apparent.

He had spied on the supposedly unwitting sisters, and pounced on the youngest of them, 'Philippa by name', at that time eight years old and nearest in age to Prince Edward, who was nearly seven. He had then subjected her to a minute and terrifying scrutiny. Apart from some criticism of her remaining baby teeth (they were 'not so white'), he had found little fault with her solid physiognomy. Her hair, betwixt blue-black and brown, was 'not uncomely'; her forehead large; her eyes blackish-brown and deep; her nose, though 'somewhat broad at the tip and also flattened', was 'yet no snub-nose'; her mouth was wide and generous; her ears and chin were 'comely enough'; she was of middle height for her age, well taught, and of 'fair carriage'.

'Her neck, shoulders, and all her body and lower limbs are reasonably well shapen; all her limbs are well set and unmaimed; and nought is amiss so far as a man may see. Moreover, she is brown of skin all over, and much like her father; and in all things she is pleasant enough, as it seems to us.'

Years afterwards, the court rhymester Hardyng remarked how unerringly the bishop's celibate gaze had fastened upon Philippa's 'good hippes', and his expert assessment of 'full feminine' potentialities became, with some reason, the cause of wonder in palace circles as child followed child from the royal bed. At the time, his appraisal of the little girl, which accords so faithfully with the bronze casting in Westminster Abbey of the queen at sixty-ish, had been shut away in his diocesan archives at Exeter, and the project had been shelved.

Now, seven years later, Isabella decided to reopen it. She took her son Edward to Valenciennes and negotiated the betrothal with Count William. Philippa, in matronly middle age, fondly related for the avid pen of her compatriot and secretary Jean Froissart her well-remembered idyll in the summer air of the unenterprising Belgian plain.

Froissart tells us: 'In those days had Count William four daughters, Margaret, Philippa, Joan and Isabel; among whom Edward devoted himself most, and inclined with eyes of love to Philippa rather than to the rest; and the maiden knew him better and kept closer company with him than any of her sisters. So have I heard from the mouth of the good Lady herself, who was Queen of England, and in whose court and service I dwelt.' When in due course Edward became king and was asked whether he would stick to his engagement, 'he began to laugh, and said, "Yes, I am better pleased to marry there than elsewhere; and rather to Philippa, for she and I accorded excellently well together; and she wept, I know well, when I took leave of her at my departure."'

Philippa's rose-tinted reminiscences dwelt only on the romance. She did not recall the high bargaining, the down-to-earth considerations that had endorsed her love match; that the papal dispensation necessary for the marriage of the cousins spoke merely of 'one of the daughters' of the count of Hainault; that she in fact had not been specified by name until two months before the ceremony, lest she should die suddenly, as a fifth sister had already died, and so default the contract. Nor did she tell that her dowry had been demanded in advance and instantly deployed by Isabella in hiring a mercenary army of seven hundred Hainaulters, with requisite shipping, led by Count William's brother, Sir John of Hainault, for the descent on England.

* * *

It was not a huge force with which to invade a kingdom of above three million souls, but the money would stretch no further, and in view of the growing exasperation with the Despensers, and of the extensive supporting preparations known to be going on in England, it was hoped it would be sufficient. So it proved. Before the insurgents sailed from Dordrecht, King Edward's interceptory fleet had already mutinously scattered, to plunder their old foes on the coast of Normandy; so the band of émigrés made easy passage. Besides John of Hainault with his mercenaries, Isabella, Mortimer and Prince Edward, they included an impressive leavening of royal sponsors: Edmund of Kent, the king's half-brother; John of Brittany, earl of Richmond, the king's cousin; Isabella's cousin, Henry, Lord Beaumont – all with their retinues; and to lend sacerdotal approbation, Bishops Stratford of Winchester and Airmyn of Norwich.

Next day, 24 September 1326, they landed at Orwell, near Harwich, within the territories of the Earl Marshal, Thomas Brotherton of Norfolk, the king's other half-brother. So far from resisting, he made haste to join them, as did also Henry Wryneck of Lancaster, and in the wake of these great magnates many lords of East Anglia and the Midlands soon came riding in. Edward and the Despensers had prepared for a fierce defence of London. Poised as the rebels now were to the east and north of the city, they could either march upon it frontally, or, if their plans to reduce it from within made that unnecessary, remain free to pursue the royal government in its expected flight to the Despenser stronghold in the west.

The struggle for London was brief, and an early essay in the effective use of propaganda. Edward intended, from his peremptory position in the Tower, to overawe the citizens and requisition money and men through the compliant mayor. On news of the landing he called upon Archbishop Reynolds to dig out a papal bull denouncing invaders (originally provided for use against the Scots) and have it read at Paul's Cross, excluding, however, his queen, his son, and his brother of Kent from its provisions. He also put a price on Mortimer's head, but these predictable measures made small impact.

Isabella was more imaginative, and it is possible to suspect in her theatricals the ever agile hand of Bishop Orleton of Hereford, who, with Henry Burghersh of Lincoln, had now openly joined her camp. She wooed London from afar with slogans, already widely circulated, of an end to tyranny and the return of civic liberties. When her first proclamation fell flat 'for fear of the King', she adopted more personal tactics. Dressed in sorrowful black she trailed through Bury St Edmunds, and put it about that Hugh Despenser had so far destroyed her family life that 'the King carried a knife in his hose to kill the Queen, and had said that if he had no other weapon he would crush her with his teeth'. She did not say what she must have known, that she should expect no better, given that what she was doing was the highest treason. Two more-savage centuries later, Henry VIII would destroy his wives on far less pretext.

Sympathy and indignation lapped around Isabella. When she reached Dunstable, only forty miles from London, the startled king realized that, far from being a monarch commanding from his Tower, he was more like a rat in a trap. Without a blow being struck he had lost his capital, his kingdom and his heir. On 2 October, only a week after Isabella's landing, he packed up his Great Seal and his Privy Seal and the crown jewels, and with Baldock the Chancellor, the two Despensers, the two loyal earls of Warenne and Arundel, and a small retinue, fled, as anticipated, to the west.

On the flight of the king his control of the city collapsed. A further appeal from Isabella appeared overnight on Queen Eleanor's cross in Cheapside, and soon copies were posted everywhere on window shutters and on walls. On 15 October the mob seized Hamo de Chigwell, the obsequious mayor, dragged him off to the Guildhall 'crying mercy with clasped hands', and made him proclaim death to the queen's enemies. His mayoralty was soon taken over by Richard de Bettoyne, Mortimer's former accomplice. Agents of the Despensers were butchered, the house of the Bardi, their bankers, was sacked, as were the mansions of the King's ministers, Baldock, Arundel, and Stapledon. John de Gisors, Mortimer's second accomplice, like de Bettoyne, was rewarded, and became Constable of the Tower, where he released, from the palace part, Isabella's other three children, John of Eltham, Eleanor, and Joan, aged five, who had been left there for safety by Edward on his flight; and from the dungeons, a whole tribe of Mortimer's relations, kept as hostages by the Despensers.

Archbishop Reynolds, long since on the fence, hurriedly called Convocation at Lambeth, but on finding that most bishops had already joined the insurgents he too deserted his king and patron, sent a golden *douceur* to Isabella, and fled to his mansion in Kent on the bishop of Rochester's horses, leaving his neighbour and brother-in-Christ to follow as best he might. He was wise. Good Bishop Stapledon, riding from the same conference to his already gutted home, the Inn in the Temple, met the riot at its height. As Treasurer he was inevitably hated, and as the only chief minister still in town he stood no chance. He made for sanctuary in St Paul's, but was pulled down in the churchyard, dragged out to the old cross in Cheapside, and there beheaded with a butcher's chopper. His headless body was left lying until two charitable drabs spread a sheet over it, and it was shovelled into an unhallowed grave at a place long after known as 'lawless church'. Eventually, he was reburied in his own cathedral church at Exeter, which he had done much to beautify.

On the day of the outbreak, from their point of view wholly satisfactory, Mortimer and Isabella, accompanied whether he would or not by young Prince Edward, were already far away to the west in pursuit of his father. At Oxford they heard Orleton preach on the egregious text 'I will put enmity between thee and the woman and between thy seed and her seed.' At Gloucester, Isabella received the parcelled head of Bishop Stapledon, the first of several such grisly tributes that were soon to come her way.

Meanwhile the king and his party had reached Bristol, where they dispersed, leaving the elder Despenser to cover their escape. Now sixty-four, he may have felt this was the last and best service he could do his king, though the respite it gained was little more than the time it took Mortimer, Kent, Brotherton, Lancaster and other magnates to pass a savage sentence on him, and see it carried out:

> Sir Hugh, this court denies you any right of answer, because you
> yourself made a law that a man could be condemned without right of
> answer and this law shall now apply to you and your adherents. [This
> was a reference to the trial of Thomas of Lancaster, in which Kent, one
> of his present fellow judges, had also taken part.] . . . Wherefore, the
> court awards that you be drawn for treason, hanged for robbery,
> beheaded for misdeeds against the Church: and that your head be sent
> to Winchester, of which place, against law and reason, you were made
> Earl, . . . and because your deeds have dishonoured the order of
> chivalry, the court awards that you be hanged in a surcoat quartered
> with your arms, and that your arms be destroyed forever.

It would have been convenient if the king could have died in battle, but as that clearly was not going to happen a nice point now arose. The rebels, or 'Contrarients' as they preferred to call themselves, were anxious that all should be legal; but there was no precedent for the deposition of a king. It was obvious that a parliament was necessary, but only the king could call a parliament. At Bristol it was learnt that Edward and Hugh the younger had slipped away by sea, and that seemed to offer a way out. Since the king had left his kingdom, a regent should be appointed, and a regent could call a parliament on his behalf. On 26 October 1326 Prince Edward was proclaimed Custos of the Realm and two days later writs were issued under his seal as earl of Chester and duke of Aquitaine for a parliament to meet at Westminster in the presence of himself and his mother, since he was still a minor.

King Edward, however, unlucky to the last, having indeed set out for Despenser's isle of Lundy, had been driven by gales on to the coast of Wales. Accordingly he had not left his kingdom after all, and his son's summons was not valid; he himself must be induced to issue new writs for his own deposition. And he had the Great Seal with him. The hunt moved north of the Severn to Hereford. Here, as Bishop Orleton proudly entertained his royal mistress and her son in his cathedral town, Henry of Lancaster, guided by a certain Rhys ap Howel, went out to fetch her husband in.

On 16 November he was found hiding in Neath abbey, with Hugh Despenser, Baldock the Chancellor, and a clerk or two (who were hanged out of hand). Orleton met Lancaster and his prisoners at Monmouth and, after days of haggling, returned to Hereford with the Great Seal. Writs for a parliament in the new year could now be drawn up in the proper form, except than an ominous provision was made for the king's absence, should he be unwilling, or unable, to appear.

Lancaster took the king to his newly regained keep at Kenilworth, where lately Edward had himself been used to play the host. The bloodbath followed. Arundel was hacked apart at Shrewsbury. Baldock, as a cleric, could not be executed. He was sent to Orleton's London house in Old Fish Street Hill, but was so roughly handled by the mob that he died in Newgate jail. The grand *coup de théâtre*, the destruction of Hugh the younger, was staged at Hereford. Like his father, he was judged guilty by 'manifest ill-fame', and the outcome differed little, save that in his case he was hanged from a spectacular gallows fifty feet high. Warenne alone of all the king's adherents managed to keep in being; perhaps because he had married a French wife, Joan of Bar, a great friend of Isabella, and daughter of Edward I's eldest daughter, Eleanor. Warenne had abandoned Joan of Bar since 1313 and had been living with Matilda de Nerford, by whom he had several children. Nevertheless Joan of Bar, though childless, was still his wife and would have been beggared by his attainder.

The question of the king's deposition occupied Parliament for most of January 1327. There was some idea that if the king could be shown to have broken his coronation oath, his subjects were discharged from their allegiance. Yet, in the fourteenth century, the theory of contract did not count for much. A king, once anointed, was divine. No reason whatever could carry for breaking faith with God. So well was this realized that it was not thought wise to allow Edward to appear in person. Accordingly, at the opening session, Bishop Burghersh suavely made out that when Stratford and he went to Kenilworth to beg the king to come to Parliament, 'he utterly refused to comply therewith; nay, he cursed them contemptuously, declaring that he would not come among his enemies, or, rather his traitors'. This report had a plausible ring; it was also highly convenient. The spectre of majesty in chains need not be conjured.

To escape the constitutional impasse, Mortimer fell back on public clamour. Through his agents in the city, he decreed a mass procession to the Guildhall, where everyone had to swear to the cause of the queen and her son, to the Ordinances, and to the freedom of the city. The swearing took three days, and all the time the people were harangued by the bishops. Orleton started on an admonitory theme, 'A foolish King shall ruin his people'. Next day Stratford kept up the pressure with 'My head is sick'. Finally Archbishop Reynolds, on the significant text 'Vox populi, vox dei', declared that Edward of Caernarvon was deposed, by the unanimous will of all the magnates, clergy and people of the realm, and that his first-born son, the Lord Edward, was now king in his place. So far as words could do it, the deed was done.

All the same, it did not all go off quite smoothly. First, Reynolds was taunted as a turncoat, and mistakenly tried to buy himself back to favour by distributing free wine. Then, his old enemy William Melton, archbishop of York, at the head of a rival phalanx of loyalist bishops (Stephen Gravesend of London, Hamo Hethe of Rochester and John Ross of Carlisle), repudiated the oath. Far worse, and most unexpectedly, the Lord Edward, aged fourteen, suddenly turned awkward. He refused to meet the great assembly in Westminster Hall to be presented as their king and receive their acclamation. He demanded to be convinced that his father had not only relinquished the crown of his own free will, but had expressly ordered that his son should take it up.

His plucky stand was technically correct and could not be gainsaid, though it caused his wretched father more misery rather than less. The king's abdication now had to be unequivocal and public, and in the middle of January an impressive cavalcade set out for Kenilworth. Bishops Burghersh and Stratford first went in to have further words with the king in private. When they had done, he came swaying out to meet the deputation, a gaunt Grand Guignol figure in a long black gown, his face ashen and tear-streaked below his vivid hair. Before a word was spoken, he fell headlong to the floor. They brought him round, and Orleton repeated the stark alternatives. If he accepted deposition, he would be treated honourably, and the crown would pass quietly to his son. If he refused, the position was uncertain. Left to choose between Mortimer and his rightful heir as his successor, Edward replied, with tears, that since his people so greatly hated him, he would make way for his son. Next day in Parliament, a Lancastrian knight, Sir William Trussel, who acted as a kind of spokesman, renounced allegiance on behalf of the whole kingdom to Edward of Caernarvon, and the Steward of the Household broke his staff.

* * *

The reign of King Edward III began officially on Sunday, 25 January 1327, 'by Order and Consent of Parliament'. His Peace, published to the sheriffs a week later, emphasized that in taking 'upon Us the Government of the said Realm', he was merely 'yielding herein to Our Father's good Pleasure'. On 1 February he was knighted by Henry of Lancaster, and proceeded, as the custom was, to knight many others, among them three sons of Mortimer. He was crowned the same day in Westminster Abbey by Archbishop Walter Reynolds, the last ordinal function of that unworthy man, for he died the following November, possibly 'of grief and horror of mind'. The gold coins scattered on Coronation Day showed a hand stretched out to save a crown from falling.

When Edward opened Parliament for the first time on 3 February, he was provided with a highly respectable Council of Regency, including both archbishops and both his father's half-brothers, and not over-weighted by Mortimer's adherents, though to be sure Orleton, the Treasurer, and Hotham of Ely, the Chancellor, were both very much Mortimer's men. Mortimer himself steered clear of it. He left the Council to bear full responsibility while he, in the way of favourites, ruled obliquely through the queen.

The ruin of so many enemies made possible the distribution of rewards to those who had shared in the risky enterprise. The efficient fiscal machinery developed by Despenser continued to run smoothly and, once the escheats and fines came pouring in, there was plenty of money to hand. Even so, Mortimer's disbursements were so lavish that scarcely a third of the crown revenues were left for the use of the Council.

The House of Lancaster, whose great power and prestige had done so much to make success easy, was suitably recognized. Except for those of Lincoln and Salisbury, which Thomas had lost when his wife ran away, Henry was restored to the remaining titles and estates of his brother – High Steward of England, earl of Lancaster and of Derby. And there were renewed petitions to make dead, cantankerous Thomas into a saint. 'Like a river descending from some pleasant place to water Paradise', his eulogy asserted, his memory gave 'a wholesome temperature and fruitfulness by its Celestial Dew to the soil of England, dyed red with the effusion of his sacred blood.' He was still working miracles and, as late as the suppression of the monasteries in the 1530s, his belt and hat were reputed to be helpful to women in labour.

Isabella's income soared to the staggering figure of £13,333 a year, contrasting strongly with the 100 marks a month (£800 per annum) allowed to Lancaster for the maintenance of her fallen husband. She arranged a pension for the helpful John of Hainault and paid off his soldiers; and, still out of the public funds, defrayed her debts in France prior to the invasion. She was awarded, as she conceived to be her due, all Hugh Despenser's plate and jewellery; and it was probably now, too, that she acquired her London mansion in Lombard Street. Nor did Mortimer neglect himself. He had his attainder reversed, and re-entered his family estates, augmented by a huge block of Despenser lands and some of those of Arundel. With the not inconsiderable portion of his wife Joan de Glenville in addition, he was virtually king of Wales.

Bishops Oreton, Burghersh, Stratford, and Airmyn of Norwich, lynch-pins of the conspiracy, received back their confiscated temporalities, and the crown undertook not to use that form of pressure for the future. Pope John XXII did not allow himself to be forgotten. A sharp man of affairs, he had taken advantage of Edward II's weakness to demand vast arrears of a tribute extorted from King John, in similar circumstances, a hundred years before. On proclamation of the new reign, the Council, not daring to offend him, promised to pay 500 marks a year. Charles the Fair of France also expected to be remembered for his patience over Aquitaine while his sister's hazard was being decided in England. On 31 March he renewed his promise to vacate the occupied districts; but, this time, only on payment of a war indemnity of 50,000 marks, in additon to the 60,000 *livres* already due. As the money was not available, no withdrawal took place, and the once proud English dominion in southern France 'was reduced to the maritime strip, without any deep hinterland, between the mouth of the Charente and the Pyrenees'.

The Scots were less placable. Rightly though rudely they ascribed tentative gropings towards a permanent settlement by their mortal enemy to his impotence, and the fiery Bruce confronted the new English stripling with a 'Defiance', saying that he would do to him as he had done before in his father's reign at the battle of Bannockburn near Stirling. The insult was unspeakable. Many in England had fathers or brothers to avenge upon the Scots, whose irritating ditties had in the intervening thirteen years kept their triumph smartingly alive. War was inevitable, and Mortimer felt it might at least distract attention from the state of things at home. A message was sent asking Sir John of Hainault to return, and he obligingly began to remuster his so recently disbanded forces. On 29 April 1327 at Notting-ham, Mortimer, already on his way north with the whole court and government, ordered a general commission of array to meet at York in three weeks' time. The response was willing. Knights' fees were honoured, esquires and men-at-arms flocked to the banners of their lords; cities and corporations, as required by their charters, provided archers at their own expense; many soldiers of fortune joined in of their own accord – in all, some 50,000 men bore down on the fair city of York, the second largest in the realm.

At York, great preparations were made for the reception of the 2,000 Hainault mercenaries, whom Mortimer and Isabella had now come to look on as their personal bodyguard. They were given the best billets in the town, and steps were taken to protect them from exploitation by the natives. According to Jean le Bel, who was among them, 'as much was to be bought for a penny as before their arrival. Good wines from Gascony, Alsace and the Rhine were in abundance and reasonable; Poultry and other provisions at very ordinary rates. Hay, oats and other necessaries for horses were daily brought to the strangers' lodgings, so that they were all extremely satisfied.' Indeed, they were far more satisfied than the envious English, who hated the guttural foreigners, the 'Hunaldi', as the chroniclers called them. Trouble soon started.

On Trinity Sunday, 7 June, Isabella and her sixty maidens gave an exotic feast of welcome for Sir John of Hainault and his knights at the Black Friars, where she lodged with the young king and Mortimer. 'There might be seen a numerous nobility well served with plenty of strange dishes, so disguised that it could not be known what they were. There were also ladies most superbly dressed, who were expecting with impatience the hour of the ball, but it fell out otherwise; for, soon after dinner, a violent affray happened between some of the Hainaulters and the English archers who were lodged with them in the suburbs.'

The pampered aliens had been making free with the townsmen's wives and daughters. Angry burgesses set on them, and were joined by Lincolnshire archers. When they fled to their billets to arm, the Hainaulters found the windows shuttered and the doors slammed in their faces. Caught in a lethal rain of clothyard arrows, they fell in swathes, and many, panicking, were drowned in the river Ouse. After dark, led by their officers hastening away from the goodwill banquet, the Hainaulters counter-attacked. Part of the city was set ablaze. In the morning, in the still-drifting smoke, there were eighty English archers to be buried in St Clement's churchyard. The English were ordered out to more distant quarters. Grumbling, the soldiers humped their kit. A strong guard was mounted around their allies, who thereafter went out very little, slept on their weapons, and kept their horses ready saddled for escape.

Stores were counted, pavilions and siege engines loaded, carts and wagons drawn up in convoy. On 28 June, Sir John of Hainault was paid £7,000, half his agreed remuneration, in advance. To prevent further quarrels, on setting out he and his troops were to keep close behind the king. Next week, 'the King and all his Barons began their march from the city of York in good order, and gallantly armed with trumpets sounding and banners waving in the wind'. It was young King Edward's first experience of active warfare. So far, cosseted in his mother's seamy entourage abroad, and hunting down his betrayed and solitary father in the West Country, he had received less than his proper share of training as a knight. King now, he was eager at last to see how the flower of English chivalry, in full panoply, would expiate years of humiliation upon a despised and barbarous foe. He thrilled to the march.

They rode to Durham, 'a long day's journey, at the entrance of a country called Northumberland, which is wild, full of deserts and mountains, and poor in everything except cattle'. Seeing no sign of any Scots, they went on towards Newcastle and joined up, as planned, with the advance forces of the Earl Marshal and commander-in-chief, Thomas Brotherton of Norfolk, the king's uncle.

The Scots were, in fact, none the less in the field with some 25,000 men, about half the English number. Bruce, now slowly dying of leprosy, was not there in person, but he had experienced commanders: Sir James Douglas, whose berserk audacity matched the cunning of his leader, Lord Thomas Randolph; and the earl of Moray. Except for the knights, who rode fine bays, the Scots were mostly mounted on fast little moorland ponies. Their hardiness dismayed the English. They lived on little scones made of oatmeal taken from their saddle-bags and mixed with water and baked over a fire of twigs on metal plates carried under the saddles. They drank from streams, and devoured cattle caught by the way, skinned and stewed in their own hides. They had no baggage train. Thus lightly equipped, they lightly came and went.

Unknown to the English garrisons at its extremities at Newcastle and Carlisle, the Scots had already crossed the Tyne, and were harrying the country miles behind the English advance, as far back as Darlington. In mid-July the army turned south in search of them. In due course they came upon ruined villages, scorched crops, half-crazed peasants, and other signs of devastation. At last they perceived a curl of smoke only a mile or two ahead. Eagerly they went towards the smoke; yet however pressingly they lumbered after it, it recoiled before them. Mile after mile, hour after hour, over hills and through valleys, past treacherous bogs and into dangerous defiles, the teasing little wisp of smoke curled up in front of them, dancing now here, now there, neither nearer nor farther off, but always the same distance, just a mile or two ahead.

After days of vain pursuit, the army halted at evening in a wood on the bank of a small river, while the king took shelter in a tumbledown monastery nearby. At a council of war it was decided that, heavily burdened as they were, they would never catch up with the Scots: that, on the contrary, as the Scots would sooner or later have to recross the Tyne, it would be better to return there at once to cut them off. At midnight the call to arms was sounded. They abandoned their cumbersome wagons in a laager in the woods, and each man carrying what he could, they set off pell-mell towards the north 'not waiting for father, brother, or friend'.

There were frequent alarms. Those behind kept hearing shouts as though battle had been joined. They clapped on their helmets, couched their lances, and made forward at best speed, to find only that the 'first battail' had put up some deer and were noisily giving chase. At vespers, having ridden hard all day, the cavalry reached the Tyne and rode across, though with difficulty, because of the large, round, slippery stones. By the time the foot soldiers came straggling up it was too dark to cross, and they had to spend the night on the southern bank, 'many not appearing till the morning, and some few never after seen'.

In imitation of the Scots, the mounted troops had fastened loaves of bread behind their saddles, but they had not done it right, and in the heat of the ride the bread had become sodden with the horses' sweat. There was nothing else to eat. There was nothing to drink, apart from the river water, 'except for some great lords, who had bottles among their luggage'. There was no forage for the animals, nor any trees or stakes to tether them to. The knights had to lie down on the river bank in their armour as they were, holding on to their horses by the bridles.

Next morning it began to rain, and it rained for a week in solid sheets, as it can on Hadrian's Wall at the height of summer. The river grew impassable, and the army had to remain perilously divided, horse on one side, foot on the other. There was nothing in sight, save for the endless, windswept, drenched Northumbrian hills. What little firewood could be found was too wet to burn; there was no way to shoe the horses' hooves. The squires used their swords to cut down brushwood and build a few leaky shelters. The armour rusted, and the leather harness rotted.

When the rain stopped at last, they found they were lost. Some country people, happening that way one afternoon, told them they were midway between Newcastle and Carlisle. Sumpter horses were sent off at once to fetch provisions, and in response to a proclamation from the king shrewd tradesmen came out with their wares from both towns, and sold them at great profit, 'sixpence the loaf, which was not worth more than a penny, and a gallon of wine for six groats [two shillings], scarcely worth sixpence'. Tempers were frayed. The Hunaldi were grumbling in their guttural language, and the Lincolnshire archers were wistfully fingering their bowstrings.

The young king took charge. He found a place down river where it was possible for the horses to cross, and though some were drowned, for the water was still in flood and swimming was little practised, at least his army stood reunited on the southern bank. He then declared that whoever first brought him news of the Scots should have a knighthood and a pension. The young esquires leapt enthusiastically to horse and galloped off.

Soon Thomas Rokeby, a Yorkshire esquire, came spurring back. He had found the Scots, he said, not more than a few miles distant just beyond the river Wear. He had gone so close that he had been taken prisoner, but their leaders, on hearing his errand, had willingly forgone his ransom on the single condition that he would bring the king to where they lay. The king knighted him on the spot in front of the whole army. Then, when all had made confession and prepared themselves for battle, they turned about once more and went southwards to the Wear.

The Scots were impregnably encamped on the southern bank on a hill overlooking the river, a pouring torrent full of tumbling boulders that would of itself have been dangerous to cross even had there been no opposition and no enfiladed slope beyond to climb. Edward declined the trap. The Scots equally refused his wily challenge to come down and fight the thing out on open ground. Edward reckoned that the Scots would soon be running out of oatmeal, and that he only had to hold them where they were to come to grips. So the armies stood face to face across the river, so close they could read the blazons of each other's shields.

By night the Scots lit bonfires, made outlandish cries, and played instruments so hideous that the English thought the din deliberately intended to prevent them sleeping. On the fourth night they made even more row than usual; in the morning they had vanished without trace. They were found again a few miles upstream, at Stanhope Park, where the English again doggedly confronted them. After dark, Sir James Douglas crossed the river well below the sleeping armies, and crept alone into the English lines. An educated man, he had an unexpected command of English, and so was able to stroll about unchallenged, exclaiming from time to time with gusto 'What, no Ward? Ha! St George!' He then rejoined his waiting ambuscade and charged full tilt into the camp crying 'A Douglas! A Douglas! Ye shall die, ye thieves of England!' He made straight for Edward's tent, cut it down about his ears, and so rode clear, still crying into the distance 'Douglas! Douglas for ever.'

Early in August the Scots once more slipped away at night by crossing a marsh, supposedly impassable, to the rear of their position, and returned to Bruce in jubilant impunity with their more portable plunder. On the site they had vacated, the English found hundreds of slaughtered cattle, some of them dressed ready for stewing in their own skins as cauldrons, and numberless pairs of worn-out rawhide shoes, presumably discarded after new ones were made.

Young Edward is said to have cried for shame and disappointment. This humiliatingly unsuccessful expedition did more even than the outright defeat of Bannockburn to force England's eventual recognition of Bruce as king of Scotland. But there was no time for recrimination. It was imperative to terminate Edward's first, inglorious campaign. It was late August; the period of feudal service having expired, the host was needed at home to get in the harvest. Back in Durham, the knights were cheered to find that their baggage wagons, left in the woods a month before and never expected to be seen again, had been brought in by the townspeople and stored in barns, each with a little flag saying which was which. At York, the Hainaulters at once sat down to make out extra claims for horses lost and other expenses additional to their wages. These came to such a discouraging total that there was not money enough in York to meet it; but Sir John went surety for all, accepting a draft on the London Treasury for £4,000, and a lien on the crown jewels if necessary. A heavy escort was provided to see the allies through the doubtful fens of Lincolnshire, where the dreaded English archers lived; and so at last, from Dover, at the end of August 1327, the Hainaulters went home.

* * *

Before the country was denuded for the Scottish expedition, it had been deemed wise to provide for the greater security of the former king. In April 1327, warrants had gone out to two of Mortimer's knights, Sir John Maltravers and Sir Thomas Gurney, to remove the royal prisoner from the indulgent keeping of Henry of Lancaster at Kenilworth to that of Sir Thomas Berkeley at Berkeley castle near Bristol. Lancaster was no longer altogether trusted by Mortimer, and he was also due to go on the campaign; while Berkeley was indebted to Isabella for retrieving his castle from the Despensers, and had lately married Mortimer's daughter Margaret.

The journey was a risky one, for Edward of Caernarvon still had friends who believed in his regality; moreover, in disordered times a wandering king was of tempting monetary value. It is possible that the indignities put upon him on the way – he is said to have had his beard shaved off with cold water contained in an old helmet, and to have been made to go by turns in rags, or wearing various incongruous forms of headgear – were no more than clumsy efforts to keep up his incognito. He arrived safely, and was received in proper style by Sir Thomas Berkeley.

At some time after the army of England had marched north into the wilds (regular allowances for Edward's upkeep were ordered, at least until 5 July 1327), Thomas Dunhead, a Dominican friar, led an attack on Berkeley castle and carried off the one-time king. He was taken perhaps to Corfe, perhaps to Bristol, with the aim of escaping overseas, but he was soon recaptured, while Dunhead suffered a frightful death. News of the attempt reached Isabella while she was alone at York, and it made her tremble. Her treason against her husband had turned, in her mind, to dread. By fits and starts, on the one day, stirred by guilt, she would send a kindly message, on the next, out of terror, dark orders to his jailors to guard him well.

Her indecision did not help Gurney and Maltravers, who realized that the affair could not end well for them, whatever happened. If Edward escaped again, they were doomed, whether or not he was retaken. If they killed him, with or without orders, they were sure to be disowned. They resolved to have him die from natural causes. Thomas Berkeley, a man of noble rank whom Edward could talk to, was refused all further access. By cold, damp and hunger, they tried to bring on pneumonia. They tried to send him mad, by keeping him awake, by talking gibberish, by staging fantasies and hallucinations, not the least bewildering of which was the sudden alteration in his treatment according to Isabella's change of mood.

Finally, since it was well known that foul vapours carried the plague, they removed him to a cell over a pit full of stinking carrion. But Edward's body was too strong to die, and his spirit too naive to break. He survived all. His chief complaint remained, as it had been throughout, that he was not visited by his wife and family.

When Mortimer reappeared from the North, he looked urgently into the case of Dunhead's insurrection. Agents informed him that there was another plot afoot in Wales. There was no room for further hesitation. He sent one William Ogle to Gurney, with cogent instructions of fiendish ingenuity, and orders to see them carried out.

On the night of 21 September 1327, while Lord Berkeley was away, the villagers were startled by scream after scream ringing out from the castle. In the morning, abbots, knights and burgesses were brought from Bristol and Gloucester to view the body of the dead king. There were no visible marks of violence. They were told he had had internal trouble during the night.

He was buried in Gloucester abbey by the monks, where afterwards his son raised a splendid shrine, a flourishing place of pilgrimage. The pillars flanking it were encircled with figures of stags, said to have drawn the body there from Berkeley. But at the time, when the young king first heard the news at Lincoln, he dared not lavishly express his grief, and kept his feelings to himself. Isabella 'bore a very troubled countenance', and appointed a day for anniversary prayers to be said for her husband's soul.

* * *

A month or two later, Edward was riding south to receive his bride. That August, Bishop Orleton had been sent to Avignon to buy the pope's dispensation for the marriage. The see of Worcester happening at that moment to fall vacant, Orleton, for the second time in ten years, bribed Pope John to 'provide' him to it, much to the indignation of Isabella, who lost her customary fee of gift as a result. He returned in October with the necessary permit, and Bishop Northborough of Coventry then set off for Hainault to fix definitely on Philippa. Philippa's passport was issued in November 1327, and after a proxy wedding at her home in Valenciennes, she came ashore at the port of London just before Christmas in the charge of her ever-ready uncle Sir John of Hainault, making his third visit in just over a year. She was met by the king, and by Isabella, her mother-in-law to be, and the mayor and aldermen turned out to welcome her.

There followed a cold New Year's journey northward by way of Leicester up to York, where the court had remained after the Scottish expedition to await the opening of Parliament in February. They rode into the city side by side, the tall, fair, regal, fifteen-year-old bridegroom and his dumpy, pleasant, capable-looking bride. On Sunday, 24 January 1328, they were married in York Minster by Archbishop Melton, with Dr

Hotham, bishop of Ely, in attendance. There followed, for the space of three weeks, 'great rejoicings and noble show of lords, earls, barons, knights, highborn ladies and noble damsels, with rich display of dress and jewels, with jousts too and tourneys for the ladies' love, with dancing and carolling, and with great and rich feasts day by day'. Philippa was not crowned at that time, nor until two years later, by which time she was noticeably pregnant. Isabella was in no hurry to become a dowager.

The main business of the parliament at York was to reach a final settlement with the Scots, who sent a delegation of a hundred knights led by the dashing Lord James Douglas. It was natural that the embattled Robert Bruce, now dying, should have wished to see all he had fought for triumphantly confirmed. Even so, the terms eventually agreed (they were ratified by Parliament at Northampton on 4 May 1328) must have amazed him by the completeness of his victory. The Border was established on the old line from Berwick-on-Tweed to Burgh-on-Sands, as though Edward I had never been. Bruce was recognized as autonomous king of Scotland. All relics and trophies were to be returned, the jewels captured in Edinburgh, the Black Rood of Scotland, and an over-rated parchment known as the Ragman Roll (rigmarole?) bearing all the homages due to Edward I. It is said that the Stone of Scone was preserved for England only by the refusal of the abbot of Westminster and the people of London to give it up. Bruce's heir, the four-year-old David Bruce, was to take in marriage King Edward's younger sister, the seven-year-old Princess Joan of the Tower. In return for all this, the restoration of certain Border lands to individual English noblemen was to be negotiated later, and the Scots were to pay a war indemnity of £20,000 for damage done.

The money, the only asset from the Shameful Peace, did not find its way into the Treasury. A third of it, 10,000 marks, was paid openly to Isabella under the Privy Seal, perhaps to offset her disbursements to the Hainaulters. The remainder disappeared; just as, it began to be remembered, all the royal treasure carted off to Wales by the old king and Despenser had likewise disappeared. What, it began to be asked, had Mortimer been up to? How, if not by bribery, had the Scots been able to decamp so unexpectedly from Stanhope Park, leaving all those leather cauldrons ready for boiling in the morning? What, for that matter, had really happened to the old king?

Yet it was not so much Mortimer's by no means unique cupidity that set the tide against him. What mainly rankled, as with Gaveston and Despenser before him, was his presumption. His ancestors, the Monthermers, had been no more than a decent county family settled in the Marches by William the Conqueror. Yet this Roger Mortimer had dared to have three of his four sons knighted with the king at the coronation, and was now marrying his seven daughters one after another into the greatest households in the land. He treated Edward with step-fatherly familiarity, would remain seated in his presence, and sometimes preceded him in procession, talking back jokingly over his shoulder. He would not allow the earl of Lancaster, the king's official guardian, nor his two royal uncles, to be alone with him, and set spies (a Sir John Wyard was one of them) over his words and actions.

In the spring of 1328, Mortimer gave sumptuous entertainments for the royal family; Round Table tournaments at Bedford and Hereford for the weddings of his daughters Joan and Beatrice; and in June, there were progresses to his castles at Ludlow and Wigmore. In July they all went north in state to Berwick to attend the promised betrothal of Princess Joan to David Bruce. There was no real harm in all this ostentation; the Round Table, for instance, did no more than recall a fabulous spectacle given by Mortimer's grandfather before Edward I at Kenilworth. None the less, he gave great offence; the more so since as much of the expense as possible was charged to the public cost. As Dr Joshua Barnes said, 'all of it in general smelt rank of a Popular Air and a vainglorious Humour'.

At the Salisbury parliament in October, Mortimer, contrary to his own decree, attended with an armed escort, and required the king to create him earl of March. True, the king's brother, John of Eltham, became at the same time earl of Cornwall, but that did not make any the less ominous Mortimer's choice of such a firebrand title.

Henry of Lancaster by now cared no better for Mortimer than his brother Thomas had done for Hugh Despenser. Mistrusting Mortimer's intentions, he kept clear of the Salisbury parliament and lay in arms at Winchester. He was joined by both the king's uncles, by many of the now supplanted Council of Regency, and by most of the former enemies of the Despensers, some of them, like Stratford, bishop of Winchester, flying headlong from Salisbury to avoid arrest. When Mortimer bore down on them, they fell back on their old stronghold, London, where they raised a force six hundred strong.

On 6 January 1329, Mortimer sacked Lancaster's southern citadel of Leicester, destroyed the parks and woodlands, drained the fishponds, drove off the game and cattle, and carried away all he could lay his hands on, down to the ornaments from the churches. Lancaster marched north to Bedford ready to give battle, but the royal uncles again changed sides, and thus deserted he was forced to accept penal terms, a huge fine of £11,000 against himself, exile for many of his adherents, and yet more forfeited lands for Mortimer. It was clear that Mortimer still held superior power, and could wield it lawfully through his domination of the king. Everything depended upon whether the king, so far obedient to his mother and helpless in her master's hands, would or would not throw them off when he grew older.

* * *

Charles IV, the Fair, died on 1 February 1328 at the age of thirty-three. He was the fourth king of France to die in fourteen years, and unless his third wife, Jeanne of Evreux, whom he left pregnant, could contrive to bear a son, he was the last Capetian. In any event a regency was necessary, and the obvious choice was his first cousin, Philip of Valois, a responsible man of thirty-five, a great prince of the blood, whose family was much at the hub of affairs, rather as the House of Lancaster was in England. Two months later the widowed queen gave birth to a daughter, who had less title to the throne than the daughters of Louis X and Philip V, already passed over 'because of the Imbecility of the Sex'. None of the girls was considered a possible candidate for the crown.

Philip of Valois was the nearest male claimant through male parentage to the throne. But it could be said that although, as a woman, Isabella was personally disqualified, her right of blood continued. In the matter of bearing children she was clearly far from 'imbecile', and her claim could pass intact to her eldest son. In this view, Isabella's son, Edward III of England, was the only grandson of Philip the Fair, while Philip of Valois was a nephew.

All the practical advantage lay with Philip. He and his family were well known in France, he was already regent, and his accession would reunite to the crown the important fiefs of Valois and Anjou. As for Edward, he lived across the sea, was the present representative of those ever disloyal vassals the Plantagenets of Aquitaine, and he was still a minor. Within days of the birth of the posthumous daughter of the late King Charles, Philip called a council under his own presidency, and had no difficulty in becoming king as Philip VI.

Embroiled though she was in England, Isabella did not fail to lodge a protest. Many letters of complaint were written to noblemen of the English interest in Brabant, in Gascony, Foix, Languedoc and Navarre. On 16 May she sent her old friend Bishop Orleton to press her case in Paris. But it was no more than a formal gesture. Complicating and expensive foreign wars had no place in the plans of Mortimer and Isabella. A fortnight later, with the general agreement of the French Estates, who were wearying of the cost of these too frequent coronations, King Philip VI was duly crowned at Rheims in the presence of all his vassals-in-chief, save one.

He took prompt steps to strengthen his position. He bought off the several girls he had disinherited. He went to Flanders where, at Cassel, he soundly avenged the stain of Courtrai (as bad as Bannockburn) a quarter of a century earlier, restored the grateful Louis of Nevers as count, and returned to Paris a hero. It remained for him to obtain fealty from the twelfth peer of France, the only one with a contrary claim, and the only one who had not yet given it, Edward, duke of Aquitaine.

Philip's ambassadors (who included the future Pope Clement VI) arrived in England in March 1329 to summon Edward to perform his homage to his new overlord. The court was at Windsor, busy patching up the hollow settlement with Lancaster, and never less in a position to negotiate from strength. It would seem that Isabella lost her temper, declared roundly that 'the son of a King should never do homage to the son of a Count', and made unpleasing remarks about the 'foundling King', as Philip was called by the Flemings, who detested him. But the outburst was shrugged off and explained away as female posturing; the French ambassadors were genially beguiled, and were got rid of without any definite commitment having been made.

Philip was not prepared to tolerate the so customary evasions of the English monarchy. He sent again to say that if homage was not done at once, he would, like Charles IV and Philip the Fair before him, reduce by force the contumacious duchy. So urgent was his tone that on 14 April 1329 a reply was sent by the hand of Sir Bartholomew Burghersh, brother of Bishop Burghersh and a reliable Mortimer man, apologizing for the delay and promising that Edward would follow in person shortly.

Philip made imposing preparations for his triumph. He fixed the date, in June, and the place, in Amiens cathedral. He invited the kings of Bohemia, Majorca, and Navarre to be his guests for the occasion, and they all accepted. The whole city of Amiens was taken over and parcelled out to house the princes, dukes and peers of France and their splendid equipages. Provision was also made to receive the modest though, in the circumstances, eagerly anticipated party expected to arrive from England.

Edward's attitude to the whole notion of doing homage to his cousin Philip had been from the first clear-cut. He did not like it. To demand a repetition of the vows he had only recently made to Charles IV seemed designed to rub in the indignity. Still, he had no choice. And at least, since his mother and Mortimer had decided, for prudence' sake, not to stir from home, he would be going on his own. It would be his first independent act of state. He prepared himself accordingly to make the best of it.

The figure that swept up the aisle at Amiens on 6 June was very different from that presaged by memories of his inept father, or by the cringing letters prepared for his seal by Mortimer's clerks; and from the reedy boy who not long ago had been seen following about Paris in the shadow of his peremptory mother. His fair hair gleamed on the shoulders of his long crimson robe, powdered with leopards of gold, falling gracefully over his straight limbs. He had his crown on his head, his sword by his side, and spurs of gold on his heels. Jewels flashed fire from him in the pale sparkle of the candles. 'His face was like the face of a god', it was said.

Philip watched his approach, startled and uneasy. Outwardly, he cut no mean figure himself, enthroned, crowned, sceptred, in royal-blue velvet embroidered with golden fleurs-de-lis. Yet something in the unstudied manner of the advancing youth, his wholesomeness, his plenty, his assurance, chilled and strangely depressed the middle-aged, henpecked, self-made Valois king.

Edward was flanked by his two royal uncles. Behind him came, instead of the small posse of 'horse-strangers' that had been allowed for, three bishops, four earls, forty knights, and, stretching far down the road outside the church, a thousand horse of war. There was an emphatic sprinkling of young men: Henry of Grosmont, representing his father, Lancaster; Thomas Beauchamp of Warwick, not yet of full age; John de Bohun of Hereford and Essex; William Montagu, Edward's soldierly personal friend; and a bright young squire of Hainault, Walter Manny, who had come to England in Philippa's retinue as her carver. Whatever their relations were with Mortimer, they all stood four-square with their king.

Edward did not quibble. When asked by the chamberlain of France in the age-old phrases, did he become the king of France's man for the duchy of Guienne and its appurtenances, as his ancestors, kings of England and dukes of Guienne had done before him, he stepped up to the throne, bowed slightly, placed his hands between those of Philip, and answered, '*Voire*' ('Truly'). The deed was done. Edward had done homage; any claim he might have to Philip's throne was dead, on pain of sacrilege. So solemn was the moment, it was not remarked that he had not gone through the full rubric of liege homage. He had not put off his crown and spurs, nor ungirt his sword, nor knelt to his overlord on a cushion; nor indeed had he kissed him on the mouth as was demanded.

Officials on either side were left to make good the details. There was to be a double marriage, in consolidation of the entente, between Philip's son John and Edward's sister Eleanor, and between John of Eltham and the French Marie. Yet to be settled were the long-lingering problems within Aquitaine itself – the 50,000 marks and 60,000 *livres* already owed by Edward; the uncertain borders, the still occupied provinces, the razing of castles loyal to Edward but rebellious to France – all these causes of friction remained critical. The English agreed to appoint commissions to look into them, and five days after the ceremony at Amiens, abruptly returned to England.

Returned too abruptly, the French councillors thought. Thinking it over, they felt they had been cheated. What, after all had the house of Valois gained? True, Edward had done a form of homage, but his homage had looked more like defiance. He had transformed a picturesque feudal observance into a confrontation between kings, between nations; England against France.

* * *

In February 1330 Philippa was five months gone with child, and Isabella at last agreed to permit her coronation. She rode on a palfrey from the City to

Westminster, squired by the king's two uncles, Thomas of Brotherton, earl of Norfolk, and Edmund, earl of Kent, on either side, disguised as simple grooms. Such charades were not uncommon in the fourteenth century, displaying a gracious condescension in the great, and at the same time their healthy confidence in their own inviolability. In later and more deadly days these cheerful conceits were discontinued for fear of condoning fatal errors of identity, until revived by Henry VIII, who was safely unmistakable. In the present instance the sequel, though unrelated to Philippa's coronation, was terrible indeed. Within a month the royal Edmund, earl of Kent, degraded in real earnest, stood stripped to his shirt, with a halter round his neck, pleading for his life before Parliament at Winchester.

Kent, unreliable and impetuous as ever, having been party to Edward of Caernarvon's deposition, and having attended his official though not his actual funeral, had become so stricken with remorse that he allowed himself to be convinced that his half-brother was not really dead, and he engaged in a conspiracy for his rescue. The true facts were, and remain, obscure. To disclose a real plot, Mortimer had planted a sham one of Gordian cunning.

Mortimer put it about that the former king was indeed alive and well, and living in state at Corfe castle in Dorset. He arranged for Sir John Daverill, the governor of Corfe, to hold masques and dances on the battlements, so that weird figures moving distantly in the garish light of torches were seen from time to time by the country people in the village below. In due course, a Dominican friar came to the earl of Kent at Kensington, and told him in a roundabout way that he knew, from a spirit he had conjured up, the whereabouts of his brother Edward. Kent sent him to investigate at Corfe, with bribes for Daverill. After being kept till nightfall in the janitor's lodge, the friar was dressed in a dark cloak and brought into a shadowy corner of the Great Hall, where he saw by rush lights on the distant dais a regal figure served at dinner with every mark of deference. He reported to Kent, who went down to Corfe in person and, with further bribes, begged Daverill to be admitted to the presence. Daverill pleaded fear of Mortimer, whereupon Kent gave him a letter sealed with his own seal for delivery to the distinguished prisoner.

On the first day of the parliament at Winchester, Kent was seized at Mortimer's order. He admitted writing the letter handed in by Daverill, which was now read; also another one to Sir Bogo of Bayonne, a decoy; also, that his wife, Margaret Wake, had likewise written letters. In his terror, he confessed to far more than was known for certain. Many enemies of Mortimer now here in Parliament, he said, had approached him at various times with offers of help. William Melton, archbishop of York, and Stephen Gravesend, bishop of London, had remained always loyal to Edward II, and Sir Fulk Fitz-Warin had assured him at Westminster that the rescue would be the finest thing ever attempted. Sir Ingelram Berenger had discussed it with him often, the last time in his room over the chapel at Arundel castle. Henry, Lord Beaumont, and Sir Thomas Rosselin, already exiled by Mortimer, had conspired in Paris in the duke of Brabant's bedroom. Kent's wife's brother Thomas, Lord Wake, and Lord John Peche (both of whom managed to flee the country); William, Lord Zouch, Mortimer's kinsman and rival in Glamorgan – all these, and Henry of Lancaster, now almost blind, were held on tenterhooks for their parts, real, trumped-up, or two-faced, in the convenient and far-flung confederacy, and for the most part their lands were forfeited to Mortimer.

For Kent there was no hope. He was condemned, and his immediate execution ordered, it is said, without reference to the king, his nephew. Supervision of the sentence would normally have fallen to the Earl Marshal, Thomas of Brotherton; but as he was the brother of the prisoner, and was suspect himself, the warrant was sent straight to the bailiffs of Winchester for action on 19 March 1330. Kent was none too popular; even so, his plight aroused much sympathy. No one could be found in the town of Winchester to carry out the sentence. The execution had to wait, the livelong day, until towards sunset a condemned felon hastily brought from the Marshalsea at Southwark saved his own life by the chop of an axe.

The judicial murder of the earl of Kent conclusively decided Edward to dispose of Mortimer. There had already been strange and occult stirrings in that direction. The chronicler Henry Knighton has a story that, after the homage at Amiens in June 1329, Philip VI tried to abduct the king of England, though what he stood to gain is far from clear. What seems more probable is that the English nobles then in France for the ceremony, and others already there as refugees from Mortimer, aimed, with or without French help, to do as Mortimer himself had done, and invade England from the Continent. The conversations mentioned in Kent's confession, supposedly held in Paris, may have had something to do with it. At all events the affair came to nothing. Bishop Burghersh of Lincoln, who was Mortimer's watchdog on the Amiens expedition, got wind of it, and hustled his party back to England.

In September, Edward's friend and personal equerry, Sir William Montagu, was sent with Sir Bartholomew Burghersh on an errand to Pope John at Avignon. Eluding his officious colleague, Montagu gained a private audience with the pope, and explained Edward's situation. On his return to England he provided his royal master with a much-needed loan of 2,000 marks from the estate of the late queen of Navarre, of which he had been made executor. The king's former tutor, Richard de Bury, now Keeper of the Privy Seal, next wrote to the pope arranging that the use of the words *Pater sancte* in a letter to the Curia would indicate that it was Edward's own, and had not been dictated to him by Mortimer. A specimen of Edward's signature was attached – the earliest surviving autograph of a king of England – and also a sample of his handwriting. With touching confidence in the pope's discretion (a trust not misplaced in this case, for the letter was found only in 1911, still safely buried in the Vatican archives), Edward told the pope that knowledge of his design against Mortimer was confined to these two, Bury and Montagu.

Unlike his father, Edward III had of necessity acquired early the valuable art of giving his trust and friendship to men not only of ability but of complete integrity, and of setting each to the task he was best fitted for; with the result that he was not once betrayed during his long reign in a treacherous age. His habitual discernment was never more fortunate than in this initial crisis.

Richard de Bury has become justly renowned as a lover of books. When bishop of Durham, his episcopal visitations took the form of a furious rooting about in damp monastic crypts to rescue mouldering manuscripts. On his ambassadorial missions he browsed at large all over Europe. He was corruptible only with books. 'No one can serve books and mammon,' he declared. In 1345, the year of his death, there appeared his *Philobiblon*, a treatise on the care of books and on rules for the use of a library he intended to found. He inveighed mock-seriously against the natural enemies of books, then so precious and so painfully constructed; the 'whimpering child' who traced over the gilded letters with sticky fingers; 'that two-footed beast', the housewife, who, 'spying them in their corner with no defence but the webs woven around them by spiders now defunct, seized them with frowning brow and bitter words'; and those 'shameless youths' who use straws as markers and so break the back, or scribble in the margins 'whatsoever frivolous stuff may happen to run at the moment in their heads'. He left his collection to the then-projected Durham College at Oxford, of which university he was a distinguished son. But his grand bequest did not materialize; he had spent so much on his books that they had to be sold to pay his debts.

Bury was the son of Sir Richard Aungerville, a knight of Bury St Edmunds. After his father's death he was brought up by John de Willough-by, a friendly priest. His selection, when an unobtrusive Benedictine monk at Durham, as tutor to the royal heir apparent was most likely due to Isabella, perhaps at the time when she enthroned Louis de Beaumont as bishop there, whom in due course Bury was to succeed. Indeed, Bury seems to have stirred a keener taste for books in Isabella, still sufficiently young to be his pupil, than he did in her son, his proper charge, whom she persuaded to hand over to her without reluctance seven French romances beautifully bound in red, white and green leather. During their penurious stay in France, Bury, as treasurer to the young duke of Aquitaine, sent mother and son part of the ducal revenues. Then, to escape the consequent rage of the king, he fled to join them in Paris, where he marvelled at the glories of the university, 'whose rays gave light to every corner of the round world', and which had not yet sunk, as he later deplored, to become the home of 'torpid traditionalism'.

He was humanist and progressive. Like his friend Petrarch a rediscoverer of the classics, he sympathized with William of Occam and the Nominalists, the avant-garde philosophers of the day. But, a true man of his times, he had other abilities besides scholarship, and Edward, while avoiding his inducements to the higher learning, typically made the best use of them on his accession, both in overseas diplomacy and at home, showering him with prebendaries and sinecures, and appointing him in time to the highest offices, Chancellor and Treasurer. For his part, Bury, finding Mortimer no more admirable than the Despensers, devoted himself wholly to the service of his young king.

The wisdom of Dr Bury teamed well with the knightly qualities of Sir William Montagu. The Montagus, descended from Drogo de Mont Aïgu who had come over from Normandy with the Conqueror, had since prospered quietly on their estates about Shipton Montagu in Somerset. Their recent history was typical of those houses of the minor nobility – the Berkeleys, Badlesmeres, Burghershes, Despensers, Mortimers – who were trying to climb into the caste of the high baronage, except that the method they pursued, of unswerving duty to the crown, was an unusual one.

Sir William's grandfather, Simon Montagu, had rendered signal service by both land and sea to Edward I in Wales, Gascony and Scotland. He had been rewarded with a baron's writ, as well as the hand and heritage of Princess Aufricia, a husky maiden in distress, sole relict of the ancient kings of Man after the massacre of her father, Fergus, and her brother Orry by the marauding Scots. She had fled to England with nothing but her long tresses and her claim to a lost kingdom, a suppliant for King Edward's austere justice. Aufricia's touch of Viking blood refortified the old Norman strain of Montagu.

Their son William, second Lord Montagu, was in his turn no less faithful to Edward of Caernarvon. Like others of that scapegrace prince's friends, he fell foul of the old king's temper and spent a short spell in the Tower. He was none the less among the hundreds knighted with the prince at Westminster, as also was Mortimer, than whom, however, Montagu then followed more loyal courses. In the wreck of the royal fortunes after Bannockburn, when Steward of the Household, he outwitted Lancaster and the Ordainers, whose chronicler reviled him as 'the author of falsehoods even worse than Piers [Gaveston] himself'. Displaced by Pembroke's middle party at the settlement of Leake in 1318, he was sent off to be Seneschal of Aquitaine, where he died the following year.

His heir and namesake, William, third Lord Montagu, born in 1301, likewise grew up at court, with the third Prince Edward. It may be that Edward II, remembering his own mishandled upbringing, chose this son of one of his few trustworthy friends as a suitable companion for his successor. Eleven years older than the prince, correct, accomplished in the lore of chivalry, and with all his wits about him, he rapidly won the boy's admiration, as he also earned the regard of the king his father. On his coming of age, his lands, in wardship to the crown for the three years since his father's death, were released to him promptly, an usual favour in the greedy times of the Despensers; and at Dover in September 1325, when he embarked with the prince to join Isabella at the court of France, Edward II knighted him as a mark of personal trust.

Thereafter the young men were seldom separated. Bear-warded in Isabella's train in Paris, and into treason at the Harwich landing, they had to watch their idea of majesty progressively degraded. All during the pursuit of the prince's father, the futile Scottish expedition, Mortimer's terrorizing of the Salisbury parliament, and the shame of the Amiens homage, they shared the deepening disdain of a Hamlet and a Horatio.

Whatever hand the secret royal conclave may have had in the earl of Kent's conspiracy, and it seems probable they had one, its fatal outcome committed them to action, for it was now clear that Edward was in personal danger. So long as Mortimer had control of a stripling king he could keep up some constitutional show; but how long would the growing Edward endure his tutelage? It was Mortimer's way to cut short such questions; no more than any other tyrant could he stand still. Plantagenet blood held no deterrent magic for him, and parliamentary pogrom was his crafty method; deposition of Edward II at Westminster and his subsequent murder, the unsprung trap for Lancaster at Salisbury, the annihilation of Kent at Winchester – where did his ambition tend? Where, and at whom, would he strike next?

After Winchester, Edward lay close at his manor of Woodstock, near Oxford, all through the spring and summer of 1330. Destined to make way for stately Blenheim Palace, rambling Woodstock, already two centuries old, had been a favourite haunt of the kings of England since it was built by Henry I, who used it as a menagerie for lions, lynxes, porcupines, and other strange animals arriving from abroad. Henry II kept Fair Rosamund there. Henry III, finding it hard to house the three leopards sent him, in compliment to the arms of England, by the Emperor Frederick II, 'Stupor Mundi', and finally nonplussed by the marvellous elephant given him by St Louis, removed the more unmanageable creatures to the Tower of London, where he provided a long chain for the white bear, so that it could fish in the river Thames. In Edward's day there was still, all the same, a fair quantity of game at Woodstock, enclosed by the seven-mile wall of the park, and he hunted contentedly, out of Mortimer's reach.

Here, at ten in the morning of Friday 15 June 1330, Queen Philippa gave birth to her first-born son, Edward of Woodstock, the future Black Prince. The event was greeted with the formal if sometimes misplaced joy always accorded to a new heir to the throne. Philippa breast-fed him, a wholesome practice and, as Dr Barnes, writing in 1688, remarked severely, a lesson to 'the delicate Madams of our Time, who think it below their Care'. The child was more responsive to his mother's attentions than, for example, his great-uncle Thomas of Brotherton had been. He, when his mother Margaret of France had tried to feed him, spat it out, to the huge if insular pleasure of Edward I, who cried, 'God give thee Grace, my boy, I see thou art right English in thy nature.' Possibly owing to undernourishment, young Thomas of Brotherton had nearly died of smallpox, but was cured by Sir John of Gaddesden, the great physician of the time, who dressed him all in scarlet, in scarlet bedclothes in a scarlet room.

In honour of Prince Edward's birth, the customary outlay was not skimped. A pension was found for Joan of Oxford, his nurse, as also for Matilda Plumpton, his 'rocker'. Thomas Prior received a fat reward for bringing the good news to the king, though, as the royal family were all together at Woodstock, his pains could hardly have been unbearable. Edward gave Philippa, for her uprising, a robe of red velvet in three pieces, with facings of pure miniver; for her churching, a coat and hood of cloth of gold; and for the great banquet, a third extravaganza. At this last revel, hangings and logs for the Great Hall were to be borne in mind. There were also to be a coverlet of scarlet cloth and miniver for the infant's cradle, and two coffers for his chamber. The king appears to have gone too far in commanding 'a coverlet of fine cloth of gold for the bed of my said Lady and a kerchief'; some Wardrobe clerk objected in stiff Latin 'not known hitherto'. The more serious implications of the occasion must have been apparent. In addition to his own safety, Edward now had a dynasty to protect. What was more, Isabella was said to be with child by Mortimer, though nothing seems to have come of it in the end.

Mortimer's dreaded *démarche* came in the late summer of 1330. He moved the court to Nottingham, and on 6 September a Great Council was called to meet there in six weeks' time. To forestall any inclination to stay away, the usual writs of summons bore a minatory rider. When the Latin had been translated for the barons, it was found to read:

> Know ye, that if (which heaven forbid), the said business should
> happen to be impeded by your absence, We shall bear as heavily on
> you as may be.[4]

The Council opened no less menacingly than was to be expected from such a tone. Mortimer's Welsh archers were everywhere in Nottingham town and castle. Yet for all their vigilance, on the fifth day Mortimer fell victim to a plot as ingenious as any of his own in that it took advantage of his own mistakes.

Mortimer had made careful plans for what he knew would be a decisive confrontation. He was well aware how far his self-elevation, his ill-gained wealth and his rashly chosen title earl of March had roused resentment. He may have heard that privately his own son Geoffrey, whom only recently he had enriched with the earl of Kent's estates at Castle Donington, scornfully called him the King of Folly. He rightly suspected the designs of the little knot led by Montagu and Bury who, in fact, shrewdly appealing more to pride than to fear, were urging the young king to drastic action. By coming so far north as Nottingham, he had boldly entered the jaws of the earl of Lancaster, whose enormous fine was still undischarged, and who was still smarting from the sack of Leicester: Lancaster certainly would not stay away this time.

Mortimer had every reason to take strict precautions. Nottingham castle, sturdily built by the Conqueror and towering on rocks above the river Trent and the little town, seemed to offer the segregation he desired. When, therefore, Sir Edward de Bohun, as deputy for his brother the constable, who was unwell, began to make arrangements for the meeting of the Council, and allotted apartments in the castle to Lancaster, as his precedence as senior earl demanded, Mortimer berated him. The castle, said Mortimer, was reserved, except during the hours of session, for himself and the Queen Mother, for the king, and for his guard of 180 men at arms. Lancaster and the other great men of the realm must be found lodgings in the town.

His wariness led to his undoing. In addition to offending the barons further, it enabled his enemies to mature their schemes out of his sight. Out in the town, Montagu swore in an action group to rescue the king from his duress. Among them was Sir William Elland, governor of the castle, who explained that they could never force direct admission, because his normal garrison had been displaced by Mortimer's, and the gates had been fitted with new locks specially brought for the purpose by Isabella, who at night slept with the keys under her pillows. But there was another way in. The solid-looking rocks on which the castle stood were riddled with caves and crevices once used as prehistoric dwellings. Unknown to Mortimer, one of these to the westward had been extended into a tunnel ascending by rough-hewn stairs to emerge inside the castle keep. It is probable that the passage was not, as has been supposed, part of the ancient Saxon defences against the Danes, but had been completed just before the Council met. Otherwise it is most unlikely that Mortimer would not have known of its existence.

On Friday 19 October, after the meeting of the Council, the lords took their leave as usual from the castle. Montagu's party then appeared to flee the town, as if in dread of arrest. Late at night, guided, it is said, by Sir William Elland, they entered the secret passage and joined the king, waiting alone in the castle ward. They clattered up to Mortimer's chamber, burst in, and found him in consultation with Henry Burghersh, bishop of Lincoln, the Chancellor. There was an affray. Montagu with his own hand cut down two knights of the bodyguard on duty at the door, Sir Hugh

Turplington and Sir John Monmouth. Isabella, wakening to sick awareness, cried out from her apartment, '*Bel Fitz, Bel Fitz! Ayez pitié du gentil Mortimer.*' But no one else thought Mortimer *gentil*, and nobody had pity on him. He and Burghersh were hustled off down the secret passage, without interference from the unenlightened Welshmen on the battlements.

Next morning in the town, Mortimer's sons and associates were seized, and King Edward proclaimed the arrests to the startled citizens. He declared that his former advisers had been guilty of maladministration, and that for the future he would govern for himself, with the advice of the great men of his kingdom. Mortimer and his fellow prisoners were carted ignominiously away towards London and the Tower, whence he had escaped seven adventurous years before. The earl of Lancaster, though nearly blind, turned out to hear the cheers of the crowd, and flung his cap in the air for joy.

Edward's first purpose on assuming the government was to break the pattern of tyranny, of hatred and revenge that had ruled for two tumultuous decades; to sort the confusions and to calm the fears. From the first there was a strain of assurance and of moderation that had been lacking hitherto; a tendency not to judge too harshly nor to enquire too closely; to mend damaged purses and not probe vulnerable consciences too deeply.

Passing through Leicester three days later, Edward summoned a new parliament to meet at Westminster in one month's time. From Woodstock, where he rejoined Philippa and his infant son, he invited the people on 3 November to lay their long-neglected grievances before him, and ordered the sheriffs to see that the knights and burgesses were less corruptly chosen than in the past.

Except for the inclusion of the Commons and a thickening of the clergy, the parliament that met in Westminster Hall differed little in composition from the terrified concourse he had rescued at Nottingham. A handful of Mortimer's nobles were absent, a like number of his enemies restored, and three additions were made to the bench of judges.

On the first day of the session Mortimer was arraigned for judgment by his fellow peers. Though the numerous charges were specific enough, he was not called upon to make any answer, nor was any effort made to prove them. Indeed, it is doubtful whether the evidence was at hand, or if it had been, whether it would have been politic to do so. As had lately become the insidious rule, the charges were all declared to be true, notorious, and known to all the land; Mortimer was condemned unheard as a traitor and a felon. Three days later, on 29 November 1330, he was dragged on a hurdle from the Tower to the elms at Tyburn, and hanged as a common criminal. On the whole he was treated with consideration. The more hideous aspects of the penalty for treason were omitted, and after hanging for two days only, at the king's command he was cut down and buried in the fashionable Greyfriars church at Newgate. Many years later he was removed to his native Wigmore. By contrast, the shrivelled members of Hugh Despenser, whom he had cut to bits at Hereford four years earlier almost to the day, were only now permitted decent burial.

Mortimer's adjutant, Sir Simon Bereford, less worthy brother of the learned judge Sir William, and Sir John Daverill, the phantasmagorical governor of Corfe castle, were likewise condemned by the Lords. They were hanged on Christmas Eve. These three deaths were the limit of the official bloodshed. The regicides, Gurney, Maltravers, Ogle, and the mysterious Sir Bogo of Bayonne (for his part in the earl of Kent affair), had prices set upon their heads but, as they had vanished, the severity was more apparent than real. Gurney was captured the next year at Burgos in Castile. He was brought to Bayonne, and after a strangely long delay was handed over, at the king's special order, to the master of a vessel bound for England, only to have his head hacked off at sea because, it was rumoured, he inconveniently knew too much. Nothing more was heard of the others, except that in due course Maltravers was restored to favour and returned to England with a royal pardon. His wife's brother, Sir Thomas Berkeley, as lord of the castle where the former king had been done to death, and as a son-in-law of Mortimer, stood trial to clear his name, and was acquitted; though here again there were some who thought that the inquiry was superficial.

Edward was far more lenient with Isabella than had been his zealous predecessor Edward the Confessor with his own mother, Emma, whom, on the first breath of scandal touching her, he had made walk blindfold over nine burning ploughshares. At his command, all reference to Isabella was struck out of Mortimer's indictment, except one clause which said that he had so far played upon her fears that she dared not go to the king her husband to offer him her bed, 'to the great dishonour of the King and the whole realm': certainly a mild assessment of the part that she had played. It was eloquent of the strength of the king's prerogative that no word of criticism of his tolerance was heard.

She was first confined at the manor of Berkhamsted while her fate was being decided, but spent Christmas with the court at Windsor, and was then sent to comfortable retirement at Castle Rising. Her income was settled at £4,000 a year, later compounded for her original revenues from Ponthieu. In these comparatively straitened circumstances, her rate of living proved a burden to the citizens of Lynn, who had to 'purvey' to her meat, swans, wax, wine, sturgeon and lampreys. Her children remained fond of her. King Edward, besides visiting her often, sent letters and gifts, now a wild boar for roasting, now a falcon, now a pair of love-birds which she fed on hemp seed and kept in her bedchamber; and, quite frequently, consignments of Gascon wine, three pipes (105 imperial gallons) at a time. As the years passed she was given greater liberty, appeared at court, and retained a certain diplomatic influence: in 1348 she was proposed as a mediator for the peace with France and in May 1354 was asked by the pope to plead with the king for the release of the duke of Brittany. For her sins, she collected relics, and took the veil. When at last she died at Hertford castle in 1358 she was buried in the Greyfriars church, close to her Mortimer, where she was soon after joined by her youngest daughter, Joan, the unfortunate queen of Scotland, who towards the end had come to share in her seclusion.

An act of oblivion closed the case of the earl of Kent. Then, after the penalties, came the rewards and pardons. Henry of Lancaster was released from all the forfeitures and charges piled upon his house from time to time during the last ten fractious years, and the king even made one more belated application for the canonization of Henry's late brother, Thomas. Thereafter for nearly fifty years Edward had no more devoted friends than his mighty Lancastrian cousins.

Thomas, Lord Wake, Hugh Audley, Henry, Lord Beaumont, and other refugees from Mortimer's spite returned from France into the king's good grace. The architect of victory at Nottingham, Sir William Montagu, was formally pardoned for the homicide of Mortimer's two knights, and was rewarded, not over-lavishly, with an annuity and a slice of Mortimer's lands; as were also his lately converted associates, Sir Robert Ufford (from those of Maltravers), and Sir Edward de Bohun, deputy constable at the decisive moment; Sir William de Clinton; and Sir John Neville, who had been wounded in the struggle. Queen Philippa's young carver from Hainault, Walter Manny, for some unrecorded gallantry, received the knighthood of the Bath, an honour which he, like the others, would many times requite in years to come. Dr Richard Bury retained his office as Keeper of the Privy Seal, and three years later, by the king's arrangement entered upon his bishopric of Durham in the presence of the whole royal family.

If Edward was wisely careful not to be too generous to his friends, he was too shrewd to waste the talents of his former enemies. Henry Burghersh, bishop of Lincoln, Mortimer's chief minister, was soon released from the Tower and, though displaced as Chancellor, re-emerged in 1334 as Treasurer. His brother, Sir Bartholomew, lost the Cinque Ports, but soon became warden to Isabella's dower in Ponthieu. Both thereafter gave invaluable service to the crown. Sir Oliver Ingham, a well-known Mortimer man, and suspect ever since his unexplained loss of the Agenais in 1324, was confirmed in his appointment as Seneschal of Aquitaine, where he remained faithful for fifteen years until his death. Sir William Trussel, who had proclaimed the deposition of Edward II, was sent on an important embassy to France. Isabella's covey of disaffected prelates, Airmyn of Norwich, Hotham of Ely, and particularly the many clerics of the Stratford family, were pressed unhesitatingly into the royal administration. Only for Adam of Orleton could the king find no forgiveness. When for the third time the slippery bishop secured his own preferment from the pope, this time to Winchester from Worcester, Edward furiously protested, though vainly, citing his complicity in his father's murder. Orleton was left to the judgment of heaven, manifested, so the chroniclers say, in the blindness of his old age.

All grants of lands made since the king's accession were cancelled. The disinherited and the despoiled came expectantly to court with their deeds and proofs of title. It was pleasant, perhaps also moving, to pardon young Hugh Despenser, the third generation of that much-lopped tree, from the disabilities he had incurred for tigerishly defending his castle, as a lad of eighteen, against Isabella in the interest of his grandfather and father. (This third Hugh Despenser was later prominent at the crossing of the Somme in the Crécy campaign, but died without sons. His nephew Edward continued the line, served at Poitiers, and became a Knight of the Garter.) A similar application on behalf of Sir Edmund Mortimer, eldest son of the late tyrant, on the other hand, Edward firmly resisted, retorting that he himself would determine if and when such clemency was opportune. The royal rebuff is supposed to have broken the young man's heart, for he died that very year. Part of the reason was probably that Edward could not at that time afford to give up so much valuable wealth. Many years afterwards, in 1355, flushed with his spoils from France, he finally allowed the petition of the tyrant's grandson, Roger, that the trial of the first earl of March had been irregular and should be quashed. This line too continued, and in course of time became scion of the Yorkist title to the throne, in the blood-soaked fifteenth century.

Some of the many settlements were not free of animosity. It was found necessary to repeat and to extend the statutes against tournaments and duels, and wearing arms to Parliament. In consequence, two lords, for drawing daggers on each other in the presence of the king, were committed to the Tower for contempt.

Other settlements, though amicable, were complex. The family of the earl of Kent, for instance, naturally requested and were granted full restitution of their lands and titles sequestered under Mortimer. So too was Richard 'Copped Hat' Fitzalan, heir to the earl of Arundel who had been slaughtered on Isabella's orders for supporting the Despensers. His nickname 'Copped Hat' could mean topped, beheaded, perhaps in joking reference to his father's inadvertence in backing the wrong side. The question then arose, what was to become of Arundel castle? It had been taken from the earl of Arundel on his arrest and given to the earl of Kent, only to fall quickly forfeit to the crown on Kent's attainder. It was agreed at last that young Copped Hat Arundel should buy out the children of Kent from his enormous regained fortune; and as they were royal wards, Edward would have use of the much needed money. Arundel was further enjoined to forgive Lord Charlton of Powis, one of Mortimer's sons-in-law, for taking part in his father's execution. The Kents in their turn were consoled with the valuable manor of Castle Donington. Seized from Alice de Lacy, heiress widow of Thomas of Lancaster, by the younger Despenser, it had gone on his downfall to Edmund of Kent, and thence briefly to Geoffrey, a younger son of Mortimer. It was now returned to the Kents, and passed in time to Joan, the Fair Maid of Kent, later the wife of the Black Prince and mother of Richard II.

Having settled his peace on the nobility, Edward determined to spread it over all the land, where conditions had become anarchic. Country life was precarious at the best of times, because constantly in motion. Each day saw in procession all the varied company of the *Canterbury Tales*, citizens of every degree going about their ordinary affairs, watched hungrily from dark shadows in the narrow streets and from forest verges of the lonely roads by the secret eyes of footpads, and by impostors scheming to undo them. Townsmen who combined to chase robbers from their boroughs or to starve out felons from the frid-stools and sanctuaries only served to drive them back upon the highways, where expectation of violence was the rule. Travellers knew their danger, banded themselves together, and took shelter in specially provided chantries. The clerks of Oxford were permitted to go armed upon the roads, though at no other time.

Normally, the accepted risks were justified, and most journeys ended safely; but the last two riotous decades had not been normal. The heads and limbs of noble victims of political miscalculation adorned gates and walls in grotesque profusion. In the wake of rebellion and rapine, accentuated by calamitous years of famine and pestilence, misery flourished; and the poor paid dismally for their crimes of despair. Between August 1322 and November 1323, eight prisoners died in Northampton jail alone from hunger, thirst and cold. Hugh Maidenlove, escaping from Norwich castle, had to carry his fellow sheep-stealer William Clerk on his back to sanctuary in the church, because his feet had putrefied in prison.

In the courts, injustice triumphed. In 1330, Alisot of Upatherle petitioned the crown about her husband, Henry, who had been taken prisoner at Bannockburn sixteen years before. When at long last he made good his ransom and went home, he found that his neighbours had occupied his fields and plundered his goods. His return was unexpected and unwanted. They raised the hue and cry against him as a vagabond, and he was locked up in Gloucester castle pending the visit of the justices. Henry regained his liberty and brought a writ against his enemies, but they set upon him in the open town and beat him nearly to death. The laconic reply of Mortimer's judges to Alisot was callous. 'If the husband be alive, the complaint is his; if he be dead, the wife's complaint is nothing.'

With the law both powerless and perverse, ruffians sought their own redress under the greenwood tree. Imperious outlaws like the self-styled

'Lionel, King of the rout of raveners' from his 'Castle of the North Wind' issued threats and commands at once whimsical, regal and intimidating. Their rough deeds were celebrated in popular songs and ballads, not because they had any idea of levelling class differences, but because their truculence satisfied a homespun craving to get even with the insolence of office.

More damaging than the Robin Hoods whether of fact or fable was the lawlessness in higher orders of society. Warlike retinues complete with horses and mail raided selectively, sometimes on their own account, sometimes wearing the livery of a powerful master and under his mainten-ance, or paid protection in the courts. Great ladies, too, were known to subscribe this summary method of settling disputes.

The Folvilles of Leicestershire were conspicuous among these bands of robber knights. In 1322 Sir Roger la Zouch ravaged the manor of Loughborough, formerly owned by his lord, Thomas, earl of Lancaster, but transferred on his decapitation to the elder Despenser. La Zouch was brought to trial before his neighbour, Sir Roger Beler, who having, more prudently than he, deserted Lancaster and joined the Despensers, was now a judge and a baron of the Exchequer. Enraged at Beler's spiteful treatment of him, la Zouch called in Sir John de Folville, lord of the nearby manor of Ashby Folville, and his six murderous brothers, to avenge his quarrel, which they did when the chance arose some four years later. Led by Sir Eustace and the Reverend Sir Richard, an outlawed incumbent of the family living, the Folville brothers waylaid Judge Beler as he was riding from his home at Kirby Bellers to the Leicester assizes. The aged justice and his escort defended themselves vigorously, but after a pitched battle he was at last cut down and slain by Eustace.

The fall of the Despensers followed shortly, whereon the Folvilles were all pardoned by Mortimer for dispatching, as it now seemed meritoriously, an odious placeman of an odious regime. Thus encouraged, during the next few years Sir Eustace achieved at least three more murders, a rape, and three robberies, all scot free. In 1329, making use of another shift in the wind of politics, four of the brothers earned a further general pardon for their earlier crimes by helping Mortimer sack the Lancastrian city of Leicester. But after Mortimer's execution they found contract work for rich protective patrons hard to come by, and so in 1332 they resumed, unsponsored, their profitable attacks on itinerant judges, now being sent round in unusual numbers in an attempt to enforce the law. They fell upon the future Chief Justice Richard Willoughby on his way to Melton after the assize at Grantham, dragged him with them 'from wood to wood', and extorted an enormous ransom. This time King Edward himself sent a powerful commission of Trailbaston to the Folville country, but little was achieved. The only member of the gang they caught, and he was not a Folville, turned out to be a priest, immune from lay prosecution. He was freed by a bench of which Willoughby was himself a member.

Thus, after twenty-one years of unexpiated crime, Sir Eustace died quietly in his bed. His career had not been exceptional. Though Knighton, the Leicester chronicler, found his murder of a royal justice worth a mention, it was with approval rather than otherwise, for Sir Roger Beler had been, no less than was Judge Willoughby for that matter, as oppressive and corrupt as he was hated. Each in his turn, Sir Roger Beler and Sir Eustace de Folville were laid reverently to rest in their respective and adjacent parish churches. Sir Roger, at Kirby Bellers, lies peacefully beside his wife, immortalized in age-old alabaster. Sir Eustace, at nearby Ashby Folville, has his head pillowed by two angels, and his violent hands (now broken off) devoutly clasped upon his stony breast.

The worst disorder was in the eastern counties, and Edward, who loved hunting in any form, spent the summer of 1331 riding about between Havering Bower, Bury St Edmunds, Norwich and Lincoln, rounding up wrong-doers and imposing his personal justice, not altogether unindulgently. Several wild young bloods of about his own age, more obstreperous than vicious, were hauled before his Westminster parliament in October, where they were fined and induced to mend their ways. At the next session in the new year, the lords recommended local justices of the peace who should be answerable to the king for keeping order, and the bishops, whose temporalities were favourite targets of the vandals, uttered dire threats of excommunication. It seems that their stern deliberations were disturbed by unruly youngsters as much in need of correction as their seniors, for a testy statute read 'let no boy or other person, under pain of imprisonment, play in any part of Westminster Palace at bars (prisoner's base) or other games or at snatch-hood' while Parliament is sitting. But the frequent repetition of all such bans, whether on tournaments and armed gatherings, on night prowlers, on maintenance, or on children's games, shows them to have been in vain, until Edward found, in foreign fields, a more exciting outlet for his subjects' energy.

* * *

While the confrontation with Mortimer was brewing, the new King Philip VI of France had been fidgeting away about Aquitaine. For all the commissions that had been appointed since the unsatisfactory ceremony at Amiens, nothing further had been done about the castles due to be returned by Philip; the dismantling by Edward of others hostile to Philip; the huge sums of money owed by Edward, or the royal marriages that were to seal the settlement; or, come to that, about the incomplete rendering of liege homage. Philip was aware that the disrupted state of England worked in his favour, and the wonder is that he was patient for so long. It may have been out of deference to his cousin Isabella for, as her downfall approached, his attitude stiffened. In the summer of 1330 he occupied

Saintes and Bourg and ordered Edward to appear again before him to confirm the homage properly, upon pain of further seizures.

Edward was sanguine enough not to be too alarmed at the cold clutch of a lawyer's summons, but the use of force he took seriously, and he was in no position to resist. He was moreover presently engaged in delicate negotiations inside France concerning Scotland which he did not want Philip to find out about or hinder, since the reduction of Scotland must necessarily precede the onslaught he already had in mind against his unsuspecting fellow monarch. So he continued to speak Philip fair, while keeping king's messengers dashing across the sea. At the same time, he sounded the neighbours of Aquitaine and his queen's relatives in Hainault for possible assistance in his threatened provinces, where before long he placed in charge two of the most able of his former enemies, Oliver Ingham in Aquitaine and Bartholomew Burghersh in Ponthieu. At last, when prevarication would no longer work, he conceded to Philip on 30 March 1331 by Letters Patent that the homage he had already done should be construed as full liege homage, and that for the future his successors should follow the form prescribed by Philip. In that way he hoped at least to avoid the disagreeable personal abasements that accompanied the taking of a sacred oath he had no intention of keeping.

Philip would have none of it, and Edward realized sulkily that he would have to go in person. He cancelled his Easter parliament and, to hide his shame, disingenuously gave out he was going to France to keep a vow he had made before his deliverance from Mortimer. Five days later he sailed clandestinely, with John Stratford, his Chancellor, William Montagu, and a dozen of his closest counsellors – a crestfallen little party, whose gloom was only faintly brightened by the opportunity their incognito afforded them to go in disguise, dressed up as merchants. Philip received them tactfully, in the obscure wooded village of Pont-Sainte-Maxence north of Paris. He offered to knock 30,000 *livres* off Edward's debt, because of the damage since done at Saintes and Bourg; he also pardoned the rebellious vassals of Gascony, and agreed that after all their castles need not be destroyed. The homage was completed smoothly, and Edward set foot in England again on 20 April, after only a fortnight's absence. The meeting had been kept as brief and as friendly as was possible. It was not through any clumsiness on Philip's part that it was to prove to be their last.

After so much tedious duty done, it was time for relaxation. Sir William Montagu, cheerfully holding his sovereign exempt from his own prohib- ition, proclaimed in the king's name a three-day tournament to be held in London at the opening of the Michaelmas parliament. Edward was decidedly in favour of the idea. He loved feats of arms. And whatever else could be said of tournaments, when his liegemen with their bannered retinues came clopping endlessly into town they would certainly provide an impressive show of strength, and he had no doubt that the Londoners were in need of such a lesson. During the late troubles they had become too far aware of their own importance. They had mutinied against the king his father; they had killed his father's ministers Stapledon and Baldock, and had clamoured for his father's deposition. When the rest of the nation was in turmoil, they had declared the young prince John of Eltham as their regent, and had calmly gone on with their ordinary business. Just lately, they had disturbed the new royal peace by arguing fractiously with the earl of Lancaster about payment for the men he had made them raise against Mortimer. It would do no harm to show them what was what.

The Guilds had mixed feelings about the tournament. On the one hand, it would bring custom to the city. On the other, it would obstruct the traffic which rumbled daily to and from the London docks; and it would lead inevitably to the much-dreaded fires. However, the mayor, John Pulteney, was of patrician leanings and had keen sporting tastes. A draper of Candlewick Street, now in the first of his four terms of office, he had a pack of boarhounds in the country, and his mews of falcons was the best in London. He delighted in the ceremony and clash of knightly combat, and was looking forward to entertaining many valiant visitors during the festival, no fewer than four lordly 'lances', at his spacious Pountney's Inn, where they would dine off trenchers of solid gold. He therefore cajoled his aldermen to fall in with their young king's reasonable desire to celebrate in his own capital. Pulteney later built the magnificent Penshurst Place in Kent, 1341, and died in the Black Death of 1349. Pountney's Inn was afterwards the London residence of the Black Prince until 1359.

On the day, the broad thoroughfare of Cheapside was cordoned off, the market stalls removed and pavilions and galleries erected. The cobbled roadway, a rare convenience, was sanded over to keep the chargers' hooves from slipping. The lists ran from the Great Cross eastward as far as Sopar's Lane. In the centre, by the church of St Mary-le-Bow, a balcony of timber spanned the street from side to side. On 21 September 1331, in brilliant autumn sunshine, 'therein Queen Philippa, and many other ladies, richly attired, and assembled from all parts of the realm, did stand to behold the jousts'.

The king and Montagu, sportively dressed as Tartars, each by a silver chain led a palfreyed damsel, gowned in crimson velvet, to the arena, through madly cheering streets and blaring music. They then took their places for the opening hastilude, or general mêlée. The advance was sounded. As the knights hurtled together, the ladies in the balcony thrilled forward to the rail above the point of impact.

With a splintering crash, the stand collapsed. Amid shrieks, a flurry of brilliant silks upturned and scattered into a sea of plunging hooves and disconcerted weapons. In the confusion, ladies were bruised and cut, many knights unhorsed and trampled.

The king got up. His bodyguard instinctively closed in about him, as on a battlefield. They were too shocked to notice the figure that he cut, in his dishevelled fancy dress. His rage was terrible. An accident. But there had been too many accidents. From Gaveston to Mortimer, the reek of treachery still hung about. It would have gone hard with the carpenters had not Queen Philippa flung herself at his feet imploring their pardon.

The angry moment passed. Her prayer was granted. The carpenters went free. The offending structure was cleared away, and in time replaced by a solid tower of stone. A new reign had begun, when passions would be less wild; when men would trust each other, and work together in a common cause.

TAKE A SOLDIER, TAKE A KING

King: A good heart, Kate, is the sun and the moon; or, rather, the sun and not the moon; for it shines bright and never changes, but keeps his course truly. If thou would have such a one, take me; and take me, take a soldier; take a soldier, take a King. And what sayest thou to my love?

Kate: Is it possible dat I should love de enemy of France?

Henry V, Act V, scene ii

TAKE A SOLDIER,
TAKE A KING

Historians tend to say that in 1331 the kings of France and England were far from thoughts of war. They suggest that during the next six years, while Philip was preoccupied with dreams of a Crusade, and while Edward pursued an irrelevant campaign against the Scots, the situation slipped, through a difference over feudal rights and duties in Aquitaine, until there was no going back.

Such a view is incomplete, and for a proper understanding of Edward's character, misleading. He was a true son of his age, an age when war still had a certain lusty innocence. Fighting was both a favourite sport and also a normal means of livelihood, the accepted way to fortune and to fame. To keep his throne, Edward had to have the goodwill of his vassals. This he had for the moment achieved by the overthrow of Mortimer. He must now weld them together in some foreign enterprise with good prospects of external gain. There was plenty at hand for all in the wealth of France. To make safe the crown of England, he had already decided that he would beggar France.

Yet he had to move with caution. He was the new king of a small country of little military renown, and at present in a state of fearful weakness. One false move and he would be crushed. The treaty of Northampton had left the Scots in full ascendancy; prudence as well as pride demanded that they should be reduced before he tackled France. He knew that Philip, if his suspicions were aroused, would rush to rescue his invaluable old Scottish alliance. So he had to create a situation where the Scots would appear as the aggressors, and at the same time he had to hoodwink Philip.

Living on his estates in Normandy was Edward Baliol, the feckless heir of the John Baliol whom Edward I had adjudged to be king of Scotland in preference to Robert Bruce. In 1328, Edward Baliol's Yorkshire servant killed a Frenchman in a quarrel. Instead of handing him over to justice, Baliol 'maintained' him in his castle and smuggled him back to England, for which King Philip seized Baliol's lands and imprisoned him, a harsh penalty, probably influenced by the knowledge that twice already Baliol had been invited to return to England and revive his father's claim to the throne of Scotland.

Baliol languished in prison until, in 1329, Henry, Lord Beaumont, arrived in France as a refugee from Mortimer. Beaumont, a Frenchman, brother of Louis de Beaumont the ill-read bishop of Durham, was related to the royal families of both England and France. By marrying the heiress Alice Comyn, he had acquired a title to the Scottish earldom of Buchan. He had been stripped of his rights by the Shameful Treaty of Northampton, and though there had been some vague promise of their return, nothing had happened, and in the idleness of exile he perceived a way through Baliol to reassert himself.

Through his influence with his kinsman, Philip, Beaumont begged Baliol out of prison, but then shipped him off to Yorkshire. On Mortimer's execution in November 1330, Beaumont too returned to England, and with others who had been similarly dispossessed, the 'Disinherited' as they called themselves, joined in raising an army for the resurrection of Baliol's claim to the Scottish crown.

Their activities were not unknown to Edward. Two passports for Baliol, the second only ten days previous to Mortimer's arrest at Nottingham, bore Edward's seal. Indeed, it is likely that Baliol offered him lordship over a conquered Scotland in return for his assistance. The proposal was a tempting one, for by the deaths of Robert Bruce and Lord James Douglas, and the mysterious sickness of Lord Thomas Randolph the regent for Bruce's son, the six-year-old King David, the Scots were unusually short of fiery warlords, and divided between themselves. On the other hand there were dangers. Under the treaty of Northampton, if Edward broke the Scottish truce he stood bound to refund to the pope the £20,000 paid up by the Scots and long since spent by Isabella; and Pope John XXII, who had French predilections and an unrelenting avarice, would certainly persist in its collection. More serious was the probable reaction of King Philip, and the effect upon the already delicate situation in Aquitaine. For the moment, therefore, Edward dissembled. He loudly denounced Baliol, forbade him to cross his territories, and refused to countenance his claims. During the parliament of March 1332, Scotland was not once mentioned; and, when the Scottish truce expired in May, Edward remained conspicuously peaceful in the south.

Meanwhile the Disinherited had got together a force of about three thousand men with archers and necessary shipping. They sailed from Ravenspur, and on 6 August landed at Kinghorn in the Firth of Forth. In a week of lightning victories, they took Edinburgh and Perth. Many of the remaining Scottish chieftains were killed or captured in battle at Dupplin Moor, while others made haste to join the victorious Baliol, as did many English noblemen, with or without their king's permission. To the general amazement, on 24 September 1332, Baliol was crowned king at Scone.

So far, Edward had carefully kept up his cousinly pretences with the cordial Philip. He had humbly performed the second homage that had been required of him. He had proposed that his small son and heir, Prince Edward, should be married to Philip's daughter Jeanne. Philip had warmly invited him over to discuss it, and Parliament approved the visit; but Edward then backed out. Instead, when conciliation was no longer vital, he married his sister Eleanor to Reginald of Gueldres, a far less friendly match from Philip's point of view, the more so since Eleanor had been promised at Amiens to the French heir John. But that did not deter Edward, when it suited him, from later declaring that it was Philip who had broken off both marriages.

Philip, fired by Pope John with an uncharacteristic zeal against the Mamelukes in Armenia, next proposed to Edward that they should launch a joint Crusade. Edward heartily agreed, but asked to defer the venture for three years until his return from Ireland where, he said, he was committed to an expedition. Quixotic ramblings about Crusades were, he thought, an excellent distraction for Philip's mind at present; to show he shared Philip's enthusiasm, he studied Roger de Stavegney's treatise *Du Conquest de la Terre Sainte*; and to sound yet more convincing about his reason for delay, he had the records searched, to see what had been done about the Irish in the past. The facts were less straightforward than he made them seem; he was, certainly, preparing for an expedition. But it was not to be an expedition against Ireland.

On the departure of the Disinherited from Ravenspur, but not soon enough to stop them going, Edward repeated his proclamation against Baliol. To emphasize his disapproval, he confiscated Henry Beaumont's lands in England, though they were quietly restored a few months later. Now, on the news of Baliol's astonishing success, it was time for him to fling aside the mask. He had won the opening round. He had a strong foothold from which to conquer Scotland, and Philip was in no way ready to prevent him.

In September 1332 horrid news was announced to Parliament. The Scots had crossed the Border. Lord John Randolph had gone to France to treat for the revival of the 'Auld Alliance'. The kingdom was in danger. Parliament, in patriotic rage, granted an exceptional aid and begged the king to divert his Irish army towards the new seat of peril. Edward needed no second bidding. He prorogued Parliament to York, and set out for the North, leaving the Chancery, Exchequer, and all the cumbrous machinery of government to follow as soon as possible. On his way through Notting-ham he paused to call out his commissions of array against the Scots. He had every reason to be satisfied with the turn events had taken; he had deceived everyone.

* * *

Seeing her husband depart on what was evidently to be a long campaign, Philippa retired to Woodstock, to prepare for the birth of her second child and first daughter, Isabella, a princess whose sad matrimonial story was so much part of the time she lived in that it deserves description. She was all her life a sacrifice to her father's diplomatic schemes. When she was three she was unsuccessfully betrothed to Peter, the Infante of Castile, who eventually married her younger sister, Princess Joan of the Tower, though Joan died of plague on arriving at Bordeaux in order to complete the marriage in 1348. At seven, after Otto of Habsburg, duke of Austria, had eagerly sought Isabella's hand for his young son, she was proposed for Louis de Male, the heir of Flanders. But, with a change in the political spectrum, it looked likely, when she was twelve, that the elderly Duke John of Brabant would have her. But then Louis of Flanders became a prospect again. Since he was at that time held prisoner by his own people at the disposal of the English, the affair seemed promising; but sooner than treat with the slayers of his father, who had just been killed at Crécy, he broke parole a day or two before the wedding, escaped to France, and married Margaret of Brabant instead.

Isabella was next offered, unavailingly, to the emperor-elect, Charles IV of Bohemia, a widower and, as it seemed, finally, to Bérard d'Albret, son of the great Gascon nobleman loyal to Edward III. The nineteen-year-old Isabella was dispatched to Bordeaux with an expensive trousseau only to decide, almost at the moment of disembarkation, to change her mind and return home. After that she continued to receive generous gifts from her father and to live a life of extravagant independence. In 1365, however, at the relatively advanced age of thirty-three, she appears to have fallen in love. Conveniently for Edward, her choice was Enguerrand (or, as the English called him, Ingelram) de Coucy, one of the most distinguished of the noble French hostages then being luxuriously interned in London after Poitiers. In the hope of binding the powerful Coucy more firmly to England, Edward made him earl of Bedford. When the war with France broke out again, Coucy evaded the issue by going to fight for the pope against the Visconti. Eight years later he returned to Isabella, welcomed by all. But he soon went back to France, taking the elder of their two daughters with him. Isabella died three years afterwards, aged forty-seven. Her life had been all frustration; though she did have the honour of becoming, before the end, the first Lady of the Garter.

* * *

Baliol met Edward at Roxburgh on 23 November 1332, and duly promised to do homage for his conquests up to date. Edward then sent his prepared answer to the expected protest of the pope about his breach of the Scottish peace, saying that his army bound for Ireland had been diverted only because of Scottish truculence. A slight reverse occurred, fortunate in that it lent colour to his explanation. On Christmas Day Lord Archibald Douglas, who as a proper Scot did not get drunk until Hogmanay, fell on the drowsy Baliol and drove him half-clothed to seek English protection at Carlisle. That winter the Scots rallied behind Douglas, fortified Berwick and made forays across the Border.

The parliament so hastily called to York was late in assembling, partly because of the winter roads, partly because of a renewed quarrel between the two archbishops as to whose cross had precedence in the other's territory. When finally it met in January 1333, Chief Justice Sir Geoffrey Scrope was consequently able to make use of the latest news, and declare that as the Scots had renewed the war, King Edward had a free hand for the future. Edward dissolved the parliament, and sent his Chancellor Stratford over to France offering triumphant proof to Philip of Scottish culpability.

The new campaigning season of 1333 began in March. To mark the occasion, Edward invested his small son as earl of Chester, and then set off from Pontefract for Berwick, bringing with him scaling ladders, covered towers, trebuchets, manganels and other heavy engines requisite for a siege. The Scottish garrison of Berwick was soon pressed so hard that it had to agree to surrender if no help came by 20 July, and Archibald Douglas, the new regent, hurried to the relief with the main Scottish army. On the very evening before the time was up, he came upon Edward's much smaller forces trapped, as he thought, on Halidon Hill, with between them and the safety of their borders, the river Tweed in full flood at their backs. He advanced to the attack. This was just as Edward hoped. He had his men-at-arms dismounted on the crest of the hill to receive the charge, and the slope up which it must come was enfiladed by banks of archers. The military mind is slow to learn. The Scots had experienced the English longbow time and again since Falkirk at the turn of the last century, so much so that Sir James Douglas, otherwise a civilized and valiant knight, had made it a rule to cut off the bow-hand of any English archer who became his prisoner. And yet now his surviving half-brother, Archibald, like many French and other commanders after him, marched recklessly into the trap prepared. Edward executed a swift, crushing, and on his side almost bloodless victory. Berwick, the prize of the action, fell to the English.

> Skottes out of Berwick and of Abirdene,
> At the Bannokburn war ye to kene,

sang the jubilant English Borderers.

As Philip of France had avenged the defeat of Courtrai at Cassel, so had Edward no less completely avenged Bannockburn at Halidon. The Scots were scattered. Their boy king David and his girl wife, Edward's sister Joan, were withdrawn for safety to Dumbarton fortress on the Clyde. Baliol's future in Scotland seemed assured. Leaving him to exploit the victory, Edward went south to make the most of his new fame in ostentatious pilgrimages to Durham, Westminster, St Paul's, Windsor,

Canterbury – anywhere he could be sure of an adoring crowd. In the winter he went north again to obtain money from his parliament at York, ready to complete his conquest in the spring.

In February 1334, Baliol handed Berwick over to Edward, and by mid-summer was able to do homage for the entire country, making Edward master of the whole rich south up to and including Edinburgh. Edward, satisfied, returned to Windsor. But the Disinherited, having victoriously re-entered their estates, soon fell out among themselves. Baliol allowed himself to be drawn in, supported Mowbray against Henry, Lord Beaumont, then changed his mind, and as a result was chased out of Scotland altogether and fled to Berwick. In November Edward had to mount a second invasion to restore him. The price in lives was not severe, apart from the loss of Sir Edward de Bohun, hero of the coup at Nottingham, drowned in the Solway Firth while driving home a herd of stolen cattle. But the £12,000 the expedition had cost was formidable; and the season was too late for decisive action. Edward spent Christmas impatiently at Roxburgh.

In July 1335 Edward launched a third massive expedition. At the outset many knights were made, and many gifts distributed. The king gave his friend Sir William Montagu, in addition to several manors, a splendid courser caparisoned with the arms of Montagu (argent, three fusils conjoined in fess, gules); while he for his own part received an unexpected tribute from his father-in-law, William, the Good Earl of Hainault, 'a very gorgeous princely helmet, richly beset with precious stones and with the coronet and other things, in the same manner as the Earl himself was used to wear on festivals'. Edward, delighted, gave the messenger £100, and proudly wore the helmet.

Since the much-weakened Scots were reduced to skirmishing, the main thrusts of the summer advance, Edward's from Carlisle, and Baliol's from Berwick, were unopposed, and their planned meeting at Perth was easily effected. But on the flanks, in the fens and crags and forests, things were better suited to Scottish interference. The earl of Moray, now in his turn regent for King David, chased the count of Namur and his dashing young brother, who had come free-lance to Edward hoping to gain favour for their uncle Robert of Artois, in a running fight ending on the hilltop in Edinburgh where, some say, the brother's beautiful virago lay among the fallen, and the rest were captured in the ruins of the castle. Since they had no real place in the Scottish quarrel, Moray not only agreed to forgo their ransom, but escorted them courteously to the Border. There, hearing that Queen Philippa was at Bamborough castle with her children, and rashly unable to resist going after so great a prize, Moray was himself taken and carried off a prisoner to London.

The Scots were now leaderless. Though the cadet branch still flourished in Sir William Douglas, the Knight of Liddesdale, the proud title of the fighting Douglases had passed, on the death of Sir Archibald at Halidon Hill, to an obscure clergyman known despondently to his fierce countrymen as Hugh the Dull. King David had been shipped away to France, and his place in safe-keeping at Dumbarton taken by young Robert Stuart, Bruce's grandson and only other heir. The Peace of Perth which Edward was able to impose on 18 August 1335 was virtually a capitulation.

Yet scarcely had he turned his back on the defeated clansmen and gone south than David Strabolgi, earl of Athol, one of the Disinherited whom he had left in charge, was killed in renewed fighting in the forest of Kilblain, and all the dispersed embers of resistance flared anew. Soldiers as great as William Montagu and Henry of Grosmont, heir of Lancaster, were quite unable to reduce the castle defended by Black Agnes, countess of Dunbar, sister of the captive earl of Moray. Once when the English tried to mine her walls under cover of a much-prized contrivance called a sow, she cried down merrily that she 'would soon make that Sow cast her pigs', and it was destroyed accordingly, by a shower of missiles from above. Montagu could do nothing with her. 'Came I early, came I late, I found Agnes at the gate', he is supposed to have protested. Baliol, incompetent to rule his so-called kingdom, was preparing yet again to leave it, and was well-nigh penniless. Contemptuously, Edward put him on a pittance of five marks a day, and, in May 1336, ordered him to go by sea to Perth and there await his coming with a further expedition.

In the summer of 1336 Edward made a fourth, and for the time being final, progress through the fastnesses of Scotland. This time he rode to the farthest north, past Inverness, 'farther than ever his victorious grandfather Edward the First had penetrated, even beyond Caithness and the mountains, where the Highlanders and Wild-Scots inhabit, where the extremities of Scotland are washed by the Deucaledon sea'. He encountered nothing. He hunted wolves and bears, no doubt; but found few rebels in sparse and distant regions where he was more like an explorer than a conquering king.

Back in Perth, he found Baliol waiting, and also his own twenty-year-old brother, John of Eltham, now earl of Cornwall, who had completed a notable *chevauchée* up the western route, the last of his brief career, for he died a few months later. The news from home was pressing. Leaving Henry of Grosmont in charge, and having furnished his main bastions, Stirling, Edinburgh and Berwick, Edward went down to York, where he buried Philippa's short-lived second son, William of Hatfield, in the minster. Then he ordered his muniments to be packed up, the waggons loaded, and led his government back to Westminster, satisfied that, though Scotland had certainly not been brought to order, at least his back was safe. As intended, the Scots had been made harmless before France could combine with them against him. Philip's effort had been too little and too late; raids on the Channel Islands and the southern shores of England, money, and a few horsemen galloping about in Scotland, were all that he had made of his opportunity. Edward was now free to turn to his main purpose, the attack on France.

For that, he had to thank his own duplicity and Philip's indecision. During the four years of the Scottish war, Edward had continued to write disarmingly to Philip, and from time to time had sent embassies to negotiate on Aquitaine. In July 1333, before fighting his great battle at Halidon Hill, he had, for fear of French reprisals, fortified Dover, and warned his sailors not to offer provocation.

His fears were at that stage needless, for Philip was still lost in his dream of a Crusade. The pope had already granted him a special tax on the clergy towards the cost, and in that summer of 1333 the Holy War was preached and Philip was proclaimed its leader. He was eager to be off; but, as shrewdly unwilling to leave Edward in arms behind him as he was keen to have the lustre of his company, he sent again to suggest that they should go together.

Edward, or his counsellors, scented a good bargain, and in April 1334, when Scotland was apparently subdued, a powerful embassy consisting of the Chancellor, Archbishop Stratford, Dr Richard Bury, Sir William Montagu, and Chief Justice Scrope arrived in Paris to argue that Edward would by all means go on the Crusade, if only Philip would first do his part towards making a settlement in Aquitaine. Philip was about to offer concessions. But on 14 May, King David, with his queen Joan and a handful of his Scottish advisers, arrived at Boulogne in a ship sent by Philip to rescue them from Dumbarton. The result of their instant loud objections was that the English envoys, who had gone to bed with the prospect of a general agreement well in sight, were abruptly roused to hear that a new, and crippling, condition had been added to the terms. There could be no settlement over Aquitaine unless Scotland was included in it. No peace without peace in Scotland. The deal was off. The Scottish war resumed. French depredations recommenced in Aquitaine, and Philip dimly began to imagine himself as lord of France, Scotland and England all together.

At about this time, Robert of Artois arrived in England. He had once been Philip's closest friend and, at his doubtful accession, his chief supporter. He had since fallen into dispute with his aunt Matilda over the family inheritance in the Pas de Calais. After a case had gone against him, Robert produced charters to prove his rights; but they turned out to be forgeries. Soon afterwards, his aunt Matilda and her daughter died, perhaps by witchcraft, more probably by poisoning. Philip, suspecting Robert's complicity, had seized the county of Artois, and their former friendship turned to bitter hatred. Driven out of France, and hounded from place to place by Philip's rancour, Robert of Artois came, an implacable exile, to Edward's court, where he was received with considerable interest. By now, Edward's focus had shifted away from defeated Scotland towards

France. Baliol the Scot was already on the shelf, and Robert of Artois, next in a long line of useful *agents provocateurs*, was soon whispering in Edward's ear.

In December 1334 Pope John XXII died and was succeeded by Benedict XII, the 'White Cardinal', a Cistercian from the county of Foix. The choice of Benedict surprised no one more than himself; 'they have chosen an ass', he said, a statement with which the poet Petrarch heartily agreed. He was as corpulent as he was bibulous, and the phrase 'drink like a pope' became current in his reign. He was altogether different from his predecessor, the meagre, thin-voiced, wavering Pope John, quarrelsome and superstitious, who had died recanting his own heresy of the Beatific Vision. Nevertheless, for all his metaphysics, Pope John proved to have had a sharp business eye. His coffers were found to be bursting with gold, both coin and ingots, a fabulous fortune, sufficient for twenty such projects as the great Palais des Papes he had begun to raise at Avignon. The worldly Benedict, on the other hand, despite his self-indulgence, was strictly scrupulous financially, and readily released part of his unexpected and indecent wealth for Philip's use against the Infidel. A vast fleet began to come into being in the harbours of Provence, particularly at Marseilles. A sailing date for the Crusade was fixed, as 1 May 1336.

Philip wanted, if Edward would not go with him, at least to secure peace in Scotland before he left. Early in 1335 he sent ambassadors to York, and scared Edward into granting a short truce. But it was a one-sided intervention in favour of the Scots. Edward temporized by trumping up an ancient Lancastrian claim to Provence in favour of his friend and cousin Henry of Grosmont. As soon as the truce was over, he made his third and most massive attack upon the Scots, culminating, as already noted, in the decisive treaty of Perth. Philip's reply was a threat of invasion, real enough for Edward's son and heir to be sent for safety to Nottingham castle, though it came to no more than a few skirmishes in Aquitaine, and the dispatch of a few French ships and men to Scotland.

Pope Benedict now intervened. Outweighing his interest in Philip's Crusade was the interest of the church in avoiding a conflict between the two great kingdoms of the West, and preventing either of them driving the other into the arms of the church's enemy, the excommunicated emperor Louis IV. He restrained Philip and, in November 1335, secured from Edward a further six months' truce in Scotland. Edward appeared to be so far hopeful of peace as to tell the king of Armenia, who was as usual questing round for aid against the Turks, that he was ready to go 'as soon as certain hindrances (in Scotland and Aquitaine) had been removed'.

By February 1336 the position had, however, worsened once again. Edward, whose tone was hardening as the end of the Scottish war came more clearly into sight, formally demanded from Philip the return of his Gascon territories. At the same time he began to put out feelers among his friends and relatives in the Low Countries about possible alliances against France, and ordered all his subjects between sixteen and sixty years of age to come under arms against a threatened French invasion.

At Easter, Philip, with King John of Bohemia, the king of Navarre, and other notable would-be Crusaders, made a state visit to Avignon to receive the pope's holy banner preparatory to departure. The visitors were royally housed in Villeneuve-lès-Avignon, the papal annexe across the river Rhône. On Good Friday, Benedict preached the Crusade so movingly as to reduce them all to tears and lamentations. But no sooner had they gone than he wrote to Philip saying that peace in Europe must come first, that Philip had misdirected the clerical taxes awarded to him for the Crusade from sacred to profane purposes, and that the whole affair was cancelled.

If he intended to force Philip to make peace, he had the opposite effect. Philip had been dissuaded by the church from attacking Edward in Aquitaine or in Scotland when he had the best chance of doing so; from allying himself against Edward with the emperor; more lately, from trouncing Edward for his breach of vassalage in harbouring Robert of Artois – all for the sake of an imminent Crusade, the bright prospect of which was suddenly extinguished. In this way, the cancelled Crusade helped to provoke the great quarrel it had been engendered to assuage. When Edward marched off on his fourth and last excursion to the North, Philip declared for Scotland and sounded the advance in Aquitaine. When Edward returned to Perth, he found that twenty-six French galleys, in the name of his small rival David, had harried Jersey and Guernsey and the Isle of Wight, and were sailing on towards Scotland. Worse, he learned that Philip had moved his great crusading fleet from Marseilles northward to the Channel ports.

The appearance of the main French fleet in the 'nearu sees' let slip the war that was to last for a hundred years. At Perth, on 18 August 1336, the leopards of England gave out a deep long-echoing growl. Edward sent to his admirals of the southern, the western and the northern waters, ordering his ships to put out to sea, 'calling to mind that Our progenitors, the Kings of England, have before these times been LORDS OF THE ENGLISH SEA on every side; and seeing it would very much grieve Us, if in this kind of defence Our Royal Honour should (which God forbid) be lost or any way diminished in Our time . . .'

No wonder, in that hard winter of 1336, there were signs and portents. At Leighton, not far from Huntingdon, the chroniclers say, a calf was born with two heads and eight legs. In frozen January the pussy-willows came into flower like roses. The elderberries were as big as blood-red cherries. A great comet with a fiery tail streaked through the sky from east to south in that dark winter.

* * *

In January 1337, the burial in Westminster Abbey of Edward's brother, John of Eltham, whose embalmed remains had been brought down from the North, marked the end of the Scottish campaign. The parliament which followed in February was directed towards war in France.

The grave enterprise was heralded by an appropriate distribution of new honours. No fewer than seven earls were belted, and their dignity supported by suitable additions to their properties. Sir William Montagu became earl of Salisbury; Henry of Grosmont, heir of Lancaster, became earl of Derby; William de Clinton, earl of Huntingdon; the extinct and long-coveted Marcher earldom of Gloucester was conferred upon James Audley; William de Bohun was made earl of Northampton; and Robert Ufford, earl of Suffolk. The redoubtable Hugh Courtenay was confirmed in the remaining seventh earldom, of Devon, which had been promised to him two years previously for the curious reason that only so could he augment his income by the amount of £18. 6s. 8d. the 'third penny' of the estate of his mother, who had been countess of Devon in her own right. The other six were younger men, all personal friends of the king, well-tried companions of the Nottingham coup and of the Scottish war. The earldom of Cornwall, left empty by John of Eltham, was elevated to a dukedom and given to Prince Edward, who thus, at the age of just under seven, became the first duke in English history. He in turn dubbed a score of new knights. Though some of them, like John Pulteney, the wealthy mayor of London, may have been favoured more for their financial than their military promise, they too were mostly soldiers, such as young Edward Montagu, the third Montagu brother to be honoured. Simon, a churchman, bishop of Worcester since 1334, was promoted to Ely at the same time.

The next question was, how best to attack the king of France? Edward's defiant claim to be lord of the English Sea had been magnificent, but it was far from true. Of naval power as a special arm there was as yet little idea. A navy was thought of only as a means of carrying men and materials to a theatre of war, and a naval action as a land battle made inconvenient by having to take place at sea. There were, indeed, two admirals, for the waters north of the Thames, and for the south and westward; but they were always soldiers. For all Edward's brave words, the royal fleet consisted of no more than a dozen cogs, flamboyantly painted, lying in the Thames at the king's command, backed up by the ancient duty of the Cinque Ports, now usually evaded, to provide fifty-seven vessels with crews, 'the King's pirates' as they were commonly called, for a certain period each year.

These were no match for the proud fleet got together at the pope's expense for the abandoned Crusade, now riding at anchor in the French Channel ports. Any further shipping would have to come from wool-merchantmen, fishing yawls, wine ships and contrabanders, reluctantly withdrawn from their normal occasions at a loss of revenue both to their owners and to the realm; and they would still have to be fitted out as warships, with the addition of wooden 'castles' fore and aft. A large expedition to distant Aquitaine was out of the question. Even by the short Channel route there had, except for King John's unhappy venture, been no main invasion since the Conquest, and that itself had succeeded only by the thinnest margin. The best way would be to take a small force to the nearest land frontiers of France, and to rely on alliances there to build it up from resources already on the right side of the water.

Such a notion was by no means new, and over the years English kings had deliberately arranged marriage alliances in the Low Countries. Duke John III of Brabant was Edward's first cousin (his mother was Edward II's sister Margaret). The count of Gueldres had married Edward's sister Eleanor. The margrave of Juliers was husband to one of Queen Philippa's sisters, Joan. William, the Good Earl of Hainault, who had recently sent the splendid helmet, was a friendly father-in-law. The German emperor, Louis IV of Bavaria, to whom all the others were vassals, had married another of Philippa's sisters, Margaret.

Though well disposed to Edward as a family connection, and in some cases themselves uneasy about French intentions, these rulers of small countries were not to be easily welded into a grand alliance. They did not believe that factious little England, embroiled with barbaric frontiersmen, could successfully challenge the fame and power of France. They did not trust one another and did not share Edward's hearty confidence that, on his unconvincing showing in Scotland, he would lead them to victory across their dykes and polderland. They thought he would be driven out, leaving them to face alone the dreadful vengeance they had seen applied by Philip of Valois to the Flemish rebels at Cassel. In general, their enthusiasm dwindled the nearer they were to the projected scene of action. Juliers and Gueldres, buffered behind the Meuse away to the east, were fairly hopeful; Brabant, sandwiched in the middle, was more dubious; Hainault, in some ways the most promising ally, was, because of its open frontier with France, the most cautious of all. Only Robert of Artois, the self-appointed adviser already at Edward's court, had no qualms, because his French county was already confiscated and he had nothing to lose.

Edward had, however, a stronger argument than family feeling to bring to bear. The Low Countries, urbanized and heavily populated, all depended for their existence on the manufacture of cloth, and therefore upon a steady supply of English wool to feed the looms. Suddenly, in the parliament of August 1336, the export of wool from England was forbidden, and the flow of the precious raw material stopped.

It has been claimed that the ban was part of a far-seeing plan to help the manufacture of home-made cloth in England. Certainly, the wearing of foreign cloth was prohibited at the same time as the export of raw wool, though that proves nothing. Weavers facing ruin in their own countries were encouraged to come to ply their trade near the source of wool supply, among them Thomas Blanket of Bristol, perhaps so named for his fame as a maker of blankets. Queen Philippa used her influence in their favour; during the 1340s, whenever she went that way, she always visited Norwich to see her follow Netherlanders at their work. But the main expansion of the English cloth trade did not occur until much later, and Edward's concern lay more with putting diplomatic pressure on his potential allies than with the fostering of an infant industry at home.

In any case the restriction could not last long, lest England herself should starve. It was not for nothing that the Chancellor sat upon a woolsack. Wool was 'the sovereign merchandise and jewel of this realm of England'. Although artificial shortage was an effective short-term weapon, as Edward I had shown some sixty years before, and although its resumption, when it came, enabled exporters at home to make a kill at famine prices, such resumption could not be long delayed.

In April 1337, when the effect of the embargo began to bite, there arrived at Valenciennes, in Hainault, Henry Burghersh, bishop of Lincoln, the former confidant of Mortimer, but now a valuable ambassador in Edward's service. With him came the two new earls of Salisbury and Huntingdon, and a few clerks learned in the law. The old earl of Hainault, bedridden with gout, freely promised his support against the French, as did his brother John of Hainault, who in the past, for the sake of his niece Philippa, had so stoutly if mistakenly assisted Isabella. The embassy moved on, in July, to Brabant, where Duke John received them equally civilly and allowed himself, after some hedging, to be bought over for £60,000 and a release of wool.

The English emissaries had brought with them a company of forty fine young gentlemen who caused excited comment by going about with one eye covered by a patch of silk. Though they would give no explanation, it was rumoured that before they had set out from England they had sworn to their ladies never to take the patches off until they had done some feat of arms in France. They had been well provided with money by King Edward, who had, strangely, found it necessary at the same time to urge them to rub up their French. They lost no time in making themselves agreeable, though no doubt Bishop Burghersh pursed his lips in disapproval. As they galloped round, their foreign charm, their mystery and dash, made no less sensation than their liberality. Before long a veritable market in alliances was flourishing with Juliers, Gueldres, Berg, Cleves, and other outlying principalities.

Flanders was less easy to persuade. The greatest of the cloth-making states, she was the only one that owed allegiance not to the emperor but to the king of France. Industrialization in her cities had produced a powerful class of burghers whose commercial interests diverged from the old-fashioned feudalism of their rulers. Unable to understand the new demotic stirrings, the French kings naturally took the part of the counts, who were their vassals, and a generation of bitter strife had recently ended in the forcible restoration of the French count, Louis of Nevers.

Flanders had been hit hardest of all by the wool embargo, and while Count Louis blamed England's malice and locked up English nationals, the citizens blamed the count's French alignment and were all for making terms with Edward. At King Philip's order, Count Louis cut off the head of the popular champion, Sigur of Courtrai, known fondly as the Lord of Courtesy. Fanned by anger and by the fear of ruin and starvation, sedition flared. Count Louis was driven, first into hiding, and later to seek refuge in France.

His place, and much of his wealth, were taken by Jacob van Artevelde, a prosperous burgess and a former brewer of mead, whose attributes, unusual then, would now seem familiar. He had almost hypnotic oratorical powers and used them to the full to work up a public clamour to discard the French connection in favour of the English. He was shrewd, greedy, and ruthless. Once established, he sustained his people's republic as a personal tyranny. He swaggered through Ghent with a posse of bravoes, to whom a mere glance from him, not so much as a nod, meant the instant dispatch of an erstwhile friend as he chatted to him amiably in the street. His spies were everywhere. At the twitch of his finger in Ghent, a knife flashed in Ypres, a noose tightened in Bruges. His power was absolute.

To Jacob van Artevelde in Ghent, therefore, Bishop Burghersh next addressed himself. It was bargaining between titans. Flanders could afford the English a broad front for entry into France and useful ports nearby, and she had a score of her own to settle with France by regaining her occupied towns of Lille, Douai and Béthune. But she could not for the moment dare again to defy her rightful overlord, nor face the interdict and enormous penalty threatened by the pope for doing so. Wool, and money, were thrown into the balance, and a firm promise of Flemish neutrality was eventually obtained. More, Burghersh felt, might follow later, as the fear of France receded, and the Flemings saw with envy how their neighbours prospered under the English alliance. To rub in the point, their chief rival in the cloth trade, Brabant, was told that a wool monopoly, or staple, discontinued since 1328, was to be set up for her in Antwerp, so that her mills in Brussels and Malines would flourish once again.

When Burghersh and his mission got back to Hainault, the old earl had died, and his successor, Philippa's brother William, less decided than his father had been, told him on behalf of the new allies that he must come to some arrangement with the emperor, their common overlord, before any irrevocable step could be taken against France. So Burghersh set out for the Rhineland, buying up the emperor's brother Rupert of Bavaria in passing.

The Emperor Louis IV had no love for Philip of France, who had persuaded Pope Benedict to continue the excommunication passed upon him earlier by Pope John. Philip, moreover, had lately married his heir, John, duke of Normandy, to Bonne of Luxemburg, daughter of the emperor's energetic rival King John of Bohemia. The emperor therefore agreed, on 26 August, to make his brother-in-law, King Edward, Vicar of the Empire, which would give him the needed authority over his allies. He even promised to send some German troops himself, in return for a huge payment of 300,000 gold florins (about £45,000).

Burghersh's embassy had done well, far better than Philip in comparison. On 24 May 1337, Philip had formally confiscated the duchy of Aquitaine, and though this was no more than Charles IV and Philip the Fair had done before him – no more, indeed, than was his vassal Edward's just punishment for harbouring Robert of Artois – peace thereafter was out of the question. Since then, Philip had joined in the scramble for allies, and had been generally worsted. A treaty with Alfonso XI had gained him an important advantage, the Castilian fleet, and King John of Bohemia was in his pocket. But in his belated approaches to the emperor he found himself forestalled; and nearer the theatre of action, in his own fief of Flanders, his protégé Count Louis of Nevers was a poor match for Jacob van Artevelde. The town of Cambrai, the bishop of Liège and Henry of Bavaria were the only other pickings left for him. On 7 October, Edward, now full of assurance, appointed the duke of Brabant as deputy leader of his now formidable alliance and declared himself king of France and England.

It was natural that when Burghersh and his companions set out on their journey home, Philip should use his navy to try to intercept them from Cadsand, an island in the mouth of the Scheldt still held by the count of Flanders. Edward got wind of it; English ships in the North Sea broke up the attack, and afterwards captured two vessels laden with Scottish lords and ladies, as well as French soldiers, horses and treasure, on their way to Scotland. Later that autumn, Sir Walter Manny, once Queen Philippa's carver, since knighted and appointed Admiral of the North, retaliated by landing on Cadsand. The Flemish defenders, the first victims of the English longbow on Continental soil, were thrown into disorder. After rescuing Henry of Derby, hard-pressed in a tussle, single-handed, and burning the inhabitants of Cadsand in the church where they had taken refuge, Manny drew off safely, taking among his prisoners the bastard brother of Count Louis, who quickly changed to the English side. Manny's panache brought him a fortune in ransoms, £8,000 – in due course, when the king could afford it.

In Flanders and in Aquitaine as well as on the seas the first arrows had now sped. Sensing that the conflict would be long and would entail much misery, Pope Benedict, who genuinely wished to avert the war looming between the Christian princes of the West, sent two cardinals to England. On their approach to London just before Christmas 1337, they were met,

79

as became their state, by an imposing group of clergy led by Archbishop John Stratford and his brother Robert Stratford, bishop of Chichester, then Chancellor; a mile outside the city, the young Prince Edward, performing his first public duty, waited on them with the laity. The king received them in person at the gate of his palace of Westminster, with due honour, and took them into the Painted Chamber. But their mission was foredoomed. One of the cardinals, a Frenchman, was so prejudiced in his address that Archbishop Stratford rose and furiously contradicted him. There was no hope of peace, and though a delay in the invasion plan until midsummer was tactfully attributed to respect for the pope's appeal, it was largely because of the shortage of English shipping, and most of all for lack of English money.

The first great foreign war since John lost Normandy had somehow to be paid for. The king, who was still supposed to bear the main cost of his military adventures, had a personal revenue of about £30,000. With the addition of what could be made from wardships and marriages, forfeitures, compulsory knighthood, scutages for unperformed knight's service, and from other feudal aids on special occasions, such as the knighting of his eldest son, it was still barely enough even to keep his household on the customary scale.

For years past, Edward had exploited every device, however trivial, for increasing it. In 1333 he had extended to the clergy, much to their indignation, an aid to celebrate the marriage of his sister Eleanor. Pilgrimages were profitable: the Holy Blissful Martyr of Canterbury brought in a steady £400 a year, and many applications were therefore made to the pope for the canonization of new saints. In 1336, £60,000 worth of treasure Edward II had lost in Wales was welcomed back at the Exchequer. The judges were ordered to increase their fines. To induce austerity, the wearing of silks and furs was forbidden to those with less than £100 a year; all tournaments, and all sports except archery, were discontinued. Edward took to his own use, as Philip of France did also on a far larger scale, all monies that had been set aside for the Crusade. In 1337 he assumed temporary ownership of all alien priories and forced the occupants to pay him rent. The unpopular Lombard merchants in the city of London were accused of usury and all their wealth was locked up in the Tower. In 1338, as the date of invasion drew near, all the tin of Cornwall and Devon was appropriated to the crown, and concessions were sold to dig mines for gold and silver in those counties. Abbeys were forced to surrender their plate and the very ornaments were taken from the churches. Finally on 28 February 1338, the hereditary crown of state was pledged to the archbishop of Triers for 50,000 florins (£7,500).

The king could usually count on his parliaments to supplement his resources by a subsidy of one-fifteenth of the value of movables throughout the land, and of one-tenth in the richer boroughs and the demesne lands that would otherwise be liable to royal tallage. In 1334 the total amount was standardized at about £38,000, allotted out by counties. The clergy generally followed suit, though they insisted on doing so outside Parliament by their own vote in Convocation. The fear of the rest of the country that the clergy might not be able to pay their share led to increasing resentment at the extra-territorial demands made on them by the pope.

Subsidies were voted in each year of the Scottish war. In 1336 there were two, and in 1337 a tenth and a fifteenth were granted in advance for each of the next three years so that the king could anticipate them for credit purposes. Though the grants, never a formality, became more and more conditional upon the prior satisfaction of grievances, and though some account began to be asked of the uses to which they were put, the king's necessity had at least come to be taken for granted. Edward was better off in that respect than Philip of France, whose commissioners had to bargain province by province with the Estates of the People and were sometimes met with blank refusals. Philip's demand for aid in 1337 brought in so little that he was unable to pay his officials for collecting it.

The wool customs had always been a royal prerogative and provided the king, aside from other legitimate revenue, with useful extra ways of raising ready money, either by direct speculation or by more or less shady dealings with financiers, and of bringing to bear economic pressure, whether individual or diplomatic. The standard export duty (6s. 8d. on the sack weighing 364 lb, with a further 3s. 4d. from foreigners, about 5 per cent of the average value) was not high, but it was extra-parliamentary, and the king by declaring *maltôtes* could vary at will the conditions and the rates and so create artificial prices and a marginal profit he could then negotiate with merchants to raise credit. From one such attractive scheme, the Dordrecht bonds, depending on the abundance of cheap wool at home as a result of the embargo, its enormous value overseas, and payment for the king's share in the form of later credits against the customs, Edward hoped to make a heady sum of £200,000. But things went wrong, and he ended by cheating the merchants for not much gain. Since the burden fell in the end on the producers, there was a growing demand that the wool trade too should be controlled by Parliament, where the ultimate losers could protect their interests. In 1336, in the hope of avoiding further sudden *maltôtes*, the king was formally assigned new duties worth £70,000 a year; and in February 1338 a despairing Parliament offered him pre-emption of half the wool in the kingdom, 20,000 sacks, on condition that the rest should be left untampered with for his subjects.

Edward's option was at once absorbed, premortgaged like all his expected revenues as security for the enormous sums he had to borrow. Loans had long been a necessary factor in royal administration, but from a sober figure of around £16,000 each year at the beginning of his reign, his debt to the Italian finance houses of Bardi and Peruzzi alone had soared, in a decade, to £125,000. And he had not yet paid his Continental allies the £124,000 due before the end of 1337, to say nothing of the cost of raising the army and the fleet. Even if his assets had not been spent in advance, loans would still have been needed to fill the long interval before their realization. The assessment, conversion into coin, and collection of the taxes, passing through many hands, invited corruption: the amounts received at the exchequer seldom came up to expectations. On arrival at Antwerp, for example, Edward was to find that of the 20,000 sacks of wool he had been promised, and for which he now stood indebted to the Bardi, only 2,500 had been delivered.

Before his departure for the Continent, Edward set out, in the Walton Ordinances, the means for the government of the country in his absence, since in this case it clearly was not possible, as had been done in the Scottish campaign, for him to conduct it personally. But the Ordinances had no realistic hope of achieving the smooth administration he intended. The division of powers and duties between home and overseas was disastrously unbalanced. All his trusted statesmen, Bishops Burghersh and Dr Bury of Durham, John Stratford the archbishop, Earls Montagu of Salisbury and Bohun of Northampton, and Geoffrey Scrope, the Lord Chief Justice, were either abroad already or would sail with him and his Admiral, Sir Walter Manny. William Kilsby would bring both the principal instruments of authority, the Great and Privy Seals. With these for his foreign council, and with his queen's brother-in-law, the margrave of Juliers, as his personal link with his allies, he would direct war policy from afar and pass back tall orders to the government at home for the money to execute it. While left behind in London, the newly appointed Chancellor and Treasurer, wielding an unimpressive 'seal of absence', and under the nominal regency of his eight-year-old son, would be expected to fulfil his distant demands for a swift and ever-increasing flow of credit.

Edward's expedition, delayed three months by lack of shipping, sailed belatedly from Walton-on-the-Naze on 16 July 1338. The truce with France agreed with the pope had terminated, and after settling in at the abbey of St Bernard at Antwerp, his first care was to call his kinsmen and allies to honour the obligations they had entered into with Bishop Burghersh the previous year. They were in no hurry to do so. They begged time to deliberate, and when they reassembled at the castle of Louvain, which the duke of Brabant, their leader and Edward's host, had placed at his guests' disposal, the duke himself was missing; they insisted that they could not proceed without him. At last, at Hal near Brussels, they promised to declare for Edward as soon as the emperor had formally appointed him his deputy.

So, leaving his lords and knights to hunt and dance their way once more through the admiring countryside, and after borrowing a further £100,000 from the Brabanters to cover expenses rightly expected to be heavy, Edward led a gorgeous embassy up the Rhine, through Cologne, where he gave royally to the fund for the great cathedral then being built, to Coblenz, where the emperor was to meet him. On 5 September an elaborate ceremony before an illustrious audience went off smoothly, except that Edward, when required to kiss the emperor's foot, refused point-blank to do so. The difficulty was got over, and at last the two monarchs were safely enthroned side by side in the market place, Louis in all his ancient Holy Roman finery, Edward wearing a glittering imperial crown, specially made for the occasion, and far surpassing the one he had had to pawn. A German knight behind them brandished aloft above their heads an enormous naked sword. Then Louis denounced Philip of Valois, and declared Edward suzerain over all his subjects west of the Rhine.

On his way back, Edward ordered his new vassals to meet him at Malines, in Brabant, a summons none now dared to disobey, except the bishops of Cambrai and Liège, who had joined Philip's side. There, once again wearing his great crown, and towering on a throne five feet above everyone else, he caused the emperor's warrant to be read. But by now the season was too late for campaigning, and he dismissed them with orders to appear on 8 July 1339 at Vilvoorde, north of Brussels, ready to attack Cambrai.

At Louvain he found Queen Philippa waiting, big with child once more, and surrounded by her ladies, some of whom perhaps had come to temper the chivalrous excesses of their still one-eyed knights. He carried the court back to spend Christmas at Antwerp, as being 'more commodious for the Queen to lay her belly in', and there, on 29 November 1338, his third son, Lionel, was born. The wet weather, and Philippa's mourning for her father, prevented the usual martial celebrations, but on her churching Edward gave her over £500 for her wardrobe, quickly spent by Philippa, ever a leader of fashion, on the long-denied fine cloths and laces to be found in the city booths of her native Low Countries.

Naturally, Edward received rebukes from Pope Benedict for his dealings with the excommunicate emperor, for his war-like attitude to his cousin of France, and for his unrepentant harbouring of the rebel Robert of Artois. He left his defence to his clerical secretaries, and they gave as good as they got. What chafed him more was the scarcity of his resources. Apart from satisfying his importunate allies, he now had to keep up prodigious state and, for example, to set up a mint at Antwerp, stamping out golden *écus* bearing the eagle of the Empire over his own name. The home government spoke of 'mighty aids' in wool, and he borrowed against its credit, though little of it arrived. In May he had to suspend all payment of his debts in England. At last July came, and his army reassembled for his gambler's throw. Snatching up a final loan of £54,000 from some merchants in Malines, he set off to his rendezvous near Brussels.

His allies took weeks to concentrate. On 1 September he sent off their formal defiance by hand of Bishop Burghersh and the Windsor Herald to Philip, now with his army fifty miles away at Compiègne. Then, without waiting for the duke of Brabant, who, once more missing, refused to commit himself before battle was actually joined, Edward advanced through Valenciennes towards Cambrai. Skirting the town, Sir Walter Manny, winning the race to be first on the soil of France, had the first brushes with the enemy, in which a young squire, John Chandos, soon to be famous, first came to notice.

Meanwhile, at Compiègne, Philip, having ordered his heir, John, duke of Normandy, to reinforce Cambrai, occupied Edward's county of Ponthieu, and marched his main force forward to Péronne. It was a formidable feudal host, comprising all the great vassals of France except Edward himself, and Louis of Nevers, who was immobilized in Flanders. There were no fewer than three kings in Philip's company – his cousin Philip of Evreux, king of Navarre; blind King John of Bohemia; and the young exile David of Scotland, in care of Sir William Douglas. With a greatly superior force, working on interior lines, and with the ability to disrupt Edward's sea lanes at will, every advantage lay with Philip; and yet he was unwilling to engage. An older and a wilier man, he knew how little Edward's hard-bought alliances were worth, and could afford to wait until the patchwork invasion fell to bits. After all, as his advisers told him, he had nothing to win by battle; defeat might cost him France, but victory could not gain him England.

Edward, for his part, had little leisure. Once again, the campaigning season was slipping away towards the time when the autumn rains would waterlog the plains. Financially and politically he was compelled to strike a single crippling blow; nor did he doubt his ability to do so, provided only that he could induce Philip to attack. For he knew that recent developments in warfare had been greatly in favour of defence. Just as an up-to-date fortified town defied assault unless treachery or starvation intervened, so the once irresistible charge of mounted armour would henceforth fall like sickled wheat before the arrows of waiting and well-sited archers. Finding therefore that Cambrai was strongly held he did not lay siege, but, disregarding Robert of Artois's desire to strike westward to his own territories, he crossed the French frontier and went south towards Péronne, where he hoped to goad Philip into action.

Philip remained watchful and, as time went by, Edward's alliance began to show the expected sign of strain. The tardy duke of Brabant had at last come in, but the other allies, hearing that the French were becoming daily stronger, grew restless, saying that their provisions were running low; testily, Edward supplied them from the ample waggons which, since his early experiences in Scotland, he always carried with him. Then William, the new earl of Hainault, Philippa's brother, conveniently deciding that his feudal duty changed when he crossed from the Empire into France, rode over to the enemy – who scorned his casuistry not much less than did his former comrades.

Planning to draw Philip after him, Edward feigned to turn away, and bore eastward into the salient of Thiérache. Deliberately provocative, his men foraged and plundered, laying waste French villages. Their cruel deeds were not at all of the sort that Froissart proclaimed would 'encourage all valorous hearts, and show them honourable examples'. At Origny a whole community of nuns was raped, and the convent burned. At Hendecourt, the country people and an abbeyful of monks, determined to defend themselves, built a barrier against Sir Henry of Flanders and his troop. Their burly abbot, seeing Sir Henry flourishing his sword incautiously too near, reached through the palings, grabbed the blade, and pinned the knight helpless between the woodwork and the press of friends who tried to drag him clear. After a lengthy tussle the abbot wrested Sir Henry's sword from him, and for years afterwards the monks displayed it proudly to visitors who passed that way.

Edward's tactics proved successful. Philip, no longer able to restrain the mounting anger in his ranks caused by the allied atrocities, advanced in pursuit from Péronne to Saint-Quentin whence, in response to a challenge, he replied to Edward's joy that 'if he would choose out a place not fortified with trees, ditches or bogs, the King of France without fail would afford him battle'. Edward richly rewarded the herald of such welcome news with furred gowns and other gifts.

And so, early in the morning of 23 October 1339, near the village of Buironfosse, the armies of France and England, which were to meet time and again in the next hundred years, first prepared themselves for action on the traditional battlefield of Europe. Edward, inviting attack on carefully chosen ground, had his men drawn up in three formations, commanded by Gueldres, Brabant and himself, in the way that had served so well at Halidon Hill: dismounted, in line, interspersed and flanked by wedges of archers projecting slightly forward towards the enemy. Escorted by Robert of Artois, Reginald Cobham and Sir Walter Manny, he rode on a white palfrey up and down the English ranks ranged under their leaders, his cousin Henry of Grosmont, earl of Derby, his friend William Montagu of Salisbury, lately advanced to Earl Marshal on the death of the king's uncle, Thomas of Brotherton; Bohun of Northampton, Audley of Gloucester, Ufford of Suffolk, Beauchamp of Warwick, Fitzalan of Arundel, young Lawrence Hastings, newly made earl of Pembroke, and Sir John Chandos, now knighted. 'It was', says Froissart, 'a glorious sight to see these two armies standing in the field, their banners and standards waving in the wind; their proud horses barbed, and Kings, Lords, Knights and Esquires richly armed, and all shining in their surcoats of satin and embroidery.' In fact, the armies were not so close together as Froissart pictured them; they were a few miles apart, and could not see each other's dispositions. Plain, silent, ominous country was, as usual, all the common soldiers saw.

Towards noon, a hare started up in view of the French, and caused such a hullabaloo that the turncoat earl of Hainault, placed ignominiously in the rear detachment, supposed that the English were attacking and, as the custom was, hastily dubbed fourteen new knights, forever afterwards known as the Knights of the Hare – 'Lions in the hall, and Hares in the Field', as a later chronicler contemptuously dismissed such carpet warriors. Young Hainault, humiliated for the second time, withdrew from the battle altogether, and marched furiously homeward.

Nothing further happened all day. According to Froissart, Philip was dissuaded from the attack by a discouraging forecast that came post-haste from his uncle, King Robert of Sicily, a noted astrologer of the day. More probably, he perceived in time the trap that was set for him, as Edward suggested in his matter-of-fact account, the earliest surviving English military dispatch:

In the evening three spies were taken who said that Philip was a league and a half from us and would fight on Saturday. On Saturday we went in a field a full quarter of an hour before dawn, and took up our positions in a fitting place to fight. In the early morning some of the enemies' scouts were taken and they told us that his vanguard was in battle array and coming towards us. The news having come to our host, our allies, though they had hitherto borne themselves somewhat sluggishly, were in truth of such loyal intent that never were folk of such good will to fight. In the meantime one of our scouts, a knight of Germany, was taken, and he showed all our array to the enemy. Whereupon the foe withdrew his van and gave orders to encamp, made trenches around him and cut down large trees in order to prevent us approaching him. We tarried all day on foot in order of battle, until towards evening it seemed to our allies that we had waited long enough. And at vespers we mounted our horses and went near to Avesnes, and made him to know that we would await him there all the Sunday. On the Monday morning we had news that Lord Philip had withdrawn. And so would our allies no longer abide.

His allies, indeed, were gone like the wind. Philip, leaving strong garrisons in Douai, Lille, and especially the exposed Tournai, returned to Paris. Edward made his way back for a second Christmas at Antwerp with his queen. He did not feel festive. So much diplomacy, so much military expertise, so much expense, all wasted on a nullity! He had not, after all, rescued Aquitaine in the fields of Picardy. On the contrary, his Gascon vassals were even then falling away before French inroads and, that same winter, an attack on Bordeaux itself was frustrated only by the resource of the Seneschal, Sir Oliver Ingham. Yet Edward could not cut and run. Having gambled so deeply, he could not but go on. He had hard thoughts, both of the home government and of his relations-in-law, his allies.

* * *

As for the home government, in September Edward had sent a powerful trio – Archbishop Stratford; William de la Pole, the merchant who was running the Antwerp wool staple; and his old tutor, Dr Richard Bury – back to England to report to Parliament. Though, they said, they had no brilliant successes to relate as yet, the king was then before Saint-Quentin, with excellent prospects of a great victory, hampered only by lack of money. Parliament was sympathetic in principle, but grumbled about extortions made without their consent under the Walton ordinances, and adjourned to discuss what help they were going to give. Then came the disappointment. When they re-assembled three months later, they offered 30,000 sacks of wool – 2,500 down and the rest to follow if the king accepted the conditions they now sent to Antwerp for him to study. Edward was not pleased with the conditions, and a miserly 2,500 sacks was of little use to him. Much had happened besides the catastrophe at Buironfosse since he had first made his appeal. He had new commitments, and in desperation borrowed further from de la Pole on the security of the customs.

His alliances needed constant bolstering. By way of good will he made William of Juliers earl of Cambridge with £1,000 a year. He also considered yet another marriage for his daughter Isabella, this time to the son of the duke of Austria; and at Christmas he called Prince Edward over to Antwerp to betroth Margaret, the four-year-old daughter of the duke of Brabant; but these plans came to nothing, in the latter case because of French intervention with the pope, who refused the necessary dispensation.

It seemed as though something more might now be made from the earlier dealings between Bishop Burghersh and van Artevelde of Flanders. The Flemings were suffering badly from the wool embargo, and partial relaxations only increased the desire for more. Van Artevelde saw from the past year's posturings that the French king's violence was not much to be afraid of after all. He had also succeeded in driving Count Louis entirely out of Flanders, and his grip was more than ever solid. To bring pressure on him, Edward pretended to offer poor Isabella, once again disposable, to Count Louis's son: and then invited van Artevelde to a conference of the allies to be held in Brussels. Alarmed at the threat van Artevelde came, with a large entourage.

The crux was how, if they joined the alliance, the Flemings could rebut the charge of rebellion against their rightful overlord, the king of France. The solution, though specious, was simple: Edward, not Philip, was the king of France. Edward moved his establishment from Antwerp to Ghent, and in the market place there, on 23 January 1340, proclaimed himself king of France and England, receiving liege homage from all the chief men of Flanders. In his new style, the arms of the two kingdoms were to be quartered above the arrogant motto *Dieu et Mon Droit*. So hasty had been the pronouncement that, when Edward wrote to explain his action to the pope, his new seal was not yet ready for use. Philip viewed both the impudence of the Flemings and Edward's presumption with patrician calm. His annoyance was not that his cousin had taken his arms, for through his mother, Isabella, Edward had some heraldic right to do so, but that he had quartered them wrongly, setting the leopards of England superior to the fleurs-de-lis of France. 'This is that which We disdain exceedingly. For thereby it should seem, he prefers that inconsiderable isle of England before the mighty Kingdom of France.'

The old title of duke of Aquitaine, absorbed in the new, was dropped. Thus casually, the old quarrel over feudal rights became a dynastic struggle between the royal houses. At the same time the neutrality of Flanders blossomed, as it now lawfully could, into a full treaty. Van Artevelde promised action without reserve in the renewed assault, planned to begin that midsummer with an attack on Tournai. His agreed terms were the return of the frontier towns of Lille, Douai and Béthune; protection from papal sanctions (Edward undertook, in the event of an interdict, to provide his own priests to read Mass in the Flemish churches); the removal, to the detriment of Brabant, of the wool staple from Antwerp to Bruges; and, shortest but stiffest clause of all, 140,000 *livres* (£28,000).

The sum of 60,000 *livres* was to be paid in advance, in Bruges, Ghent and Ypres, by Pentecost. Edward saw that his only hope was to return at once to England to dragoon something out of his dilatory subjects. His clamorous creditors were reluctant to let him go, but were told it was that or nothing, and in the end it was arranged that his army, commanded by William Montagu, earl of Salisbury, the earl Marshal, and Robert Ufford, earl of Suffolk, should remain as guarantors of his return; and that Queen Philippa, who in any case would be lying-in again in March, should stay in Ghent with her children, Isabella and baby Lionel, as personal surety. Her crown, in its turn, had to be pawned to some merchants in Cologne; none the less she settled dutifully to her task of getting on with van Artevelde, receiving him frequently in her apartments in the Abbaye Saint-Bavon, and in due course becoming godmother to his son Philip.

Edward sailed from Antwerp with the prince, his heir, and landed at Orwell on the morning of 21 February 1340. He at once called Parliament for 29 March. His most noticeable resemblance to his father was his sense of theatre, and the *mise en scène* for so important an occasion was superb. In the presence of their sovereign lord, enthroned, proudly pathetic, the Lords spiritual and temporal and the Commons of the realm were told, probably by Archbishop Stratford, then once again about to take the helm as Chancellor, that the king's debt for his country stood now around £300,000; if nothing were done, all his policy would founder, and for his honour and for theirs he would have to return abroad as a hostage, until restitution had been made. If, however, sufficient help were given, the king now had in hand new strategies that could not fail to put all to rights.

Swept with emotion and caught off balance, Parliament granted him at once, going well beyond the usual fifteenth and tenth, a ninth all round alike in town and country for the next two years, while the clergy voted a tenth. But they were not so overwhelmed that, as he had hoped, they failed to repeat their previous conditions. The hated *maltôte* was to go (though after some argument it was allowed to continue for a further fourteen months); sheriffs were to answer for their deeds as tax-collectors; royal purveyances (exactions of goods and services) were to be curtailed, feudal tallages and extra-parliamentary aids abolished, and the raking-up of shady ancient fines and perquisites discontinued. They also asked to see the accounts of de la Pole and other merchants with whom the king had dealings. Nor was the great news that their king of England was now king of France as well received as a matter for applause and celebration; rather, it was regarded doubtfully, as leading possibly to sinister enmeshments, and Parliament insisted on a statute to the effect that Englishmen should never be subjected to France thereby. All this was far from satisfactory; but Edward needed the money and could not afford to cavil.

It was time to turn to the other, no less pressing question that had brought him home, the protection of the kingdom. In recent years Philip, cautious though he was on land, had been making the most of his superiority at sea. During 1335 and 1336, while Edward was still in Scotland, young David, from his French exile, had raided Jersey and Guernsey. For fear of French invasion, it had been found advisable to remove Prince Edward from the Tower to Nottingham castle, and to order all able-bodied men from sixteen to sixty to go armed. Next year Philip brought north the Genoese squadron he had hired to harry the coasts of Aquitaine, and, together with other vessels impressed from Norman and Picard seafarers, added it to his massive Channel fleet. When in reply the English reinforced the Cinque Ports with sixty extra sail, and successfully attacked Boulogne in swift caravels under cover of fog, hanging twelve French ships' captains from their own mastheads, the pace of sea warfare quickened.

Between 1337 and 1339, under admirals Hugh Quiéret, Peter Béhuchet and Nicholas Barbenoire of Genoa, tough professional sailors all, the French raided at will Harwich, Hastings, Dover, Portsmouth, Rye, Folkestone, the Isle of Wight, burning all ships at anchor or still building in the ports. In March 1338 Béhuchet overran all the Channel Islands, with the exception of Castle Gorey in Jersey, which held out, leaving garrisons in

Alderney and Sark and in Castle Cornet in Guernsey. Though the rest were retaken in 1340 after the battle of Sluys, Castle Cornet remained in French hands for seven years, until it fell to a three-day combined assault by English forces, the Jersey and Guernsey militias and Guernsey seamen. The French defenders were massacred.[5]

In the autumn of 1338, off Middleburg, the French intercepted a convoy laden with bullion received in exchange for wool in Flanders and overwhelmed the escort, the *Christopher* of Exmouth, running to 300 tons, and the *Edward*, the two latest and greatest ships and the pride of the English fleet, taking them captive with their smaller charges, the *St George* and the *Black Cock*. At nine o'clock one Sunday morning in October, while the people of Southampton were in church, fifty galleys rowed up Southampton Water, crowded with armed men who ravished women, hanged men in their own houses and fired the town during all that day and the ensuing night. Afterwards, the surviving townsfolk of Southampton set about building themselves a wall. At Plymouth, where French raiders fell to burning the great ships under construction in the harbour, that doughty old man the earl of Devonshire, more than earning his belated coronet, went for them with his local militia and cut them down in droves. But mostly the French had it their own way.

While Edward and his army were lingering in Antwerp, the threat of invasion deepened. French ships were seen in the mouth of the Thames, and piles were hastily driven into the mud of the river bed. As in 1940, church bells fell silent, allowed to peal only as a signal of alarm. That invasion was no mere scare was shown later on, when detailed plans were found in the ruins of Caen during the Crécy campaign, and were read out both at Paul's Cross and in Parliament. Prince John, duke of Normandy, was to maintain a landing in England for at least ten weeks; and, if opportunity so offered, to place himself on King Edward's throne.

Nevertheless, this parliament in the spring of 1340, as others later did when similarly led, agreed without question, in the face of mortal peril at home, to send what remained of its forces overseas. Concern was shown, it is true, for the security of the Channel coast; for the stricken town of Southampton, where a resolute governor was sent, with a garrison and provisions. The bishop of Winchester, the egregious Adam of Orleton, was to keep his nearby manor in a state of warlike readiness. In the Isle of Wight, the King's Butler was enjoined to deliver wine and coals to cheer the constable of Carisbrooke castle in the event of siege, and the common people were solicitously, though not very helpfully, warned to look out for themselves. The bailiff of Jersey, where a certain jurat, one William Payne, had deserted to the enemy, was sternly told to arrest his goods, and to choose a more loyal jurat in his place.

Yet the main endeavour was now diverted from home defence towards the king's forthcoming midsummer offensive on the Continent. Measures already in hand as precautions against invasion were given a new agressive impetus. Committees were formed to look after separate aspects of the preparations. To hold the Scots during the denudation of the country, reliable captains were dispatched to Roxburgh, Edinburgh and Stirling. Commissions of array were ordered at Newcastle and Carlisle. Berwick was provisioned. The useless Edward Baliol's pension was increased.

Timber crashed down in the royal forests as the building of new ships was hurried on. The fleet was to concentrate: nine royal vessels from the Thames, and twenty-one others from the Cinque Ports (they were to pay only half the cost this time, without prejudice as regards the future) would rendezvous at Winchelsea under their admiral, William de Clinton, earl of Huntingdon; a hundred more, many of them wine ships taken off the Bordeaux run, from Portsmouth and places west, were to gather (also at their own cost) at Dartmouth, under Richard, earl of Arundel. As many as possible were to be of 100 tons or more, about 60 feet long by 20 on the beam. Merchant ships, seldom of greater burden at this period, were round and tub-like, clinker-built with overlapping ribs, one-masted and square-sailed, slow and unhandy. Other shipping come in off the high seas was to be directed to safe harbours. The 'great ships' were to be fitted with stone-throwing artillery, mangonels or trébuchets. Weapons of unheard of violence were seemingly being prepared, since one Thomas Brookhall was excused all his debts for providing 32 tons of powder; and it is known that the captured *Christopher*, for one, carried an armament of three cannon. Granaries and marine warehouses at Sandwich and Southampton were to be stocked up. Crews were to be made up with pressed men. As for soldiers to man the ships, numbering about twenty-five to each on average, allowing for stores and horses, and for the ship's cat that every merchant-man was compelled by law to carry, all those who had received the king's pardon for crime must repair immediately to the sea coasts under penalty of forfeiting it. All was to be ready before the end of Lent.

And all was to be ready assembled for the king at Orwell, when he went there to embark at Whitsun. Bishop Burghersh of Lincoln, it was specially stated, was to sail with him, because of his unique influence with the allies. The kingdom was to be entrusted to Prince Edward, with Archbishop Stratford, old Henry of Lancaster and the earl de Warenne as his experienced counsellors. Warwick and Huntingdon, two admirals, were to join them on their return from delivering the expedition.

Then came a hitch. Philip, not unapprised of what was happening, knew that Edward was preparing to go back to Flanders; why not take the chance to intercept him? If Edward did not sail, he faced ruin; both his alliance and his credit would be gone; and worse, unimaginable shame, his queen would remain a pawn in foreign lands. He would have to sail; and what then – his death? his capture? Philip ordered his whole colossal fleet to Sluys, the port for Bruges, gateway to the cloth towns, the key to Antwerp.

Word came to Ipswich from Reginald of Gueldres overseas. A mighty French armada was assembling in the mouth of the Zwin; it was the talk of everyone. Edward should watch out. Admirals Hugh Quiéret and Peter Béhuchet were sworn on pain of death to present him alive or dead in Paris. Edward hoped that his brother-in-law was exaggerating. But Lord Robert Morley, admiral north of the Thames, back from a sweep, confirmed the news. A vast floating garrison lay in wait, many great ships among them; sleek crusaders from the Mediterranean, two-, even three-masters, some of these of 300 tons and more, towering Castilians from the Atlantic main, easily out-topping the little ships of England; sturdy, weather-beaten Genoese carracks, carvel-built and fast; swift, scudding galleys; Norman and Picard cogs, an old familiar foe. All manned to the top-castles. Upward of four hundred sail in all.

Edward had only about two hundred. He delayed long enough to send Bishop Burghersh scouring the harbours down to London, and went himself to Yarmouth where the herring fishermen were lurking, trying to escape interference with their summer catch and the horrid prospect of fighting hull to hull alongside their enemies from the Cinque Ports, whom they hated at least as much as they did the French. Between them, they rustled up sixty more, and that would have to do, for time was getting short. Edward ordered all aboard.

Then Archbishop Stratford intervened. Stratford was a mature states-man who admired and loved his 'cumly King', and had served him faithfully from his boyhood, twice already before this as Chancellor; with a handful of others he had stood by the king in that dark hour in 1331 when they slipped away to France to undergo the humbling second homage; and only recently he had skilfully piloted his policy through Parliament. But as chief peer of the realm and as chief minister, he now had a duty to speak out. He had long regarded Edward's French enterprise with misgiving, and had found his own part in it unworkable; to plunge into it once more, after the lesson of Buironfosse, was folly. It would beggar the finances, and impoverish the church which it was an archbishop's first duty to protect. With the added dangers now newly apparent, it could lead to the loss of the fleet, invasion, possibly even to a king's ransom, crippling to any nation (as the French were to find out later in the century).

So he begged the king not to go. It was a classic encounter between May and January. Stratford had graduated from Merton before Edward was born. Edward, 'looking upon him as one whose blood Age had Frozen', spoke tartly, in the idiom of the time, of those 'who feared where no fear was', and said he would cross in spite of him. Stratford resigned the Chancellor's seals in favour of his brother Robert, bishop of Chichester. Fortunately Robert too was an experienced minister, taking office now for the fourth time. But Stratford cannot really have hoped so easily to evade his personal liability.

Edward sailed soon after midnight on 22 June, just two days before he was due to meet his allies. He was in the cog *Thomas*, the best ship available for his *Salle du Roy*, or flagship, since the loss of the *Christopher*. He had told Admiral Warwick that he in person would command the action, so important was the occasion, though he was no great sailor and was usually seasick. His ship-master was John Crab, a rugged former enemy he had won over to his side in Scotland. The reserve was brought up by Lord Robert Morley with the northern detachment. Morley had in charge a precious cargo, bevies of countesses, knights' wives, and other ladies, going over to attend Queen Philippa in Ghent. He kept them very heavily guarded.

On the afternoon of the next day, 23 June, off Blankenburgh, they sighted the phenomenal French array. Sluys was a narrow harbour, fast silting up, and their concentration had been too dense. The port was crammed with ships, so tightly packed that they had no room to move; it is said that their masts looked like a forest. The Genoan Nicholas Barbenoire, his instincts outraged, had begged that they should move out into more open water. But Quiéret and Béhuchet, good seamen though they also were, refused. Here, they said, Edward could not slip past them; here, they would bring him to book; Barbenoire was but a mercenary after all, whereas their lives depended on it.

Edward asked Crab, unnecessarily, who he thought they were. And Crab replied that no doubt they were the same villains as had spoiled Southampton and taken the good ships *Christopher* and *Edward*. They dropped anchor for the night, and Edward ordered John Chandos and Reginald Cobham to take land and ride about among the men of Bruges who were clustered on the shore, waiting a chance to attack the French in the rear. Chandos and Cobham reported back. The enemy were indeed about four hundred vessels strong, among them nineteen of the biggest ships they had ever seen. They were ranged side by side in three close lines, and in the forefront, sure enough, lay flauntingly the gallant *Christopher*.

It was the vigil of St John the Baptist, Midsummer Eve, when by pagan custom, time out of mind, people all over England would be going out into the woods to collect green birch, long fennel, St John's wort, orpin and white lilies, for garlands to deck their doors. The dark streets of London would be made light as day by bonfires, with feasting and dancing. The city watch would march through Cheapside with a thousand cresset lanterns swinging on poles, followed by dancing processions, pipes whiffling and drums thumping, the mayor on horseback with his gilded footmen and torchbearers about him.

Next morning, Saturday 24 June 1340, Edward deployed his fleet, a shipload of men-at-arms between every two of archers, and sailed towards the enemy. He then sheered away, as if running for England, and the French, fearful of losing him, made ready to pursue. While they wallowed confusedly, fouling each other in the harbour mouth, he put about and came back on their half-beam with the wind and the tide behind him. The blaring alarums of the French, the answering shouts and hunting-calls of the English, made a hideous din on the quiet waters, clearly heard by the Flemings on the shore. Before the fleets had closed enough for the quarrels of the French crossbows to have effect, at bowshot range of about a furlong the first English cloth-yard arrows flew, shower after shower, hissing and thudding into their huge congested target. Under their cover, the troop carriers made for the big ships of the French main line; and they, bewildered, reeling, dazzled by the Midsummer Morning sun, had small opportunity to exploit their close-quarter skills, the dropping of great stones from their superior castles fore and aft, or from dinghies lashed aloft to the ships' crow's-nests; or the crafty scattering of dried peas on enemy decks. They were grappled, boarded; the line disintegrated. Ships fought singly, hand to hand. The *Christopher* was quickly captured, her alien crew dispatched, and sent remanned back into action; the *Edward*, the *St George* and the *Black Cock* were also retaken. The *Rich Oliver* of England was rescued from four Genoese galleys, themselves then overwhelmed. The huge *James of Dieppe*, trying to make off with her prize, a small ship of Sandwich belonging to the prior of Canterbury, was accosted and subdued after a fight so bitter that next morning four hundred dead were found on board. As one by one the French ships struck, they were methodically chained together by their captors, made helpless, so that only a skeleton guard need be kept back from the battle.

The second line put up less resistance. Successively boarded from the flank under a creeping barrage from the archers, stumbling about their cluttered decks unable to escape the deadly flights, goaded, mail-clad Frenchmen in their hundreds jumped, fell, or were jostled into the reddening sea and sank like stones. The Flemings set on the wrecks and drifters in the shallows. Morley, with his reserve, sailed in to complete the kill, bringing with him the ladies, hemmed in together by their escort, flushed, ribbons flying, hair straying out from chaperons wrapped about careful braids, craning over the bulwarks.

After nine hours of action, dusk fell at last on the long day. Barbenoire, who had kept his head and his own good counsel, was able to sail his squadron of thirty Genoans out to sea, and though Edward sent his captain John Crab after him, he got away into the gloaming. Quiéret and Béhuchet died with their ships, though there is no proof of the story that Béhuchet was hanged from his own yard-arm. The French flagship, *Saint-Denis*, and 230 other craft were taken.

Fighting continued here and there about the port far into the night. Edward stayed on board the *Thomas*, where, Froissart says, 'there were great noises with trumpets and all kinds of other instruments'. It was hard to say, out of all the galaxy with him in the thick of battle, whom most to praise. A young squire, Neil Loring, was knighted for his special valour, and awarded £20 a year for life. Next day, Sunday, Edward received the leading men of Bruges on board, and attended a thanksgiving Mass in Sluys. On Tuesday he made pilgrimage on foot to Our Lady of Ardenburg, an ancient church about three miles away. That done, he mounted and rode on ahead of his army into Ghent, to Philippa, and his new son, John, who had been born there in the spring.

At first, his victory, not uncostly, seemed only a prelude, haphazard and undesigned, to his coming summer campaign. It was, none the less, prodigious. Looking back in pride a few years later, when he was rich enough to introduce gold coinage into England, he struck the famous noble, showing himself standing in the cog *Thomas* with his sword and shield, bearing the quartered arms of France and England; and on the other side a biblical *riposte* to Archbishop Stratford's qualms: 'Jesus crossing, he passed through the midst of them.' He had, as if by miracle, made good his callow boast to be lord of the English Sea.

* * *

Meanwhile, inland on the French frontier, fighting, if it had ever really stopped, had begun again. Philip had duly persuaded Pope Benedict to lay an interdict on the Flemings, and had used the now powerful garrisons in his outpost towns to ravage their territory. Van Artevelde had mounted a counter-invasion. While going from Ypres with their English contingent to assist him, William Montagu of Salisbury and Robert Ufford, earl of Suffolk, when passing Lille just after Easter 1340, fell into an ambush. Ufford was one of Edward's best officers, like Montagu the Earl Marshal and his close friend, with whom he had fought side by side in the coup at Nottingham. Both were seasoned soldiers of about forty; it is far from clear how they were so easily captured. They were carried ignominiously in a cart to Paris, where they only survived Philip's command for their summary execution at the chivalrous intercession of King John of Bohemia. Now they lay in prison in the Châtelet pending the discharge of an enormous ransom.

Philip had sent his son John, duke of Normandy, from Cambrai to make similar attacks on his other dissident neighbour, Hainault, thereby again convincing the duty-torn new earl that his true loyalty lay after all not with Philip but with Edward. Young William complained bitterly of the French outrage to his and Philippa's mother, Lady Jeanne de Valois, who was also Philip's sister. Since the death of the old Earl, her husband, the virtuous widow had withdrawn from the world to the lovely abbey of Fontaine-au-Tertre, so far as it was possible to withdraw at all in that much-battered countryside. Poor lady, she could only sigh at her son's tale of distress. Her own convent was soon to be attacked in error by her nephew John's marauders, though mercifully only to the extent of burning. Earl William took the more robust advice of his uncle John of Hainault, changed sides yet again, crossed furiously to England to see Edward – and on his way back whipped up the other allies.

Thus the situation now was that William of Hainault, van Artevelde and the duke of Brabant were marching against the main French forces, which were led ostensibly by John of Normandy but in reality by Philip in person, who posed as a common soldier to avoid rebuke by the pope for his aggression. The French were besieging the castle of Thine-l'Evêque, stormed the year before by Walter Manny in his first swoop across the border. Hainault was all for attacking, but Brabant prudently advised him to await the arrival of their joint leader, the king of England, whom they hourly expected.

Everything waited upon Edward; and when it was learned that, flushed with a great victory at sea, he had come at last, his allies raced back to Valenciennes to greet him. There, van Artevelde treated them all to one of his most inspired harangues. It was so eloquent that his high-born audience, perhaps with malicious reference to his bourgeois origins, declared admiringly that he ought by rights to be not only ruler but count of Flanders. Edward, as promised, had brought with him priests, who released Flanders from the inconvenience of the interdict. He then called a rally at Vilvorde north of Brussels. His battle strength was the same as the year before, with the considerable addition, besides his own English reinforcements, of the Flemings, and of Robert of Namur, the nephew of Robert of Artois, who had fought for him in Scotland and was the husband of another of Philippa's sisters, Isabella. The plan was for Robert of Artois to go with Henry of Flanders and a detachment of the Flemings westward to Saint-Omer, prior to resecuring his own county, while the rest attacked the Tournai salient, of particular interest to van Artevelde. Edward began the campaign by sending another insulting challenge to his enemy, this time calling him plain Sir Philip of Valois, a challenge rejected by King Philip as improperly addressed. By the end of July, the large allied army was encamped before Tournai, completely surrounding it on every side.

There was never any hope of taking Tournai, unless in time by famine, for Philip had thoroughly fortified it. Even by famine there was little hope; from the first, the duke of Brabant played a double game. Soft-heartedly, to say the least, he allowed the *bouches inutiles* to pass out of the town to join the French at Arras; later, it was rumoured by his many critics, he also let in supplies through his part of the perimeter. In any case, Edward's main concern was not with Tournai but, as before, to tempt Philip to give battle; this, though he advanced from Arras to Bouvines, only ten miles west of Edward's position, Philip once again declined to do. However, the allies were well provisioned, and settled down to a summer siege of Tournai.

There were the usual flourishes and excursions in the country round about, the usual miseries and accidents of war. Earl William of Hainault, bold soldier now, seeking revenge on France, broke into Saint-Amand with battering rams and laid about inside the little town giving quarter to none. Owing to confusion in a fog between the banners of Sir William Bailleul and Sir Robert Bailleul, two brothers fighting on opposite sides, in a nearby skirmish at the bridge of Cressin, a hotly contested crossing, Sir William's men joined Sir Robert's by mistake. In soldiers' yarns, Lord Beaujeu, holding Mortain for the king of France, won fame for his remarkable sword. Immense and glittering, it was furnished with a fearsome steel hook under the hilt, with which its proud owner deftly clutched many an unwary adversary and hurled him to muddy death in the river Scarpe below.

After a nine weeks' siege, Tournai showed no sign of yielding, nor Philip of attacking. Robert of Artois's assault at Saint-Omer had gone wrong; his borrowed Flemings did not like him and had no interest in his selfish cause, save plunder. One night they fell into a panic for no apparent reason, slashed down their tents, trussed their waggons, and ran away home. When Artois and Sir Henry of Flanders brought the strange news to Edward's camp at Tournai, it was supposed they must have been be-witched. The allies were in constant friction; the Brabanters in particular, who had lost the precious wool staple to the Flemings, were liable to go home too. The season was getting late again, nothing had come from England, and Edward could not pay them to keep the field.

Philip likewise had his troubles. He had lost his fleet, and his men were dying like flies from fever in the hot weather and the swampy air round Lille (L'Isle, as the old spelling was). His astrologer uncle, Robert, king of Sicily, so sagacious that before now he had kept his end up in dialectics with the poet Petrarch, was worrying him again, with further gloomy presages about the fate of France should the war continue. Philip was therefore open to the peace-makers sent to him by the pope. King Robert, a pretended neutral, was strongly French in sympathy. His son had been killed in the raid on Southampton a few years before, while trying to carve out an English province for himself. Philip's sister, Lady Jeanne de Valois, riding around the armies in her litter from the abbey of Fontaine, so busied herself with one and the other of her warring kinsmen that on 25 September 1340, at Espléchin, halfway between the camps, a truce was signed to last until Midsummer Day next following.

The truce pretended that the war so far had been a non-event. Flanders was released from papal sanctions; in return, Count Louis was to be restored. All prisoners were to be paroled, subject to payment of their ransoms before the truce expired. The truce was to extend to Scotland. Nothing specific was said about the original cause of the conflict, Aquitaine; but it was envisaged that more would be settled at a peace conference to be held in Arras. In fact, the conference added little; Ponthieu was returned to Edward, and the truce prolonged by two years until June 1343, though this clause did not apply to Scotland. Included in the high-powered English delegation were Henry of Grosmont, earl of Derby, Dr Richard Bury, and the tireless Bishop Henry Burghersh, who died in Ghent immediately afterwards. Described by Walsingham as 'a covetous, worldly wretch', in the end Burghersh had served his country well, twice Treasurer, once Chancellor, and had earned his distinguished burial in Lincoln cathedral.

Edward returned to Ghent in anger. His great enterprise had failed. His allies had proved false. All that was needed now, as before long happened, was for the emperor to be bought off by Philip, and to withdraw his support and his commission. On top of it all, news had come that the citadel of Edinburgh had fallen to the Scots. Sir William Douglas, the Knight of Liddesdale, perfidiously using his unwarranted command of English (as his elder cousin, the great Sir James, had done during the expedition of 1327), had gained access under the pretence of delivering coal. All had been ruined for lack of money, Edward thought. In July, Parliament had been called to hear his modest letter to his son, un-emotionally recounting his great victory at sea. It had been a popular victory. In London they were singing songs:

> Two hundred and mo shippes in the sandes
> Had oure Inglis men won with thaire handes;
>
> The Kogges of Ingland was broght out of bandes;
> And also the Cristofir that in the streme standes.[6]

Edward had hoped it would bring Parliament to his aid. What had they done? Certain merchants had advanced some £30,000 in cash towards his foreign liabilities, and to buy back the crown jewels. Certain bishops had raised credit to put 20,000 sacks of wool at his use overseas; 500 sacks more of Gloucester wool were assigned for Philippa's debts. All these were loans to pay old scores, and were charged against old grants that had not yet been collected and now began to look as if they never would be. Nothing new had been voted. And the wool disappeared in transit. William of Norwich, the pope's representative at Ghent, reported he had often heard Edward say 'He had not all the time of the siege received one penny out of England.'

His overseas council had warned him. Kilsby, the Keeper of the Seals, and particularly Burghersh and Scrope, the Lord Chief Justice, now also lately dead at Ghent – those two loyal men, both gone – had especially warned him that the home government was rotten to the core, and that Archbishop Stratford was to blame. In his disillusionment, Edward felt they had been right to blame Stratford. Edward's fancies mounted with his anger: Stratford was the diplomatist who had first arranged the war, the archbishop who had insisted that the new title of king of France be sworn upon the holy cross of Canterbury; but he was a sham friend, who had let him go to almost certain death at Sluys. Stratford was a traitor. How many times had Edward not told William of Norwich, 'I verily believe the Archbishop would that for want of money I had been ruined and slain!'

At Ghent, the fawning hospitality of the newly restored and keen-to-be-reconciled Count Louis of Flanders pleased him not one whit. Far from it. He decided to go home at once; but he was bankrupt, *en désastre*, and his creditors were threatening; there could be no question this time of leaving the royal family behind. His cousin, the faithful Henry of Derby, who had already raised nearly £1,000 to retrieve the crown of state, and whose freely offered jewels, all he had with him, Edward had now pawned for £1,500, had to stay as surety instead, in prison at Malines. Henry too cursed Stratford. Of the many services the great soldier was called upon to render to his king, this was the most irksome. Though Edward seems to have feared lest Philip might be able to purchase and secure the royal hostage from the Brabanters, Henry was not in real danger; he was, for example, allowed to buy passes to take part in tournaments. But it was months before he managed to redeem himself, at frantic personal expense, through the good offices of the Leopardi.

Edward, with Philippa and the little boys Lionel and John, William Kilsby with the seals, William de Bohun, earl of Northampton, his army commander, and a few others, left Ghent suddenly and secretly for Zeeland, a safe Hainault province, whence they set sail for England, piloted by Walter Manny. After a frightful three-day crossing they landed at the Tower, unannounced, at one in the morning on St Andrew's Day, 30 November 1340. There they found the other royal children, Prince Edward, Isabella and Joan, well, but quite unguarded except for their three servants, a clear example of the easy-going carelessness the king had come to punish.

The Constable of the Tower, Sir Nicholas de la Bèche, was missing from his post. He was rounded up and clapped into one of his own dungeons. The mayor of London followed him. The whole city, for having raised only a quarter of the loan it had been asked for, was declared amerced. The respected Sir John Pulteney, four times mayor, and the rich merchant William de la Pole were put in prison (de la Pole had declined to better the £100,000 he had already found for the king). The Chamberlain, John Molins, was most harshly treated; his lands were confiscated, and he languished in jail six years under a charge of treason before at last he obtained his pardon.

Almost all the officials of Chancery and the Exchequer were arrested; and many of the judges, Sir Richard Willoughby, Scrope's deputy as Lord Chief Justice, and William Shareshill, later his successor. The Chancellor, Robert Stratford, and the Treasurer were arraigned and given the choice between the Tower, or going to Brabant to relieve Derby in prison as pledges for the royal debt. When they pleaded clerical immunity, Edward sacked them. Saying he would have no more ministers who could not be made to answer for their crimes, he appointed laymen in their place, Sir Robert Bourchier becoming the first lay Chancellor on record.

Special eyres (circuit courts) were ordered for the trial of those detained, and the customary bail by compurgation was disallowed. Further afield in the shires, whole nests of maladministration came to light. Stringent commissions of Trailbaston were sent roundabout, and flagitious sheriffs, escheators, coroners, justices, customs men were dismissed in droves. The wonder is that the country could continue in its daily round, for surely never were the persistent tendrils stifling government so vigorously torn down. And yet the country did continue. A wonder? Or a lesson? So long as the draconian measures stopped at discomfiting corrupt officials they were viewed not without relish by the people, who shared the king's disdain. Walsingham, for instance, was ashamed 'that so worthy a Prince should from his own subjects find such unworthy dealing'. Only when the inquisitors nosed into private sins, into forgotten crimes and evaded taxes, did they meet resistance, and in places violence.

At the doomful moment of the king's return, Archbishop Stratford was at his palace of Lambeth. When the guards came for him, he had wisely disappeared. He took sanctuary with the monks of Christchurch, Canterbury, hard by the bones of the hallowed martyr, his precursor. He knew Edward well. He knew his present peril; but he also knew that the swift Plantagenet temper faded as suddenly as it flared. If he could gain time he might avert a murder direful not only for himself, but in its consequences for both the king and the country. Within the cathedral precincts he was safe. He must use that safety to confuse the issue, to elevate the dispute to the lofty plane of constitutional theory; for nothing disarms action more than arguments of principle. Thus, a personal quarrel came to embrace high matters, the liberties of the church, the rights of peers, the king's prerogative, Magna Carta and the common law, whereto all states of society were party; and devolved in the end, as it had begun, upon the supply of wool.

Sir Nicholas Cantilupe came to Canterbury with orders for the archbishop to go overseas at once, to answer for debts that were properly not the king's but his. This thin assertion, so constantly emphasized that probably it was Edward's true belief, Stratford brushed aside, since it had no legal value. In due course it was repeated in more tangible form when Kilsby, one of Stratford's active enemies, appeared at Canterbury with bum-bailiffs from the duke of Brabant. Stratford refused to see them, so they tacked a summons warning him into court at Louvain to the High Cross outside the priory gate, and after dinner at the prior's expense, departed.

On 29 December, St Thomas Becket's Day, the archbishop preached in

Canterbury cathedral. Having deplored, as the saint had done before him, his fault in preferring the king's service to his pastoral duties, he proceeded to lay sentence of excommunication on any who should violate Magna Carta or the liberties of Holy Church, engage in arbitrary arrests, or falsely bring any prelate into the king's hate or anger. It was no more than a formal renewal of a traditional imprecation; the royal family was specifically excluded, and no actual names were used. All the same, it was a dreadful if theatrical ceremony, the bells of the cathedral dolefully tolling, and the candles being suddenly extinguished.

Stratford then wrote a personal letter to the king explaining his action, warning him against his evil counsellors, and begging him, twice, to call Parliament, promising there to submit himself to the judgment of his peers. The Steward of the King's Household arrived, breathless from haste or agitation 'as if he had come a long journey', with a verbal reply from Edward. It was not convenient to hold Parliament then. The king wished Stratford to come to a private discussion of the nation's finances. Stratford said that he feared to obey. He would come only to full Parliament which, as a peer but no minister, was where he belonged. The king sent a safe-conduct under his seal. Stratford mistrusted it; rightly, since that same day the sheriff of Kent received orders to produce him to the Council, orders which did not envisage his return. Stratford later maintained that he personally never received orders to attend the Council, and therefore had not disobeyed them. He sent out a spate of vindicatory departmental letters, of a sort none was more expert to write then he, to the Chancellor, to the bishops, to the king and Council, repeating the threat of excommunication, and especially condemning an undeniable abuse, double taxation of the clergy without their consent, and their arrest in default of payment.

By this time Edward's passion had cooled, and he dropped his designs on the archbishop's life. What he most needed now was a public counterblast to Stratford's all too effective politics. Edward himself was no dialectician. It was generally supposed that the person (though naturally he disclaimed it) who took the royal case in hand was none other than Adam of Orleton, who hated Stratford for having opposed the release of his emoluments when he got himself made bishop of Winchester – a virulent old war-horse brought out of stable to tackle the archbishop in the paper lists.

The king's indictment against Stratford was ready by 12 February 1341, in the form of an open letter to the bishop of London; professional, expectably florid, set out in clerico-legal Latin. While outlining the general causes of complaint, it did not spare the archbishop's private character. He had been 'an heavy and unnatural Step-father', who had 'compelled Us to plunge Ourselves into the Devouring Gulf of Usury'. In mishandling, and perhaps misappropriating, the royal finance, it went on, he had been 'a Mouse in the Bag, a Fire in the Bosom, a Serpent in the Lap, a Broken

Reed'. Edward's old taunt from before Sluys was alluded to, that in his late refusal to attend the king as ordered, Stratford had once more 'feared where no fear was'. The bishop of London was to see to the wide promulgation of the letter.

On Ash Wednesday, the archbishop preached again in Canterbury. After his sermon, he caused Orleton's accusation to be read, as he was obliged to do; the *Libellus Famosus*, the infamous libel, as he called it. He went on, fluently and without much difficulty, to repeat and destroy each of the charges one by one. He scorned 'the malevolus pleasure of the dictator of your letters'. He had never been a 'Mouse in the Bag', or any such thing. On the contrary, he claimed, according to the vulgar saying,

> Ultra posse viri
> Non vult Deus ultra requiri.
>
> (God expects from man no more than he can.)

He had crossed the sea thirty times in the service of the king, of the king's late father, and of his illustrious grandfather; and since the present wars began he had received precisely £300 from the Exchequer against his considerable expenses. There was no doubt that the archbishop was winning the paper war.

The king, for want of money, was at last compelled to call a parliament. On Thursday 26 April 1341, Stratford entered the Painted Chamber with his related bishops, his brother, Robert of Chichester, and his nephew, Ralph of London, but was called away to the Exchequer for examination there. On Friday he refused to go again to the Exchequer, though he was prevented, in the king's name, from taking his place in Parliament. The crucial day was Saturday. When he once again appeared, his way was barred by the royal guard. He protested his rights, as chief peer of the realm, his summons by writ, the ancient title of his church of Canterbury. When they still opposed him, he vowed that he would not move from the spot until the king admitted him. As he stood there, passing sycophants and *claqueurs* mocked the old man, and muttered 'Traitor!' At whom, holding aloft his great cross of Canterbury, he thundered balefully, 'The Curse of Almighty God, and of His Blessed Mother, and of St Thomas, and mine also, be upon the heads of them that so inform the King. Amen.' Two of the king's lieutenants, William Montagu and Bohun of Northampton, hearing the uproar, came hurrying out and promised the furious priest to see what they could do.

Inside the chamber, the old earl de Warenne, earl of Surrey, supported by his nephew Richard of Arundel – a family dedicated to the rights of peers since the day when the earl's grandfather had brandished his ancient sword at Edward I over *Quo Warranto*, complained that those who should be foremost in Parliament were being excluded, while those, not peers, who had no right there were let in. 'Lord King', he growled, 'how goes this

Parliament?' In spite of his widely practised and much talked of amatory athletics, de Warenne was a magnate of senior importance, lately become more so through a rich windfall of treasure conveniently found in a cave at Bromfield as a result, it was said, of the incantations of a Saracen doctor. The last of the Warennes because, despite fathering at least eight bastards, he had no legitimate offspring, he was notably pious and his words carried weight.

After Kilsby and other ineligible commoners had consequently left the assembly, the archbishop was at last admitted. But that was not the end, for he at once demanded his right of trial by his peers, to clear himself of the thirty-two articles against him. Towards evening the peers arranged a suitable compromise, whereby Edward allowed Stratford to kneel and ask his pardon. Edward agreed to drop the charges, and Stratford his embarrassing insistence on being tried. The Commons were then called in, and business proceeded. Before Parliament rose, a committee was appointed to look into the case, and, if satisfied, to shelve the papers with the Privy Seal. Two years later they were destroyed, at the king's command, as untrue and contrary to reason. The noble adversaries lived happily ever after, or rather until Stratford's death in 1348.

There remained the reckoning. The king still had, as he said, to attend to the common affairs. He by his rage, and Stratford by his subtlety, had stirred up more than they had bargained for. In all three estates of the realm the grievance of capricious arrest rankled; all three had been reminded of Magna Carta; all three demanded statutes confirming their old liberties. They asked for nothing new. Nor, though his present agreement was the price extorted for his much-needed subsidy, was the king's prerogative for long infringed. Six months later, of his mere initiative he declared the statutes void. No new parliament met until April 1343, and when it did so his arbitrary edict was approved. It was not the content of the statutes, but the confidence and unanimity behind them that had been unusual. The king, not Stratford, had been judged in Parliament. The purse strings had tightened. In future there would be unwritten rules to the unwritten process of parliamentary government.

* * *

It is hard to say how Edward got out of his financial difficulties. Any idea that he economized would be quite mistaken, even if cheeseparing could have made much difference to his enormous liability. To a large extent he seems simply to have left his debts unpaid. The duke of Brabant became noticeably less cordial than before and, like van Artevelde and the Emperor Louis, began to look to France for a more reliable source of stipend. At home, Edward made use of the growing frenzy about spies, and against foreigners in general, to ward off importunate claimants. The Peruzzi collapsed unpaid and unpitied in 1343; while the Bardi, though they escaped insolvency, struggled on only in a much diminished way on the occasional pittance he allowed them. In the name of security, likewise, he refused to lift his hand as promised from the assets of alien priories. Fortunately, too, rich native merchants like William de la Pole had somehow remained as rich as ever, and as a result of his castigation were ready with their loans. So he was able to get on without recourse to Parliament, while at the same time his friends, and the rest of the crown jewels, managed to reappear by degrees from loyal limbo.

Preparations for war continued unabated. Edward never regarded the truce with France as anything but a pause for breath to be concluded as soon as possible. Before doing so, however, it was once more necessary to do something about Scotland. The Scots had taken advantage of Edward's preoccupation with the Low Countries to recover much of the territory they had earlier lost. In the autumn of 1339, while the French and English were counter-marching about Buironfosse, Robert the Steward, regent for the exiled King David, had taken Perth. A year later, in the summer of 1340, while Edward lay before Tournai, Sir William Douglas, leaving young David in his comfortable retreat at Château-Gaillard on the Seine, had returned to the Tay with a flotilla of French ships laden with troops and supplies of war. As has been mentioned, he entered Edinburgh by a ruse. He then marched south across the Border and attacked Newcastle, where he was repulsed by the constable, Sir John Neville; and his right-hand man, John Randolph, earl of Moray, was taken prisoner, apparently for the second time.

In September 1340, the inclusion of the Scots in the terms of the truce of Espléchin temporarily halted their activities. As far as Scotland was concerned, though, the truce was to last only until Midsummer Day next following. In order to be ready at its expiry, King David with his queen, Joan, Edward's sister, was brought back secretly from France by the same devoted sailor who had rescued them from Dumbarton seven years before, and landed at Montrose on 4 May 1341. Robert the Steward and Sir William Douglas rallied to David, and a large Scottish army concentrated at Perth. The moment the truce ended in June, they took Stirling, and pressed on across the Tweed past Roxburgh and Berwick, the two last strongholds still in English hands, on towards Durham, ravaging as they went.

The threat could not be ignored. As soon as he had completed his high-handed revocation of the Stratford statutes on 1 October 1341, Edward set out at the head of an army. As he rode through the autumn forests of the Midlands and over the endless windswept hills towards the North, he was in a gloomy mood. Driven out of France without any obvious foothold to return to, let down by intransigent ministers, encumbered by debt, worsted in Parliament, here he was once again, as so often before in the fifteen years since his accession, compelled to repeat his first futile pursuit of a barbarous enemy who, he knew, would vanish into the wilds before he reached them. By 4 November he was in Newcastle-on-Tyne, where he learned that his provision fleet, battered and scattered by a North Sea gale, was indefinitely delayed. He waited morosely at Newcastle, at a low ebb.

As Edward expected, the Scots began, on his approach, to draw back towards the Tyne, and came early in December to the castle of Wark. It stood on a hill just south of the river, in desolate Northumbrian country about forty miles west of Newcastle. Edward had given it, in 1331, to be held by his friend Sir William Montagu, since become earl of Salisbury, as part reward for his share in the arrest of Mortimer. It was well garrisoned, and well stocked. As the Scots passed by below it, winding through the woods towards the river, the governor of the castle, who had a sharp eye for such oppotunities, spied from the battlements the rich plunder they were carrying away from England in their baggage train.

The governor made a sally, stalked and fell upon Sir William Douglas's unsuspecting rearguard, and safely regained his base, driving with him 120 heavily laden pack-horses. Furious at the barefaced resort to his own favourite tactics, Douglas reared in pursuit, stormed up the hill, and violently assailed the castle, by that time adamantly closed against him. King David, coming up with the main army and seeing the useless wastage of his men, decided, since he knew that Edward was held up far away, to make camp for the night, and to prepare assault engines for a full attack the next day. The attack went in at dawn and lasted the short day through, without advantage, until the winter nightfall, when David again gave orders for a resumption in the morning.

* * *

At this point, a romantic legend intrudes, tantalizing because of its occasional approximation to known fact, and also for the suggestion it contains of a darker side to Edward's character.

Within the castle at Wark, so the story goes, was a lady, described as 'one of the most beautiful and estimable women in England'. During the fighting, according to Jean le Bel, 'she much comforted the defenders, and from the sweetness of her looks, and the charm of being encouraged by so beautiful a lady, one man became as good as two'. For all that, when they saw the Scots preparing for a grand assault, and knowing that they could not long withstand it, the defenders determined to send to Newcastle[7] for help from Edward. No one was keen to attempt the break-out, so at last the governor said, 'I am very well pleased, gentlemen, with your loyalty and courage, as well as for your affection to the lady of this house; so that out of my love for her and for you, I will risk my own person in this adventure.' He added that he did not doubt that the king would quickly send sufficient aid, and that they would be well rewarded for their staunch defence.

'This speech cheered both the lady and all present. When night came, the governor prepared himself to get out of the castle privately, and unseen by any of the Scots. Fortunately for him, it rained so very hard all that night that none of them quitted their quarters; he therefore passed through the army without being noticed.' Towards daybreak he met two Scots foragers driving oxen and a cow towards their army half a league away. He maimed them both, killed the cattle to deny them to the enemy, and said, 'Go and tell your King that I have passed through his army and am gone to seek help from the King of England.' He then spurred away. On hearing his message the Scots, whose attack on the castle was being badly hindered by the rain, decided to cut their losses and make off with the large amount of booty still remaining to them. In the morning they decamped across the Tyne into the forest of 'Gendours' (Jedburgh?), 'where the wild Scots lived at their ease'.

Next day Edward arrived with his army and occupied the site the Scots had left. It had been a gruelling march, and he knew it would be useless to pursue them. So he pitched camp, and said he would go up to the castle to see the lady of it, 'whom he had not seen since her marriage'. As soon as he was disarmed, he set off, taking ten or twelve of his knights with him.

The story continues:

As soon as the lady knew of the King's coming, she set open the gates and came out so richly beseen that every man marvelled at her beauty. . . . When she came to the King she kneeled down to the earth, thanking him for his socours, and so led him into the castle to make him cheer and honour as she that could right well do it. Every man regarded her marvellously; the King himself could not withhold his regarding of her, for he thought that he never saw before so noble or so fair a lady; he was stricken to the heart with a sparkle of fine love that endured long after; he thought no lady in the world so worthy to be beloved as she.

Thus they entered the castle hand in hand; the lady led him first into the hall, and after into the chamber nobly apparelled. The King regarded so the lady that she was abashed; at last he went to a window to rest him, and so fell into a great study. The lady went about to make cheer to the lords and knights that were there, and commanded to dress the hall for dinner.

When she had all devised and commanded them she came to the King with a merry cheer, (who was in a great study) and she said 'Dear sir, why do you study so, for, your grace not displeased, it appertaineth not to you so to do; rather ye should make good cheer and be joyful, seeing ye have chased away your enemies who durst not abide you. . . . Sir, leave your musing and come into the hall if it please you; your dinner is all ready.'

'Ah fair lady', quoth the King, 'other things lyeth at my heart that ye know not of, but surely your sweet behaving, the perfect wisdom, the good grace, nobleness and excellent beauty that I see in you, hath so surprised my heart that I can not but love you, and without your love I am but dead.'

Then the lady said, 'Ah right noble prince for God's sake mock nor tempt me not; I can not believe that it is true that ye say, nor that so noble a prince as ye be would think to dishonour me and my lord my husband, who is so valiant a knight and hath done your grace so good service and as yet lieth in prison for your quarrel. Certely sir, ye should in this case have but a small praise and nothing the better thereby. I had never as yet such a thought in my heart, nor I trust in God, never shall have for no man living. . . .'

Therewith the lady departed from the King and went into the hall to haste the dinner; then she returned again to the King and brought some of his knights with her, and said, 'Sir, if it please you to come into the hall, your knights abide for you to wash; ye have been too long fasting.' Then the King went into the hall and washed and sat down among his lords and the lady also. The King ate but little, he sat still musing, and as he durst he cast his eyes upon the lady. Of his sadness his knights had marvel, for he was not accustomed so to be; some thought it was because the Scots were scaped from him.

Curiously, this romantic episode is not mentioned in any contemporary English source, but comes down purely through the foreign chronicles of Jean le Bel and Froissart. So far, the two accounts are virtually word for word the same. But now there comes a sharp divergence. Le Bel, the originator, changes suddenly to a harsher, more admonitory tone:

But he had other things at heart, for the love of that lady had so keenly entered his soul that, either by struggle or denial, he could not rid himself of it; and in the end the shaft of love pierced him so sharply that he did something for which he was bitterly blamed and reproved; for when he could not have his way with the noble lady either by love or by prayer, he had it by force, as you will hear hereafter.

Le Bel's successor and continuator, Froissart, in his earlier versions simply omits the damaging allegation, and goes straight on with the remainder of le Bel's narrative:

All that day the King tarried there and wist not what to do. Sometimes he imagined that honour and troth defended him to set his heart in such a case to dishonour such a lady and so true a knight as her husband was who had always well and truly served him. On the other part love so constrained him that the power thereof surmounted honour and truth.

Thus the King debated in himself all that day and all that night. In the morning he arose and dislodged all his host and drew after the

Scots to chase them out of his realm. Then he took leave of the lady saying, 'My dear lady, to God I commend you till I return again, requiring you to advise you otherwise than ye have said to me.'

'Noble prince,' quoth the lady, 'God the Father Glorious be your guide, and put out of you all villain thoughts. Sir I am and ever shall be ready to do your grace service to your honour and mine.' Therewith the King departed all abashed.

But, in his late Amiens edition, Froissart, evidently thinking le Bel's accusation too weighty to be totally ignored and his own description of the king's emotions over-delicate, adds a sprightly additional anecdote not recorded by le Bel or anyone else, inferring that the incident was quite light-hearted, and that the lady, less severe than she appeared at first, to some extent led Edward on: an innuendo Froissart had already made when first introducing her as the most beautiful woman in England by altering le Bel's 'and the most estimable' (*vaillant*) to 'most alluring' (*amoureuse*). The passage suggests that the king wagered with her for her favours and tried to arrange, by allowing himself to be defeated, to have a reason for returning later on:

So he called for chess, and the lady had it brought in. Then the King asked the lady to play with him, and she consented gladly, for she wished to entertain him as well as she might. And that was her duty, for the King had done her good service in raising the siege of the Scots before the castle, and he was her right and natural lord in fealty and homage.

At the beginning of the game of chess, the King, who wished that the lady might win something of his, laughingly challenged her and said, 'Madam, what will your stake be at the game?' And she answered, 'And yours sir?'

Then the King set down on the board a beautiful ring with a large ruby that he wore. Then said the Countess, 'Sir, sir, I have no ring so rich as yours is.'

'Madam', said the King, 'set down what you have, and do not be so concerned over its value.'

Then the Countess, to please the King, drew from her finger a light ring of gold of no great value. And they played chess together, the lady with all the wit and skill she could, that the King might not think her too simple and ignorant. The King, however, deliberately played poorly, and would not play as well as he knew how. There was hardly a pause between the moves, but the King looked so hard at the lady that she was very much embarrassed, and made mistakes in her play. When the King saw that she had lost a rook or a knight or some other piece, he would lose also, to restore the lady's game.

They played on till at last the King lost, and was check-mate with a bishop. Then the lady rose and called for the wine and comfits, for the King seemed about to leave. She took her ring and put it on her finger, and wanted the King to take his back as well. She gave it to him, saying, 'Sir, it is not appropriate that in my house I should take anything of yours, but instead, you should take something of mine.'

'No, madam,' said the King, 'but the game has made it so. You may be sure that if I had won, I should have carried away something of yours.'

The Countess would not urge the King further, but going to one of her damsels, gave her the ring and said, 'When you see that the King has gone out and has taken leave of me, and is about to mount his horse, go up to him and courteously give him his ring again, and say that I will certainly not keep it, for it is not mine.' And the damsel answered that she would do so.

At this, the wine and comfits were brought in. The King would not take of them before the lady, nor the lady before him, and there was a great debate all in mirth between them. . . . After this, and when the King's knights had all drunk, the King took leave of the lady, . . . and he watched until the knights and damsels were busy taking leave of one another. Then he came forward again to say two words alone: 'My dear lady, to God I commend you till I return again . . .'

and so on, as before.

Froissart, having suppressed le Bel's censorious though reluctant allegation against Edward (just as he also suppressed the promised evidence in support of it that le Bel had provided no less reluctantly in a later chapter) leaves us with what is no more than a romantic vignette. The king, skirmishing after the wild Scots far from home, makes a pass at the *châtelaine* of the castle and is virtuously repulsed. Why then did Froissart find it necessary to vary it in different versions of his chronicle? Why, as becomes apparent when it is looked into, is the whole thing so garbled, so obscure?

Not for reasons of propriety. The fourteenth century was a time of unprudish tolerance of sexual intrigue. There was nothing in Froissart's story to shock a society grown accustomed to Jean de Meung's erotic nuances in *Le Roman de la Rose*, which Christine de Pisan certainly objected to, but only on feminist grounds; a society bawdy enough before long to enjoy the Wife of Bath, and the rude satire of *Les Quinze Joies de Mariage*. It is true that the king emerged from Froissart's story in none too good a light, but the king was the one character whom there was no effort to disguise, and it may be that the part allotted to him would be seen by those in the know as no more than he deserved. There is no proof of Edward's amorous propensities beyond the rather monotonous *enceinture* of Queen Philippa – in June this year, 1341, she had given birth at Langley to Edmund, yet another son. But his household was evidently not austere. One monkish chronicler found it necessary to reprove the sauciness of the court ladies, '*effoeminatorum in Regno Angliae dominationem . . . reprimendam*'. And the conscientious William of Norwich told the pope that his master, Edward, had been heard to complain, at Ghent, that Stratford, in addition to his other misdeeds, 'hath told my Wife such things of me, for which if he had been credited, he would have provoked Us to much mutual discord'. Indeed, the mention of the king as checkmated by a bishop may itself have been a sly reference to Archbishop Stratford's tale-bearing ways. It can be expected that in love, as in so much else, Edward was the Pantagruel of his age. It is probable that he was boisterous; that there were pouncings and scufflings on spiral stairways; and that his forward young ladies well knew what they were all about. Far from being satisfied with the story of his risqué game of chess, they would be astonished that it had the pale climax Froissart thought it desirable to give it.

It was because he was trying to transform what le Bel had presented as unpalatable fact into a pleasant fable, and not because formal romance demanded delicacy, that Froissart took refuge in evasion. That the king had a violent love affair with a married woman was apparently far too widely known to be silently dismissed. Instead, he discreetly clothed it in the tradition of courtly love. An examination of the sources may suggest why.

The prime authority is the chronicle of Jean le Bel.[8] Le Bel lived approximately between 1290 and 1370. He was a poet, a learned cleric, and a not very godly canon of Liège; in his old age he fathered twin natural sons, Jean and Gilles, to whom he left great riches. He was well acquainted with the court of Hainault, and also a man of action. He and his brother Henry had served with the mercenaries who went to England in 1327 to assist in the young King Edward's early Scottish campaign. Thereafter he seems to have settled at Valenciennes, and in about 1352 to have begun, on commission from Lord John of Hainault, his history of the great war between France and England, editing the knightly memories of his acquaintances. His chronicle began with his experiences in Scotland, ran on until 1361, and was left uncompleted at his death.

Le Bel favoured the old chivalry. He idolized '*le noble roi Edowart*', and at one point felt obliged to apologize at length for preferring him to his adversary of France. He would do nothing if he could avoid it to diminish him. On the other hand, he was a thorough scholar, scorning the *romans rimés* of the day. He was careful to qualify events he was not sure of with a 'so I have heard tell', saying again and again, '*si m'en tairay à tant*' ('so I will leave it at that'). Moreover his natural allegiance was more French than English, and when he began writing, his patron, John of Hainault, had lately transferred his loyalty from Edward to Philip. Le Bel was therefore under no pressure to spare the feelings of English royalty. He would report what he believed to be the truth, even to the detriment of his hero.

All the same, from the verbal nature of his sources, le Bel is not always accurate about names, dates or places. In the Scottish campaign of 1327, for instance, although he had himself been present, he credited Sir William Douglas with the deeds of his uncle, the great Sir James. He had not been back to England since 1327, and for the episode at Wark in 1341 he would have depended much on John of Hainault who, as Philippa's uncle, had hearsay knowledge of what happened at Edward's court. So that in this case there was more room than usual for confusion, as he seems to have realized.

On Jean le Bel's death, his uncompleted chronicle disappeared from view. It was adopted and continued by his more famous protégé, Jean Froissart, the peripatetic Hainault chronicler. In 1341, the year in question, Froissart was at most an infant, so that for all the earlier part of his work he relied on his predecessor. This he was the first to admit, and with good reason, since, when a copy of the lost text of le Bel was discovered in the middle of the nineteenth century, it was found that Froissart had transcribed it almost word for word. Froissart continued to add to, and amend, his chronicle until his death in about 1400, and the several versions show considerable variations.[9]

Froissart was first and foremost a vastly popular story-teller, the Rudyard Kipling of the age of chivalry. He was less precise and more given to poetic licence than le Bel. And unlike le Bel, he was susceptible to English sensibilities. As secretary and loyal pensioner of Queen Philippa from his early days, he would have been at pains to tone down any of his material that, as time went by, seemed to reflect discredit on her memory or on that of her immediate circle. Comparing the two texts, it can be said that, though liable to genuine error, le Bel is the better authority. Froissart is chiefly of interest for what he, or his informants, found it advisable to exclude or alter in le Bel's account.

There is no need to doubt the main outline of the story. Le Bel, in his version, gives none of his cautious warnings, and Froissart, who during later visits to both England and Scotland had a chance to check it, does not in general differ from him. The time, late autumn 1341, is firm enough. Edward did make an expedition to the Border then, and there is no other occasion at about that time when he could have done so. The place, Wark castle, is also clear, once the tiresome circumstance has been mastered that there are two Warks in Northumberland, some fifty miles apart; this one appears to have been on the Tyne, the more southerly of the two.[10] What of the action and the actors? The king, without doubt, is Edward. Who is the governor of the castle? Who is the lady and what became of her? For, as the matter stands so far, the king, though worsted for the moment, had every intention of returning to the attack.

Le Bel states that the governor of Wark was Sir William Montagu. He adds, by way of identification, that this was not William Montagu, earl of Salisbury, who owned Wark, but another, 'son of the sister of the Earl of Salbri, and was called Sir William Montagu after his uncle who had the same name'. Froissart adopts this confusing information without demur. The waters are already beginning to go cloudy.

Le Bel says, and the sense of the story hangs on it, that the earl was not at Wark, because he was at the time a prisoner in Paris. That is not quite true. The earl had indeed been taken prisoner at Lille at Easter 1340, and sent to Paris with the earl of Suffolk. But under the truce of Espléchin in September 1340 they had both been released on parole. By the end of the year Salisbury was free and back in England and, like Suffolk, strenuously trying to raise his ransom. He was very much in evidence at Westminster during the 'Stratford' parliament in the spring of 1341. Some say that, after the parliament, he went on crusade against the Moors in Spain, though in fact he did not go to Spain until two years later, with the earl of Derby. Or, he may have gone to settle his kingdom of Man, inherited from his grandmother, Princess Aufricia, and restored to him by Edward from the Scottish spoils after Halidon Hill. At all events, though he was not in prison in the autumn of 1341, we are assured he was not at Wark either, but had put a lieutenant there in his place.

The only other William Montagu then living was the earl's son and heir. He was at the time a boy of thirteen, and, though he may have been present at Wark, it is scarcely likely that one so young could have achieved the feats of arms demanded of the governor. Sir William Dugdale, the renowned seventeenth-century genealogist, perceived the difficulty and, at a loss for a credible William Montagu, cast about for another more likely Montagu, and lit on the earl's youngest brother, Edward. It is hard to see who else it could have been, since the only remaining Montagu, the middle brother Simon, was a bishop secluded in the cloistered calm of Ely. G. F. Beltz and Dr Barnes agree with Dugdale.[11] Sir Edward Montagu, a wild, unfavoured, chip-on-the-shoulder soldier of fortune, aged about thirty-six in 1341, was every way fitted for the bold, violent deeds ascribed to the governor in the story.

The lady of Wark, and her relationship to the governor, is even more difficult to place. Le Bel calls her, from first to last, the countess of Salisbury, and Froissart to that extent faithfully follows him. But evidently hoping to clear up a faint ambiguity, le Bel, when reintroducing her in a later context, mentions, but for the only time, that her name was Alice: '*la vaillant dame de Salbri, Alis nommée*'.[12] Froissart arbitrarily and without explanation changes this to 'the noble lady, Catherine Countess of Salisbury'. And since the text of le Bel then vanished, Alice was thus displaced by Catherine, until le Bel's text came to light again five hundred years afterwards.

Of possible ladies for the part, therefore, the obvious candidate was long considered to be Catherine Grandison, the earl's wife, and the reigning countess in 1341. She was the youngest of three daughters of William, first Lord Grandison, who was descended from the ancient house of Grandison, dukes of Burgundy. She was also the sister of John Grandison, bishop of Exeter from 1327 to 1369. At the time in question she had been married to the earl for fourteen years, and was the mother of William Montagu junior, of his small brother John, and of several daughters. But the earl was the king's best friend, and Catherine had been governess for some time to her own and the royal children at the manor of Woodstock; it seems nonsense to suppose that the king 'had not seen her since her marriage', or that she could so suddenly have touched off the 'sparkle of fine love' that struck him dumb at Wark. They had known each other well for years.

On these grounds Miss Margaret Galway[13] selects Joan, the Fair Maid of Kent, as the only other person with any right to be called countess of Salisbury at the time.[14] Miss Galway has effectively disposed of Catherine Grandison as the object of the king's lamentable advances. And she has also detected, incontestably, a later conspiracy of silence designed to hush up the whole thing. But she has not carried the conclusions that follow from her discoveries far enough. She has not differentiated between the honest mistakes of le Bel and the deliberate confusions introduced by Froissart; nor has she seen the full significance of the latter. They were not, as she suggests, inspired by a simple drawing-room concern to shelter the good names of a noble king and of a subsequently great and gracious lady. Their real purpose was more grim. Le Bel had come too near the truth; and the truth had to be concealed.

Consequently, Miss Galway would seem to have picked the wrong card in this game of find-the-lady. Joan's name was never mentioned in this sense either by le Bel or Froissart at the time, nor at all until two centuries later, when the fame of her amatory exploits had made her a Helen of Troy, and it had become the fashion to see Joan in everything. It was, for instance, bruited that she was the reason why King John of France returned of his own accord to die in captivity in England, although she was then living far away in Aquitaine.

Joan's life was certainly spectacular enough for her to be considered for a star part in any romantic drama of the time. She was the third of the four children of Edmund, earl of Kent, the king's uncle, who had been beheaded by Mortimer, and his wife, Margaret Wake of Liddell. Her first appearance was at Arundel castle in April 1330 just after her father's execution. There, with her mother and the other children, she was held in detention so severe that, for lack of an older sponsor, she, though not yet two years old, had to stand as godmother to her newborn brother, John. On Mortimer's fall soon afterwards, the family was restored. Joan and her brothers and sister became royal wards and, like many political relics of the period, were taken into the care of good Queen Philippa. She thus came to Woodstock and into the schoolroom of Catherine Grandison, allegedly her rival for the lead part in this tale of Edward's misdoings. There, Joan can hardly have failed to play with two small boys of about her own age: Catherine Grandison's son, William Montagu junior, and Prince Edward, heir to the throne. Both were destined in due course to become her husband.

As she grew up, her precocity and her royal lineage – for at that stage it cannot have been her eventual unexpected wealth – soon got her into trouble. Among the orphans at court was Thomas Holland, the son of Sir Robert Holland of Lancashire, an unprincipled knight, once the lieutenant of Thomas of Lancaster, whom he had betrayed at Boroughbridge. Sir Robert had in turn deserted Edward II for Mortimer, and in October 1328, while riding incautiously through Henley woods at the summons of his latest mistress, Isabella, he had been attacked by Sir Thomas Withers and retainers of Henry, the new earl of Lancaster, with whom Mortimer was by then in conflict. Robert Holland's severed head was sent to the new earl in revenge for his original treachery.

After his father Robert's murder, young Thomas Holland had been befriended by Isabella, had survived her disgrace, and had, full of am-bition, grown into a keen young squire at the court of Edward III. He had been one of the dashing blades in silk eye-patches who galloped expen-sively about the Low Countries before the outbreak of war, and seems to have returned to England in the King's entourage after the Buironfosse détente, while Queen Philippa, Joan's royal guardian, stayed on in Ghent. Alerted for overseas service again in the spring of 1340, when he was about twenty and Joan twelve, the minimum marrying age for girls, he swept her into marriage vows before witnesses and then into bed, in those days a binding if unorthodox contract. He then left her, to serve at the battle of Sluys and at the siege of Tournai. Thereafter, he pursued his knightly career by fighting for the Teutonic Order in their long-standing Crusade against the heathen Lithuanians in East Prussia.

Not long after Holland went to Prussia, the king and his friend the earl of Salisbury both came home from their respective misfortunes abroad, the earl from prison in Paris, the king from bankruptcy in Ghent. The king, unaware, among the many more urgent wrongs committed in his absence and exciting his wrath, of the entanglement his valuable ward had got into without permission, arranged to marry Joan to Salisbury's son and heir, her former schoolmate, William Montagu junior. Joan, not caring to increase the king's already towering anger, nor to appal her formidable mother, Margaret Wake, by revealing that she had already married Thomas Holland, went through with the wedding to William Montagu, on or before 10 February 1341, when the castle, manor and town of Mold in North Wales were settled on the young couple as man and wife. Thus, at the age of twelve, Joan had already collected two husbands within a few months of each other, and both marriages were in valid form.

She had, no doubt, a rather anxious time of it. Fortunately Thomas Holland, on completing his tour in Prussia, did not at once come home. He was ordered to Aquitaine to guard the frontiers at Bayonne, and continued thence to join another Crusade, against the Moors in Granada, taking part in the siege of Algeciras. By the time he got back to England late in 1343, Joan had been the established wife of William Montagu for two years. Holland saw readily that his part in the affair, if known, would not benefit his standing with the royal family, and wisely agreed to keep silent, in return for his appointment as steward of her household. So after their marriage in February 1341, Joan and William Montagu were unquestionably the newly-weds of the season, blessed by the king her guardian, approved by his father the earl of Salisbury, admired by all.

It is not therefore impossible that Joan, a new bride, was present with her husband William Montagu and other members of his family at Wark in the autumn of 1341. But that does not necessarily make her le Bel's lady of the 'castle of Salbri'. She was only thirteen, and it remains unlikely that even Joan would have been capable of the poise required of the countess by the story. Miss Galway makes the point that Joan was legitimately countess of Salisbury; but she was so only briefly: her husband William Montagu did not become earl until he came of age in June 1349, and their marriage was dissolved by the pope in November, five months later.

The legendary reputation of the Fair Maid of Kent may explain, but it scarcely requires, her identification with the seductive beauty whom Edward met at Wark. That reputation was assured by the other fabulous excitements of her colourful life. She was doubly a wife at the age of twelve and then divorced by the pope and awarded to Holland. Later, by the death of her mother, Lady Wake, and of her brothers, she was the rich countess of Kent in her own right. She was loved by and, as soon as she was accessible, the bride of the nation's paragon, the Black Prince. Thereafter, she was Princess of Wales and duchess of Aquitaine; mother of Richard II and, in his minority, arbitress of the kingdom; Dame of the Garter, second only to King Edward's long-suffering daughter, Isabella. As a boy-king's widowed mother, she was dragged from her whirlicote on the road from Canterbury and kissed by murderous Kentish peasants, and besieged in the flame-girt Tower not only with her royal son but also with, among others, her original husband, William Montagu, now become an elder statesman. All this is ample stuff for legend. To make her also the dame of Wark is altogether too much.

Furthermore, if Joan were the dame of Wark, it is pertinent to say that for King Edward to have permitted his son and heir afterwards to marry his own leman is surely inconceivable. And to anticipate again, if she was the lady of Wark she must also, in Miss Galway's view, be accepted as the inspiration of the Order of the Garter. This in turn would mean that at the famous ball at Calais after Crécy, not only would she have had to humour both her existing husbands, Montagu and Holland, both there present and not then on the best of terms, as well as the prospective third, her gallant Prince of Wales. She would also have had simultaneously to attend to the arcane entreaties of the king, the prince's lovesick father. It suggests an evening programme daunting enough to make any girl let slip her garter; but it is too much for credence. If garter there was, it was not Joan's. The great Order, so strangely designated, and so strangely neglected by those devotees of chivalry, le Bel and Froissart, coming into being so shortly after the siege of Calais, commemorates a less frivolous origin, a more pathetic heroine.

By and large, it is quite probable that le Bel, recounting the tale of Wark by hearsay, and knowing that some *dame de Salbri* was involved, was uncertain which one was meant: whether the countess Joan, famous at the time when he was writing; or her mother-in-law Catherine Grandison, countess at the time when it occurred; or indeed whether it was neither of them, but the only one whose name he stated, a third, named Alice.

Miss Galway thinks the whole episode a pastiche, composed by embarrassed chroniclers so as to convey, without giving anything away, that the king engaged in a long and not very creditable love affair of which this purposely garbled incident was the beginning. As for the elusive Alice, Miss Galway thinks that no Alice could rightly be called countess of Salisbury, and that she did not exist. She says (p. 39), '"Alice" is clearly composite. *Qua* wife of the [until recently] imprisoned first Earl of Salisbury she represents the Countess Catherine; *qua* flame of Edward III she represents Countess Joan, the wife of the second Earl.' An involved explanation, but the only one possible, granted that the names 'William Montagu' and 'countess of Salisbury' were the real names of the people le Bel was thinking of. All becomes very much clearer if it is admitted that le Bel, aware of his own uncertainty, determined to pinpoint the lady beyond all doubt by adding the one thing he was sure of, that her name was Alice.

For there was an Alice. She was the wife of Sir Edward Montagu who was almost certainly the governor of Wark and who, on setting out to seek help, confided 'the lady of this house' to his garrison in possessively conjugal terms, 'out of my love for her and for you'.

Except that she was an important five years older, her circumstances were so nearly parallel to Joan's that the two could easily be confused. She was also closely enough knit into the house of Montagu to allow of her being mistakenly called the countess, although she never was; after all, during most of the century, the very mention of Montagu would conjure in the popular mind the earldom of Salisbury.

She was the youngest of the three children of Thomas of Brotherton, Earl Marshal, earl of Norfolk, elder brother of Edmund, earl of Kent,

Joan's father, and, like Edmund, half-uncle of the king. Alice was therefore Joan's first cousin; both were step-cousins of King Edward, and all three were grandchildren of Edward I. Her mother, also Alice, who had married Brotherton in about 1320 and died in 1330, had been the daughter of Sir Roger Hales, coroner of Norfolk.

Alice was born early in 1324.[15] In February 1333 her father, Brotherton, betrothed her to William Montagu junior,[16] then aged five, but the marriage did not take place, perhaps because she was considered to be too much the older. Instead, William Montagu was married, in 1341, to her younger cousin, Joan of Kent, as has been said: while Alice, for her part, was married to William's uncle Edward Montagu, some twenty years her senior, probably about March 1337, when he was knighted and granted an exchequer allowance of £100 a year, at the same time that his elder brother became earl of Salisbury.

Alice's father, Thomas of Brotherton, died in the late summer of 1338, leaving Alice and her sister Margaret as his heiresses. In December Edward Montagu, who was at that time with the king at Antwerp, stood as proxy for Alice to receive her share of her father's estates in England, and early in 1340, at Ghent, did 'homage for all the lands which he and Alice held in chief of her inheritance by reason of their common offspring'.[17] It thus appears that Edward Montagu and Alice had by then acquired their first child, who was a son named Edward, and perhaps also their second, Audrey of Etheldreda, probably so called after the patron saint of Ely, where the middle Montagu brother Simon was now bishop.

In 1341, Edward Montagu was back in England. In October he was paid off with £200 in wool on account of his army wages and arrears of his annuity. Sometime that autumn, when the Scots, on the conclusion of the truce, came swarming across the Border, his brother Earl William sent him north to take charge of Wark on his behalf. Edward took Alice with him.

In late November or December, Wark was attacked, and after riding through the night Edward Montagu arrived at Newcastle, drenched and travel-weary, to call for the king's assistance. The king, who perhaps had heard how attractively his girl-cousin of Brotherton had turned out, set off next morning, and did not require her exhausted husband to accompany him. When he raised her from her curtsy, he found that Alice, now about eighteen, had flowered out of all recognition from the leggy girl she had been when he last saw her, at her wedding four years earlier, before he went abroad. King Edward was twenty-nine, handsome and very lusty. In his own eyes he was, at that moment, a world-disgusted and frustrated soldier, deserving consolation. The Scots had gone; he had time on his hands. Alice was beyond all accounts lovely, and she bowled him over.

* * *

On leaving Wark, the king rode off towards the north, and after a perfunctory hunt round for the Scots, made for Melrose abbey where he spent Christmas riding about the woods in a very poor humour. His cousin Henry of Derby, at nearby Roxburgh castle, arranged tournaments in an effort to engender festive cheer – an aim disappointed because Sir William Douglas and his Scots, in attendance to discuss an impending truce, disported themselves so over-energetically that there was a good deal of bloodshed. Early in 1342 Edward was back at Langley, and soon after that in London. Roxburgh fell to the Scots before Easter, and Henry of Derby completed an unsatisfactory peace on 20 May.

Le Bel did not suggest that Edward called again at Wark on his way south to renew his pressure on his reluctant cousin; and Froissart was at pains to agree on the point. Unfortunately, in his attempt at a complete cover-up for Edward he let slip the careless – but conclusive – information that the 'Countess' was indubitably Alice. He says that Edward, impressed by her fidelity to her husband, deliberately did not return by way of Wark but instead, when passing by, sent the young lad, William Montagu, her nephew, with a message: 'William, tell the Countess, your aunt, that she should rejoice', since he had her husband's welfare much in mind. Now Alice was William's aunt by marriage, whereas Catherine Grandison was his mother, and Joan of Kent his wife. Only Alice could be his 'aunt'.

For the moment, Alice had warded off the unsought attentions of her king and cousin, though she cannot have imagined it would be for long, for it could not be thought that Edward would be so easily foiled of his wayward heart's desire. She faced a predicament her cousin Joan could have taken in her stride by the light of nature, but which she, in her seemliness and modesty, was not equipped to deal with. The king, never patient, would not be a gentle lover. He would hunt her exuberantly like a tremulous quarry. He would trumpet his passion, expecting her to receive it dutifully, as though it were a blessed visitation. She had nothing to fear from Queen Philippa, for she was incapable of spite; but Montagu, her husband, was another matter. Fierce, middle-aged, resentful, Edward Montagu would not be complaisant. And she had her children to think of. There was no one she could turn to. Her father, the king's uncle, had been dead three years. Her worldly sister Margaret would tell her to make the most of her good fortune. Helpless, she burrowed fretfully into her insecurity.

The king's next move soon followed. The early months of 1342 were taken up with preparations for the invasion of Brittany then in prospect. Edward summoned a Great Council to meet at Westminster on Easter Monday (1 April), in order to discuss his final plans, and then postponed it for a month 'for certain reasons' so that it would follow conveniently upon a mammoth tournament arranged to take place at Northampton during the Easter vacation to launch the enterprise. Invitations were accepted by

Queen Philippa's brother, William of Hainault, and Sir John, his uncle. Young Prince Edward, old Henry of Lancaster, Henry of Derby, his son, and all the great men of the kingdom were to be there without fail, and as many splendid ladies. Edward Montagu was expressly ordered to have his wife there, '*la vaillant dame de Salbri, Alis nommée*'.[18]

The more surely to bait his trap, and to keep his promise to Alice that he had her husband's interests much in mind, the king called Edward Montagu to attend the Great Council by personal writ. A Great Council was an assembly of lords without the commons, and though his writ did not then and there create him a baron of the realm, as a similar summons to a full parliament would have done, it was a step in that direction, and an honour Montagu would not dream of disobeying.

He 'very cheerfully complied with the King's request, for he thought of nothing evil; and the good lady dared not say nay. She came, however, much against her will; for she guessed the reason which made the King so earnest for her attendance, but was afraid to discover it to her husband, thinking, at the same time, by her conduct and conversation to make the King change his mind. . . . The ladies and damsels were most superbly dressed and ornamented, according to their different degrees, except the Countess of Salisbury, who came there in as plain attire as possible. She was not willing that the King should give up too much time to admire her; for she had neither wish nor inclination to obey him in anything evil, that might turn out to her own or her husband's dishonour.'

Alice's tactics were successful. The dancing and the feasting lasted for fifteen days, and the tournament went off without mishap, except that many valuable knights were injured on the eve of the expedition, and the promising Lord John Beaumont, son of Henry Beaumont, former leader of The Disinherited, and doubly brother-in-law to Henry of Derby, was killed. Alice's virtue seems to have been preserved once more. But not for long.

Le Bel gives a second solemn warning that he has bad news to tell of the conduct of King Edward, 'the noble King Edward, who was full of all nobility and gentleness, for never have I heard tell any evil deed of his, save one, of which I will speak, and the force of love drove him to it'.[19] This warning, like the first, was suppressed by Froissart. Then, a few pages later, le Bel plunges into his scandalized chapter 65.[20] Its bald chapter heading reads, 'How King Edward gravely sinned when he ravished (*efforcha*) the Countess of Salisbury'.[21] Admittedly *efforcha*, or in Latin *raptus*, is capable of two meanings. It can mean, on the one hand, raped, or, on the other, abducted and despoiled of her property: a doubt under which the good name of the poet Chaucer, likewise accused of the rape of Cecily Chaumpaigne, still languishes. But in the present case the text that followed left no doubt that the carnal sense was the one intended:

Now I must tell you about the evil deed King Edward did, for which he was much to blame, for it was no small thing, as I have heard tell. You well know how he was so enamoured of the beautiful countess of Salisbury that he could neither give her up nor accept her refusal nor change her answer either by humbly begging or by hard words. It happened after he had sent the valiant Earl of Salisbury, the good lady's husband, into Brittany with Sir Robert d'Artois, that he could not refrain from going to visit her in the pretence of inspecting her country and its fortresses, and entered the marches where the castle of Salisbury was, and where the lady dwelt. He went there to see whether he would find her any better disposed than formerly.

The good lady made him as much honour and good cheer as she could, as she well knew she ought to for her lord, although she would have preferred him to have gone elsewhere, so much she feared for her honour. And so it was that the King stayed all day and night, but never could get from the lady the answer agreeable to him, no matter how humbly he begged her. Come the night, when he had gone to bed in proper state, and he knew that the fine lady was in her bedchamber and that all her ladies were asleep and his gentlemen also, except his personal valets, he got up and told these valets that nothing must interfere with what he was going to do, on pain of death. So it was that he entered the lady's chamber, then shut the doors of the wardrobe so that her maids could not help her, then he took her and gagged her mouth so firmly that she could not cry out more than two or three times, and then he raped her so savagely that never was a woman so badly treated; and he left her lying there all battered about, bleeding from the nose and the mouth and elsewhere, which was for her great damage and great pity. Then he left the next day without saying a word, and returned to London, very disgusted with what he had done.

The good lady never again knew happiness, nor carried herself joyfully, nor went in company with good folk, so great was her anguish of heart. Soon afterwards, it happened that the good King went to Brittany to help those he had sent there, as you have heard, and then returned to England with the Earl of Salisbury also.

When the Earl reached home, he quickly noticed his wife's distress, especially when she would not go to bed with him as usual. Challenged, she sat beside him on the bed, sobbing, and told him all about it from beginning to end, as she had always intended to do sooner or later.

No wonder that the good knight was overwhelmed with grief and disgust, remembering the great friendship and honour the King had always shown him, and the great deeds he had done for him who had now so shamed and betrayed him and the best woman living. The wonder is he did not despair. I am sure he was never happy again.

When they had somewhat recovered, he said they could no longer live together, having been so disgraced. He would go to another country for the rest of his life, and she would remain as a good wife should, as he was sure she would be in future. She should have half his property for herself and for his child her son whom she would bring up, for she would never see him again; and he would have the other half for his own use as long as he lived, wherever he might be, but he thought and prayed it would not be for long.

He then left his wife and took his young son with him to London, who was only twelve, and publicly reproached the King for his shameful deed, saying that he renounced all he held of him in favour of his son, for they would never meet again. He then left the royal court, and his son, and went overseas; and all the lords of England were deeply shocked, and everybody blamed the King.

He went to join the King of Spain who was fighting the King of Granada, and had laid siege to a strong town called Algeciras, where he died, as did many other lords before it was won. And I well believe that the good countess did not live long after, for no decent woman could live long in such distress. *Si m'en tairay à tant. Dieu leur face pardon.*

It is difficult to know what to make of this damaging story. Needless to say, Froissart omitted the whole chapter, remarking tersely, in his Amiens edition only, that he had never heard of any such thing in England. Le Bel certainly would have dearly wished to do the same, but what he believed to be the truth constrained him, and his modern editors say that they have found traces of the matter in other French sources.[22]

It is probable that the 'castle of Salbri' here referred to was not that of Wark, as the former one had been. It is clear that Alice was at the Northampton tournament at Easter 1342, and it is unlikely that she would then have gone back to the Border, so exposed to the Scots, after her husband had left for Brittany; nor could Edward reasonably have pretended that he wished to inspect the defences of Wark which he had seen so recently. The castle meant here was more probably at Bungay, in Suffolk, the main seat of Alice's Brotherton estates, where she and Edward Montagu normally lived.[23]

Edward Montagu had been alerted for service overseas since August the previous year, when he had engaged to raise six knights, twenty men at arms, twelve armed men, and twelve archers for forty days, at wages totalling £76 to be met from the local wool subsidy for Suffolk, though the indenture was at that time postponed. Robert of Artois, too, had been preparing for Brittany since November 1341, and Montagu may have accompanied him as le Bel indicated, when his delayed advance party finally sailed with Northampton's main army from Southampton in mid-August 1342. The king, who was mustering his own later expedition, stayed in London until they left, when he moved to Eastry near Sandwich, where he remained until shortly before he in turn sailed from Portsmouth in *la George*. While at Sandwich, he had trouble in assembling the always rebellious ships of the North for 'Our passage', and had to threaten their captains with the Tower; so it may be that during September or October, when making a voyage of impressment up the East Anglian coast, Edward visited Alice, now alone at Bungay, and had his way with her. Though that is not to say he resorted to brutality. Such a thing would have been completely out of character, as le Bel, in making the accusation, repeatedly protested.

The rest of the narrative is full of perplexity and doubt. There is no telling who the small son of only twelve was supposed to be. Nor does the account of the 'good knight's' division of his property make much sense, since the property was really Alice's and he had only a life interest in it as her husband.

No Montagu died at the siege of Algeciras. Earl William, it is true, went there with Henry of Derby in 1343, but he went straight from Brittany, before, not after, he returned to England. He certainly did not die there in shameful exile, nor did he break with the king. He died, much regretted, of wounds honourably sustained in a round-table tournament at Windsor in January 1344. His brother Edward, for his part, lived on, notably active, until he died in the second plague in July 1361.

As for Joan of Kent, she certainly did not die of grief and shame. She went on to enjoy fame and fortune, and a comfortable middle-age spread, for another forty years. Catherine Grandison, after Earl William's death in the lists, had dower in his possessions, and took the veil; she died during the Black Death in April 1349. But when Alice's ultimate fate is studied, the glass slipper suddenly fits at last, and everything falls into place.

For all his errors and inexactitudes, le Bel was on the track of the real truth. Incontrovertible public records show that poor Alice was in fact battered to a lingering death at Bungay, though not in 1342 as le Bel supposed, but nine years later, in 1351. And not, indeed, by the king, but by her husband Edward Montagu, then recently estranged from her and living, temporarily out of royal favour, as a disreputable cattle-rustler.

The records also show that the king's reaction to the outrage was most strange. Perhaps fearful of Montagu's rage at his betrayal, as depicted by le Bel, and of the possible exposure of his adultery, far from avenging the murder of his royal cousin, the king took urgent and effective steps to cover the whole thing up. Criminal proceedings begun against Montagu and his accomplices were stopped. Edward Montagu had become a peer in November 1348, and the notoriety of a trial by his fellow lords would have been invidious. He was confirmed in life enjoyment of Alice's Brotherton estates, which since she had been a tenant-in-chief would normally have escheated to the crown. Wardship of her two young unmarried daughters, Maud and Joan, was restored to him by the king's 'special grace'. He was re-employed in the public service and continued to attend Parliament until his death. No whisper of the affair survived in any English chronicle, and it may be that only Froissart's discretion, coupled with the popularity that led to a rapid multiplication of his manuscript, preserved his own version from the same oblivion as le Bel's.[24]

But all this was still far off in the future when the king embarked for Brittany in the autumn of 1342.

* * *

During 1341, developments on the Atlantic coast of France seemed, to the watchful Edward, to offer a new footing in place of the one on the north-eastern frontiers he had lost in the previous year. One of King Philip's major vassals, John III, duke of Brittany, on return from doing his feudal duty at the siege in the swampy air around Tournai, fell ill and died at the end of April. For all his valiant efforts with three wives, he left no children, and his inheritance was disputed.

His possible successors were his niece, Joan of Penthièvre, the daughter of his deceased younger brother, Guy; and his half-brother John, son of their father's second marriage to Violante, heiress of Narbonne and of de Montfort. Duke John III had foreseen the situation that would arise should he die childless. He mistrusted the intentions of John de Montfort, and had married Joan of Penthièvre to Charles of Blois, King Philip's nephew, son of his sister, Margaret of Valois, on the understanding that Philip would guarantee Joan's right to the duchy of Brittany if the need arose.

When Duke John III died, John de Montfort saw that the scales were laden against him, but he had the advantage over his Valois rival, Charles of Blois, in that he was present on the spot, and that because of their ancient spirit of independence the Bretons resented their threatened assimilation into the royal demesne of France. He therefore made haste to seize the chief towns in Brittany, including Nantes, the capital, and the Atlantic port of Brest, as well as the ducal treasure which lay hidden at Limoges. He then called on the tenants-in-chief of Brittany to come to Nantes to do him homage as Duke John IV. But they, more respectful of French power than the simple townsmen who had less to lose, demurred. None of them appeared save one, Sir Hervé de Léon, who was there already, and who deserted as soon as he saw the chance.

Fearful of impending invasion by Charles of Blois, de Montfort crossed to England, ostensibly to do his homage to Edward for the titular earldom of Richmond which pertained traditionally to the dukes of Brittany, but in reality, by becoming Edward's vassal, to secure a powerful and willing ally against the wrath to come from Philip. Edward had a triple interest in his cause: first, to prevent the Breton seabord coming under French control, to the peril of his sea lanes to Aquitaine; second, to make as much mischief as he could, with renewed hopes of coming to grips with his enemy on Continental soil; and third, if all went well, to gain a permanent lodgment for an attack on France, and far easier access to his isolated provinces further south. He promised de Montfort his active support, and went to work at once to raise the necessary troops and shipping. De Montfort, much heartened by Edward's activity, returned to Nantes.

It mattered nothing, as the chroniclers were swift to observe, that in Brittany Edward and Philip were both going directly contrary to the positions they had so hotly taken up over their respective titles to the throne of France; for, in Brittany, it was Edward who was supporting the male line and Philip who defended the claim through the female. Circumstances alter cases, and they both wanted the control of Brittany. Philip formally summoned de Montfort to Paris to hear the question decided by the peers of France. De Montfort obeyed, but before ever the case came on, anticipating not only defeat but personal danger, he fled headlong back to Nantes, disguised in the merchant's garb appropriate to such extremities. Sure enough, not only did the peers find for Charles of Blois, but Philip confiscated de Montfort's existing earldom because of his treasonable dealings with the king of England. By way of consolation, on 24 September 1341 Edward duly confirmed him in the earldom of Richmond, but owing to the lateness of the season and his forthcoming expedition against the Scots, was unable to provide more tangible help that winter. Charles of Blois, backed by Prince John, duke of Normandy, descended on Nantes, and by the end of November de Montfort was back in Paris, a prisoner in the donjon of the Louvre.

All seemed over, as town after town fell to Charles of Blois; but he had reckoned without the resistance of de Montfort's energetic countess, Joan of Flanders. Made adamant, as mothers sometimes are, more by concern for the future prospects of her small son, John, than for her luckless husband's plight in Paris, she abandoned her French obedience, and was followed by her brother Louis, count of Flanders, Philip's pensioner at the other side of France. When at the onset of winter Charles of Blois bore down on her in Rennes, she refused to yield, and carried the infant off to Hennebont in the heart of de Montfort territory, pursued by Charles of Blois, who proceeded to lay siege to the town.

Hennebont, picturesquely situated near Lorient on the southern coast of Brittany, had a strongly fortified harbour open to the sea down the long estuary of the river Blavet. Throughout the ensuing 'war of the two Joans' it was to be a main redoubt of the de Montforts, and from the first the countess defended it ferociously. As the enemy approached she had the church bells ring the alarum, and rode about the town on a fiery courser, armed *cap à pied*, cheering on her loyal Bretons. She drove the women to the ramparts, whence they threw down stones and pots of quicklime on their assailants, and made them shorten their skirts so as to be more nimble at the task. Seeing from a high turret that the attackers were all busy at the walls, she made a sortie and destroyed their camp, so that they spent the rest of the cold weather in discomfort, sheltering themselves as best they could with trees and branches. The siege lasted through the winter and into the spring of 1342 without sign of ending, though food was beginning to run short in Hennebont, since Don Luis de la Cerda of Spain, maintaining the blockade for Charles of Blois, used his powerful fleet to patrol the sea beyond the estuary.

Don Luis, more of a sailor than a soldier, was a story-book pirate king, bloodthirsty and greedy, yet secretly a grandee with the bluest of blue blood running in his veins. He was the rightful heir to the throne of Castile, set aside in infancy by his uncle Alphonso XI, the Implacable, the cruel though crusading king now reigning. Don Luis was also descended directly from Blanche, a daughter of St Louis of France. Expatriate from Spain, he had become a soldier of fortune at the head of a motley following, an early example of those Free Companies that were so to terrorize Europe later in the century during the brief intervals of official peace.

In view of his French connection, Don Luis had engaged himself on the side of Charles of Blois and France against de Montfort and the English. He had kept on terms with his uncle, and since Alphonso was still bound by treaty to help Philip against Edward, he had at his disposal a large part of the Castilian fleet, perhaps as many as thirty-two great carracks, carvel-built in the latest style, of 200 tons or more, as well as many shallow-water galleys, with which to fill the gap left by the destruction of the French ships at Sluys. Throughout the Brittany campaign he gravely troubled the de Montfort allies not only on the high seas but by his sudden amphibious appearances among the islands and inlets of the craggy Breton shore.

While Hennebont held, all was not lost to the de Montfort cause in Brittany. While Charles of Blois left for the north to raise extra levies among his Franco-Breton partisans, and to be more centrally placed against the English expeditions he rightly guessed would soon be on their way, Prince John of Normandy was taking an unconscionable time to muster the main French forces in his support. In the meantime Edward responded to the repeated calls for help from the valiant Countess Joan. On 10 March 1342 he ordered Sir Walter Manny to take a small *coup de main* contingent of fifty archers, fifty men at arms, twelve knights and thirty-two esquires with himself as banneret, direct by sea to the relief of Hennebont. Manny had been preparing since November but, as always in this war, there was difficulty with his shipping. On 4 April his vessels were still at Southampton, on strike for lack of pay, and he did not reach Hennebont until late in May.

Having once arrived, his mission was accomplished with predictable élan. As he sailed up the Blavet, the countess de Montfort, rising from a despondent council meeting called to discuss surrender, looked down from from her high window and saw him entering the haven. She clasped her hands and cried, 'I see! I see the succours of England coming! There's the cross of St George.' The dismal conference gave place to a celebration banquet, at which the staple provisions brought by Manny no doubt furnished a welcome supplement to the excellent, though to the long-beleaguered garrison now tedious, shellfish of the country. After the wine and comfits had gone round, Manny expressed displeasure at a great French siege engine which kept thumping stones against the walls. Straight from table he led a party down and silenced it. They were duly rewarded by the countess, who gave them smacking kisses in the street below. The siege of Hennebont was raised, and skirmishes reached out as far as Quimper, Quimperlé and Auray round about.

Brittany was roughly divided in allegiance by a line from Brest to Rennes, the north being mainly French-speaking and for Charles of Blois, while the south was Breton and for de Montfort. From Edward's point of view the alignment was a geographical misfortune, since it meant that the French could move rapidly by land against the south anywhere between Rennes and Nantes, while the English relief, denied the northern coastline, must come in little ships unsuited to the Atlantic weather rounding Ushant and beating into Biscay, to say nothing of the risks of interception by Don Luis. Edward's plan was therefore to secure, from Brest, the western part of Brittany between Saint-Brieuc and Hennebont; to march against Rennes and Nantes, the two extremities flanking any French advance; to capture the important southern harbour of Vannes and reinforce it by sea from England; and if necessary then to confront in strength the main French army.

Not that things turned out so cut-and-dried in the event. Many localities were undecided, waiting on the fortunes of war as they wavered this way and that. The impression of the actual fighting is one of small rose-red fortress towns defying siege, of nobles changing sides, covering huge distances overnight, sometimes even reportedly appearing at the same time in places far apart – a confusion no darker now that it seemed then, as armies without maps or communications vanished into the gnarled Breton terrain, into hamlets whose outlandish names had never been heard before.

On 27 March 1342, William de Bohun, earl of Northampton, had been nominated to the chief command in Brittany. After the inaugural Easter tournament at Northampton, he took leave of his wife, Elizabeth Badlesmere, as soon as his belligerent guests had departed from his county town, and went to Portsmouth to press on with his arrangements. On 13 July, wages were promised for all his captains, Warwick, Suffolk, Devon and other lords, each with a hundred or so men. On 20 July he received his marching orders. In mid-August he sailed with an army of about 3,000, accompanied by Robert of Artois with a separate detachment for a separate mission, long held up for want of shipping, about 250 strong. After a (possible) sea encounter off Alderney and Guernsey, where the French still held Castle Cornet, he landed at the friendly port of Brest.

He then struck north-east for the Channel coast and invested the town and harbour of Morlaix, sealing off the cape of Finistère. Blois came from Rennes to the relief of Morlaix, and on 30 September, Northampton met his advance outside the town in a prepared position that was to serve as a pattern for more famous victories of the future. He had his cavalry and men-at-arms dismounted, their battles interspersed with wedges of archers as at Halidon Hill, on the crest of a gentle slope, with the hidden dykes or 'pots' of Bannockburn in front of them, and a small wood behind. Blois obligingly attacked in three massed waves, the English archers did their work, and the day was won. Northampton resumed his interrupted siege of Morlaix, which shortly fell.

In the meantime Robert of Artois had separated from Northampton and gone off to pursue the mission originally allotted to him by Edward on 3 July, to join Walter Manny and the Countess Joan at Hennebont, and then capture Vannes. Away to the south, Manny had been carrying all before him. At Quimperlé, Don Luis of Spain had so enraged the country people by his piracy and pillage that they set on him with machetes and pitch-forks, and so roughly handled him that he barely managed to slip out of harbour in a single galley, leaving the town, the rest of his flotilla and all his loot to fall into the hands of the delighted Manny. The whole south coast lay open to the countess; and Charles of Blois, though badly mauled at Morlaix, hurried down. At his approach, Manny shut himself up once more in Hennebont, where Blois and Don Luis renewed their siege. Despite help from numerous French knights passing on their way to and from the Crusade in Granada, they were no more successful than before. The countess was as vigorous as ever, and the people of Hennebont, veterans now, had learned that English woolpacks made an excellent padding for their walls. Then Robert of Artois arrived with his relief force.

Charles of Blois did not like the steely interfering English fingers now closing in on his small ducal array. He raised the unprofitable siege of Hennebont and withdrew to Nantes, waiting for either the tardy French army of the duke of Normandy or the more certain grip of winter to take the pressure from him. Manny, thus set free, sallied out from Hennebont and joined Artois before Vannes, which they captured by a brilliant night attack. Remaining there in personal charge, Artois sent part of his force north towards Rennes to cover the flank of Northampton's intended southward march, while Manny returned for the third time to the countess at his base in Hennebont.

Their hasty dispersal from Vannes was a mistake. Olivier de Clisson, the able Bloisian governor, who had escaped to Nantes during the night assault, came back in a week or two with reinforcements of quite unexpected strength. Late in October, Robert of Artois, going out from Vannes to give him battle, was outnumbered and, on falling back on the town, found the gates closed against him by the citizens. De Clisson re-entered Vannes, while Artois, caught in the open, stumbled away to Hennebont, mortally wounded.

In England Edward, who had been at Sandwich throughout September 1342 collecting shipping for his own expedition, and perhaps planning a surprise landing in Flanders, now denuded by the French, decided after all, because of the endless delays, to intensify his efforts against Brittany before winter came. Apart from the feud between the Cinque Ports and the fishermen of Yarmouth, the shortage of money was acute, and he had to send urgent orders to Westminster that the sailors must be paid, 'for truly they are so in misery they can scarcely be kept together, and otherwise neither We, nor you, will have any peace'. In the end, his fleet had to return to Portsmouth to pick up some of Northampton's transports now back from their first voyage. Finally he was able to board the good ship *George* with Henry of Derby and William Montagu of Salisbury, his Earl Marshal. He sailed on 23 October, landed at Brest, and spent two weeks at the little town of Rosiers just across the Elorn estuary.

In mid-November he marched off from Brest, and Northampton, coming down from Morlaix, joined him at Carhaix, the plumb heart of Brittany. Salisbury and Suffolk were sent east to Rennes, where the garrison proved obstinate and one gruff Breton in particular, Bertrand du Guesclin, all too well known to the next generation of English soldiers as 'de Clakyn', first came to notice. Edward and the main force headed south, taking Ploermel, Malestroit and Redon, important towns on the Oust, in passing, until late in the month they came in front of Vannes. There Edward learnt to his dismay how the city had been won only to be lost again, and of the death in battle of his 'dear cousin', Robert of Artois, the persevering exile from the other side of France.

On 25 November, from Grand-Champ north of Vannes, he wrote home to Philippa, '*Douce coeur*' as he addressed her, asking her to see that his instructions to the Chancellor and Treasurer about the honourable burial of Artois in London were properly carried out. But '*Douce coeur*' had other sorrows of her own. Two months later young Prince Edward, guardian of the realm, was still trying to arrange the interment not only of Artois, but of '*dame Blanche, ma soeur*', his baby sister, who had died almost as soon as she was born. There was not money enough even for royal funerals.

Removing to a small port south of Vannes to await the navy and the reinforcements due to come from England, Edward sent Northampton, Warwick and Hugh Despenser (son of Hugh the younger, hanged high at

Hereford sixteen years earlier), with four hundred men to Nantes, where, though Blois fled before them, the city held; a siege was in progress by 5 December 1342. Edward had now crossed Brittany unmolested from its north-western port of Brest to its capital in the south-east. The Bloisian army had been driven out, the three great cities Rennes, Nantes and Vannes all lay almost within his grasp, and his investing forces were well distributed to intervene whichever way the expected French onslaught from the east should come. For now, if ever, was the time for the mighty power of France to restore its humiliated vassal.

King Philip in person joined his son John, who was mobilizing ponderously at Angers, and, with Charles of Blois, advanced purposefully westward into Brittany. Now that the line of attack was clear, Edward fell back from Nantes, abandoned Rennes, and concentrated his whole army north of Vannes. He had, as before at Buironfosse and Tournai, intended to bring about a major engagement, but he had not expected such a full French turn-out in the dead of winter, and he had hoped to have Vannes in his hands to receive the fleet from England, of which there was no sign. As it was he was facing two ways at once with, behind him, a hostile town between him and the sea where Don Luis prowled, and in front, steadily approaching, the full French army. This time he might have over-reached himself. He sent repeated though fruitless messages home for speedy help.

Philip halted at Ploermel, twenty-five miles to the north. The garrison of Vannes, reassured by his presence, made a violent sortie against the English rear but were driven back, with the loss of their leader, Olivier de Clisson, and Godfrey de Harcourt, a Norman knight. They were briefly made prisoner, but soon afterwards were exchanged for Lord Ralph Stafford, taken on the English side. The French army came closer into open battle country, pennants flying, harness clattering, steam rising in the winter air. For the third time in four years the two kings faced each other in array, an impressive tableau, menacing but sterile.

For Philip still did not attack. He held to his wise counsel that Edward stood to gain more and lose less from a battle than did he. It was, besides, unnecessary; for at that same moment his southern vassals, led by Bertrand, comte de l'Isle, of Bergerac, in far-off Aquitaine were chipping steadily away at Edward's once proud heritage, the first cause and the ultimate prize of the whole conflict. Down the Dordogne as far as Libourne, and in the Garonne valley almost up to the walls of Bordeaux itself, the French were pressing on, rewarded with tracts of the rich wine lands that they conquered. English prestige was falling; more and more of the uncertain Gascons were going over to the enemy, and the Seneschal's efforts to buy their loyalty out of the shrinking ducal revenues and ruined vineyards meant that there was no money left to pay the garrisons, which led to still more desertions. So Philip only had to wait, to resist euphoria, to encourage Charles of Blois by a sufficient show of force, while the deadly work of attrition went on in Aquitaine.

Edward, true to his defensive ethos, had no intention of attacking either; nor had he ever been in worse case to do so. He was uselessly tied down, equally far from Aquitaine and Paris, either or both of which must be his decisive theatre. The Brittany venture had been expensive for little gain; less expensive certainly than his previous effort to buy over the whole Netherlands, but the cost of garrisons was heavy enough, and his captains, their engagements expired, expected payment. It was a cheerless Christmas; both sides longed for winter quarters, and the encircled English were also hungry. So, when the ever-ready papal cardinals suddenly appeared protesting peace, a truce was rapidly agreed at the priory of Malestroit near Nantes, on 19 January 1343.

The armies broke up, each side retaining what it held pending a general settlement. Edward took shelter for a month at Hennebont with the grateful countess, Joan de Montfort. Then, when his ships were ready, and he was satisfied that Philip had duly returned to Paris, he sailed for home on 22 February, taking with him his hostess and her small son John.

As usual on returning from abroad, his convoy was shattered by a frightful storm. Tossed wildly in ripping winds the vessels were separated. The king's cog was driven before a northerly gale down almost to the coast of Spain. He reached Weymouth on 2 March, and as soon as he had sufficiently recovered went on pilgrimage to Our Lady of Walsingham, to Canterbury, and to his father's shrine at Gloucester, to give thanks for his deliverance from the waves. He was convinced that the tempest had been raised by the spells of his necromantic enemy, King Robert the Wise of Sicily, who, had however, unknown to Edward, died in January, and could not charitably be supposed to have carried on his malice from beyond the grave.

The countess and her son, in the care of the earl of Northampton, at last limped safely into Plymouth. Six months later she was locked up in the castle of Tickhill in Yorkshire, supposedly because, always overwrought, her recent energies had swamped her reason.[25] Young John de Montfort, whose father was still Philip's prisoner in the Louvre, joined Queen Philippa's nursery of important orphans. He was installed with a tutor in the Tower, and remained in England as a useful diplomatic prospect for the future. In due course he married Princess Mary, Philippa's ninth child and fourth daughter.

* * *

Apart from conditions concerning guarantees and the exchange of prisoners, the truce of Malestroit had in the main confined itself to leaving things as they were until September 1346, at which time the pope would decide the whole issue between the crowns of France and England. Both sides were to send full embassies to Avignon to present their own and their allies' cases. All concerned were to accept the pope's award, given not as a judge but as an impartial friend of peace.

The pope, in short, was to take the quarrel between Edward and Philip into his own hands. This was sound feudal practice. Any sovereign could arbitrate disputes to prevent the unnecessary spilling of blood, as King John of France would before long stop the duel between Henry of Derby, by then duke of Lancaster, and the truculent Duke Otto of Brunswick at Saint-Germain-des-Prés in Paris; and as Richard II would stop Boling-broke and Mowbray in the lists at Coventry. How much more was the Holy Father, spiritual sovereign of all Christendom, entitled to end blood-shed between nations. None could question his right to intervene.

Yet all the Avignon popes were French in sympathy, some more so than others, and much depended on the outlook of the pope concerned. The Curia maintained a permanent secretariat for diplomacy, whose methods of persuasion were none the less cogent for being based upon theology. But the curial bureaucracy, for all its deep grounding in history and canon law, its agility with scriptural authorities, its devotion to precedent, and its sonorous jargon, inevitably reflected the foibles of the pontiff of the day. A change of pope could drastically alter the chances of the hoped-for peace.

Such a change had recently taken place. In May 1342, Benedict XII was succeeded by Clement VI, who reigned for the next ten years. Benedict, to be sure, had been far from abstemious, and had depleted the treasure left by his thrifty predecessor, John XXII. But personally self-indulgent though he was, Benedict's strictness with others had been a byword. While, for example, he gladly accepted the thousand mule-loads of plunder, the twenty captive Moorish princes, and Ferrante, the beautiful Arab charger, brought to him in triumph by Alphonso of Castile after his great Christian victory at Salado, he did not fail to scold Alphonso soundly, if ineffectu-ally, about his mistress Dona Leonora de Guzmán. His firm stand against venality, especially regarding marriage dispensations and nepotism (he had declared that a pope should have no relations), had made him exceedingly unpopular with his cardinals, who lost money through his scruples. Politically, he had been a genuine friend of peace and, within the limits of his French birth, impartial. When Nicholas de Flisco, Edward's envoy, was spirited away from Avignon by Philip's agents, Benedict had rained down excommunications, and hanged some of his own officers from the window of the inn where the abduction had occurred.

In comparison with that of his successor, Benedict's extravagance had been as nothing. Clement VI, Cardinal Pierre Roger of Limoges, was of exalted lineage, a scholar with a fabulous memory, and one of the few popes of whom Petrarch did not wholly disapprove on intellectual grounds. He was famous for his delicacy of speech and courtesy of manner; once, when he preached in Paris, the whole university and town turned out to hear him. At the same time, however, he was a sybarite, an addict of the rich and rare. On being reminded of the greater moderation of John and Benedict before him, he remarked. 'Ah! my predecessors never knew how to be a pope.' His generosity was as lavish as his luxury; during the plague year of 1348 his charitable coffers were wide open. He could never bear to send away the humblest religious empty handed, and although in consequence his carriage as he rode to Mass was showered with petitions, he complained only because some of them had stones wrapped up in them the better to make sure of their aim.

A Frenchman through and through, he had no idea that the Holy See should ever return to Rome, and set out, an enthusiastic Pontifex Maximus, to ennoble Avignon as a fit residence for the Vicar of God. He extended Benedict's solid beginnings of the great Palais des Papes on a magnificent scale. He rebuilt the first four arches (the only four now standing) of the Pont d'Avignon, to provide easy traffic over the Rhône to Villeneuve, the annexe where he lodged important visitors and, some say, other sparkling though less meritorious adornments of his court.

Not content with that, he took the opportunity, when it offered in 1348, of buying up the whole city at the bargain price of 80,000 florins (about £11,500) from the fair Joanna, queen of Naples, grand-daughter of Robert the Wise of Sicily. Joanna was already in his debt; she had been married as a girl, against her will, to an uncouth Hungarian husband and Clement had protected her from a well-supported charge that her servants had hanged him naked from her balcony just as he was climbing into bed with her. Joanna had then married her more presentable lover, the prince of Taranto, and after being chased from her kingdom by her furious brother-in-law, Louis of Hungary, they had arrived at her city of Avignon in penury. She needed the money badly. So Clement bought the city from her and, accepting her excuse that her distaste for her first husband had been due to witchcraft, pardoned her as well. Joanna used the money to win back her kingdom of Naples, but her later history was far from happy. The prince of Taranto turned out to be no good. She married two more husbands: James, the beggarly king of Majorca, who deserted her, and the quarrelsome *condottiere* Otto of Brunswick, who almost came to blows with Henry of Derby. In the end, Louis of Hungary caught and imprisoned her, and she was strangled at her prayers. She was much admired by Petrarch and later by the poet Mistral, and has been called the Mary Stuart of the South.[26]

Clement's varied interests cost money, and had somehow to be paid for. He could not afford Benedict's laudable precepts about the probity of the Holy See. His court became a bourse for the receipt of bribes, the sale of expectancies and preferments. His haughty Cecily, viscountess of Turenne, was always in his vestibule, raking in contributions like a croupier. 'Semiramis with her quiver', Petrarch called her; '. . . there is no clue to lead you out of this labyrinth: . . . the only means of escaping is by the influence of gold; . . . for, to say all in one word, even Jesus Christ is here bought with gold.'

His chronic shortage of money led Clement to reach out as far as England for sees and benefices, and to demand taxes from the clergy, arousing ever louder protests against his papal provisions and bulls. Edward mistrusted, and soon came to scorn, the good faith of such a pontiff. He could never hope to whisper as effectively in Clement's ear as did Clement's fellow Frenchman Philip, nor did Edward ever have as much cash to spare, and so he was continually worsted. At Philip's behest, Clement adroitly weaned the emperor, Louis of Bavaria, though an excommunicate enemy of successive popes, away from his English alliance, and then deposed him in favour of Charles of Moravia, husband of Philip's sister Blanche of Valois, and son of Philip's old friend King John of Bohemia. Clement's prejudice against England was well known. When, even though infidels were in firm possession of them, he proclaimed Don Luis of Spain as king of the Fortunate Isles (as the Canaries were then called), it became a popular joke that the British Isles were the Fortunate Isles he really had in mind.

From the first, therefore, the truce of Malestroit was a sham. The Flemings were supposed to be released from interdict, but the pope did not release them. Philip was supposed to release de Montfort from the Louvre, but took two years about it. The Scots were enjoined to keep the peace, but carried on as usual. When Edward drew Clement's attention to these things, Clement replied blandly about recovering Smyrna from the Turks. In retaliation Edward occupied Vannes, declared by the truce an open city in the hands of the Vatican. Thus the years 1343–6 were years of complaints, denials, excuses, and of keen diplomacy in preparation for the resumption of the war.

It was obvious to Edward that positive action was urgently necessary to rescue Aquitaine, now reduced to a narrow coastal strip between Bordeaux and Bayonne. All idea that the power of France would collapse like a house of cards as the result of a single battle in the north was a dangerous daydream. Even before he left for Brittany, his Seneschal, Sir Oliver Ingham, had come home to report that the situation of Gascon arms and Gascon money was critical and would soon be desperate. Direct English help was vital.

The preliminary need was to win over Alphonso of Castile from his French alliance, or at least to prevent the interference of his fleet with the English sea lanes to Bordeaux. Accordingly, as soon as the armies broke up before Vannes in Brittany, Henry of Derby and William Montagu, earl of Salisbury, set out for the Crusade in Spain, as did also many of their friends and enemies – the Constable of France, Raoul, comte d'Eu, among the latter. But unlike their fellow travellers, who were mostly going to finish the winter campaigning side by side more comfortably in the sunny South, the two earls had a delicate mission to perform.

They paused on their way through Aquitaine, and at Bayonne picked up Thomas Holland, who was guarding the frontier there. Fortunately, the awkward circumstance that he was the secret husband of Salisbury's supposed daughter-in-law was not known to them at this time. They travelled down to Algeciras, beside Gibraltar, and won crusaders' due renown at the great siege then entering its final stage. They earned further favour with the Spanish admirals by sailing with their galleys in an attack on Ceuta, on the Moorish coast of Africa, and got back to England in November 1343.

They had made some progress. They had approached Alphonso with a proposal of marriage between his heir, Pedro, and Edward's ever-disposable daughter Isabella, though their efforts did not bear fruit for several years. By then, Isabella had been replaced as bride-to-be by her sister Joan, who then died of plague at Bordeaux on her way to her wedding. They had made friends, and had gained a valuable insight into the intricacies of Spanish etiquette, wherein the French had so far held a damaging advantage. They learned that the way to handle blunt Alphonso was through his Sevillian mistress, Leonora de Guzmán. They so charmed everyone that Don Luis ceased his piratical attacks forthwith, and on renewal of war between France and England two years later, the Castilians observed strict naval neutrality.

Meanwhile Edward was reorganizing his home government ready for the enormous demands soon to be made on it. What he wanted and had not as yet achieved was a concept wholly new, an administration able to finance the war and provision it effectively even if cut off from him for months on end. He soon relinquished his resolve to have no more clerical ministers. Laymen were not only less educated, they were more expensive. While churchmen could be satisfied with bishoprics and preferments, laymen wanted salaries and mansions within range of Westminster. The discontent was mutual. The first lay Chancellor, Sir Robert Bourchier, who had a salary of £600 and had been renting the bishop of Worcester's house, soon went back to a less complicated soldier's life and joined the Brittany expedition. The same happened with William Kilsby, the Keeper of the Privy Seal. Kilsby was in some kind of minor clerical orders, and Edward tried to persuade the incorruptible Pope Benedict to provide him to the see of York, but to his annoyance was over-ruled in favour of William Zouche, whom he had just dismissed as Treasurer. Fortunately, the insidious Kilsby was no great loss, and Zouche was later to redeem himself as the fighting archbishop of Neville's Cross.

Edward needed new men. Of his old and trusted clerical advisers, Henry Burghersh of Lincoln was dead, and Archbishop Stratford, though reconciled, was aged. His former tutor and man of all work, Richard de Bury of Durham, died at the age of fifty-eight in 1345, the same year as Orleton of Winchester, a shrewd servant though never a friend. He found their successors in Thomas Hatfield, who followed Bury, and completed his dream, Durham College at Oxford, on money made out of mining Durham coal; in William Edington, who took Orleton's place at Winchester and became first prelate of the Order of the Garter; and in John Thoresby, later, on the death of Zouche, archbishop of York. These three priests, Hatfield, Edington and Thoresby, were typical of the professional ministers Edward was to cherish and rely on for the remainder of his life. Devoted, expert, never in the way and never out of it, they divided the great offices of state between them for the next twenty years. They found ways of meeting his often high demands, and took from his shoulders both the odium and the weight of home administration.

Buffered by good sense and tact, Edward's government fell into an easier routine. Finance became less his personal concern and was centralized in the Exchequer, while his subjects came to recognize their national duty to supply the king's necessities. In return, he flattered them by seeking their advice on foreign policy, and listened to their grievances.

Not that the change happened overnight. The parliament that met in the spring of 1343, the first in the two years since the Stratford controversy, was still in a querulous mood. The elevation of Prince Edward to be Prince of Wales was acclaimed, but that was the limit of their affability. They confirmed, though not without comment, the king's high-handed repeal of the Stratford statutes. They protested violently against Pope Clement's extra-national exactions and appointments, but the clergy could not support them against the head of the church, and since the king was himself making use of papal provisions to find places for his ministers, they could get no further for the moment. Far worse trouble was therefore stored up for the future. So in small things is the seed of greater sown. Small grievances neglected would lead in time to wholesale convulsions, to the Henrician Reformation and to the Puritan revolution. For the present, however, Parliament merely grumbled about the prerogatory *maltôte*, but ended by permitting it for the next three years. A year later, in June 1344, they were more cordial. More of them than usual arrived at the proper time, and they were congratulated for it by the king. They demanded a fuller consideration of their petitions in return for grants; but they withdrew charges against William de la Pole and Reginald atte Conduit, the king's merchant banker friends, and voted subsidies for the next two years provided they were spent, as intended, on preparations for the war.

Edward's consultations with his parliaments gradually became less of a confrontation and more of a partnership in a common enterprise. There was no further constitutional crisis until the end of his long reign. He embodied the growing self-assertion of his people. His warlike policy was popular, and when once it began to show a profit, he did not have to search for soldiers. The chance of fortune and a pardon for past crimes were enough to bring plentiful recruits for adventure overseas, though service in bleak Scotland was naturally less sought after. Grooves were worn spontaneously in the sandstone porches of village churches where men sharpened arrows for archery practice after Mass.

Edward's eventual strength was his opponents' weakness. A competent national assembly such as was growing up in England had no counterpart in France. The representatives of the provinces, on the rare occasions when they were called, met only to hear and to obey, not to debate policies and vote money for them. Philip was less king of France than chief of a confederation of great nobles, and was always hard put to it to keep up his ascendancy. His administration, though labyrinthine, did not reach beyond the royal demesne; for national revenue he had to depend on feudal dues collected, if at all, in towns and regions, or else upon debasement of the currency and other dubious means. At first his essential shortcoming was hidden because, in comparison to England, France was prosperous and large, a people of twenty million against England's three or four. For some time yet, Philip had money enough to arrange alliances, to satisfy the pope, to enlarge his capital estate by buying Montpellier from King James of Majorca, and the kingdom of Arles, the Dauphiné, whereof in due course in 1349 his grandson the future Charles V became the first French dauphin. But as the war developed and expenditure increased he had to impose taxes directly on his people, first the *fouage* on every hearth and then the hated *gabelle* on salt, a monopoly that was continually cursed down to the Revolution, and was blamed upon the Jews as a tax on sun and sea-water. When the *gabelle* was introduced, Edward took his chance to sneer that Philip was indeed the author of the Salic Law. Consent to such measures depended upon the king's personal prestige, and Philip lacked charisma. For all his knightly aura he was privately a mediocrity, under the thumb of his lame wife, Jeanne de Bourgogne, *la trop crueuse femme*; he was hesitant, peevish, and as time went on *dolent et angoisseux*. He would never be able to stir his Frenchmen as the flamboyant Edward led his English.

Edward deliberately used his dramatic instinct to cultivate his heroic image. In the present interval of enforced peace and internal rearrangement, he was considering how he could strengthen the already considerable bonds he had formed with his peers and leaders in war, his friends and cousins, his chivalrous elite. What they all shared was a joy in battle. Feats of arms, whether real or make-believe, were their livelihood, their proof of virtue, their daily exercise. About now Henry of Derby was made captain of a club of knights and sought Edward's permission to hold annual jousts at Lincoln. Edward, no less than he a devotee of sport, decided that he himself would found a new knightly order, and at once envisaged the greatest order that ever was, in keeping with his own huge sense of majesty.

Perhaps the idea unfolded in his mind as he strolled at his palace of Windsor, with one or more of his eight vast alaunts sniffing gravely, more or less at heel. As he looked out over the valley of the wandering Thames and its sleepy royal town, Windleshore as the Saxons had called it, he mused about St George, the patron saint of England, and about the magic of King Arthur's name. This Windsor, his birthplace, would be the home of his new brotherhood of arms, the grandest, the most permanent, of all Round Tables there had ever been. Henry III's picturesque old rookery would be transformed into its Caerleon. And it should meet every year on St George's Day. At the New Year's games next ensuing he would announce his great invention.

On 1 January 1344, invitations to a New Year's tournament were sent out more widely than usual since, as for the moment there was peace, the Scots and even the French could be included. On Monday 19 January the guests began arriving in great numbers, and their arms and achievements were laid out for the customary review. There were many fine ladies present, whom Edward showed personally to their places for the banquet in the hall, where logs blazed and minstrels wearing specially splendid tunics played in the gallery. Queen Philippa was 'most nobly adorned', and no less so the king's mother, Isabella, making a rare appearance from retirement. Alice, too, was surely there, though the only indication of her presence is that le Bel, in his curiously slim account of the grand occasion, interpolated here his second cryptic warning that he would soon have bad news to tell of King Edward's misbehaviour. There were altogether so many ladies that the lords and knights had to sit at separate tables in pavilions in the courtyard. After the feast came revelry; 'dances were not lacking, embraces and kissings alternately commingling'.

Three days of hard tilting followed, with running at the ring and other displays of skill. At the end, when the ladies had adjudged the prizes and had tactfully awarded three of the six to Edward, he declared that 'no lord or lady should presume to depart but await until the morning to know the lord King's pleasure'. Next morning, after Mass in St Edward's chapel where he had been christened, the king, in a gown of very precious velvet, with the crown on his head and sceptre in hand, went in procession with his High Steward and his Earl Marshal, Henry of Derby (representing his father the earl of Lancaster), and William Montagu of Salisbury, followed by the queen and the newly created Prince of Wales, to make oath on the Bible 'that he would begin a Round Table in the same manner as the Lord Arthur, formerly King of England appointed it, namely to the number of three hundred knights, a number always increasing, and he would cherish it and maintain it according to his power'. Six earls present confirmed the vow. 'Which being done, the trumpets and nakers sounding all together, the guests hastened to a feast complete with richness of fare, variety of dishes, and overflowing abundance of drinks; the delight was unutterable, the comfort inestimable, the enjoyment unalloyed, the hilarity without care.'[27] The jousts were then resumed for several days until damped by the death on 30 January, at the age of forty-two, of the Earl Marshal, William Montagu of Salisbury, from buffetings received in the lists. Tournaments, originally lethal and sometimes seditious mock battles in the open country, had by now been refined into organized spectacles with elaborate rules. They were contests, in a measured arena, between knights whose lances were blunted by *rockettes* or *coronels*, which would grip the opponent's armour without piercing it. Even so, Montagu's fate indicates that the risks were still far from negligible.[28]

Edward allowed no time to be lost in starting on the building. On 16 February 1344 William Ramsey, the king's mason, and William Hurley, the king's carpenter, were commissioned to take what they wanted, materials, skilled tradesmen and labour, from all over the country for the king's works at Windsor, with the waggons, drays and Thames barges necessary to carry them. Hurley was to make a gigantic Round Table (very probably the one now preserved at Winchester College) and Ramsey a great circular tower to house it. Speed and durability were the king's priorities, and whatever the two fastidious craftsmen, designers of the octagonal lantern at Ely, may have thought of it, the grim edifice began to rise. Stone and timber poured into Windsor. The bridges were strengthened to take the weight, and sanded against skidding. By March, seven hundred men were at work hewing setts, mixing mortar, sawing wood, forging metal at wages ranging from seven shillings a week for master masons to twopence a day for labourers, the same rate as an archer. The new order was duly inaugurated in April on St George's Day. Then suddenly the activity slackened; the labour force packed up its tools and left. Expenditure was cut to one fifth, for the king had found that 'much treasure must be got together for other affairs'. The Round Table faded like an insubstantial pageant, to reappear four years later in another, more exclusive guise.

The 'other affairs' were, of course, the war with France. Since the truce of Malestroit early in 1343, Philip had been seeking out and punishing those he thought had betrayed him during the Brittany campaign. Olivier de Clisson was seized and on 2 August beheaded without trial or explanation at Les Halles in Paris. His goods were distrained, and his wife and children banished. Other arrests followed. On 29 November, ten other Breton knights and squires were beheaded in Paris, also without trial. The executions caused astonishment in France, because de Clisson in particular was thought of as a gallant knight who had recaptured Vannes for Charles of Blois and had killed Philip's sworn enemy Robert of Artois. It was believed that the unpopular queen, Jeanne de Bourgogne, had been responsible.

The news was brought to Edward by Henry de Malestroit, hitherto a clerk in the French royal service, whose father and brother were amongst those put to death, and who had himself escaped only because he was a priest. Edward knew very well that de Clisson, when briefly his prisoner before the truce, had come over to the English side, and since his release had been working as a de Montfort agent. So while it was no doubt distressing for Edward to have his embryonic secret service scuppered in this way, spies are always expendable, and he could not blame Philip for avenging old treasons in Brittany, now momentarily a backwater. He gave asylum to de Clisson's small son and namesake Olivier, who joined young de Montfort in Philippa's home for refugees; and he allowed the widowed mother, Jeanne de Belleville, who owned considerable estates in Aquitaine, to marry one of his most deserving knights, Sir Walter Bentley. Otherwise he did nothing for the present. He did not care for Henry de Malestroit, whom he perhaps suspected of being a double agent. He sent him back to a job in Vannes, then loosely in English hands, where he was soon caught by the French, carried to Paris, unfrocked, chained in a dung-cart, and pelted to death.

Early in 1344 Philip struck again. He not only forbade his subjects to take any part in Edward's festivities at Windsor, he proclaimed a rival tournament of his own in Paris, and cynically used the sportive occasion to trap three suspect Norman knights. Unlike the Bretons, they were given a form of trial. On 31 March they were convicted by the royal court of conspiring to make Godfrey de Harcourt duke of Normandy in place of the king's son John. On 3 April they too were beheaded, and their heads impaled on the gates of Carentan, to the subsequent misfortune of that town. Godfrey de Harcourt, their leader, got away to England.

This time Edward reacted violently. De Harcourt had been taken prisoner at the same time as Olivier de Clisson at Vannes, and like him had joined the English. He owned the valuable property of Saint-Sauveur-le-Vicomte in the Cotentin of Normandy, and Normandy, unlike Brittany, was at that moment a sensitive area in Edward's thinking. The Norman conspiracy was no old outdated treason like the Breton one, but a live element in an as yet undeclared design, and Philip's percipient action was a gross interference with Edward's future plans.

Henry of Derby dissuaded Edward, only with the greatest difficulty, from executing in reprisal poor Sir Hervé de Léon, a prisoner in the Tower since his capture at Hennebont by Manny in May 1342. Instead, Hervé was set free on condition of an enormous ransom, and was made to carry a very rude defiance to Philip; he died as soon as he had fulfilled his thankless task. Edward raked up the Breton executions as proof that Philip had broken the truce in Brittany. He told Pope Clement in no uncertain terms that he held himself at liberty to resume the war, and that his long-debated peace embassy would never now arrive at Avignon. He kept the Norman Godfrey de Harcourt at his court, a suitable replacement for the dead

Robert of Artois. He sent young William Montagu north with Edward Baliol to watch the Scottish Border, collected his two years' subsidy from Parliament, and pressed on with his elaborate project for a grand assault on France from several different quarters.

The concept he had in mind was the most ambitious ever yet undertaken from the shores of England. Nineteenth-century critics inclined to say that Edward had little strategic vision, and squandered the country's resources in order to march about in France, gaining in the end only the slim reward of the little port of Calais. But the nineteenth century stands corrected by the twentieth, for his plan was in essence the same as that adopted for the recapture of France just six hundred years later. First, an expeditionary force would sail south to recover Aquitaine; after that it would strike northward, like the Anglo-American forces from southern France in 1945. Then, from the north-east, a large Anglo-Flemish army would drive down by its old route past Tournai and Lille towards Paris, like the Russians rolling remorselessly towards Berlin. At the same time, a third landing from England in the west would break out from Normandy, heading east. At any rate the two strategies were similar.

So grandiose a scheme needed complex preparation, and when on 28 June 1344 Edward ordered his Admiral of the North, Robert Ufford, earl of Suffolk, to marshal all shipping, he was merely declaring his future intention. A good year must elapse before it could become fact. In the meantime emergency measures must be taken to stave off the disaster looming in Aquitaine, where wine exports had dropped from their peak of 100,000 tons in 1309 to about one-tenth of that amount, and further alienations of ducal property in an attempt to reduce desertions to the French were ruining the treasury. Things became worse with the death of the staunch Seneschal, Oliver Ingham, and the appointment by King Philip in March 1344 of John, duke of Normandy, as overlord of all French provinces in the neighbourhood, where he was already making a tour in force and taking up his homages.

In the spring of 1344 Henry of Derby was sent out for the second time to revive the hard-pressed Anglo-Gascons. Ostensibly going on pilgrimage to St James of Compostela, he kept suitably disarming company with his sister Eleanor, widow of Lord John Beaumont killed at the Northampton tournament, and Richard 'Copped-Hat' Arundel who was having an affair with her. Derby and Arundel had further talks about neutrality with Alphonso of Castile and the kings of Portugal and Navarre, and went on to see Pope Clement at Villeneuve-lès-Avignon, though all they seem to have gained there was the dispensation necessary for Arundel to divorce Isabella Despenser so that he could marry Eleanor instead. Back in England they reported that the outlook in Aquitaine was not good, but their delaying tactics had been for the time effective. In February 1345 Lord Ralph Stafford, whose son had lately married Derby's baby daughter Maude, was sent out as Seneschal in Ingham's place with a small but, as it proved, adequate holding force to prepare the way for Derby's expedition.

By this time three great fleets, some 450 ships in all, were assembling in the English Channel ports: at Sandwich, under the northern Admiral, Ufford, to take the king to Flanders; at Portsmouth, at the disposal of William de Bohun, earl of Northampton, for Normandy or Brittany; and at Southampton, 150 vessels manned by 3,000 seamen were getting ready to carry Derby to Aquitaine. The last had obvious priority, and on 13 March 1345 Derby entered into indenture with the king to have an army of 2,000 ready to sail on 14 May. An advance of pay at the current rates plus a *regard* for overseas was arranged for the first six months, with more to follow if he should stay longer. Derby's army comprised 500 cavalry, 500 mounted archers, 500 foot archers, and 500 Welsh foot-soldiers. Of these, Derby himself was to provide 250 cavalry and 250 mounted archers. Rates of pay were six shillings and eightpence (half a mark) a day for himself, bannerets four shillings, knights two shillings, esquires one shilling, mounted archers sixpence. Foot archers as a rule got threepence or twopence, and common spearmen twopence. Derby's associated retinues, apart from Ralph Stafford, who had already gone, were those of Lawrence Hastings, earl of Pembroke, Sir Walter Manny, and James Audley. The foot archers and Welsh spearmen were to be found by royal commissions of array. The shipping was provided at the king's expense by Richard of Arundel, as Admiral of the West. Derby was ready by 11 June, but his fleet had the longest haul of the three proposed expeditions and there were delays in equipping it for sea.

In the meantime unforeseen events had altered the arrangements. The bargaining with the pope about the truce had induced Philip at last to release John de Montfort from the Louvre on parole in Paris, and de Montfort fled to England about Easter 1345. An opportunity had thus arisen for a quick limited operation to restore him to his duchy, and so secure the rear of the intended future landings in Normandy. On 24 April Northampton was commissioned once again for Brittany; on 20 May, de Montfort did formal homage for Brittany to Edward; and by 11 June, while Derby was still preparing at Southampton, they had already sailed from Portsmouth. They landed at Brest, and de Montfort headed for the south, where Charles of Blois had re-entered Vannes and was making progress; but in September de Montfort died of a burning fever outside his cherished town of Hennebont. His death removed the main purpose of the expedition, and having taken advantage of the fact that Blois was preoccupied in the south to capture Roche-Derrien in the heart of the Bloisian country in the north, Northampton left Sir Thomas Dagworth in charge in Brittany and returned to England in December 1345, to be ready for next year's more important campaign in Normandy.

A greater setback to the main plan had by then occurred. While

Northampton was taking his chance in Brittany and Derby was still preparing for Aquitaine, the king had been organizing his own third arm of the attack, from Flanders. Jacob van Artevelde still kept his iron grip on the Flemish cloth towns, and was still trying to keep out Count Louis of Nevers, who with French help had been making ground against him. Edward had agreed to bring a substantial force to Flanders, when he and van Artevelde would declare Count Louis deposed in favour of Edward's eldest son, who would become duke of Flanders. They would then together make an invasion of north-eastern France mightier than the one they had attempted five years before, in 1340.

In June Edward had announced his resumption of the war and gone to Sandwich to embark. He appointed his second son, Lionel of Antwerp, as regent in his absence, and on 3 July sailed with the Prince of Wales and a sizeable fleet for the port of Sluys, the scene of his former triumph. There, van Artevelde had come from Ghent to greet him, and at dinner on board Edward's *Salle du Roy*, the *Catherine*, in the presence of his principal burgesses van Artevelde made one of his inflamed orations in favour of exchanging Count Louis for the excellent Prince of Wales as duke, and for an ample dole of wool.

His speech was not as well received as usual. His burgesses said doubtfully they must consult their townships, and hastily dispersed. In fact when they had been gone a week or two in silence, it began to seem that something had gone wrong. Van Artevelde revealed that there had lately been industrial trouble between the weavers and the fullers, and in particular that the dean of the weavers, one Gerard Dennis, had been stirring up the *canaille* of Ghent against his beneficent rule. Edward, who needed to preserve van Artevelde, sensed that it would be prudent to provide a guard to take him back to Ghent; and wondering whom to charge with this possibly disagreeable mission, soon thought of the very man, Sir John Maltravers. Maltravers, who had fled from England with a price on his head for his part in the murder of Edward II and the execution of the earl of Kent, had now turned up in Sluys entreating pardon. He was in some financial distress, and by van Artevelde's death he stood to lose what money he still had left. He was granted a provisional pardon, and put at the head of five hundred Welshmen to see van Artevelde home.[29]

They got van Artevelde safely back to Ghent, but the atmosphere there was far from cordial. The streets were strangely empty except for groups of whispering citizens who 'began to run three heads under one hood'. Soon van Artevelde was barricaded in his house in the Place de la Calandre, vociferously accused of embezzling his enormous wealth in England. Desperately, he used his hitherto unfailing tongue to reason with the mob from an upstairs window; but this time it did not save him, and he went the eventual road of many rabble-rousers. His house was invaded, in spite of stiff resistance by Maltravers and his Welshmen; and when he tried to make off from the back, van Artevelde was cornered in the stables and his head split open to the teeth with an axe. Edward and the Prince of Wales, who had wisely remained on board ship at Sluys, had no alternative but to weigh anchor and head for home, where they arrived on 26 July.

Edward put a brave face on his disappointment, and on his son's humiliating first experience of glorious war; perhaps he remembered that his own, in Scotland, had not been much better. On 3 August he told his sheriffs that he had stabilized the state of affairs in Flanders, where loyalty to him had never been firmer; indeed, that autumn a delegation from Bruges, Ypres and other Flemish towns, concerned for their wool supply, came to Westminster to deplore the rash action of the Gantois, and to beg his pardon.

Something might yet be salvaged from the Flanders project, but other events of the year 1345 in the north-eastern theatre were no less disturbing. The increasing pressure by Pope Clement on the Emperor Louis, leading up to his deposition in favour of the French choice, Charles of Moravia, and to his death from apoplexy while hunting bear, removed the cement from Edward's original Netherlands alliance. The slippery duke of Brabant at last openly joined the French. Then, Philippa's brother and brother-in-law, William, earl of Hainault, and William of Juliers, earl of Cambridge, were killed while dealing with a revolt in Friesland. The heir to Hainault was Earl William's sister, the dowager Empress Margaret, but in the interim his uncle John of Hainault, long Edward's staunch supporter, became regent, and Philip somehow managed to buy him over to the French side for good. Edward's influence in the Low Countries had declined abruptly. A limited action might still be possible; but all hope of a decisive march into France from the north-east, the intended hammer to meet Northampton's Normandy anvil, had disappeared. Of his three campaigns, those in Brittany and Flanders had met misfortune through the death of their principal protagonists. There remained the third, in Aquitaine. It was imperative that it should succeed at once, deprived as it now was of any diversion in the north. When Edward got back from Sluys he learnt with relief that his cousin of Derby had sailed from Southampton three days earlier.

Henry of Derby landed at Bordeaux, where he was anxiously awaited, on Tuesday 9 August 1345. There he renewed acquaintance with those lords of the Bordelais whose loyalty and interest still lay with the *Roi-Duc* and whose retinues were ready at his service: the brothers Bernard and Bérard d'Albret; and Pierre de Grailly, who had married the last heiress of the supreme *Famille de Bordeaux*, together with his son, Jean de Grailly, who, on his mother's death, had attained the title Captal de Buch. Bordeaux was a busy port on the Garonne, a great walled city of some thirty thousand souls, as large as London, with an ancient castle called the Ombrière and the noble Cathédrale Saint-André. With Derby's help, these men would raise Bordeaux, though they did not yet guess as much, from its present dolour to its apogee of fame.

The army of two thousand Derby had brought with him was not a large one, but half of them were longbowmen, whose full significance had not yet penetrated as far as Languedoc, and half of the whole force was mounted. There was not yet a French national army in the neighbourhood to oppose them. Fighting was local and sporadic, the object of each side that of winning over wavering Gascon lordships and of establishing a predominance. For Derby, the essential thing was speed, in case the crumbling loyalty of the duchy should disintegrate entirely.

Within a few days he left Bordeaux with his Gascon allies and sped up the Garonne to join his relative Ralph Stafford, the Seneschal, who was holding the south-eastern approaches to Saint-Macaire. Hearing that the main concentration of the French Gascons under Bertrand, comte de l'Isle, was at Bergerac about fifty miles due east of Bordeaux, he left the Garonne valley, struck out across country, and took them by surprise. Under an unprecedented storm of arrows, and harried by Manny's lightning cavalry charges, the defenders shut themselves up within the ramparts. Derby brought some of his naval transports up the Dordogne from Bordeaux as reinforcements, and on 24 August the comte de l'Isle retreated to La Réole, thirty miles away on the Garonne. Only a fortnight after he had set foot in Aquitaine, the prestigious stronghold of Bergerac was in Derby's hands.

Bergerac commanded the Dordogne, one of the main approaches to Bordeaux. The ease of its capture and the tempo of the attack caused a sensation among the usually slow-moving warriors of the country. It yielded a number of ransomable prisoners and a gratifying amount of plunder. Knighton says that 50,000 marks from Bergerac later went to the building of Derby's manor of the Savoy; others, that a mint of gold was found there. Since the enemy had gone south, Derby left Bergerac in garrison and went north. He skirted Périgueux, on the river Isle, the most northerly of the three rivers leading to Bordeaux. Finding it strongly fortified, he tackled nearby Auberoche where, surprisingly, the gates opened to him without a blow. Here too he left a garrison, in the care of Sir Frank Halle, and retired towards Bordeaux, to Libourne, picking up towns and castles as he passed.

Meanwhile, Duke John of Normandy had been ponderously leading his army home after his *chevauchées* in force and the collection of his homages. On hearing of the fall of Bergerac, he came south again, and when Derby turned away from Périgueux was hovering not far off to the north, while Pierre, duke of Bourbon, was also advancing from the south. Derby had thought it best to slip away before they closed their trap between him and Bordeaux. Encouraged by their approach and by Derby's departure, the comte de l'Isle returned from La Réole and laid leisurely siege to Auberoche. He had brought 'four great engines from Toulouse', so that Sir Frank Halle and his garrison were soon battered into hopeless straits. They sent a messenger to Derby, but the unlucky fellow was caught, searched, loaded into one of the 'great engines', and catapulted back into the streets of Auberoche with his message round his neck, where his remains were viewed with dismay and lamentations by the citizens.

Another messenger successfully reached the earl at Libourne. Derby reckoned that his best chance was to dash for Auberoche and attack de l'Isle before the dukes of Normandy and Bourbon to the north and south could intervene. There was no time to wait for Pembroke and Stafford, who were on detachment duty, but he had Walter Manny with him and his own crack retinue; so he sent word to the others to follow, and set out at top speed.

They arrived undetected at Auberoche and spent Tuesday 21 October 1345 lying up in the woods close behind the camp of the far more numerous but oblivious besiegers. Then, as dusk descended, and the enemy could be seen gathering round the woodsmoke of their fires, they attacked. A hail of arrows fell on the camp from the edge of the wood some two hundred yards away, nice bow-shot range, followed as at Bergerac by a pouring cavalry charge. De l'Isle's knights, all unbuckled in their tents, frantically fastened on their armour. At the height of the slaughter, Frank Halle came down from the castle with his men and joined on Derby's flank. All was soon over; many important lords were taken, including the comte de l'Isle. In the generous custom of the time, Derby personally attended them at dinner in the castle, off their own provisions, before attaching them to ransom to the tune of £50,000. While the good-mannered if exhausted feast was going on, Pembroke arrived in time to have a bite too.

The effects of Auberoche were widespread and immediate. The whole Franco-Gascon army in eastern Aquitaine had been destroyed. Duke John of Normandy pulled off northward almost as far as Tours, where he began to mass a great national army to retrieve the damage in the spring. The duke of Bourbon fell back to winter at Agen, covering Toulouse.

Derby, all danger of interference now removed, went south without delay to attack La Réole on the Garonne, the third valley of access to Bordeaux, which it controlled as effectively as did Bergerac the Dordogne and Auberoche the Isle. The defences of La Réole were thick and strong, so he built two enormous beffrois, movable towers covered in by leather screens, and wheeled them against the walls. While archers on the protected platforms engaged the defenders on the battlements at eye level, a group of miners from the Derbyshire Peak and the Forest of Dean methodically sapped the foundations. The town of La Réole was doomed, and on 2 November was persuaded to surrender upon terms, though the castle held out longer. Meanwhile Ralph Stafford went thirty miles further up river to Aiguillon, strongly sited in the crook formed by the confluence of the Lot with the Garonne. Totally demoralized by the lightning defeats elsewhere, Aiguillon succumbed on about 10 December without resistance.

Derby was by now Henry, earl of Lancaster, since his father, blind old Henry Wryneck, had died on 23 September 1345, in between his son's crashing victories of Bergerac and Auberoche, and had been buried in the Newark, the collegiate church of his new hospital in his favourite town of Leicester. The new earl of Lancaster spent Christmas and the spring of 1346 at La Réole, where his wife, Isabella Beaumont, evidently came to join him, since their daughter Blanche was born early in 1347. Sir Walter Manny, who could not bear inactivity, set out to search for, and apparently found, the bones of his father, who had been murdered there twenty-five years earlier while returning from a pilgrimage to St James of Compostela. He bundled the remains reverently together and conveyed them to their native Valenciennes in Hainault. Earl Henry spent his time more prosaically, pacifying the intermediate districts round about. He did it with tact and delicacy, asking each township simply, without bombast, to return to its obedience to *le Roi-Duc*, and offering concessions on the wine duties if they did so. The result was that many communities readily agreed to such attractive terms and many local jurats accepted remunerative offices in the English service. La Réole was particularly gently treated, as became its ancient and royal associations with the English crown. Only Sir Guiscard d'Angle, at Blaye, north of Bordeaux, still strong in his French loyalty, refused all blandishment, though he too was to end up as tutor to Richard II and as earl of Huntingdon.

The charm and invincibility of *le noble Comte d'Erbi*, as the Gascons continued to call him even if he was now earl and soon to be the first duke of Lancaster, had made him a legend overnight. With a tiny force he had won back in four months all, and more than, it had taken the French eight years insidiously to gain. At the age of thirty-five he had reached the height of his fame and glory, and he thoroughly enjoyed it. For, brilliant diplomat and soldier as he was, he was also human; approachable and sympathetic. While he modestly protests in his devotional memoirs, *Le Livre de Seyntz Medicines*, that, self-taught, he is no author, and being English no great hand at French, a significant disclaimer for one of his rank and date of writing, it becomes plain none the less that he was not only a very perfect knight but a richly human personality.

Tall and fair, he was more than passably accomplished in the 'daunsying chambre'; fond of elegance and the fine rings on his fingers; fond of fox-hunting in Leicestershire; fond of wine 'to put me and my friends out of our senses, for it is a good thing to be merry'; very fond of food, especially salmon; fondest of all of ladies, particularly ladies of the humbler sort because they did not seem to mind him kissing them. For ladies, he admitted, he had sometimes stretched out his stirrups in the lists so they should admire his shapely leg. He did not take himself altogether seriously. His rueful fourteenth-century English fun was as light and clear as the period's stained glass and no less vivid. In all, he confessed as his wholesome motive a 'great desire to be praised, then loved, then lost' (*'Par grant desir d'estre preisez, puis amez, puis perduz'*).[30]

* * *

In February 1346, Duke John of Normandy, after consultations in Paris with King Philip his father, left winter quarters near Tours at the head of a large army, moving south to put paid once and for all to Lancaster and the perennial problem of Aquitaine. The king had ordered powerful national and feudal elements to join him on his march: Raoul, comte d'Eu, and Jean, Lord Tancarville, the Constable and the High Chamberlain of France, and his kinsman Otto IV, duke of Burgundy. All retinues south of the Loire were to muster at Toulouse, where Duke John also found Don Luis of Spain with his mercenary Genoese and a number of siege engines; and at Cahors, for good measure, twenty-four 'crackys' or cannon. Not without difficulty he got his unwieldy forces on the move north-westerly down the Garonne and on 5 April arrived at Agen where Duke Pierre of Bourbon was confronting Lancaster's garrison at Aiguillon, twenty miles further down river.

Contemporary estimates, always wild, place his effective numbers at 100,000. Even if they were no more than 12,000, they were still incomparably larger than the scrappy detachments by whom the fighting in Gascony had so far been conducted, and certainly larger than anything Lancaster could bring against him. Lancaster had, in addition to his original expedition of 2,000, perhaps a somewhat greater number of Anglo-Gascons, though many of them were tied down in their scattered localities. There could be no question of facing Duke John's superiority in the open field. All Lancaster could do was to defend his lately won outposts on the river approaches leading to Bordeaux – Auberoche, Bergerac, Aiguillon, and his own headquarters at La Réole – and wait for *le Roi-Duc* to assist him, for he well knew that diversions were intended for that purpose. In return, he could hope with his small decoy to detain important enemy forces in the south.

Fortunately all four towns were considerable strongholds, strategically sited and thickly walled, and during the winter they had all been strengthened and stocked ready for a siege. Fortunately, too, Duke John had not generalship enough to divide his superabundant forces to attack more than one place at a time. He seemed to think that the mere presence of his imposing, and all-devouring, army would revive the drooping Gascons' French allegiance. It was well known to be Duke John's honourable boast that he never broke his word, so when he announced that he would not leave Aiguillon until it fell to him, Lancaster reinforced it further, and took steps to keep him there for as long as possible. He put Pembroke and

Manny in command, both determined leaders, and remained on call himself at La Réole.

The siege of Aiguillon began in the middle of April. It was soon clear that Duke John had no chance of taking the place by storm, and it became a question of starvation. In this respect his huge conglomeration was a disadvantage and, if anything, the besieged had the better of it. With many fewer mouths to feed, they made determined raids on his commissariat as it drifted down river in barges from Toulouse and on his foragers rounding up cattle in the countryside, seizing the provisions for their own consumption. Lancaster, at La Réole, sometimes found opportunity to run revictualment into Aiguillon, and was always a harassment in the rear of the besiegers.

Meanwhile, in England, the six months since Lancaster's departure had passed quietly. The usual windy exchanges with Pope Clement about peace had continued, but nothing of graver domestic import happened than that Edward, always ready for a flutter on pietistic ventures, licensed a certain John Blome of London, who had had a holy dream, to dig at Glastonbury for the remains of Joseph of Arimathea, traditionally buried thereabouts, in the hope of attracting pilgrims.

The calm was apparent only. On New Year's Day 1346, Edward ordered his navy to concentrate at Portsmouth. Northampton's transports, assembed there the previous year, were still in readiness, and were now joined by the king's fleet, lying at Sandwich since its return from his abortive visit to Flanders in the summer. More ships came in from Dartmouth, Plymouth, Fowey and other western ports, and despite the usual evasions and shortfalls due to lack of money, an Armada began to grow. On 15 March he formally repeated his personal resumption of the war. On 6 April he ordered troops to man the vessels 'for service wherever he might lead them', and thousands of men, on foot or horseback, began to pour on to Southsea Common, and put up their tents and pavilions. He appointed his second son, Lionel of Antwerp, as regent in his absence, since the Prince of Wales, now nearly sixteen, was to go with him. Old Archbishop Stratford was, as usual, to be chief counsellor at home. He entrusted Queen Philippa to young John, earl of Kent, the Fair Maid's brother. William Zouche, the archbishop of York, with Lord Henry Percy, Ralph Neville of Raby, and other northern lords and clergy were made responsible for the Scottish Border. The mayor of London, Geoffrey Wichingham, was to have an ear for careless talk and spies, and to lock offenders up in Newgate. Soon an army of 15,000 men and a navy of 700 sail were gathered at Portsmouth. It was obvious to even the least deductive among King Philip's agents, of whom there must have been quite a number, that the greatest of all expeditions was urgently preparing. The only question was, where for?

It was generally supposed that the king was going to Gascony to rescue his cousin Lancaster. Edward did not discourage the idea; it suited his purpose that the duke of Normandy's great army should continue for the present to be cheaply pinned down in the south. On the contrary, he ordered his bishops to have prayers read publicly throughout the land on 6 May for the success of his forthcoming campaign in Aquitaine.

Would he thus have declared his real intention? Had he, in view of the van Artevelde débâcle, called off his meeting with the Flemings in the north of France? Why, then, had he announced that his Flemish alliance was as sound as ever? It was, moreover, nearly a year since he had taken homage of Godfrey de Harcourt for his confiscated estates at Saint-Sauveur-le-Vicomte in the Cherbourg peninsula. Since then, with an eye to his own restoration, Harcourt had been advertising the advantages of a landing in the fat farmlands of Normandy and his knowledge of the people, with their unwarlike nature, their easy riches, their lack of defences. Remembering Edward Baliol, Robert of Artois and John de Montfort before him, Edward's close attention to Harcourt, another embittered rebel from France, was surely a straw in the wind. When Edward adopted such men he put them to good use. His neutralization of Brittany the previous summer seemed designed to isolate Normandy from the rear. Would he really risk his entire forces on the long journey through the Bay of Biscay, when the whole north coast of France lay open to him just across the Channel? After all, if a landing in the north succeeded, Duke John would be recalled from Aiguillon, and Lancaster would be not only rescued, but set free to continue his conquest of Aquitaine.

Philip clearly had his doubts about Edward's plans. He set his fleet to patrol the Channel, though as he was not able to direct it to defend any particular point on the hundred-mile coast it was too scattered to be of much use. He left Duke John and his army at Aiguillon in case of a further landing at Bordeaux, but in June he recalled to Paris his two royal officers, the comte d'Eu, the Constable, and Lord Tancarville, the Chamberlain, and sent them to Caen, then as always the gateway from Normandy into the heart of France. And he set about the exacting task of raising a second grand army at Paris, for he had been forced into the position where he needed two to make sure of Edward's one. Fortunately for him he had not only his own royal retinue, as well as the feudal *levée en masse* and some 6,000 Genoese mercenaries, but also powerful allied dependants: his brother, the duke of Alençon; his brother-in-law, Charles of Moravia, the new emperor-elect, and his father, blind King John of Bohemia; King James of Majorca, from whom Philip had just bought Montpellier for 100,000 gold crowns; his old pensioner Count Louis of Flanders; and the newly acquired John of Hainault. His army was always augmenting as the summer wore on; when it came to its zenith it may have numbered around 40,000, about three times as many as Edward's.

Edward kept his secret, and his great fleet sailed from Portsmouth with sealed orders to be opened only at sea. The leading vessels seem to have left on 5 July and to have sailed west of Cherbourg to Guernsey, where Godfrey de Harcourt and Reginald Cobham led an assault on Castle Cornet, ending an eight-year occupation by the French with the slaughter of Nicholas Hélie and his garrison. The rest of the expedition, like their successors six centuries later, were held up by bad weather, and they spent an unhappy week tossing about off the Isle of Wight until on 11 July the skies cleared and they made good time to land next day at Saint-Vaast-la-Hougue a few miles north of the latter-day Utah Beach.

Surprise was complete, and there was no resistance at Saint-Vaast. The country people took to the fields, and some warships 'with castles fore and aft' caught floating in the little port were quickly burnt. As usual on great occasions, Edward had taken over the admiralcy from the earl of Warwick. According to Froissart, when his vessel beached, he jumped ashore with such enthusiasm that he stumbled, and sustained a violent nose-bleed, to the consternation of his staff, who begged him to go back on board in the face of so ill an omen. Remembering, perhaps, that similar royal accidents had happened before, notably to Henry II when in his coffin, Edward replied trenchantly, while dabbing at his nose, that on the contrary it showed the land was thirsty to receive him. Having staunched their qualms by his neat *mot*, and his own flow of blood, he briskly turned to business, the knighting of his eldest son, a ceremony that automatically entitled him to a nationwide aid in England. Then the new Sir Edward of Woodstock, Prince of Wales, in his turn duly knighted several of his own young friends. Among them were William Montagu, heir of the late earl of Salisbury and Joan of Kent's official husband; and Roger Mortimer, the grandson of the tyrant, who afterwards married Montagu's sister, Philippa.

The army was now ready to move off. First they cleared the Cotentin peninsula to their rear, a tactical precaution not ignored by their Overlord successors. The soldiers, exuberant as hounds unleashed, raped and plundered, and showed no mercy to the hated Norman 'pirates' who had so often plagued their homes across the Channel. Orchards were stripped. Cattle were herded on to the ships, and wealthy farmers were taken along for possible ransom. Barfleur was sacked, and all its shipping burnt. Pillage continued into the town of Cherbourg, though the castle defied assault.

Harcourt, having landed from Guernsey in the west of the peninsula and marched across through the familiar marshes on his own lands at Saint-Sauveur, came up with them short of Carentan; the town where lately the grinning heads of his executed friends had been exhibited was now razed to the ground 'for all the King could do'. By the time the army reached Saint-Lo, its first fury had spent itself. Edward, still with impeccable technique, turned east, marching in three columns, with his own in the centre, the fleet keeping company to the north along the coast and burning all French shipping on the way. About now he was joined by Sir Thomas Dagworth, coming from Brittany, where he had been left in garrison the year before and which was for the moment peaceful.

At the end of July they came to Caen, historic as the Conqueror's birthplace, a valuable seaport, and the vital point of debouchment into the heart of France, where they met serious resistance from Raoul, comte d'Eu, and Jean, Lord Tancarville, King Philip's Constable and Chamberlain, sent there for the purpose. But the city was unwalled, and apart from Louis of Flanders with a small contingent, no reinforcement from the king in Paris had arrived since Edward's landing. The Constable and the Chamberlain were heavily outnumbered, and after bitter fighting on the river Orne, they found themselves surrounded in the barbican at the bridge's end.

Here, Thomas Holland, Joan of Kent's other, unofficial, husband, had a stroke of luck. No quarter was being given and it was war *à l'outrance*; and the two great French lords looking out from their gatehouse were relieved to see him as he advanced towards them. He was still wearing the silk eye-patch he had vowed always to wear in action nine years earlier, and remembering him as a worthy knight, their old comrade in arms, during intervals of truce, on crusade in Granada and Prussia, they sought protection as prisoners from him and his companion, Sir Peter Leigh.

Holland and Leigh were not at all averse. These high French officers were valuable. They were handed over to the king, who sent them under heavy guard to England. Lord Tancarville, too elderly for the rigours of confinement, fell sick in prison; and though, when peace followed a year later in October 1347, King Philip offered 3,000 golden écus towards his ransom, he died. So Sir Peter Leigh lost much of his reward, and had to make do with lands Edward granted him in compensation.

Raoul, comte d'Eu, the Constable, was more adaptable. In August 1347 he struck a bargain with Edward over his considerable property bordering Calais, lately captured, and bought himself out of the dungeons at the Tower into its more comfortable quarters. Later, during the swinging days of victory he was a debonair figure at the festivities in London; he had a great way with him, especially with the ladies. He took all too well to his kindly treatment by his captors. In September 1348 he allowed himself to be approached by Henry of Lancaster about a truce in Flanders, much in England's favour; and in October 1350 Edward decided much might be gained by sending him back to Paris. But Duke John of Normandy, by now King John the Good, was less cordial than had been hoped. Disenchanted by his Constable's tiresome praises of the English court, and by tales that years before his capture the comte d'Eu had been carrying on with his late duchess, Bonne of Luxemburg, John confronted him with his treasonable letters, flung him into the Tour de Nesle, and had him beheaded two days later.

Fortunately for Thomas Holland he had already, on 16 July 1347, sold outright to Edward his interest in the pliant Constable for the enormous sum of 80,000 florins (about £11,000), as much as Pope Clement paid Joan of Naples for the whole city of Avignon; and so great were Edward's expectations from his high-placed prisoner that the money had been promptly paid.[31] Holland had made his fortune. Now at last he could lay aside his self-depreciating eye-patch, could stand up for himself and speak out boldly. He told the pope all about his early relations with Joan of Kent; of her girlish romance with him, of their secret marriage, and of how she had been given to Montagu against her will while he was away fighting the Holy War and not able to protect her. It was a well-framed application that Clement should, in plain humanity, paternally forgive their peccadillo, and in justice restore Joan to him as her rightful husband.

It is possible that the whole tale was cock-and-bull; that they had simply become lovers quite lately, while Holland was serving as her steward in Montagu's household, and that she was pregnant by him. But Joan stood by it, and Clement, always attentive to wealth, accepted it. He ordered Montagu, who had locked Joan up, to let her out, declared her divorced from Montagu and married to Holland. No one seems much to have cared in the era after Crécy, first so exalted and then so plague-ridden. In a year or so Montagu was married again, to little Elizabeth Mohun; and his subsequent dealings with Joan remained during nearly four decades quite unimpaired. Joan proceeded to bear Holland five children, several of them distinguished, and accompanied him to his important posts abroad, as regent of Brittany, as governor of the Channel Islands, as Captain General in France and Normandy, and finally in his retirement as king's tenant of de Harcourt's former estates at Saint-Sauveur-le-Vicomte, where he died, by then styled in her right, earl of Kent, in 1360. Though that was by no means the end of Joan, who was still only thirty-two.[32]

* * *

To complete the capture of Caen, the English fleet sailed up the river Orne. Its presence was timely, for the spoil the soldiers had by now collected was immense. Even apart from the wine, which they mostly drank, it was far more than they could carry. There were also prisoners, for in response to Harcourt's pleading for his Norman countrymen, Edward stopped the indiscriminate massacre and rape. Plunder, prisoners, and the sick were loaded up. With the document they had unearthed in Caen proving the French plans to invade England in 1338, they sailed, in the care of William de Clinton, earl of Huntingdon, himself a casualty, for home, where the ships and sailors were badly needed for their workaday affairs.

Edward's advance continued. On 6 August 1346, a week after leaving Caen, he had covered a further sixty miles and was approaching the Seine between Rouen and Paris. On the news of his landing, Philip had meanwhile bestirred himself, by no means over-hurriedly, from his country château of Bécoiseau and returned to Vincennes east of Paris. The mood in the capital was alarmed. Here was no vague threat on distant borders as at Tournai or at Vannes; Edward was marching rapidly through the heart of France, and possibly on Paris. Philip's duty to protect his subjects compelled him to confront the invader. He put himself at the head of his army, drew out from the abbey of Saint-Denis the Oriflamme, the Crusaders' sacred banner promising no quarter, and on 2 August reached Rouen, eighty miles away to the north-west athwart Edward's line of march on the Seine, here three hundred yards across.

Now, for the first time, Edward had a chance to measure what he was up against, and he had to make a crucial decision. He was, unexpectedly, within striking distance of an undefended Paris, and the temptation to go at once for that glittering prize was very great; for as General Zeitzer observed when discussing the Allied reconquest of Western Europe in 1944, 'It was clear to us that their primary objective must be Paris, for history has proved that he who has Paris, has France', and it was probably even more true in those feudal times than now.[33] On the other hand it was expected that as soon as Edward had shown his hand in Normandy, Duke John would raise his siege of Aiguillon and hurry north. Edward had foreseen and indeed counted on this; for to rescue Lancaster in Aquitaine, not Paris, had been his first objective. As it happened, Philip had so far shown a haughty disdain for Edward's impudent invasion, and refused to oblige him by giving up the promising stranglehold Duke John had established in the south so long as he thought he could deal with the northern threat himself. It was only now, when his very throne was in the balance, that he recalled his son to his assistance. Duke John did not leave Aiguillon until 20 August and would not reach Paris before September. But Edward could not know that; he had to assume that the duke was already on his way, and might appear in the Ile-de-France at any moment. To get caught up in a siege of Paris, between the great armies of Philip to the north and his son John to the south, would be disastrous.

Alternatively, Edward could go straight for Philip, and fight him in or near Rouen before John arrived. Apparently with that in mind, he altered course sharply to the north. When, however, he reached the Seine at Elbeuf only twelve miles from Rouen, he found the bridge destroyed; and Godfrey de Harcourt, who had been scouting ahead, reported back, after a stiff brush with his elder brother in the suburbs, with disturbing news of the odds they would be facing in a direct attack upon the city.

To tempt Philip to break cover, and as an extra inducement in case he had not yet recalled the duke from Aiguillon, Edward turned south up the Seine, feinting towards Paris. Philip, as intended, followed him out from Rouen into open country, but coasted doggedly on the north bank; all the bridges separating them were broken down or strongly held, and he showed no inclination to give battle. On 13 August they arrived, side by side, the river between, at Poissy, a charming royal retreat, the birth-place of St Louis, lying on Edward's side of the serpentine bends of the Seine less than twenty miles from Paris. It contained many noble buildings, among them a fine modern palace Philip had just completed, adjoining an ancient and high-class convent where his sister, no doubt the good and gracious Lady Jeanne de Valois, late of the no less venerable abbey of Fontaine-au-Tertre, was prioress.

Partly out of respect for royal privacy, partly because until a few days before, sylvan Poissy had seemed far removed from any possible violence, its defences had been neglected. It was unwalled, and its bridge was still intact; it was the last bridge, as Philip knew and Edward did not, leading directly to the capital, before the river swept away in a big loop to the north. Edward on the south bank could go straight on into the city. To get there first, Philip must abandon his watch on the north bank and cross now, or else he must make a long detour. When he marched out to Rouen he had deserted Paris, where panic was now growing. The enemy were almost at the gates, and he had no word that his son was yet approaching from the south. Philip lost his nerve. He raced ahead of Edward, crossed Poissy bridge, ordered its instant destruction, swept up his sister and her Dominican maidens from their convent, and rode on into Paris.

That settled it. Philip was in greater strength than had been expected, and by re-entering his Paris fortress he had castled, as in a game of chess. Edward had never intended to attack him there; he had hoped to bring him to battle in the open, and in that he had not succeeded. He must now resume his march towards his Flemish allies away to the north-east. After van Artevelde's death, Flanders had become for the time an urbanocracy, but the 'three towns', Ghent, Bruges and Ypres, were still in revolt against their French count Louis of Nevers; and on 24 June, before he sailed, they had confirmed they would honour their engagement with Edward. On 16 July, four days after Edward landed in Normandy, Hugh Hastings and Sir John Maltravers had brought six hundred English archers to their assistance, and on 2 August the combined force under Sir Henry of Flanders had set out south-westward from Ypres in his direction.

It was far from being the massive thrust Edward had once proposed to lead in person with van Artevelde at his side, but it might be strong enough to brush past the garrison opposition it was likely to encounter. His allies were already on the move, and it was dangerous to change plans when they could not be informed. He might yet meet them as arranged, though to do so he would have to get his cumbrous expedition over two formidable intervening water barriers. With luck, he would draw Philip in pursuit, and so hustle and string out his columns before rounding on him at the head of a much increased Anglo-Flemish army with the safety of Flanders at its back. It was possible. While Philip was flustered and confused in Paris,

Edward would slip across the Seine and make for the Somme with all speed.

At Poissy, examination showed that, though the central span of the bridge was broken, a single beam remained. Northampton managed to scramble over it, and formed a bridgehead on the further bank, where he beat off heavy attacks both from Paris and by auxiliaries hastily called in from as far as Amiens to defend the capital. Edward, who had with him bridging equipment and the necessary craftsmen – the great mason Henry Yevele, later in his prime to build the naves of Canterbury and Westminster, and indeed Edward's own tomb there, may have been in their number – set them to mend it sufficiently for the crossing of his heavy transport. It took them only three days to do it. Philip knew of course that the bridge was being mended, but it did not mean that Edward might not use it to encircle Paris, where the anxiety of the citizens, not devoid of criticism of himself, kept him on edge; a state Edward encouraged by sending out the Prince of Wales and other eager youngsters to exercise themselves in burning the suburbs at Saint-Germain-en-Laye, Saint-Cloud and right up to the walls at Petit Boulogne, so that the fires could be seen from the centre of the city.

While Philip was dashing from one side of Paris to another and ordering narrow penthouses to be destroyed to avoid a general conflagration, Edward at Poissy made the most of his plush surroundings, living in Philip's palaces and drinking up his best wines. On 15 August, the Feast of the Assumption, he piously proclaimed a holiday to rest his men for the extreme effort they were about to make, and kept state in his travelling regalia, a sleeveless scarlet tippet furred with ermine. At last, Philip, either to save Paris from apparently impending devastation or more probably to persuade his critics that he would not brook such insolence, challenged him to a pitched battle outside the walls, at any time or place of Edward's choosing. But by the time Edward declined, on the 17th, he was across the Seine and racing away, dead straight due north for the Somme. Philip regathered his army at Saint-Denis and set off after him on the 18th, two whole days behind.

Edward moved fast. His orders against rape and plunder, though in force since the first days of the landing, had so far been exuberantly ignored. There was no time now for such distractions, and at Beauvais, where his men broke off to raid the abbey, he had twenty of them hanged. At Poix, two mannerly knights, John Chandos and Ralph Basset, came upon two pretty girls, daughters of the lord of Poix, cringing in the castle, and to save them from their certain fate brought them before the king. Edward had them to dinner, and asked them kindly where they wished to go. They said to Corbie; and though Corbie was thirty miles distant in enemy country, he had them taken there. It was a courtesy ill-requited. Next morning after the king had left, the citizens of Poix, who had agreed to pay indemnity, fell on his assessors as they went about their duty. But the assessors had their armour on below their fustian habits; a fight developed. Reginald Cobham and Thomas Holland, in charge of the rearguard since they had been wounded ten days before just short of Poissy, turned back and exacted fearful retribution.

On 21 August Edward reached Airaines, midway between Abbeville and Amiens, five miles short of the Somme, and only about fifty miles from Béthune, where the Flemings lay. Once over the river he could hope to meet them in a day or two. But that same evening Philip arrived at Amiens. After covering a phenomenal seventy miles in three days he had caught up, was astride the Somme ahead of Edward, and less than twenty miles away. Philip was no longer fully in command. He was being rushed along like a floating straw by his impetuous lords, their pride blazing, their blood up, hunting down a desperate quarry.

Next day Warwick tested all along the swampy valley of the Somme between the strong towns of Abbeville and Amiens. He could find no crossing, and also reported a skirmish with the vanguard of the king of Bohemia's German cavalry. The enemy knew their whereabouts and were in close pursuit. There was nothing for it but to skirt wide to the west round Abbeville and try to cross down river in the last broad stretch of the estuary before it ran into the sea. Edward left Airaines hurriedly, in the early morning – so hurriedly that the French, coming up an hour or two behind, found meat cooking, and provisions and casks of wine all strewn around. Later that day he was at Acheux, having passed by Abbeville safely and returned to about five miles from the Somme.

There were no further bridges below Abbeville, and the estuary as it neared the sea was almost two miles wide. Many supplies had been lost, and the men were hungry, munching the green fruit ripening in the orchards. Edward was now in the heart of his own province of Ponthieu, but he had no knowledge of the country and he had no guide. He was in imminent danger of being trapped by a larger and more mobile army with the choice of a friendless sea or an impassable river at his back. He did as he had done when lost in Scotland nearly twenty years before, offered reward in return for information, only this time the offer was made not to his own men but to country fellows he had rounded up; and, to be fair to the hostages, in the circumstances it was probably made more persuasive by lurid menaces of the penalty for non-compliance. One, Gobin Agache, ingratiatingly revealed that there was a ford midway down the estuary where the water, though deep enough at full tide to float heavy shipping, became so shallow at the ebb as to be no more than knee high, and its broad, firm, gravelly bottom gleamed white, giving it its name of Blanchetaque. Edward marched off in the middle of the night, and at dawn on the 24th his army formed up at the entrance to the ford at Saigneville where they had to wait precious hours for the tide to fall.

Philip had guessed that Edward might find out about this last line of escape and had set Sir Godemar du Fay, a Norman knight, to guard the crossing while he was covering the eighteen miles from Airaines to come up in the rear. As the English waited, Godemar duly appeared on the distant further shore. He had imposing numbers with him, but their quality was doubtful. He had to hold Abbeville as well as Blanchetaque and Le Crotoy on the sea, and so, though he had a good force of Genoese archers and some men-at-arms on horseback, tell-tale glimpses of white peasants' smocks indicated a large bucolic element in his rank and file, armed with little more than pitchforks.

At low tide, Hugh Despenser, son of Hugh the younger, led the leading archers into the water, followed by the king and his whole army, with the drays and waggons. The footing was good, and for the first mile and a half there was no danger until they came within range of the Genoese cross-bows on the other bank. The English archers while wading in the deeper water had to carry their bows above their heads to keep them dry, and at first suffered casualties; but as they came out into the shallows they answered arrow for arrow, and as usual had the better of it. They made way to let the cavalry pass through; French knights of the locality, well versed in this form of water-sports in their aqueous countryside, dashed in to attack them, and there was a muddled, splashing conflict. Once ashore, the English horse made short work of the opposing rank and file who, in a storm of arrows, broke and ran, Northampton chasing and killing them up to the gates of Abbeville. Hugh Despenser meanwhile turned the other way, down to the river mouth at Le Crotoy, where in accordance with routine he burnt the shipping and came back with a welcome booty of food and wine.

By now, leading elements of the king of Bohemia's cavalry had reached the ford at Saigneville and destroyed a few last English units waiting their turn to cross. But by the time Philip arrived with his main army the tide was up. His elusive enemy had escaped him like the Jews in the Red Sea. He had no choice but to turn back to Abbeville and hope to rediscover them further north. Philip had two pressing worries. Owing to the extraordinary, and perhaps on his part involuntary, speed of his advance from Paris, his infantry had been left behind, straggling along far back down the road past Amiens. They were hobbling up in bits and pieces, worn out and in no kind of order, as Edward had intended when he set so stiff a pace. Edward counted that when it came to battle, his knights, dismounted, and his archers, in prepared positions, would inflict crippling shocks on unsupported cavalry. As it was, Philip did not yet even have all his cavalry. He was still expecting young Amadeus VI, the Green Count of Savoy, sprightly sovereign of the order of the Snares of Love, who owed him a thousand lances, already paid for in advance.[34] He could not wait for him. Either he must attack at once, or, if he paused to marshal his forces, risk losing

Edward altogether. Left to himself, he might have welcomed the second course; but that would not carry with his allies.

Therein lay Philip's second weakness. His huge army was cosmopolitan, comprising Germans, Bohemians, Genoese, Savoyards, Hainaulters, Franco-Flemings, Bretons, and various breeds of French who, if they did not entirely hate, did not know or trust each other. Their opponents were fewer but coherent, long accustomed to their own company and foibles, and to those of their king and leader. That night, before they left Abbeville on what was to prove for many of them a fatal day, Philip gave a dinner for his assorted kings and princes, and exhorted them to mutual forbearance; to prudence and restraint. His wise words fell on deaf ears. Angered by the indignity of the failure at Blanchetaque, his followers would not heed them.

Over the Somme, Edward released Gobin Agache and his relieved companions, who rode off his not very creditable page of history on a fine new horse and clutching a bag of gold. To Edward's disappointment, his scouts could find no trace of Hugh Hastings, or Maltravers or Henry of Flanders with their Flemings. The Flemings had in fact been held up for the last ten days at Béthune, and not knowing the closeness of Edward's whereabouts had, on the 24th, the very day of Blanchetaque, fallen back to the river Lys. Edward decided not to exhaust his troops in searching for them further, but to form up and face his over-eager enemy alone.

On the 25th, Edward laid up his men to rest in Crécy forest while he chose a suitable field of battle. After early Mass next morning, on Saturday 26 August 1346, his army, refreshed and full of confidence after the miracle of Blanchetaque, emerged from the north side of the forest and settled into a familiar position as naturally as a foetus in its womb; on foot between Crécy and Wadicourt, cresting a rise sloping gently down the way the enemy must come, their horses corralled by the waggons in a wood behind them. Each pikeman had his own spear's length of room, each archer a bundle of spare arrows to stick in the ground before him. They were ranged in three formations. The right, towards Crécy, was commanded by the sixteen-year-old Prince of Wales in the personal care of Harcourt and Sir John Chandos, and with the experienced earl of Warwick to advise him, divided by impassable broken ground from Northampton on the left. Each division was flanked at both ends by a projecting wedge of archers; and in reserve, close behind, was the king with his third battle. Everyone of note was there, except Henry of Lancaster and those with him in Aquitaine. They were meticulously reviewed by Edward, riding up and down on a white palfrey, a short white wand in hand. Then, since there was no sign of the enemy, they took off their helmets, laid their arms down in their places, fell out, ate a meal, stowed away the cooking implements, relieved themselves, talked, spat, and gambled about their prospects. The event was to surpass their wildest dreams.

Philip left Abbeville early to cover the twelve miles, a good day's march, to Crécy field. The Green Count of Savoy and others had come in during the night, and droves of country militia joined the columns by day. The roads were jammed. There was rivalry for the lead, contingents were all mixed up and there was no chance to form battle order. Four senior knights rode out and surveyed the English, now standing to their arms, ominously alert and motionless. It was getting late, and Philip's men were tired. He called a halt until the morning. But his commanders suspected shilly-shallying, as at Buironfosse and Vannes. No more of that, they thought, and took no notice. That first disobedience was their downfall. Their cause was lost. At about five o'clock, the whole rout poured down what is still called the Chemin de l'Armée into the valley of the Maye and raggedly deployed half left, rank behind rank, towards the silent enemy on the ridge above them.

Whatever the French may say, there is no need to doubt any of the favourite traditional stories about Crécy. There really was an afternoon rainshower, and the English did scurry to protect their precious bow-strings. The French did attack on horseback in overwhelming numbers, time after time, with enormous gallantry, but pell-mell and uphill, contrary to orders, after a fatiguing march and into the August sunset. Cannon did roar, 'devilish engines', as Dr Barnes says, 'managed by Persons of no Force or Courage', sending their missiles, hardly bigger than cricket balls, bounding down the hill to add, as much by their noise as anything else, to the confusion of the Genoese who, paid professionals as they were, had been sent in to open the battle with their crossbows, only to be trampled down as they fell back by the huge French destriers thundering up behind them.

The Prince of Wales was, in truth, thrown to the ground by Alençon's charge, and his standard bearer, Richard de Beaumont, did stand over him, sheltering his body with the banner of Wales. The king's command post was indeed in the famous windmill. And, when Harcourt sent urging him to commit his reserve to save his son, though there is no proof that he replied 'Let the boy win his spurs', he may well have done so. When the day was lost, the blind King John of Bohemia did demand to be led into the thick of the battle, and he was found next morning, dead, with his reins still fastened to the bridles of his devoted escorts. The prince did wear black armour, and the blind king's ostrich plumes did then and there become his badge.

Darkness spread mercy on the carnage. The archers could no longer see to shoot. Gradually, silence returned, except for the ring of desultory clashes where desperate men, many of them Germans, were still fighting for their lives; and except for groans and cries from the terrible valley out in front.

King Philip had been twice unhorsed, and twice wounded, in the thigh and in the neck. His standard bearer had been killed before his eyes, and the muddied Oriflamme would have been lost had not a resourceful knight ripped it from its shaft, wrapped it around his body under his surcoat, and galloped from the field. Lord John of Hainault found the king wandering bewildered, remounted him, and led him away by a devious route. At Labroye, when the frightened garrison demanded who it was who expected to be let in so late at night, Philip answered, 'Open quickly, for I am the fortune of France.'

He was right. No nation could afford the cost of a captured king. So well was it realized, that his apt escape was thankfully known as 'la Beau Retracte'. After a few hours' rest, he hurried back to Amiens, where he took leave of his surviving leaders, John of Hainault and the count of Namur; his brother-in-law Charles, emperor elect, now king of Bohemia; and the new Count Louis of Flanders, both of whom had lost their fathers in the battle. He lay at Amiens for some days, threatening to execute Godemar du Fay for failing to hold Blanchetaque, and the Genoese for supposed cowardice in battle. He then retired to his manor at Pont-Sainte-Maxence in the forest north of Paris, where in October his son John, at last back from Aquitaine, tried in his bluff and pious way to lift his parent's dreadful gloom.

There was no pursuit. Edward, who did not yet know the magnitude of his victory, had no intention of letting his army vanish into the night in a mad race after ransoms. He came down from his windmill and had great watchfires lit. His men, who had never stirred from their positions, not even to retrieve arrows, not even to make the most tempting captures (no prisoners had been taken), stood obediently to arms or went blessedly to sleep.

Sunday morning dawned in dismal fog. The roll was called; English losses were miraculously light.[35] Reginald Cobham and Thomas Holland, staff officers of the reserve, went down with heralds to identify the French dead by their blazons, in the valley still known as the Vallée aux Clercs. They worked all day, and their tally was impressive; 1,542 persons of quality, all mounted, about one in eight of those who had been engaged. They included King John and the count of Flanders; Philip's brother, the duke of Alençon; Philip's nephew Guy of Blois, elder brother of Charles of Blois of Brittany; Ralph, duke of Lorraine, another royal nephew; and John, earl of Harcourt, Godfrey's brother. King James of Majorca, who was not noticed for valour in the battle, seems to have escaped, only to die fighting the king of Aragon some years later.

The bodies were methodically stripped of valuables, and the spoil divided fairly between the soldiers. The wounded were cared for by the monks of Crécy Grange. Most of the dead, and their horses, were buried in great pits where they lay, and the whole battlefield was blessed, while the more illustrious were given holy ground at Maintenay. Edward and the

Black Prince attended the king of Bohemia's funeral in solemn mourning and with suitably regretful mien. If truth be told, the old campaigner (he was fifty) had not always been the flower of patient chivalry he is commonly made out to be. Once, enraged with an unfortunate doctor who had failed to cure his eyesight, he had him stitched up in a sack and thrown into the river Oder.

Northampton, Arundel and Suffolk had gone out with powerful mounted forces to look for important wanderers, and in particular for the king of France. They did not find him. Instead, they encountered, one after the other, two great bodies of French militia, left behind on the march, hurrying up from as far back as Rouen and Beauvais. They had no idea that all was already over, and in the fog mistook their enemies for their friends. They had no chance. The rule was still no quarter. The Grand Prior of France and the archbishop of Rouen were killed, and the losses among their followers were enormous, le Bel says four times as many as those in the main battle. This seems to confirm that the French at Crécy were almost entirely cavalry since the foot had not arrived. Except for the Genoese who had fought at Blanchetaque and were already in the neighbourhood, no French infantry were mentioned in the action. Edward in his dispatch, and his chaplain Richard Wynkeley, both speak only of 12,000 mounted men at arms, and no count was made of common soldiers fallen on the field. Not that it made much difference to the common soldiers whether they died on that day or the next.

The question for Edward was to what use he could put his victory. In retrospect he may have regretted his earlier decision to go on to meet the Flemings, sound though it was at the time he made it. He never did meet them, and there was no point in doing so now. Had he fought and won his victory south of Rouen, he could have entered Paris, perhaps killed or captured Philip, and won the war at a blow. As it was, he was now too far away. His army was tired, Duke John must certainly be near the capital, and supplies were running low. What he most needed, both for his immediate wants and for the continuation of the war, was a strong port as close as possible to England. On the Tuesday, three days after his great triumph, he left his shattered enemy behind him and marched north up the coast road for Calais.

* * *

At no time in the past had Calais been English, not even in the greatest days of the Normans and Angevins. Edward's predecessors had paid little attention to it. With its spacious natural basin, it had been for centuries a quiet fishing port and, because of its marshy hinterland and general inaccessibility, a lair for pirates until, a hundred years before Edward's time, the count of Boulogne in whose domains it lay had developed its strategic possibilities. Since then it had grown considerably and become comparable in importance to Plymouth or even Bristol. It boasted a double curtain of walls and a double dyke, enclosing a gaunt citadel on the west side of the town. It was fully provisioned, and strongly garrisoned under a brave Burgundian, Sir John de Vienne, a veteran of French expeditions to Scotland. His brusque rejection of Edward's formal challenge to surrender left no doubt that it would be well defended.

Edward wanted Calais for several reasons. In the short term he wanted it as an autonomous staple for English trade, not dependent on the vagaries of Brabant, Flanders or other unreliable customers; and as a handy lodgment for the renewal of the war, easy to extend since it was near the disputed territories of his dead friend Robert of Artois, whose nephew, Robert of Namur, had lately joined him. It was not far, either, from his own royal patrimony of Ponthieu; and across the marshes to the south it faced the castle of Guînes, the property of his prisoner, Raoul, comte d'Eu, with whom he was opening hopeful negotiations. Chiefly, however, Edward wanted it as a tangible monument, one almost visible from the cliffs of Dover, to his glorious if territorially unfruitful campaign, and as a permanent insult to the French.

Its strength did not deter him. It would be months before Philip could come to its aid. He had plenty of time; and if it proved hard to win it would be equally hard to lose. Indeed, once captured, Calais was, though at burdensome cost, to remain English through the changing fortunes of two whole centuries until finally lost by ineptitude in the reign of Mary Tudor who, when she died, was sure, as every schoolchild once knew, that the word 'Calais' would be found written on her heart. In much later times, in the worst days of 1940, the embers of its English heritage rekindled an inspired resistance.

As his army swung along northward up the sandy coastal road of the Pas-de-Calais, past Boulogne and Wissant, Edward prepared for a lengthy siege. On 1 September he called back William de Clinton, earl of Hunting-don, and Sir John Montgomery, with the fleet, to blockade the harbour mouth and to bring siege engines, all the cannon in the Tower, and building equipment of every kind. On arrival on 4 September, however, he found that though Calais was easy to encircle, its terrain was unsuitable for a bombardment and it must be reduced by famine only. Impassable swamps to the south offered no footing for his cannon, though that flank could be safely watched by outposts on scattered islands of solid ground. Eastwards towards Dunkirk and westward to Cap Gris-Nez, deep pow-dery sand dunes swept away out of sight along the shore. He made contact with his Flemish allies, who moved forward to Saint-Omer and controlled the eastern approaches up to the sea at Gravelines. That left only the route he had just come by from the west as the vulnerable quarter to be guarded.

In that direction there was a convenient spit of firm land about a mile square immediately below the citadel, bounded by the town walls to the east, the sea to the north, the marshes to the south, and on the west by the river Hem; the only crossing of the river was at the bridge of Nieulay in the south-west corner of the rectangle so formed. Here, when materials arrived, Edward began to build not merely a camp but a wooden town, Villeneuve-le-Hardi, or 'Nouville' to the English soldiery, to shelter his army during the coming winter, complete with streets and commodious state buildings enclosing a large square in the centre. Villeneuve-le-Hardi, though as soon as Calais fell it was to be accidentally swept away by fire, was at the time a wonder, the first complex of its kind; its progress was watched probably as keenly by the bored defenders on the city walls as by its future occupants. About 10 September, Queen Philippa left England to join the king, and went to stay in Ypres with her sister, the dowager Empress Margaret, until apartments were ready for her. This evidently happened at the end of November, for she arrived at Calais with a bevy of court ladies three days before All Saints' Day, and during the scenes of wild rejoicing and reunion she no doubt declared the place officially open in time for the magnificent Christmas celebrations soon to follow.

Provisions had been scarce at first, no less for the besiegers than for their victims. Michael de Northburgh, the king's confessor and secretary, writing home on 14 September, said that for the first time since leaving Caen, where the fleet had separated, 'now as the case stands we partly need your help to be refreshed with victuals'. That state of affairs was quickly altered. Edward arranged for regular markets to be held twice weekly in the square. They were well attended by neighbouring farmers, who welcomed them as a civilized alternative to constant armed raids on their country fairs at Thérouanne and elsewhere. Before long, a mouth-watering trade was thriving under the hungry gaze of the Calaisians.

In the early stages their situation was not desperate, for though Calais was surrounded on the landward side, the same was not true of the sea. As usual, the fleet took some time to carry out its orders, and at first only a rudimentary blockade could be maintained by Flemish vessels. The harbour was wide, and even after the English ships arrived the local fishermen, notably two, Marant and Mestreil of Abbeville, were not only adept at running supplies into the town at night but most annoyingly bored holes in English hulls below the water line. Edward had breakwaters built out from the beaches to prevent them hugging the shallows at high tide, and put soldiers aboard the ships. He also began a strong stone tower, Fort Risban, to dominate the main harbour channel, but it was many months before it was ready for use. As late as April the next year a large French convoy broke through and supplied the town, though a similar enterprise two months later was intercepted and destroyed.

In the beginning, Edward's attitude towards his proposed new colonial subjects was conciliatory. On 13 September, when Sir John de Vienne sought to pass out seventeen hundred *bouches inutiles*, he not only let them through but gave them a square meal and twopence a head to help them on their way. As time passed, however, his mood towards their obstinacy stiffened. Later on, a second application was ignored, and five hundred wretches were left wandering in misery outside the walls. By the spring of 1347, disease, especially dysentery, was rampant in both camps; desertions were frequent on the English side, and the condition of the beleaguered citizens was grim. When the place fell at last it was progressively depopulated. Many of the survivors died from eating too ravenously the food sent in to them, while the remainder, except for a necessary cadre of officials, were driven out to Guînes and left to the charity of their own king, who, be it said, did the best he could for them. Their property was divided up between Warwick, Manny, Ralph Stafford, Henry of Lancaster, and other prominent English officers, who thus acquired 'a competent portion of houses they never built, and of lands they never purchased, that so they might be obliged to people and defend the town'. All wealth and riches were locked up in one place, and much of them used to disperse the Flemings, who came thronging round like jackals. Proclamation was made for prosperous London families to emigrate on promise of easy rents and privileges, while humbler artisans and labourers crossed the straits from Kent. Before 1347 was out, a new society of English settlers had taken over the empty town, with Sir John Montgomery as its first captain, though he and his wife died in the Black Death soon afterwards.

Meanwhile, as the siege continued, and unpopular posting though it was, English spirits were buoyed up by a succession of good news of the unexpectedly widespread though natural consequences of the great victory of Crécy. In Aquitaine, the belated and not unharassed departure of Duke John from Aiguillon on 20 August 1346 had enabled Lancaster to resume his interrupted recovery of the duchy. The Agenais and the east had already been regained. To the south-east he sent his Anglo-Gascon allies, the d'Albrets and others, up the Garonne to push back the old border and spread dismay in French territory almost to Toulouse. That left the north. On 12 September Lancaster set out northward from La Réole at the head of a small fast-moving force of something over a thousand mounted men and archers. There was little opposition except from solitary garrisons, such as that of the resolute Guiscard d'Angle, who had moved up from Blaye to Niort and successfully defied him. It was really a victory march, la belle chevauchée as Lancaster himself described it, with a political more than a military object. It entirely succeeded. The lightning speed of his advance and the vast distances he covered, coupled with his already stupendous reputation, made it seem to his demoralized opponents and his stunned countrymen alike an irresistible and scorching conquest.

Forcing a crossing of the Charente at Châteauneuf, Lancaster left old ducal territory and headed through Saintonge for Poitou, realms of the king of France which had owed no English allegiance for a hundred years.

In enemy country he was very much the warlord. Ransoms were heavy, terms were strict; he left no doubt that everyone was at his mercy. He hurried forward to Saint-Jean-d'Angély and sternly exacted the release of the retinue of Sir Walter Manny, who had lately been flung into prison there; though with his usual resource Manny himself had managed to escape, it had not been without 'great trouble'. The story later went, according to Froissart, for whom, as a fellow Hainaulter, Manny was his hero, that after the fall of Aiguillon Manny had induced Duke John to give him a safe conduct across the length of France so that he could join his king in Normandy; he had then been perfidiously seized, and after a stirring encounter with King Philip in person, had duly arrived before Calais to the astonishment and delight of Edward. Though what, if he was heading for Calais, Manny was doing so far west as Saint-Jean-d'Angély is not clear; and afterwards he seems to have stayed on in Aquitaine for as long as Lancaster. Most likely he had rashly strayed too far ahead of the advance.

Poitiers on its forbidding promontory, though poorly garrisoned, had to be taken by storm. It was the capital of Poitou, and its people, rich and sullen and profoundly French in sympathy, resisted. Lancaster's troops had covered two hundred miles since starting from La Réole only three weeks before, and during eight days at this, his furthest point of penetration, they had their head. There was slaughter and pillage, rape and fire. Pope Clement complained of the robbery of churches, and demanded compensation for his clergy. The phial of miraculous holy oil given to St Thomas Becket by the Virgin Mary, and later used by Lancaster's grandson to sanctify his illicit coronation as Henry IV, was said to have been part of the treasure. When the men left for home they were so laden with riches 'that they made no account of cloths unless they were of gold or silver', or, curiously, 'of feathers'.[36]

By contrast, the returning sojourn at Saint-Jean-d'Angély was all smiles. While his officers made good permanent defences on the old line of the Charente, Lancaster dropped his ferocious mien, drank the native cognac, and gave banquets for the ladies of the town, who said he was the noblest prince that ever mounted steed. At the end of October he was back in Bordeaux after a crowded seven weeks, and on New Year's Day 1347 he arrived in England, in close company with Pembroke and with Manny. There were fresh orders for him from the king, to relinquish Aquitaine and help the Black Prince, now at home, in raising a new army, lately released from other tasks, for Calais, where an attack by King Philip was expected. He sailed in May, and was given the vital command at Nieulay bridge, where he remained for the duration of the siege.

As soon as he reached London, Lancaster paid a visit to an important new prisoner in the Tower, David, king of Scotland, whose presence there was due to a further feat of English arms in the *annus mirabilis* of 1346. When Edward landed in Normandy, Philip had called on his old Scottish allies to invade England while her strength was dissipated overseas. He had supplied men and money, and in spite of clan dissensions, even before Crécy the Scots had been ravaging across the Border. It was an obvious plan, with a fair chance of success given a good leader. But David had none of the rough cunning of his father the great Bruce, or the brilliance of the Black Douglas. Since he came back from the comfort of Château-Gaillard he had turned out a weak and profligate young man. The last of the pre-Stuarts, he was the first of Scotland's long and disastrous royal line of spoilt romantic exiles.

On news of the French disaster, and thinking that Edward might return from Calais at any moment, he decided to take his fleeting opportunity. He rallied his squabbling chieftains, and in October crossed the Border at the head of his whole army, raided Lanercost and appeared at Durham. Defence of the North had long been among the pastoral cares of the archbishops of York, and the present incumbent, William Zouche, the former unsatisfactory Treasurer who had been put there, much to Edward's indignation, by the pope, now gamely took the field with his brother bishops Kirkeby of Carlisle and Beck of Lincoln (Hatfield of Durham was in France and had been at Crécy), and with a great number of lesser though equally stout-hearted clergy. Thanks to Edward's foresight the heavenly arm was strengthened by powerful Marcher lords, Henry Percy of Northumberland, the Nevilles of Raby, Ross of Hamlake, Edward Baliol the pretender, as well as others sent home from Calais, and by the northern levies. Even so, the prospects were bad. If the Scots broke through there was nothing to stop them north of the Trent. Indeed, the monks of Durham, who had found it advisable to settle in advance with the Scots for £1,000 indemnity, sang the army out with a dismal *Miserere* as it went off to do battle at Neville's Cross on 17 October 1346.

Unaccountably, the day went well. The English archers made havoc among the massed Scottish schiltrons. The monks of Durham, now ranged on the tower of their great cathedral, their purses saved, changed their chant to a *Te Deum*. Robert the Steward, David's nephew and heir-presumptive, who became the first Stuart king on David's death in 1371, was much older than David and vastly superior in experience. He was all for retiring while there was time. David, who resented him, pressed on with the attack only to finish up alone, unarmed and wounded in the head. Realizing the implications for his country, he tried to escape, but a Northumberland squire, John Copeland, recognized him. David resisted violently, striking his assailant in the face with his steel gauntlet and knocking out two teeth, but he was overpowered. Other Scottish losses were catastrophic. The Holy Rood again changed hands and was hung in Durham cathedral. The earls of Monteith and Fife, taken prisoner, were later tried and condemned for treason in London. Fife was spared, as a cousin of David, but Monteith underwent the gruesome punishment.

John Copeland played his good fortune carefully – too carefully, many thought. He took his royal prisoner off to his own castle, nursed him watchfully, and refused to give him up to anyone except at the express command of the king at Calais. At last he obeyed orders to hand him over to Sir Thomas Rokeby, whom, as a youth years before, Edward had honoured for discovering the enemy on the Border and who was now, in his wealthy prime, High Sheriff of Yorkshire. At the year's end, David was conveyed to London, where he was met by the mayor and aldermen, and rode on a great black horse through wide-eyed crowds to the Tower. Copeland, rewarded not over-graciously by other standards of the time, was made knight-banneret with an annuity of £500.

In the new year, 1347, Charles of Blois started another distraction in Philip's favour, in Brittany, where uneasy and unusual quiet had lasted since he had departed for Aiguillon, and his opponent Sir John Dagworth for Normandy, the previous summer. Dagworth was now shipped back secretly from Calais to deal with him *coup de main*. Blois, thinking himself alone in the field, laid leisurely siege to Roche-Derrien, Northampton's recent conquest, which he bombarded with huge stones, to the terror of its captain's wife as she lay in childbed. During the brief darkness of the night of 20 June, Dagworth, taking a leaf from Lancaster's book at Auberoche, launched a violent attack on the Bloisian camp. Blois, utterly astounded and startled from sleep in his tent, fumbled vainly with his armour. He struggled out, but though he fought bravely in his quilted aketon, he was badly cut about and was dragged away more dead than alive. His condition was not improved by subsequent ill-treatment, and on his voyage to imprisonment in England he had to be attended, in accordance with the fascinating medical tenets of the day, by eight guitarists, to soothe his throbbing head.

The capture of Charles of Blois did not in the long run alter the balance of affairs in Brittany. The war of the Two Joans continued. When Dagworth went home soon afterwards, the French retook Roche-Derrien; the townspeople were all slaughtered, and the English garrison, marching out unarmed on terms to the castle of Quintin were, despite their escort, massacred to a man by ferocious villagers. Still, as Philip's nephew, Blois was a valuable accession to the promising list of important personages, the comte d'Eu, Constable of France, David of Scotland and his hapless queen, Edward's youngest sister Joan, who came south to join her husband, and his own rival, the small boy John de Montfort, now held in London either as prisoners or as more or less willing residents.

The English were having things all their own way. Only in Flanders did Philip gain a small, purely bedchamber success, and even that in the end was to prove a curse to the kingdom of France. After Count Louis of Nevers was killed at Crécy, Philip, hoping to win the Flemings over from the English side, sent them back Louis's son and successor, the sixteen-year-old Louis of Malines, suggesting among other things that he should marry Margaret, daughter of Duke John III of Brabant, now an outright supporter of the French. But Louis's assertive subjects, who did not like the French connection, kept him a virtual prisoner at Courtrai; and Edward, who liked it even less, promptly proposed instead a rival match for Louis with his ever-ready eldest daughter, Isabella. The lad objected, with some spirit, that he would never marry the daughter of the man who had killed his father, but he had little say. In March 1347 he was taken to Bergues, near Dunkirk, where Edward and Queen Philippa soon arrived from Calais with Isabella, and the young couple met. They were at once betrothed, and arrangements ordered for the wedding to follow with the least possible delay.

Louis shrewdly declared himself captivated by his bride-to-be. So well did he seem prepared to accept his lot that it was thought safe to allow him, though still in custody, to enjoy while waiting his favourite sport of hawking. In Easter week, the week of the wedding, when following his bird as it swooped on a heron in the marshes of the Lys, he slipped his guards, set spurs to his horse, and never drew rein till he was safe in France. In August that same year he married Margaret of Brabant. Their daughter Margaret of Flanders married Philip the Bold, the first great duke of Burgundy, and so gave rise eventually to the Armagnac–Burgundian civil war. Her betrothed's disappearance was naturally upsetting for Princess Isabella, though she was no doubt told in the nicest way that, as was true, it was for no fault of her own person. There were for the present no grave political results. The Flemings disowned their self-willed new young count, and remained true to their English treaty.

Aquitaine, Scotland, Brittany, Flanders: Philip's diplomatic finger could be seen in all these foiled, peripheral endeavours to compensate for the disgrace of Crécy. Calais alone symbolically held out. In consultations with his son John, the stark decision became inescapable. He must rescue Calais, and rescue it by direct attack. In April 1347, he stirred from the bosky rustlings at Pont-Sainte-Maxence and began to mobilize at Arras. By July he was ready, and had achieved, in the circumstances, a creditable muster. He had no support now from the Genoese, and Robert of Namur had lately gone over to Edward, while Charles of Moravia, his brother-in-law, had returned to Germany to make sure of his Empire as Charles IV. But Philip had the other surviving veterans of Crécy, John of Hainault and Amadeus, the Green Count of Savoy, and in addition, for what he was worth, the shifty Duke John of Brabant. He also had, as he had not before, his son John and his army of the south, under its leaders, Duke Otto IV of Burgundy, brother of Queen Jeanne; Pierre, duke of Bourbon; Gaston Phoebus, count of Foix, now at the beginning of his long career; and his younger son, Philip, newly become first duke of Orleans.

For all that, Philip had left it very late. On 25 June a French convoy was destroyed off Calais by Sir John Montgomery's fleet, with Northampton and Pembroke on board. Among the wreckage was found an axehead, thrown overboard to avoid capture, with a desperate message for Philip from Sir John de Vienne: 'Know, dread Sir, that your people in Calais have eaten their horses, dogs, and rats, and nothing remains for them to live upon, unless they eat one another. Wherefore, most honourable Sir, if we have not speedy succour, the town is lost.' Edward quizzically sealed it up with his own seal, and sent it on to its destination. Duke John went ahead to lend assurance by his presence; but however comforting, his presence was no substitute for food. Philip hurried after him.

Because of his failure to suborn the Flemings, he could not, as he would have liked, approach Calais from Gravelines to the east, and force Edward out of his western entrenchment to face him in the open on the other side of the town. Instead, he changed course at Guînes and on 27 July encamped at Sangatte five miles west of Calais. His host made an intimidating spectacle on top of the high coastal dunes, but his enemy showed no concern, and it was evident that in their perimeter behind the river Hem they were as secure from his attacks as the Calaisians were from theirs. They had been greatly reinforced from England since the removal of the Scottish threat, and no one cared to tangle with the famous Henry of Lancaster at Nieulay bridge, the only point of access. As usual, peacemaking cardinals were soon on the scene, and days of useless parley followed. At last, thinking to disengage, Philip made the formal and excusatory demand for a pitched battle, but to his dismay Edward coolly accepted it. Before dawn on 2 August, the day before the battle was due, the French camp was in flames, and the whole great concourse vanished in disorder, pursued with damaging effect by Lancaster and Northampton.

The panoply of France on the dunes at Sangatte had been clearly visible over the heads of the intervening English to the famished watchers on the walls of Calais. On the first night of his arrival, Philip's fleurs-de-lis, surrounded by the banners of his dukes and earls, appeared on the high tower of the castle, lit up by a great fire, to the noise of cheers and trumpets. The second night the fire was somewhat less. The third night it was a flicker. There were wails and groans, and all standards were taken in except the lonely flag of Calais. When finally the pitiless dawn showed up the mirage of their hopes, an empty smoking waste, that too was taken down and dropped into the moat. Sir John de Vienne, lamed from an affray with Thomas Holland, rode out on a bony nag to give up his sword and the keys of the city.

Philip's retreat, inglorious though it was, was the swiftest and most merciful way to end the siege of Calais. On 28 September 1347 a truce was signed outside the walls that was to last, with the usual breaches and renewals, for the next eight years. Afterwards, the kings departed on their ways; Philip and Duke John to Paris; on 12 October, Edward, Philippa and the Black Prince for London by way of Sandwich, after a dreadful crossing. In one of his few recorded utterances, Edward exclaimed, 'St Mary my Blessed Lady, what should be the meaning of this? That always in my passages to France the winds and seas befriend me, but in my return to England, I meet with nothing but adverse storms and destructive tempests!' Perhaps he felt a secret guilt, sensed some unhappy future, in spite of the triumph that awaited him.

Philip spent the rest of his days in hopeless dreams of invading England. He was discredited. When he asked for the requisite money, he was reminded 'how you went to these places honoured and in great company, at great cost and great expense, and how you were treated shamefully, and sent back scurvily and made to grant all manner of truces, even while the enemy were in your Kingdom and upon it'. What a way for the common estates to address the king of France! His unamiable queen, Jeanne de Bourgogne, regarded by many as his evil genius, died in December 1349. Within a month he married brisk young Blanche of Navarre, nearly forty years his junior, whom he had first intended as a consolation to his son John for the loss of Bonne of Luxemburg. John now married Joan of Boulogne instead. Philip's new marriage was the last, fond gesture of an old and broken man. Six months later, in August 1350, he was dead. Edward had been too much for him.

* * *

Edward had stayed a whole year in front of Calais. Colonel Burne, the military historian, pertinently wondered why, when he should have hurried home to face the great Scottish invasion he knew quite well was coming; why, when he could have confidently handed over the humdrum siege to Northampton or any other of his galaxy of great commanders, and have exchanged his wintry wooden barracks for the comfort of his hunting lodges and the plaudits of his people he was too good a showman to ignore. There was no military reason.

The most likely explanation is that Edward had a mistress with him. That in itself would not be sensational, were it not that the founding of the Order of the Garter immediately after, and the unusual care with which the whole affair was covered up, add piquancy to the question of who she was. The new order came into existence with a reticence quite foreign to Edward's normally ebullient nature, and strangely at odds with his loud announcement of the Round Table four years earlier. Its original articles, if any, were quickly lost. Its startling emblem and its enigmatic motto, palpable facts, are mysteries still. Le Bel and Froissart make only the briefest mention of it, and none whatever of any lady who inspired it. Nor did other chroniclers of the time give any hint of her though, by contrast, Edward's later favourite Alice Perrers was the object of noisy national concern, publicly recorded in the rolls of Parliament.

Edward himself seems to have thought it necessary to conceal his traces, for when Calais at last fell he insisted on the pantomime whereby the leading burgesses were brought out with halters round their necks, and Queen Philippa had to save them from his wrath by pleading mercy on her knees, as she had done in earnest for the carpenters in Cheapside sixteen years before. His stage management was excellent. The incident became part of the fabric of English history, and by it he established three desirable impressions: his rage at being kept so long at Calais against his will, his susceptibility to his wife's entreaties, and that at least so late as the previous Christmas he had not deprived her of uxorial company; for Philippa was once more heavy with child, Margaret of Calais, the future wife of John Hastings, son of Lawrence, earl of Pembroke. Yet the elaborate tableau was quite false. For a soldier of his stamp as for a knight of his quality, to resent so brave a defence would be impossible; and in fact when he got home he showed magnanimity and due respect to Sir John de Vienne, then in the Tower, while the chief of the burgesses, Eustace de Saint-Pierre, was showered with gifts.

Long after the event, two not inconsiderable scholars both reported a tradition current in their days, that during a ball at Calais after Crécy, a lady with whom Edward was in love lost her garter, and that he recovering it, clapped it on his own leg with the famous apothegm '*Honi soit qui mal y pense.*' Polydore Vergil, writing his *Anglica Historia* in the time of Henry VIII, said that the lady was either the queen herself or a friend of hers among her minstrels. A hundred years later still, the antiquary John Selden in his *Table Talk* announced boldly that it was 'the Lady Joan, Countess of Kent and Salisbury, her Garter'. Joan of Kent may well have been at Calais, but as has been said already, she was an unlikely candidate for the part, since at the time she was already in dispute between her first and second husbands, Holland and William Montagu (or William Montagu and Holland), and was later to marry, as her third, the king's own eldest son. Public rumour is not to be despised in the absence of other evidence; but rumour is by nature liable to enlarge, and is prone to the logical fallacy that since one thing follows another in time, it must have been caused by it. In the present case the reasoning is simple. Joan of Kent was the great beauty of her day. King Edward was in love. Therefore he was in love with Joan. The Order of the Garter came into being during the celebrations after his return from Calais. Therefore she had lost her garter there.

The garter episode, albeit with a heroine other than Joan, may or may not have happened. So politely circumstantial a story is not essential to explain the boudoir gallantry implied by the insignia of the order, which may have been spontaneous, the unprompted self-invention of its founder, a pleasing *jeu d'esprit* neither staid nor over-bold. Its muted, sentimental impropriety would have seemed a becomingly old-fashioned concession to the wild manners of the day. For the joyous, easy-going licence of the years after Crécy struck a generally more audacious note.

Giddiness ran riot. Shocked chroniclers grumbled at the wantonness of troops of girls, provocatively dressed up like men, who cavorted between the combats on richly caparisoned horses during the endless tournaments, unblushing at 'the modest outcries of the people. Ladies from the more handsome and the more beautiful, but not the better ones, of the entire Kingdom; in divided tunics, that is, one part of one kind and the other of another kind, with small hoods and liripipes flying about the head in the manner of cords, and well belted with silver or gold, even having upon their stomachs, below the middle, knives which they vulgarly called daggers placed in pouches from above'. Indelicacy did not stop there. The clerks also complained of Englishmen seduced by foreign fashions, who changed them every year, fantastic modes, 'destitute and desert from all old honest and good usage. . . . And the women were arrayed more curiously than the men, for their clothes were so narrow that they let hang fox tails sewed beneath within to hide their arses.' In that atmosphere, intimate garments fluttering in the lists would cause little comment, and a new order of chivalry with suggestive trappings would be thought no more than sporting. In adopting them, royalty merely stooped to, and did not necessarily lead, the common mood.

On the other hand, there is further evidence from near the time to indicate that Edward did have a concubine at Calais, and there may well be some connection, ball or no, between his amorous lapse and his prompt heraldic vindication of it. Some twenty-five years after Calais, towards the end of his long reign, when he was in his dotage and the Black Prince was slowly dying of malaria caught in Spain, Edward shared the effective government with his next surviving son, John of Gaunt, by that time the duke of Lancaster. Gaunt was hated. The war had gone badly, there were complaints about corruption, and he was suspected, probably unjustly, of designs upon the throne. Discontent centred, though not encouraged by them, around the dying prince, his popular wife, Joan of Kent, and their small son, Richard, the next heir to the throne if not dispossessed by Gaunt. Among the prince's friends was Humphrey de Bohun, son of the great earl of Northampton, army commander in Brittany and at Crécy. In the early 1370s some member of Bohun's household wrote a bitter lampoon against the government of Gaunt and the aged king.[37]

Since it was in Latin, it was clearly intended for an informed and limited circle, and that probably is why it alone among tell-tale documents survived. To avoid censure, it took the guise of a pretended prophecy by one 'John of Bridlington', supposedly composed early in the century, accompanied by an anonymous commentary, and newly come to light. Its burden was that the early promise of Edward's reign would decay through his own profligacy and neglect, and would reach its present nadir as a divine punishment for sin, until rescued by the accession of the prince. The decline is supposed to begin at Calais, where a woman, already married and a mother 'having milk in her breasts', would come and seduce him from his duty. She would ensnare him as Delilah ensnared Samson. She would cause him to let his army go short of bread. She would sap his martial ardour and put an end to his victories in France. She would separate him from his queen, and in fact herself become queen of England in everything but name.

This lady, whom 'John of Bridlington' calls Diana, he also calls in no uncertain terms a harlot, *clunagitata* (buttock-tossing) and *vesana* (raving, insatiable), terms so grossly abusive, even for the clerical writer that he clearly was, as to prove once and for all that he was certainly not speaking of Joan of Kent, the gracious idol of his party. Diana, he went on, would make the king commit the sin of David, who lay with the wife of his humble soldier Uriah the Hittite, and sent him unsuspecting to his doom. After the dreadful visitation of the plague, Edward would still be in Diana's toils, and would pleasure with her instead of with his wife. But he would find the consequences of his adultery graver than he expected, and would try to cloak it over with excuses. Then, says 'John of Bridlington' obscurely, from their commerce there would be a robber born (*latronem generabit*). The 'Commentator' professes doubt about his meaning: 'I do not know who this robber may be, whether it is a son of the King born at the time of the siege, or who was born next after, or that a robber of the people will arise from the evil indulgence of him who should be their protector.' Thinking, however, he had best be prudent, he says, like le Bel and Froissart when touching on Edward's love affair, 'if I say more, I shall make myself unpopular'.

The vagueness as to who 'the robber' was remains unclarified. Edward's child born at Calais was a daughter, not a son; and of his sons nearest in time, William of Windsor died in infancy, while Thomas, the future duke of Gloucester, born eight years later, cannot justly be called, whatever else, a robber; moreover both sons were born in proper wedlock. Miss Galway, who maintains that Diana was meant to be Joan of Kent, unflattering though that would be to Joan, concludes that the robber was metaphorical.

It is probable that both the robber and Diana were metaphorical, though only in part; the one, representing in the latter phases of the 'prophecy', John of Gaunt, who indeed was Edward's son, and the other, Edward's favourite of his old age, Alice Perrers. These two allies were jointly the chief public villains at the date 'John of Bridlington' was really writing, and were the true targets of his attack. But he was not attacking his modern scapegoats only. He was underhandedly exposing the old king as well. That is why his 'prophecy' harked back to Calais, years before either of them were important, and why he invented a metaphorical robber to disguise a real one active long before Gaunt's day. The allegations he obliquely made tie in very closely with actual though unmentionable past events, and they recalled more than simply an illicit love affair.

The real robber was Edward Montagu. Edward Montagu had fought at Crécy, and if the king really put him in the forefront of the battle like Uriah the Hittite, he had nevertheless somehow managed to survive.[38] He may then have been one of the lords Edward sent back from Calais to strengthen the Scottish Border before Neville's Cross.[39] If so, no doubt it was to get him out of the way before his wife, Alice Montagu, the king's cousin and lover, arrived at Calais with Queen Philippa and the other royal ladies. When they all got home again a year later, Edward's flagrant attentions to Alice, no longer in the private purlieus of Calais, but under his own eyes in the full glare of tournaments and parties up and down the country, maddened Montagu. He made off to the eastern counties, and disaster followed.

By October 1350, soon after the Black Death, Edward Montagu, the respectable soldier, was in full business as a brigand in Norfolk and Suffolk, and in very truth despoiling those it was the king's duty to protect, though he failed to do so. Resentment at the king's seduction of Alice his wife, and rage at the closure of her estates against him, drove Montagu to batter her to death. Certainly, as 'Bridlington' says, a robber had been born, and Edward found the consequences of his adultery graver than he expected. He did, too, rake over the traces, and did excuse the revengeful husband he had injured.*

'John of Bridlington's' allusions to Diana and the robber were double references: on the one hand to his all too active political enemies at the time when he was writing, and simultaneously to dim ghosts from an old, carefully buried, deeply painful royal scandal. The robber was both Edward Montagu and John of Gaunt, and the shameless strumpet was in part Alice Perrers, in part Alice Montagu, the king's belle of Calais. Poor, modest, murdered Alice Montagu, inexorably trapped between the king's lust and her husband's violence; more gently commemorated, it may be, in the Order of the Garter.

* See Appendix, pp. 175–8.

APPENDIX TO BOOK II

THE STRANGE DEATH OF ALICE, LADY MONTAGU

1 'Item, that also the said Mons. Edward [de Montagu], William Dunche and
Thomas parson of the church of Kelleshall by force of arms and feloniously did
beat Alice daughter of Thomas of Brotherton cousin of our lord the King and
wife of the said Mons. Edward at Bungay, that is to say on the Sunday next
after the feast of Saint Botolph in the twenty-fifth year of the reign of the King
who now is [17 June 1351]; from which beating the said Alice languished sick
unto death, and she died within the year and the day.' (*Ancient Indictments*,
file 114, m. 3. Quoted Cockayne, *Complete Peerage*, under Edward de
Montagu)

2 '4 June, 1361. Pardon, for good service done in the war of France . . . to
William Dunche [Montagu's henchman] of Bungay in the county of Suffolk, of
the King's suit for the death of Alice daughter of Thomas of Brotherton late
wife of Edward de Montagu.'

   Also for having 'taken by force sixteen cows worth ten marks from James,
prior of Thetford Monachorum, and impounded them until the prior bound
himself in £10 to Edward de Montagu for their deliverance; and driven away
horses and cows of the lady of Roos, the master of Kerbrook and the prior of
Thetford, at Walton, Kerbrook and Merton, and detained them until they
made fine with the same Edward by £10 for their deliverance.

   'Also for having stolen timber, chips [ostell], faget and two leaden vessels
worth £10 late of Edmund le Listere at Dickingham, a coffer late of Thomas
Home, chaplain, and twenty marks therein at Bungay priory, and for any other
subsequent old trespasses.' (*Cal. Patent Rolls*, 1361—4, p. 26)

   There is no record of a pardon being granted to Edward Montagu for any of
the offences where he is mentioned, but no action was taken against him.

3 Everything seems to have been well with Edward and Alice Montagu until
1349. Edward fought with distinction as a banneret at Crécy in August 1346 at
the head of nine knights, fifteen esquires and twenty archers (Cockayne,
Complete Peerage), and for his good services was granted a general pardon for
any felonies he might so far have committed (*Cal. Patent Rolls*, 1345—8,
p. 506). As has been said in the text, he was summoned to Parliament as a peer
on 20 November 1348, and was styled lord of Bungay, where, on 2 February
1349, the last of their five children, Joan, was born (*Cal. Inquisitions Post
Mortem*, 37 Ed. III, no. 94). In June 1349 the whole family, that is to say
Edward, Alice and their three children of sufficient age, Edward, Audrey and
Elizabeth, were granted the pope's permission in the diocese of Norwich to
choose their own confessors, seemingly a not uncommon practice during the
Black Death when priests were at a premium. (*Cal. Papal Letters*, III, p. 327)

Then things started to go wrong. Young Edward, described in June 1349 as a 'donzel' or hopeful lad, and Audrey, are never heard of again and probably died of plague later in the same year. By 16 October 1350 Edward Montagu had evidently taken to crime, because on that day a commission of *oyer et terminer* was appointed to inquire into a complaint by Margery, wife of the late William de Roos, that a band of twenty-two and more brigands had taken her cattle (eleven horses and twenty cows) at Whaddon in the county of Norfolk, driven them away to places unknown, and assaulted her servants so that her land remained untilled. The brigands included, besides Montagu himself and his crony Dunche, Thomas 'Edwardes prest montagu' and Geoffrey 'Edwardes prest montagu', two ruffians who were no doubt among those Montagu had been given permission to enrol as his chaplains (*Cal. Patent Rolls*, 1350—4). It was useful to have clergymen in such gangs because, if caught, they could claim clerical immunity.

A further commission of *oyer et terminer* was nominated on 8 May 1352, 'on complaint by William son of Reginald de la Marche of Dickyngham that Edward de Monte Acuto, *chivaler*, John le Botiller of Mershelande, Henry le Bakere and others, broke his closes and houses at Dickyngham, county of Norfolk, carried away his goods and so threatened him and his servants that he dared not stay in his dwelling place at the said town or elsewhere in those parts and his servants dared not serve him, nor could he get any to serve him, whereby he entirely lost the profit of his land there'. (Ibid.)

On 28 November 1351 Edward de Montagu, staying in England, had letters approving John de Podesye as his attorney in Ireland (for Alice's father's estates there) for two years. This licence, repeated in subsequent years, may mean that he was forbidden to leave the country. (*Cal. Patent Rolls*, 1350—4, p. 184)

4 Edward Montagu's fatal assault on Alice in June 1351 happened in the middle of this suddenly lawless phase of his career. The general trend of his criminal activities was a combination of theft together with intimidation and extortion, a gambit not unusual with the gentlemen of the day, and reminiscent of Sir Eustace de Folville.

He clearly needed money, even paltry sums; and coming when it did, his lapse was possibly because the Bungay estates had been especially badly hit by the plague of 1349, and he was desperate. But it is hard to see what he stood to gain financially by his attack on his wife, since he already had control for life of everything she owned.

He did not apparently intend to murder her. If he had, he and his cowardly associates, Dunche, and Thomas, the vicar of Kelleshall (who may perhaps have been the same Thomas 'Edwardes prest montagu' mentioned in the previous charge), would effectively have killed her then and there, instead of leaving her a battered witness to die uncertainly half a year later. It looks as though, enraged at some affront, he meant to punish her, but went too far. The affront can hardly have been his discovery of her affair with the king; for if that began at Wark ten years earlier, and had been carried on afterwards at Northampton and at Calais, it is unlikely that he would have found out about it only at so late a date. He had condoned it, lived with her, and had children by her regularly in the interval. Some further and critical incident must surely have occurred quite recently.

5 Whatever it was, it is plain that Montagu was able to bring enough pressure on the king to make him deflect the normal course of law.

Five months after the assault on Alice, from Westminster on 14 November 1351, William de Middleton, escheator in the counties of Norfolk and Suffolk, was ordered to open a routine inquest post mortem into the lands of Alice late the wife of Edward de Montagu. But this inquest was countermanded because it was testified that Alice was still alive. (*Cal. Fine Rolls*, VI, p. 288)

On 30 January 1352 the same escheator was again ordered to inquire into the estate of Alice, now dead. (Ibid.)

Ten days later, on 10 February 1352, the escheator was hurriedly directed not to meddle with the lands which Edward de Montagu holds by the law of England by reason of the death of Alice his wife, one of the daughters and co-heiresses of Thomas, earl of Norfolk, restoring any which have been taken, as at the time when the king was at Ghent in Flanders (early 1340) he took Edward's homage for all the lands which he and Alice held in chief of her inheritance by reason of their common offspring. (*Cal. Close Rolls*, 1349–54, p. 411)

Similarly, with regard to the children, on 16 November 1351, the king's sergeant-at-arms, Richard de Basevill, was sent to take into the king's hands the two daughters and heirs of Alice late the wife of Edward de MonteAcuto tenant-in-chief (Maud aged about six, and Joan, two), who are under age and whose marriages pertain to the king, and to deliver them in his name into the keeping of Elizabeth [Edward Montagu's mother, now Lady Furnivall], late the wife of William de Montagu their grandfather, until further orders. By the king (*Cal. Patent Rolls*, 1350–4, p. 181)

But on 15 February 1352 this order also was amended. Although the little girls probably went on living with their grandmother until she died in August 1354 (*Cal. Fine Rolls*, VI, p. 412), their financial value was restored by the king to Montagu: 'Although for causes shown before the council the marriage of the daughters and heirs of Alice wife of Edward de Montagu, deceased tenant-in-chief, pertains to the King, he as a special grace has granted the same to Edward, father of the heirs, who holds by the law of England all the lands of the said Alice by reason of issue raised up between them.' (*Cal. Patent Rolls*, 1350–4)

Thereafter Edward Montagu reappeared regularly in the royal service at home, especially in the eastern counties. In 1354 with the Prince of Wales he appointed proxies to treat with France. In 1356 he was a custodian of the coast of Norfolk, in 1358 a commissioner to settle disputes between the king's officers and the townspeople of Yarmouth. And in 1360 he was a commissioner of array for Suffolk. (Cockayne, *Complete Peerage*, and *Cal. Patent Rolls*, 1358–61, pp. 79, 407)

He died in July 1361 (*Cal. Fine Rolls*, VII, p. 195). Shortly before that he had married again, a second wife called Joan, by whom he left a second Audrey, aged two and more when he died, and an infant second Edward, who survived him only by three months. (Cockayne, *Complete Peerage*)

6 Of Alice's five children, as has been said, Edward and Audrey died before their mother, probably in the great plague of 1349, aged about eleven and ten.

The next was Elizabeth, born about 1343. Elizabeth was already married before the attack on Alice, for she was not claimed as a royal ward like her two younger sisters (*Cal. Patent Rolls*, 1350–4, p. 181). In February 1359 she was described as aged fifteen and the wife of Walter Ufford (*Cal. Inquisitions Post Mortem*, X, no. 564). On 15 July 1360 there was a division of further Brotherton lands between the heiresses, Alice's sister, Margaret, now the wife of Sir Walter Manny, and the three remaining Montagu daughters. Elizabeth was by then a widow (*Cal. Fine Rolls*, VII, p. 130). By the time of the inquest on her father only a year later she too was dead. Perhaps like him she died in the second plague.

Maud was born about 1345. She was declared a royal ward in November 1351. In February 1359 she was thirteen. In July 1360 she was still a minor and unmarried. She also died before her father's death the following year.

The youngest, Joan, was born at Bungay on 2 February 1349 (*Cal. Inquisitions Post Mortem*, 37 Ed. III, no 94). Like Maud a royal ward in 1351, by February 1359 she was said to be eleven, and was the wife of William Ufford, younger brother of her sister Elizabeth's husband Walter. When her father died and his life interest lapsed, she was Alice's sole surviving heir. On 28 October 1361 William Ufford was granted wardship of all lands in Norfolk and Suffolk that had been held for life by Edward Montagu 'by the courtesy of England' after the death of Alice, on behalf of his wife Joan, Daughter and heir of the said Alice, until she came of age (*Cal. Fine Rolls*, VII, p. 185). Joan had four sons, but they all died before her, and she left no other children at her death in 1375.

William Ufford succeeded his father, Robert, the famous soldier and friend of the king, as second earl of Suffolk in 1369. He outlived Joan by seven years and married again, but died without leaving issue in 1382, when his earldom became extinct. (*Dictionary of National Biography*)

BOOK III

THE NEW SUN

'Then folk thought that a new sun was rising over England.'
Thomas Walsingham, *Historia Anglicana*, I, p. 272

THE NEW SUN

On 12 October 1347, after an absence of fifteen months, King Edward, with Queen Philippa and her baby daughter Margaret, the Black Prince, and the king's famous cousin Henry of Lancaster, came home from Calais to a rapturous welcome. At thirty-five, Edward was at the height of his grace and vigour. The chronicler Adam Murimuth described him in terms which the usually sardonic Thomas Walsingham saw no reason to qualify in his history a little later:

> He was so great-hearted that he never blanched or changed the fashion of his countenance at any ill-hap or trouble soever that came upon him; a renowned and fortunate warrier, . . . clement and benign, familiar and gentle even to all men, both strangers and his own subjects or dependants. . . .
>
> His body was comely, and his face like the face of a god, wherefrom so marvellous grace shone forth that whosoever openly considered his countenance, or dreamed thereof by night, conceived a sure and certain hope of pleasant solace and good fortune that day. He ruled his realm strictly even to his old age; he was liberal in giving and lavish in spending: for he was excellent in all honour of manners, so that to live with him was to reign.

Five hundred years later, Bishop Stubbs, contradicting this glowing contemporary sketch, declared that Edward was no statesman, that his obligations as a king sat lightly on him, that he was ambitious, extravagant, ostentatious and unscrupulous. No doubt the Victorian bishop was put off by Murimuth's sad admission that Edward 'controlled not, even in old age, the dissolute lusts of the flesh; and, as is believed, this intemperance shortened his life', though such common concern at the king's loss of his normally resounding health was in itself a further compliment, since Edward none the less reached the then considerable age of sixty-five and reigned for more than half a century. As Miss McKisack says in her eloquent reappraisal, Edward's people would not have agreed with Bishop Stubbs. They wished, and perhaps, after so long, half expected, him to live forever.

He was the 'mighty victor, mighty lord', and beside him was his comfortable Philippa. Froissart, her devoted clerk and countryman, carried on the paean on her account:

for since the days of Queen Guinevere, who was wife to King Arthur and Queen of England (which men called Great Britain in those days), so good a Queen never came to that land, nor any who had so much honour, or such fair offspring; for in her time, by King Edward her spouse, she had seven sons and five daughters. . . . Tall and straight she was; wise, gladsome, humble, devout, free-handed, and courteous; and in her time she was richly adorned with all noble virtues, and well beloved of God and men.

They were a right royal pair. With their strapping and still increasing brood, they were, for those times, the very model of what a royal family should be. On their return, the country went wild with joy. For the first time the people could applaud not their king alone, but themselves as well; could share in a triumph they had helped to make. Together they had trounced the French for not being English, while there was also the age-old satisfaction of extensive plunder. Walsingham goes on:

Then folk thought that a new sun was rising over England, for the abundance of peace, the plenty of possessions, and the glory of victory. For there was no woman of any name, but had somewhat of the spoils of Caen, Calais, and other cities beyond the seas. Furs, featherbeds, or household utensils, tablecloths and necklaces, cups of gold and silver, linen and sheets, were to be seen scattered about England in different houses. Then began the English ladies to wax wanton in the vesture of the French women; and as the latter grieved to have lost their goods, so the former rejoiced to have obtained them.

At once, starting in November and continuing far into the succeeding year, there were tournaments and celebrations up and down the land. The court was always on the move, showing itself to the adoring population. Distinguished prisoners of war were released from the Tower to add to the display: Charles of Blois of Brittany, Philippa's cousin; David Bruce, king of Scotland, Edward's brother-in-law; and Raoul, conte d'Eu, the Constable of France, though his over-willing participation in the rejoicing helped to cost him his head later when he got back to France. Rich and various costumes were presented by the king on most occasions. At Windsor, King David was provided with a blue velvet harness for his horse, embroidered with a white rose on a pale of red. At Eltham, Henry of Lancaster and those of the king's side were given hoods of white cloth powdered with blue dancing men and buttoning up the front with large pearls. At Canterbury, the king and his eight challengers wore surcoats of light blue Indian silk bearing the arms of Sir Stephen Cosington, though what they were is not recorded. At Lichfield, the royal colours were blue robes with the white hoods, and the highest ladies in the land, tricked out in masks and visors, rode into town with the competitors sporting the same favours. Very soon the gay motley of the uniforms conformed to the single dominant motif that had first appeared in November 1347 in time for the Christmas games at Guildford, the emblem and the motto of the Garter. For a time they were closely associated with 'the King's Device', a White Swan gorged Or, bearing 'the King's Saying', which he appears to have bellowed out on all occasions of festivity:

> Hay, Hay, the White Swan
> by God's soul I am thy man!

Nobody knows who the White Swan was, but it is noticeable that after Edward Montagu's murderous attack on his wife, Alice, at Bungay in June 1351, the swan became mute, and was heard of no more.

The first of the annual Garter celebrations was held at Windsor on St George's Day 1348. On 6 August that year the king rededicated the old chapel of St Edward where he had been christened to St George, and Bishop William Edington of Winchester became the first prelate of the order, known however for some time yet as the Order of St George rather than of the Garter. In December the Black Prince issued Garter insignia to his own team of twelve, and the new foundation began to take its now familiar shape. The colour of the robes was blue, the royal blue of France; the material was English wool, the staple of the English victories.

When the king first envisaged his new creation four years earlier, in 1344, he had been thinking of a membership of hundreds, ever increasing; but now he suddenly decided to confine it to a mere two dozen, besides himself and his eldest son. His fortunate restriction of the numbers, so amenable to English taste, resulted in the first London club. Rigidly exclusive, its lack of specified qualifications for admission expressed an hauteur positively intimidating. The founder members seem to have had no particular attribute in common, other than being friends of the king and the prince. Sir John Chandos was not, as was Henry of Lancaster, of the noblest blood. Many of the famous warlords of Sluys and Crécy – Sir Walter Manny; Richard 'Copped Hat' of Arundel; Ufford of Suffolk, the king's old crony of the Nottingham coup; the Admiral, Clinton of Huntingdon; and the great army commander Bohun of Northampton – were originally left out in favour of comparative nonentities, though most of them were accepted later on as the stalls fell vacant. Many, but not all, were young. Some of them, like Sir Henry Eam of Flanders, Sir Sanchio d'Ambréticourt from Hainault, and the Gascon Captal de Buch, were not even English. The absence of formal rules, too, reflects both lordly nonchalance and the clubman's wily resolve not to be publicly tied down. These essential niceties escaped King John of France when a year or two later, in 1351, he founded his unsuccessful rival Order of the Star. He allowed an original membership of eighteen to escalate to five hundred, and they were sworn never to desert each other: so that when in the next year they were worsted by the English at Mauron in Brittany, ninety of them died unnecessarily, if bravely, and the order collapsed.

* * *

The year 1348 was the zenith of Edward's prestige at home and abroad. On the whole, he kept his head, and exploited his power judiciously. His occasional displays of dreadful majesty were calculated adjuncts to particular policies, and implied no rash delusions. When he met his parliament during Lent it was in a quiet key, boasting little of his victories, but emphasizing the fragility of the existing truce, and asking their counsel what should be done, whether peace or further war. Avoiding the trap of thus making themselves responsible for the resumption of the war, with the heavy demands for money that would surely follow, they replied uneasily to his unusual inquiry that their most redoubted lord and his council alone could determine such high matters, but that they would loyally abide by whatever was decided. They then pointed out the very heavy and unstatutory royal exactions that had been the price of victory, purveyancing of goods, enormous imposts on wool, especially a 'loan' of twenty thousand sacks which had evidently disappeared. They demanded that their present petitions, unlike others in the past, should be granted and enrolled before they voted him, as they proposed to do, three fifteenths for three years, always provided that the war should last that long and that the money should not be levied as an extra burden upon wool. Their attitude was far from one of bedazzlement by the king's new glory, but he accepted their terms coolly, took the money, neatly evaded most of their petitions, and dismissed them for what was to prove to be three years.

A more challenging because less familiar test of Edward's level-headedness than parliamentary tactics followed in the spring, when a group of glowing Germans, all becks and smiles, arrived with assurances that their Electors had chosen Edward to become Holy Roman Emperor, a fitting accolade for one who had already worn the vice-imperial mantle, and had so lately proved himself, for all to see, the most illustrious knight in Christendom.

The former emperor, Edward's old ally and brother-in-law, Ludwig IV of Bavaria, after many years of struggle with a succession of Avignon popes, had eventually been comprehensively cursed, both in time and eternity, by Clement VI, and declared deposed in favour of Charles of Moravia. Charles, who had married Philip of France's sister Blanche (and his own sister Bonne of Luxemburg was the wife of Philip's heir, Duke John), had strong French inclinations. He had fought for Philip at Crécy, where his father, blind King John of Bohemia, an inveterate enemy of the

Emperor Ludwig, had so heroically died. The elevation of Charles was overwhelmingly in the French interest, since it would abolish all prospect of an alliance between Edward and the empire against King Philip's throne. Charles was most ready to accept. He agreed to all the papal terms, and sealed the bargain with the lure, to Pope Clement irresistible, of gold. All the same, the new Emperor Charles IV was not yet secure. He needed the confirmation of the German electoral princes, many of whom still violently opposed the papal pretensions to imperial rights so long resisted by Emperor Ludwig. Ludwig did not take his deposition kindly, and had he lived he might have survived this crisis as he had survived many others in the past. But in October 1347 he died of apoplexy, falling from his horse while hunting. His sons, unable to agree on a successor from their own house of Wittelsbach, decided to seek the help of a powerful ally disposed as strongly as themselves against Charles IV and the French connection.

Their proposal was straightforward, if naive. At first sight it appealed to Edward, not only as a grandiose satisfaction of his vanity, but also because it opened up a new horizon, a countless array of dutiful mid-European vassals to press through his defeat of Philip of Valois. But Queen Philippa, who had some knowledge from her sister Margaret, the dowager empress, of the intricacies of imperial diplomacy, took obstinately against it, perceiving it, in a wifely way, as a trap secretly fostered by Edward's enemies. Particularly she feared that it would exacerbate the already sharp family differences between her husband and her sisters' husbands over their native Netherlands provinces, left heirless by the recent death of her brother William. Her good sense quickly dispersed Edward's cloudy aspirations. The plan would lure him into alliances whose worthlessness he well remembered, and in such baffling new enmities that he would have to abandon his main design in France; and his rivalry would drive the new emperor Charles outright into Philip's arms. The honorific offer was dangerously barbed. He used it to persuade Charles, as the price of his abstention, not to hinder him in France, and Charles gained his imperial crown with mutual goodwill instead of with rancour.

Meanwhile all over England the joyous merrymaking continued through the summer of 1348 in spite of weather abominable even by English standards. It rained and it rained. The chronicler Henry Knighton, still outraged at the 'wanton buffoonery' of the hoydens prancing in and out among the knights at the tournaments, found grim satisfaction in their discomfiture: 'God in this matter as in all others brought marvellous remedy, for he harassed the places and times appointed for such vanities by opening the floodgates of heaven with rain and thunder and livid lightning and by unwanted blasts of tempestuous winds.' In reality, the heavenly visitation he thought of in such graphic terms was more than a mere damp rebuke for frivolous sins, the inconvenience of soaked costumes and water-logged tilting grounds. Writing after the event, what he had in mind was the universal wrath that shortly followed, signs whose implications were as apocalyptic as Belshazzar's feast.

England was far from being alone in the vagaries of the weather. For some time past, while Crécy was being fought, while Calais was being besieged, travellers' stories had been drifting back to Europe of prodigious natural convulsions in the unknown East, in the deserts of the Saracens, in the endless steppes of the Tartars of the Golden Horde, in faraway Cathay. Tales of drought and famine, floods and locusts, of fiery eruptions, of mountains vanishing to become great lakes, of chasms appearing in the earth and exuding rolling balls of fire, of pestiferous vapours corrupting the middle air; of torrential downpours discharging venomous snakes and blood and, in one part, 'huge vermin with eight short legs and tails, all over black, some living and some dead, whereof the dead stank over all the country and the living became as mortal poison to whoever chanced to touch them'. There had been subterranean thunder in Canton. Everywhere between Cathay and Persia there was vast mortality. In Babylon there was no one left except for some distracted women who fell to eating one another.

Such reports were not disbelieved. In the Middle Ages, there were in everyday humdrum life many strange effects without discernible causes, and all were taken for granted as the agency of either God or the Devil. Religion so permeated knowledge that the duration of medical treatment was measured in terms of the time it took to say a paternoster. Nothing was incredible, especially in the heathen Orient. It was at about this time that the enigmatic Sir John Mandeville was setting out the account of his marvellous travels to the court of the Great Chan which, though he never left his fireside at Liège, convinced and beguiled a sophisticated public for several centuries. And if life was credulous, it was also at best precarious. Any day's journey might well end in death, whether from human or supernatural causes. Evening prayers were a real thanksgiving. When darkness fell, families, mostly unable to afford the cost of candles, huddled together on their pallets, hopefully to await the blessed sunrise. So the rumours were bandied about in the European seaports, and though allowance was no doubt made for their elaboration in the telling, it was concluded that an unexampled pestilence was raging in the East. But it seemed remote from the familiar churches, markets, forests, and ox-turned fields of Christendom. In any case there was nothing to be done. Even for common contagions the only disinfectant, though not recognized as such, was vinegar, the only prophylactic an aromatic sponge. These had no effect on a mysterious, windborne, universal scourge.

The plague reached the Mediterranean by the same channels as the warnings of its approach, by caravans bringing silks and spices through Tartary to the great entrepôt of Baghdad; from lonely trading posts operating at the limits of the known world; in Genoese galleys from the

Crimea, carrying in their rich cargoes the invisible and spectral Death (the word 'Black', though now indissociable, was a later addition). Ghost ships were found drifting in the sea with not a soul alive. The ruler of Tharsis in Aomagena (Armenia), a perspicacious pagan, wondering why he and his people had been singled out for divine displeasure when the Christians to the west had apparently been spared, suspected religious error, and set out with his court on the long journey to Avignon to discuss with Pope Clement a possible conversion. But when he was twenty days on his way he found the pestilence had preceded him. The Christians' lands were in worse case than his own where the fury was now burning out; so he turned back, hardened in his disbelief, assailed by terrified Christians. By the beginning of 1348 the Death came ashore at Messina in Sicily and the great ports of Venice and Genoa on the Italian mainland. The maddened citizens tried to drive away the deadly vessels with burning arrows, but succeeded only in scattering the plague from place to place.

From Italy it continued on its relentless way through a Europe disastrously weakened in advance. Extensively overpopulated in the previous century, now in Malthusian recession after floods, famine and disease of cattle; overworked, undernourished, unhygienic, disrupted by war and brigandage – the nations could offer no resistance. It did not pause for two years, until 1350. Having passed through Scotland, it ended its northern sweep in the furthest reaches of Scandinavia and Russia, and in the west at the Atlantic where it killed Alphonso XI of Castile, the only reigning monarch to succumb, while besieging the Moors at Gibraltar. The orderliness of its march was not apparent to people without maps or information. They only knew that when it struck the neighbouring village, it would be with them the following day. Its habit was to linger for about seven months and then move on. Its effect was generally consistent, destroying about one in three of all humanity, to say nothing of the brute creation who also perished like their owners. When it passed, it passed as abruptly as it had come, but remained endemic for as long as three centuries afterwards, recurring whenever it found a concentration of new victims not immune to it.

It was sudden, deadly, agonizing and revolting. The afflicted died in three days, or one, or sometimes in an hour or two, according to the form it took. In the common type, where raging fever was accompanied by engorged inflammations in the groin or armpits, there was a fair chance of survival if the dreaded black-bluish plague spots burst or, in a few rare cases, were successfully lanced. Those taken in the lungs died horribly and quickly, with 'an inflammation in their innards, which created acute pains about the stomach, so that they sent up blood and a loathsome cadaverous stink from within. Their jaws and tongues were dried up with heat, and black, and tainted with gore.' If it entered the bloodstream, a man who went to bed at night might well never see the dawn. Priests and doctors hurriedly ministered to the dying but often themselves died before their patients, so that it came to be thought that a mere look, even one of grateful farewell, from a sufferer *in extremis* was enough to kill. Few stayed with the sick. It was said 'the sick are served by their kinsfolk as dogs would be; food is put near the bed for them to eat and drink, after which all fly'. Thus humanity was degraded not in the body only, but in its saving graces of loyalty and compassion.

The official reason for the plague, as given by the medical faculty of the University of Paris in a report demanded by King Philip, was that God in his anger had ordained a fatal conjunction of the planets. This had sucked up the waters of the sea into an invisible but poisonous miasma, driven ever outwards before a foul blast of wind, destroying all living things as it came upon them. This explanation was orthodox and convincing. The unpredictable irascibility of God was well known from the Scriptures, and from the livid paintings on the walls of the churches; while astrology was so advanced a science that no doctor in his senses would approach a case until he had made sure the stars were lucky, any more than he would treat a patient who had not been shriven, or for that matter fail to take his fee in advance. No one questioned their authoritative diagnosis. And, as it happened, in the year of the plague there really were seismic disturbances even more dramatic than the incessant though scarcely miraculous rain in England; this was enough to inflame fearful and bemused imaginations still further. In Venice, the bells of St Mark's were set ringing without human agency. In Paris, a baleful comet named Nigra appeared at sunset, flying low. In Avignon, a pillar of fire stood over the pope's palace at dawn of day. At Villach in Germany the market place burst open in the shape of a cross, and exuded blood and water. In Vienna, Plague Maidens were often seen riding in the storms and whirlwinds.

When it came to specific remedies, the medical faculty were less assured. In general their advice was to keep calm, stay indoors, avoid coasts, swamps, dew or moisture in any form, and to burn large fires of green wood laced with aromatic herbs to purify the air. Dietary advice was plentiful: olive oil was fatal; beetroot and other vegetables, whether eaten fresh or pickled, were dangerous; some authorities thought the same about lettuce. If it rained, a little fine treacle should be taken after dinner. Fat people should not sit in the sun and copulation was to be avoided at all costs. These recommendations were really an admission of utter helplessness. Guy de Chauliac, the greatest practitioner of the day, confessed the truth: 'The plague was shameful for the physicians, who could give no help at all, especially as, out of fear of infection, they hesitated to visit the sick.'

In fear at every moment, and thrown back on their own resources, people behaved variously. None denied Langland's dictum in *Piers Plowman* that 'the pestilences were purely for sin', but they could not ignore the evidence of their senses that however cosmic in origin, the disease spread like fire from one person to another, and that, as Gentile de Foligno observed, whatever may be said about the planets, 'the immediate and particular cause is a certain poisonous material which is generated about the heart and lungs'. Some locked themselves in, until the stench disclosed their rotting corpses. Some ran away, to illusory safety in the country. Some gave up, imagined their symptoms, and threw themselves into the common pits to die atop their dead fellows. Some got drunk. Some robbed the gaping houses, and committed ruffianly outrages upon the dead and dying. Some, following animal instinct, crawled away like diseased rabbits to die in the open caves and ditches, with the difference that whereas the myxomatosised rabbit always had its eyes and guts pecked out, no living creature would touch a victim of the plague.

There were desperate affectations of belated penitence. The dicemakers of Tournai found their trade fell off so sharply that they manufactured rosaries instead. The citizens of Lübeck, when their propitiatory stack of household treasures were refused by the monasteries for fear of infection, manhandled them over the walls. Weird processions of Flagellants, wearing red stars on their heads, shuffled through Europe, dismally chanting, grovelling in the dust, and whipping themselves into doleful frenzy. Everyone looked for a scapegoat. As always, and especially in Germany, the Jews fared worst; they were tortured and massacred, accused of poisoning the wells. Perhaps the inveterate human loathing of a small, brave, intelligent and not uncleanly rodent is a lingering example of the natural desire for revenge. It became routine in the end to blame it all on poor *Rattus rattus*, the black rat, who nevertheless suffered no less direly than the men he lived with. The black rat was at worst no more than a carrier at third hand, as host to the flea that acted as transmitter of the deadly microbe now identified as the cause of bubonic plague.

Horror stories come from all parts of Europe. At Siena, no one could be found for money or friendship to bury the dead. Dogs scratched up bodies from their shallow graves, and the chronicler Agnole de Tura carried his own five children to the common pit. At Florence there were no herdsmen. The cattle wandered untended out of town to pasture on the abandoned corn, and if they survived the day returned to stable of their own accord. Boccaccio lost his father there, and also, at Naples, his beautiful though hard-hearted Fiamonetta. The historian Giovanni Villani went on writing until death snatched away the pen from his hand, for it then to be taken up by his brother Matthew. To prevent panic, lists of the dead and the tolling of passing bells were forbidden, and, to reduce infection, so were funeral processions.

The plague reached Avignon early, from Marseilles. In April 1348 it swept away Petrarch's perfect Laura. His decorous description of her peaceful end, which he did not witness, did not chime with the common experience. It is said elsewhere that 'People died bleeding at the nose, mouth and fundament, so that rivers ran with blood, and streams of putrid gore issued from the graves and sepulchres of the dead.' The fastidious Pope Clement did his best. He purchased a communal burial ground outside the walls, wherein many were over-hastily buried alive. When that was full, he blessed a stretch of the river Rhône where the corpses could be dumped. He protected the Jews, who were being burnt alive in the streets below his palace, and later on all over Christendom. He attended intercessions in his courtyard, though when the Flagellants proved to be excessive and near heretical, he banned them. He authorized autopsies on the dead, to investigate the illness. He sent doctors to attend the sick, including the excellent Guy de Chauliac, his personal physician, who, unlike many of his fellows, felt forced by shame to perform his duties, albeit in continual fear. He became one of the few to recover from the plague, though we do not know by what means this physician healed himself. Clement felt it his first duty to remain alive. He wore a magic emerald ring to ward off infection, and on de Chauliac's advice retired to his mansion at Valence, where he sat out the worst in a single room between huge fires kept blazing day and night even in the hottest weather, and so survived – for a year or two.

Paris was stricken in May 1348. Here, the attack lasted an unusual eighteen months. The sisters of the Hôtel-Dieu redeemed mankind by their devoted nursing of their charges regardless of their own losses, for the staff had to be replaced several times over; and in justice the same should be said of all priests and religious, to judge from the high rate of their casualties from the bishop of Paris downward. The royal family removed to the country, where in any case King Philip was always happier than in town. None the less, four queens were lost: his own wife, Jeanne de Bourgogne; his niece, Queen Jeanne of Navarre; and his sister Blanche, wife of the Emperor Charles; as well as his son John's queen-presumptive Bonne of Luxemburg. The path of the plague across Normandy was charted by black flags run up on successive parish churches, visible for miles in the rolling countryside. At last, at the end of summer it stood poised on the Channel coast for an invisible and invincible invasion.

The English, already becoming insular and pleasure-loving, paid little heed to what they knew was happening in Avignon, in Paris, and in their own duchy of Aquitaine. The first cruel blow struck home from far away. At Easter 1348 Henry of Lancaster and his wife, Isabella Beaumont, had staged a stately tournament at Lincoln for the envoys from Castile come to clinch the marriage he had proposed some years before between young Pedro the Castilian heir and one of King Edward's daughters. Two years before, Princess Joan of the Tower had replaced her elder sister Isabella as being more suitable in age. Now thirteen and eligible, she took leave of her parents and set out on her adventure with a magnificent trousseau. When she got to Bordeaux the plague took her and she died on 3 September.

By that time it was afoot in England, having arrived at Melcombe Regis in July. On 17 August the bishop of Bath and Wells, apparently unaware of its presence in his diocese, ordered prayers in all his churches to avert the pestilence 'which had come from the East into the neighbouring kingdom'. By the following January he knew better, and exhorted his dwindling clergy 'in the bowels of Jesus Christ' that where there was no priest to take confessions they should be made to laymen, or if there was no man, then even to a woman. At the worst, if extreme unction could not be given, faith must suffice. At the bustling port of Bristol, grass was soon growing in the streets; neighbouring Gloucester refused shelter to the refugees. In October the cultivated tones of Bishop Edington of Winchester joined in: 'A voice in Rama has been heard; much weeping and crying has sounded throughout various countries of the globe. . . . This cruel plague, as we have heard, has already begun singularly to afflict the various coasts of the realm of England. We are struck by the greatest fear lest, which God forbid, the fell disease ravage any part of our city and diocese.' He prescribed the saying of the seven penitential and the fifteen gradual psalms, and on Fridays barefoot processions through the churchyards and market places, reciting the greater litany. These pious precautions were unavailing: Winchester was struck with special savagery. Oxford soon followed. There were three mayors in a single year; the colleges and schools were all closed down. In country districts some villages disappeared forever. In 1350 someone scratched on a wall in Ashwell church in Hertfordshire 'the dregs of the people alone remain'.

London was penetrated in November 1348. The 'Flower of Cities all', though already sooty, was in appearance more pleasantly pastoral than it has since become. Fair gardens ran down to the river's edge; there was always a merry clatter of bells from a hundred steeples, and the gaunt Tower, regularly whitewashed, actually brooded white. But its hygiene did not support the poet's encomium. The sophisticated garderobes of the wealthier dwellings emptied down the walls of the houses into the Thames. In a humbler quarter, two enterprising householders managed to use their neighbour's cellar as a cesspit and were not found out until it overflowed. Mostly the privies swelled the filth already choking channels in the middle of streets so narrow that the overhanging penthouses shut out the day, where it was shovelled along by the city rakers, past the neat stalls of piemakers and greengrocers, past the squatting beggars brandishing their sore deformities at corners. The Fleet River in Holborn, supposedly a broad stream of sweet water, had become a stagnant bog of sewage. Fly-buzzed blood from the shambles ran over the cobbles, and offal floated in the river. Recalling cleanlier times past and ordaining improvement as part of the stable-door legislation after the plague had ended, the king complained in 1357 that 'when passing along the waters of Thames, we have in divers places beheld dung and lay stalls and other filth accumulated and have also perceived the fumes and other abominable stenches arising therefrom, from the corruption of which, if tolerated, great peril as well to the persons dwelling within the said city, as to nobles and others passing along the said river, will, it is feared, ensue'.

In this great city, several times larger and more cosmopolitan than any other in the kingdom, some sixty thousand people bedded down each night with their domestic animals and, of course, the companionable fleas. 'On the crowded couch of incest in the warrens of the poor' the disease made splendid cultures. It raged all through the dark and sodden winter, and through the desolate unreviving spring. The graveyards were soon full. At Greyfriars, hundreds of pathetic talismans have been found, fallen from about the necks of people long since turned to dust. Sir Walter Manny and Ralph Stratford, the bishop of London, provided between them a field called No Man's Land outside the walls at Smithfield, where during the peak period two hundred were buried every day. By the time Manny died in 1372 it had served its original purpose, and he endowed on the site his famous Charterhouse in memory of himself and his wife, Margaret Brotherton; but Bishop Stratford's adjoining sector continued for two centuries to be used for unfortunates denied church burial, as well as for suicides and those hanged at nearby Newgate. It was known as Pardon Churchyard.

The anonymous old, the weak, the wretched were the hardest hit, though the better off were by no means proof. The archbishop of Canterbury, John Stratford, died of old age before the plague arrived, but his successor, John Ufford, followed him before he could be enthroned; and the third in line, the brilliant scholar-soldier Thomas Bradwardine, King Edward's field chaplain on his expeditions and, like Stratford, a Merton man, lasted only two days at Lambeth. The city companies suffered heavily. The Cutlers and the Hatters lost all their wardens, and the Goldsmiths four of theirs. Rich Sir John Pulteney, four times mayor of London, and Robert Bourchier, soldier and first lay Chancellor, perished. Hugh Despenser, son of Hugh the younger and hero of the Somme, died this year, when all agree that no one died of anything except the plague. Joan of Kent lost her mother, Margaret, and her mother's brother, Thomas Wake of Liddell, to her personal gain. Edward and Alice Montagu appear to have lost their two elder children.

That doctors were likely to be of little avail may be judged from the material that survives concerning Master John Arderne, the first great English surgeon. Brought up as a gentleman, John Arderne had seen army service with Henry of Lancaster at Antwerp, at the siege of Algeciras, and at Bergerac in Aquitaine. Like his French contemporary Guy de Chauliac, he painfully discarded the standard Greek dogmas of Hippocrates and Galen handed down in corrupt translations from the Arabic, in favour of practical experiment ('it is hevy for to change noying custom, and most of it be olde'). His youthful unorthodoxy sometimes led to grievous complications, as when he dressed leg wounds with powdered arsenic; thereafter he specialized in gentler ointments such as Salus Populi made of mutton fat, Narbonne Plasters, or diaplosun, an external variant of his long-famous Tapsimel, based on nightshade.

A dignified Master of the Long Robe, he boldly practised surgery, an ill-thought-of, even desperate technique. He evolved a lucrative operation for *fistula in ano*, hitherto incurable, a distressing abscess common among knights from sitting for long hours on wet saddles and from a constipating diet; and he concocted anaesthetics out of opiates for his operations. Yet he was a firm believer in astrology, and he adopted for use in epilepsy a superstitious spell said to have cured paralytic spasm in those who caroused too deeply at Prince Lionel's wedding in Milan; but, he says, 'I used to write it in Greek letters that it might not be understanded of the people'. For him, as for all his colleagues, 'Gold in physik was a Cordial', and he gave much thought to his enormous fees, often supplemented by annuities for life. The rich were to be charged as much as possible to inspire their confidence. The poor could be treated free to increase prestige, though if they sent fowls or ducks in payment it was better than nothing. His rules for a successful leech were strictly formal. He must not boast, or comment on his fellows, and he should err on the safe side in his prognostications. He must be modest and discreet and his nails clean. He must not be overloud, though a little flattery did no harm, and he might 'talke of good tales and of honest that may make the pacientes to laugh, as well of the bible as of other tragedies'. To prevent anxiety, he should never whisper in corners. He must not be too familiar with 'fair wymen in gret mennes houses', nor greet them by thrusting his hands about their bosoms. At all costs he must keep sober, and the Arderne would surely have agreed with William of Salicet that 'a wise surgeon too will do well to refrain from stealing anything whilst he is in attendance'.

Arderne's household remedies, mainly herbal, were fashionably mystifying. 'Centaury cooked in wine kills snakes and all worms in the belly.' A plaster of pigeon's dung and honey applied hot was good for kidney stone. Gout could be relieved by a poultice of green laurel and honey made with the lard of a male pig. He had cured an abbot overnight like this and claimed that it 'is privy and presious and show it not but to thy son or to one as well beloved'. Heart attacks were expensive, but could be allayed by a powder taken at meals containing slime of gold and perforated or unperforated pearls. A leek chewed in the mouth was first-aid for a dog bite. Rue in any form put paid to the venom of a toad, and the toad itself could be worn round the neck as a general amulet. He also kept handy a universal preparation of fifty-eight ingredients which would cure anything.

Naturally, Arderne was most at home with soldiers' ailments. At Algeciras he had cured a man of wrymouth by applying chunks of brown bread piping hot and soaked in vinegar. *Chaude pisse* (gonorrhea) was dealt with by injecting a mucilage of parsley shaken up with oil of roses and the milk of a nursing woman in which camphor was dissolved. For burst eyeballs, the only hope was God's virtue – the whites of new-laid eggs of white fowls beaten in a brass mortar. *Sang d'Amour*, the specific for arrow wounds, ideally required the blood of a maiden of twenty taken at the full moon in Virgo, mixed with myrrh, aloes, dragon's blood and powder of alkanet, and boiled up with olive oil; though if no suitable maiden was available, a red powder would usually do, 'for now in this tymes virgines cometh full seldome to 20 yere'. Significantly, for all his widespread competence Arderne made little mention of the plague, except for the conventional warning not to take hopeless cases for fear of loss of fees and reputation, or suspicion of poisoning. The plague was beyond him, as it was beyond everyone.[40]

At Westminster, the plague virtually halted the processes of government. The parliament summoned for January 1349, probably to the king's relief, had to be cancelled. The law courts went into recess. At Westminster Abbey, Abbot Bircheston died, and twenty-six of his monks were buried in the cloisters under a huge slab called Long Meg. The abbey jewels had to be sold to meet the expenses, and fortunate Simon Langham, later Chancellor, archbishop and cardinal, was left to enjoy preferment. In September 1349, a hundred or so Flagellants appeared from Holland, and put on one of their macabre performances at Paul's Cross. Their painful antics had little appeal for the stolid English and they were rapidly deported. So the Death went on its way through the length and breadth of the land. Late in the year when the worst was over in the south, the Scots on the Border scoffed at 'the foul deth of Engeland'. But when they mustered in the forest of Selkirk to wreak advantage, they found they had enlisted an unwelcome grim recruit. They too lost one in three.

* * *

The sudden removal of something like one-third of humanity was bound to have repercussions. Their extent and permanence have since been the subject of many inconclusive and, in the case of English scholars, rather parochial studies reducing the universal to the local. For instance, they have paid scant attention to Giovanni Villani's assertion that before the plague reached Europe, the Christians, eager to profit from the affliction of their heathen neighbours, sold them all their grain, so weakening their own resistance when the time came.

Until the nineteenth century it was usual to regard the Black Death as its contemporaries viewed it, as a transient calamity quickly overcome. But Victorian respect for free enterprise, and the notion of the bondman releasing himself from servitude, led to it being looked on as a watershed between the old world and the new, 'the year of the conception of modern man'. This extreme, too, has been heavily modified. The present opinion is that if there was a single overall result at all, it was in the direction of a change already in progress, an evolution from a dependent to a contractual way of life.

The immediate effect, a drastic fall in prices for lack of consumers, was quickly reversed. The untended cattle died, the crops rotted, and as consumption increased there was scarcity, and prices soared. The peasants found themselves on the one hand starving, on the other in exceptional demand. Whereas, before the plague, there had been too many people and not enough land, things were now the other way about. They could make their terms. Those already free expected higher pay; those still in serfdom sought to buy themselves out of ever-increasing drudgery; others simply ran away to the towns of opportunity, or to the better-bolstered large estates. Faced with their sweeping acres running back to wild, with reduced production and with a nugatory force of labour unable to pay the heriot and other feudal dues, some ruined landlords took to crime, like Sir Edward Montagu in East Anglia. More tried to insist on the old order. Others gave way, sold freedom to their villeins, agreed to higher wages to keep their own and to attract their neighbour's labour, and speeded the renting of their land to tenants. There was no fixed rule.

To the authorities of the time, the trouble was obvious. Presumptuous riff-raff were exploiting their unnatural advantage. Even while the epidemic was still raging, in June 1349, the king, or the king's advisers, issued a proclamation to peg wages (and prices, but principally wages) to their level before the outbreak; and in February 1351, as soon as Parliament met again, this ordinance against 'the malice of servants' was elaborated, at the express demand of the Commons, into the Statute of Labourers. Such regulation of labour relations, enacted in Parliament by gentlemen landowners and enforced by them as magistrates, was an interference deeply resented by the rest of the country, not least by the magnates, who found their wide freedom of manoeuvre threatened. There were many prosecutions, not only of workmen but of employers; and there were a great many more collusive evasions. As in France, where similar measures carried the harsh penalty of branding, it failed by default. Its sole achievement was to inject a new strain of bitterness into society.

Bitterness and disillusion were a more fertile legacy of the Black Death than were its economic consequences. The chroniclers alleged a general falling off of moral standards, a devil-may-care recklessness; but this may be no more than what every older generation says about its successors. Certainly, men began to question old values and institutions formerly taken for granted. The church, already a principal sufferer in life and property, suffered more sorely in esteem. The concept of a spiteful God destroying his own creation was not a noble one and many did not believe it in their hearts. But though it was unthinkable to question God's justice and mercy, his earthly agents came under scrutiny. The clergy had been proved no more than human: vulnerable, greedy, sometimes cowardly.

And when their depleted ranks were filled up with elderly widowers, illiterate youths, or mendicant rogues for whom 'silver was sweet', they lost their supernatural aura, as Langland, Gower and Chaucer all made plain. As in medicine, bland authority at variance with reason was no longer blindly accepted. The same parliament which made the Statute of Labourers made also the Statute of Provisors, against clerical trespass in temporal affairs. If it is hard not to see the Peasants' Revolt as the social outcome of the plague, the Lollards were its less easily silenced moral counterpart.

The Black Death halted the war more effectively than any papal legate, not for any lessening of aggressive purpose, but for sheer lack of men and means. The Scots did not cross the Border for the next five years, and neither the English nor the French could field an army. So the truce arranged at Calais was grudgingly prolonged when it fell due, on the first occasion sponsored by two gracious pledges, Queen Jeanne of France, and Edward's mother, Isabella, deputizing for Philippa, lying-in at Windsor with her short-lived William. But behind the scenes every diplomatic dirty trick was perpetrated. Since general engagements were impossible, local issues were decided by private warfare. The historic example, the famous Battle of the Thirty, commemorated by a monument as recently as 1823, took place in Brittany on 27 March 1351 on a selected pitch at the Halfway Oak between Josselin and Ploermel. It has been seen by Dr Coulton as 'one of the last flickers of the old lamp of feudal chivalry', though it could just as well be thought a rough precursor of a football match.

The truce of Calais had brought no peace to Brittany. Sir Thomas Dagworth, King Edward's governor, had been harsh with the Franco-Bretons who retook his prized Roche-Derrien. One day he was lured from his castle at Auray, and was killed by Raoul de Cahors. This Raoul, originally a rebel against King Philip, had assisted Dagworth in his capture of Charles of Blois, and had been rewarded by Edward with a grant of lands in the Pays de Retz just south of the river Loire. This had brought him into enmity with Sir Walter Bentley, who claimed them in the right of his wife, Jeanne de Belleville, the widow of Olivier de Clisson unjustly executed by Philip, and violently anti-French. Edward arbitrated in favour of Bentley, whereon Philip regained the allegiance of Raoul, and Raoul slew Dagworth at Philip's bidding. Edward appointed Bentley to succeed Dagworth, and Brittany was once more in confusion. Neither king could overtly take part because of the truce, and Raoul and Bentley lay low for the same reason, while both claimants of the duchy, Charles of Blois and John de Montfort, were detained in England. In the end it was left to underlings to assert the honour of the two kingdoms.

Jean de Beaumanoir, Raoul's associate, and captain of the French royal town of Josselin, held a parley with Sir Richard Bamborough, Bentley's subaltern at lately captured Ploermel. Since neither had regular forces, they agreed to a battle of thirty a side, to be fought on foot, with weapons of personal choice in the manner of the old mêlée. Beaumanoir raised his thirty Bretons easily; but Bamborough, though he had Hugh de Calveley and Robert Knollys, both later famous free lances, could find only twenty native English and had to make up with mercenaries. However, he had enlisted Captain Croquart, a German, once Lord Berkeley's page and now a brigand chief with a name to make men tremble; also a soldier of enormous girth called Hulbitee, and Thomas Billefort, who wielded a colossal mace weighing twenty-five pounds. Bamborough took the field with confidence at the Halfway Oak, in front of a huge crowd of excited onlookers from far and wide.

The first shock went in favour of the English. After some hours, there was a break for drinks. 'Good was that wine of Anjou, I trow', carolled the contemporary French ditty. During the interval, Bamborough insulted Beaumanoir, calling scornfully, 'Slay thee I will not, but I will give thee for a gift to my leman.' At this, a Breton drove his spear full into his face, his visor open as it was, and when he struggled to his feet, another dispatched him. General battle was resumed. Croquart rallied the shaken English into a serried ring where they fought like lions. The steady clash of metal and the punctuating thud of Billefort's mace could be heard a mile away. Beaumanoir, wounded and weary, left the field but was called back by a gruff companion: 'Drink thine own blood, Beaumanoir, and thy thirst will pass!' Towards evening a Breton, breaking the rules, charged into the English phalanx on a heavily armoured horse and mowed them down.

That was the end. The English had lost eight killed, besides their captain. The rest were carried off to Josselin, where they were set free on light ransoms as became their valour. By common consent, Croquart was named the hero of the hour. King John of France made tempting offers afterwards to win him over, but Croquart, who was by then worth forty thousand crowns, always refused. Eventually he broke his neck training a new roan for his much-valued stable. Everyone who fought that day bore the marks for life. Years later, Froissart met one of the Bretons at the table of King Charles of France, his face still scarred and twisted almost out of human semblance. For all that, nothing had been decided about the fate of Brittany.

In 1349 the Battle of the Thirty was still two years in the future, but it is the best documented of several similar episodes that were happening at the time. This kind of thing was much to Edward's taste. Judging from the escape of the royal family, during the year of the pestilence he was medically well advised. He sensibly saw it through at Havering Bower and other quiet palaces. But inactivity chafed his spirit, and his restlessness involved him gratefully, when the opportunity arose, in surely the most irresponsible adventure ever undertaken by a king of England.

The precious castle of Calais was in the charge of one Emeric, or Aimery, of Pavia, a Lombard. There is much doubt as to who this person was. Froissart says that Edward had brought him up from a child, and loved him; though his subsequent treatment makes no suggestion of any special bond between them, such as that Aimery's son, who comes into the story later, was really Edward's bastard. He had been captain of the Calais galleys since April 1348 and presumably therefore was a sailor of distinction. Calais suffered badly from the plague. Sir John Montgomery, whom Edward had left in command on his departure in October 1347, and his wife both died of it, and so probably did at least one successor; it seems likely that Aimery had thereby gained temporary promotion *faute de mieux*. All the same, it is strange that Edward should have entrusted the hard-won apple of his eye to a little-known foreigner.

So at any rate thought Geoffrey de Charny, the resolute French governor of Saint-Omer, who saw a chance to retrieve the disgrace of France. Like other Lombards, this Aimery might be fond of gold. Late in October 1349, after cautious soundings, with or without King Philip's knowledge (though probably with, in view of the large sum involved), he proposed that Aimery should betray Calais to him for 20,000 crowns. Aimery swore to the bargain on the Sacrament, but sent a messenger scudding across the Channel to tell Edward. Edward, who at that time of plague could not launch an effective reinforcement, told him to carry on with de Charny as though nothing were amiss. In the next few weeks the details were worked out. The French attack was to go in at night, on the stroke of the New Year 1350. De Charny insisted on strict safeguards. The money was to be paid to Aimery only when the castle of Calais was delivered, and in exchange Aimery was to hand over his son as a security. Meanwhile de Charny mustered a considerable striking force in deep secrecy at Saint-Omer.

Edward sent for Sir Walter Manny, the perfect leader for the plan he had in mind. In the middle of the Christmas holidays, Manny sailed from Dover with a select party well sprinkled with the young nobility. With them went Edward and the Black Prince, who were to serve incognito under Manny's banner. They arrived at Calais after dark and were taken to Aimery in the castle. On the last night of the year, de Charny approached Calais by the only bridge at Nieulay, where he detached the Lord de Fiennes to hold it against possible interference. He then moved on to the Boulogne gate of the town, where he sent off Sir Edward de Renty, with about a hundred men, to the postern gate of the castle, where Aimery let them in. Aimery gave up his son, and received from de Renty the bag of gold, which he tossed into a lock-up saying there was no time to count it. But while he was showing his visitors over the fortress the drawbridge was quietly hauled up; and when he drew the bolts that opened the great door of the keep, King Edward bounded out at the head of his ambush and, with a great cry of 'Manny to the rescue', released Aimery and his son, and locked the others in.

A party was sent off to seize the bridge at Nieulay, which they did after fierce fighting, though de Fiennes got away on horseback. The rest assembled inside the Boulogne gate, where de Charny was waiting impatiently for Aimery to admit him, and complaining about the winter cold. The king and the prince took the French horses in the yard, and streamed out of the town by opposite sally ports to fall upon his flanks.

Because of the darkness of the swampy Calais pale, both sides fought dismounted. After their first surprise, the French, whose lances had been shortened into spears, recovered gamely, and they had by far the greater numbers. In the blundering, scattered struggle Edward came to grips with a knight of quality, later shown to be Sir Eustace de Ribemont from Picardy; though they were often separated as the battle surged between them, their duel went on all night. Twice Edward was knocked to his knees by mighty strokes, twice he fought back, and as he slammed away with his great sword he exclaimed from force of habit 'Ha! St Edward. Ha! St George', an unmistakable war-cry which revealed to the astounded Frenchmen as well as to many of his own side that the king of England was in their midst; to everyone, in fact, except his hard-pressed adversary, who did not find out until afterwards. As the New Year's dawn came up, de Charny, seeing the tall figure slashing away alone under Manny's banner (or, three chevrons sable), drove forward to make an earth-shattering capture, but his way was blocked by the Black Prince. In daylight, the English archers posted on dry spits between the marshes were able to pick out targets; Edward at last brought Sir Eustace to surrender, and by ten o'clock all was over. The remaining French, including de Charny, badly wounded, and his son, were herded off to join de Renty and his disconsolate posse in the dungeons.[41]

That evening Edward gave a feast in the great hall of Calais castle, when the prince and his friends served the first course to the captives before sitting at the high table with his father. After the wine and comfits, the king moved down among his guests. To de Charny, whose wounds had been patched by his own doctors, he only shook his head in sorrowful rebuke. But to his own prisoner Sir Eustace he gave the chaplet of pearls that he was wearing, telling him to show it proudly among the ladies, and quitting him of ransom. Sir Eustace was so charmed that he added three chaplets of pearls to his coat of arms.

Walter Manny, a baron since 1347, was further rewarded with a pardon for all escapes from the Marshalsea prison during his year as governor, a substantial indemnity, also lands near Bordeaux and on the Scottish Border. Sir Guy Brian, the standard bearer, was made knight baronet with a generous annuity. To Aimery, Edward was less gracious. The day after the battle he replaced him in command at Calais by the more estimable John Beauchamp, brother of the earl of Warwick, and exposed him, as he had done an earlier informer, Henry de Malestrit of Brittany, to the vengeance of his enemies. Aimery, once astute, behaved as if besotted.

Apparently unaware that the French owed him any malice, he led a life of careless debauchery in the small castle Edward gave him outside Calais. After buying himself out in London, de Charny raided it at dawn, caught Aimery in bed with a girl sent to him from England, and had him cut into little pieces with satisfying deliberation in the crowded market place at Saint-Omer. His girl-friend, released from whatever contract she had engaged in, settled down unremorsefully with a squire of France.

Later in that same year of 1350 the king, who now clearly saw himself as an impresario of merit, was able to stage a yet more sensational spectacle, this time not secretly in the murk of winter, but in the full blaze of an English summer afternoon.

After Princess Joan of the Tower so sadly failed in her task of marrying Prince Pedro, the heir of Castile, French influence had won back lost ground, and a French princess, Blanche de Bourbon, had been chosen in her place. Matters were not improved when the shrewd statesman King Alphonso died, also of the plague, for Pedro, then aged about fourteen, if not yet actively unhinged, was already an unpredictable young man. By the spring of 1350 the great Castilian fleet was at sea under Charles de la Cerda, even more French-oriented than his brother and predecessor, Don Luis of Spain, who had died in 1347. Charles de la Cerda was a close friend of Duke John, the heir to the throne of France, and was husband of a sister of Charles of Blois, the French-Breton leader now a prisoner in London. He had preyed on the English wineships from Bordeaux, and hampered Henry of Lancaster on his return from a foray in Aquitaine. He had then sailed on in stately insolence up the Channel to Sluys, once again a safe French landfall, where he posed a threat to the English wool trade, if not to Calais itself, so recently preserved from treachery. Early in August he was preparing to return to Spain with his English prizes and laden with cloth of Flanders.

Edward resolved to intercept the overbold marauders. He fitted out a motley fleet of some fifty vessels, and on 10 August his archbishops ordered public prayers for the success of the campaign. It was to be a tournament at sea, and very much a royal occasion. When he went down to Winchester he dragooned everyone – his queen, the Black Prince, who had in tow his admiring brother John of Gaunt, aged ten, and many founder members of, and eager aspirants for, the new Order of the Garter. Not that they required much bidding. As he embarked he was especially pleased at the timely arrival from overseas of Robert of Namur, Philippa's nephew and afterwards Froissart's patron, to whom he gave his *Salle du Roy*, or flagship, since he himself was to sail in his small cog *Thomas*, veteran of Sluys ten years before, and since become the famous imprint on his gold nobles.

Monday 29 August 1350 was spent standing-to on board. During the long wait Edward wore négligé, a black velvet jacket and a hat of beaver fur. His officers had never seen him look so well. He ordered his music to play a German dance lately brought back to England by John Chandos, and gaily made Chandos sing to it. At last towards evening, the look-out cried 'A sail!' Soon he called down 'Yes, I see two, three, four – so many that, God help me, I cannot count them.' The king ordered wine, and as they drank they fastened on their armour and closed their visors for the day. The ships formed line of battle, and the trumpets sounded.

La Cerda, with the wind behind him and his massive sheets, could easily have sailed straight on. He did not intend to do so. He had in his company forty-four huge carracks, and he had delayed in Sluys fitting his merchantment with wooden castles, and loading extra men, catapults, and tons of iron bars. He may even have proposed, as Edward declared, to lead Philip's threatened landing in depopulated England; to do that, he would have first to win the Channel. He steered straight towards the toy armament now frisking out of port to meet him.

Philippa and her ladies had been installed in an abbey high on the Downs with a broad view of the sea. The day through, she saw nothing except the sunlight tediously dappling the water. Then towards vespers she saw, bursting one after another through the summer haze, countless proud ships in full sail, pennants streaming forward with the wind, sheer sides, towering castles bristling with tiny figures like beans with blackfly; and she saw the garishly festooned English pinnaces scudding out towards them, arriving, weaving in and out. With them went her eldest and her next-to-youngest sons and, incorrigibly more boyish than either, the king their father. That was all she knew, and she could learn little from the excited exclamations of her courtiers. Goodness knows how the anxious lady passed that dreadful evening. Perhaps she had her maids dress her dark hair. It was droll, this battle of 'Les Espagnols sur Mer'.

About midnight, her menfolk clattered in, wet and grimy, safe and sound, all talking volubly. The king, it seemed, as if in the lists, had crashed head on into the leading Spaniard, making no impression although his own prow split and his ship began to fill. He scrambled aboard another enemy and flung its heavy weighted company into the sea. He had won a handsome prize, but the cog *Thomas* would be of service only as a showpiece. The Black Prince too had tried to ram, but had been holed by a stone from a springalle, or was it a trebuchet, and, sinking fast, wallowed knee-deep while the enemy threw down on him iron bars and everything they had. Happily Henry of Lancaster boarded from the other quarter, and hauled the prince and his small brother to safety before their ship went down. As darkness fell, Robert of Namur found himself grappled by an enormous galleon and towed helplessly away. He called vainly in the gloom to save the *Salle du Roy*, and would have become the only ignominious Spanish gain from the now decided battle, had not Hannequin his squire climbed aboard the abductor, cut down the mainsail with his sword, and entangled their astonished captors in its shrouds. It had been a well-fought day, though they all regretted the death, among many others, of poor Richard Goldesborough. Young John of Gaunt was no doubt packed off to bed. The rest got very merry.

As at Sluys, the longbow had outmatched the arbalest. As at Sluys, the Spaniards had overfilled their ships. About half their great men-of-war had fallen into English hands. The rest limped back into Flemish ports where they still lay in November. A year later, on 1 August 1351, an effective twenty-one-year truce was signed with King Pedro of Castile. The French had once more lost the balance of power at sea.

A week before this battle of Winchelsea, on 22 August 1350, King Philip of Valois died and was gathered (or rather the more durable bits of him after the embalmers had finished with him, were gathered) to his cousins at Saint-Denis. He was succeeded by his son, John the Good, more properly John the Hearty, a mature man of thirty, father of seven children by his first wife, Bonne of Luxemburg, daughter of the late King John of Bohemia, on whom he seems to have modelled himself. His heir apparent, Charles, aged thirteen, now became the first dauphin of the recently purchased Dauphiné de Vienne. For Edward, the change from the morose and wary Philip was a fortunate one. A knight of the old school, John was chivalrous, extravagant, generous to his favourites, a man of honour who always kept his word, and easily predictable. Yet he was also cross and hasty; knowing he was continually outwitted, he was given to sudden bear-like rages. Distinguished so far, according to Perroy, by gallantry and military incompetence, he had been given by his father all the old Angevin provinces, Normandy, Anjou and Maine, to hold against Edward, towards whom, eight years his senior, his formal enmity was tempered by huge admiration and a misplaced trust.

The disastrous tendency of John's mixed disposition became evident at once. In October 1351, a year after his accession, he revived the ancient Order of the Star in answer to Edward's Garter, and summoned its first members to their noble mansion at Saint-Ouen, near Paris, where they were to meet each year to discuss all their ventures. Among them came Geoffrey de Charny, redeemed from England, once more governor of Saint-Omer and now Chamberlain of France; John of Artois, more loyal than his father, Edward's rebel Robert, and now comte d'Eu and Guînes in succession to the unfortunate Count Raoul, lately beheaded; and Walter de Brienne, Master of the Horse, the new lord of Guînes castle in right of Count Raoul's only daughter, his wife Jeanne.

The castle of Guînes, about six miles from Calais, was a solid fortress built in the ancient style. Since the fall of Calais it had been a point of vantage from which the French could obstruct English efforts to extend their pale. At the moment they were engaged in strengthening it. Somehow, during the absence of all the important officers in the district at the long solemnities at Saint-Ouen, the castle of Guînes was taken by the English.

The English story, as given by Geoffrey le Baker and Robert of Avesbury, was that the affair was purely local and fortuitous. An English archer, John of Doncaster, had been captured in the marshes and imprisoned with others like him in the castle. He had been allowed to work with the French labourers in the daytime and, going to and fro, made friends with a companionable young laundress. In the panting intervals of their commerce, she obligingly told him that the apparently impassable moat could be crossed by way of a wall only knee deep below the surface, provided for the use of fishermen. He tried it out one night, and made his way to Calais, where he lay up until the curfew lifted, before greeting his former comrades in the town with good news of likely gain. They got scaling ladders, blacked their armour, and after darkness followed him back to Guînes. They recrossed the moat, dispatched the watchmen on the walls, surprised the garrison playing chess and hazard in the hall, and tumbled the knights and ladies from their beds. Next morning they courteously set the ladies free with their belongings, released their fellow prisoners, and with surprising competence made good their capture. Later that day they were reinforced from Calais. When Walter de Brienne, the absent lord of Guînes, demanded on whose orders they had seized the castle in time of truce, they replied on no man's orders but for their own profit. They would sell it to the highest bidder, but in order to avert the king of England's anger at their indiscipline, he should have the first refusal. Edward rapidly took up his lucky option, and in January 1352 became master of the key to Calais.

King John complained at Edward's breach of faith. Edward replied that the truce did not forbid buying and selling, and that he had done no more. John did not accept the explanation; deciding that Sir William Beauconray, deputy captain of Guînes at the crucial time, had done the selling, he had him torn to pieces by wild horses.

In seizing his chance at Guînes, Edward had done no more than de Charny had tried to do at Calais. Adaptability was the order of the day. To judge from his merry air at Winchelsea, he may for a time have intended that battle to be his last, a grand valedictory climax to the ten years of glorious war begun at Sluys. He had made the point he had always laboured. He, the habitually seasick sailor, ruled the waves, and Parliament dutifully proclaimed him king of the sea. His treaty with Castile made his realm impregnable. At home, his authority was supreme. It would be a fitting moment to conclude the general peace the church so earnestly urged, to gather up the ransoms due to him, to bask in his fame and retire to a life of ease.

Apparently with such a course in mind, he twice offered to restore David of Scotland to his throne in return for homage and an enormous payment, and was prevented only by the bitter refusal of the Scots to have him for their overlord. Yet even this gracious gesture, like all Edward's ploys, had as its hidden motive the further weakening of France. It is more likely that his peaceful mien derived more from domestic difficulties, the restrictive effect of the plague, and his inability to get money out of Parliament except with increasingly intrusive stipulations, than from a genuine change of heart. He would accept a general settlement when he could get satisfactory terms, but there was always the chance the terms could be improved, especially now that John was king of France. So for the next few years Edward played the diplomatic game, on the whole without success.

In 1352 he persuaded his prisoner Charles of Blois, whom he could persuade to almost anything, to return to Brittany as his vassal, while Edward, in exchange, abandoned his young ward John de Montfort, Blois's rival. It would have meant that both claimants to Brittany were in Edward's homage and neither in that of France. The unfortunate Blois got as far as Calais; but on entering France to see about his ransom was called to his senses by the militant tongue of his wife, Jeanne de Penthièvre, the real heiress, who reproached him with betraying the recent sacrifices of their gallant Thirty at the Halfway Oak. Her counsels quickly prevailed, the French alliance was resumed, and Blois had to return to his sad captivity in England.

The Low Countries were another theatre where French interests might be damaged. In 1345 Count William III of Hainault, Philippa's brother, had died leaving his three sisters as his heirs. Edward's prompt claim for Philippa's share was easily defeated, and the eldest sister, the dowager Empress Margaret, who had French backing, was successful. She made her son William of Bavaria her regent, but they soon fell out, and both appealed to Edward. Edward awarded Hainault to Margaret and the rest of the inheritance to William, whom in 1352 he married to Maude, Henry of Lancaster's elder daughter, already a widow though only ten. Next year the grateful William sent grain to relieve famine in England, and when his mother died in 1356 he reunited Hainault to his other provinces. Edward's new alliance to the north-east of France, though short-lived owing to the fact that in 1358 William became incurably insane, served for the moment to offset a reverse Edward had sustained in neighbouring Flanders.

There, Count Louis de Malines, who had jilted Edward's daughter Isabella, had married instead Margaret, daughter of his estranged ally Duke John III of Brabant. In 1350 they had produced a solitary heiress, another Margaret. Embassies from both France and England were quickly beside the cradle of the important infant. Edward tried to marry her to John of Gaunt, but her father, Louis, as usual preferred the French connection, and her great potential was lost to England in 1354 when she was betrothed to the boy-duke of Burgundy, Philip de Rouvre, son of the widowed Joan of Boulogne, who was now King John's second wife.

While his ministers, particularly the devoted Lancaster, struggled with these intricate affairs, Edward made the most of his unsought-for leisure. He moved grandly about the country from manor to manor, showing his splendour to the people, and enjoying the lusty pastimes proper to his rank; hunting, coursing, hawking (he was an expert judge of falcons), tilting, feasting and engendering children (his twelfth and last child and seventh son, Thomas, was born at Woodstock early in 1355). He was suitably pious and munificent, and he was a mighty builder.

His buildings reflected a character more practical than aesthetic. Whether military or charitable, they displayed a mixture of magnificence, common sense and royal whimsy. At Cambridge, he completed his endowment of King's Hall, begun early in his reign and later swallowed up by Henry VIII's huge edifice of Trinity. He built St Mary's Abbey at Eastminster; the abbey cloisters were begun; and St Stephen's chapel was converted into a college in 1353. Its walls bore paintings of the king and his family, long since destroyed, though copies have been preserved by the Society of Antiquaries. One of them may be the only surviving likeness of Edward as a young man, since a vessel the crowned figure carries may well have been one of two he is known to have possessed, containing respectively relics of St Stephen and one of St Adrian's teeth. Nearby he built a belfry with three huge bells so sonorous that, to the dismay of the inhabitants of Westminster, they soured all the beer in the neighbourhood.

Pride of place went to his great works at Windsor castle. In 1347, as soon as he could leave Sandwich after his dreadful voyage home from Calais, Edward had gone by way of Southampton, where he inspected the new curtain walls, to Winchester, to discuss with his friend and Treasurer, Bishop William Edington, his interrupted project of making Windsor into a worthy home for his new order of chivalry. Shrewd and to the point as always, Edington produced the very man he needed, William of Wykeham, a young man lately come into his service, then in his early twenties. Wykeham was of sound English stock, of secular upbringing, of marked ability, and already a student of masonic science; he was of practical outlook, and his natural ambition ensured he would make the most of his opportunities. Edward had him tonsured to get him a clerical living at no cost to the crown, and tried him out on minor tasks at first, the care of his dogs and horses. Wykeham soon proved himself indispensable, and a few years later, in 1356, became a surveyor of the works at Windsor, where John Spanlee, master mason since the Ramsays, William and John, had died in the plague, was pressing on in spite of shortages. Wykeham did so well that twenty years after he left it he returned to Winchester, following Edington as bishop, and aspired to the highest office as chancellor. The story goes that he inscribed on the finished walls at Windsor 'Hoc fecit Wykeham' and, taken to task by the king for boastfulness, nimbly protested that it meant not 'Wykeham made this', but in all accuracy, 'This made Wykeham'.[42]

Meanwhile, in the early 1350s the kingdom at large was prosperous and quiet. In 1353 the wool staple was brought home to England, to the benefit of home producers as against the king's rich money-lending friends, and Parliament was placid; while the people in general were busy reshaping their lives after the miseries of the Black Death.

Not that there were no commotions. A long, stormy winter in 1352–3 was followed by drought, and then by the famine that William of Bavaria tried to relieve with his gift of corn. To make matters worse, the Black Prince, whose reckless spending had severely encumbered his estates, chose this heedless moment to lay harsh exactions upon his tenants. The result was a serious rebellion in Cheshire, the only one of the whole long reign. The Welsh Marches were always sensitive, and the rebellion was grave enough for the king to send Lancaster, Warwick and Stafford from the adjacent counties to help his son reduce his earldom by a firm application of discreet though sufficient force. The rising was punished by a commission of Trailbaston and savage fines as a means to cutting down the prince's mountainous debts.

Then, in February 1355, on St Scholastica's Day, the brittle calm of Oxford was suddenly destroyed. A student brawl about the wine at the Mermaid Tavern led to riots. The bells of St Martin's sounded for the Town; the university church of St Mary answered for the Gown. The Chancellor calling for order was greeted with a flight of arrows, for archers denied their legitimate occupation were ready to turn their aim on less conventional targets. Neighbouring villages joined in, and the riot became a three-day battle. The townsmen set about the pampered scholars with ferocious cries of 'Havak, havak, smyst faste, gyt good knock.' Dons were scalped in mockery of their tonsure. Some thirty students were recorded killed; others disappeared secretly in the latrines and were never seen again. The Halls were broken into and the plate stolen, only Merton remaining inviolate behind its ancient walls. The schools dispersed. For some time afterwards timorous freshmen sought matriculation at the less venerable but less embattled Cambridge. The king's council took the matter up. The mayor of Oxford was imprisoned, the town placed under interdict, and an annual compensation levied which continued to be enforced for nearly five hundred years before the university, itself far from blameless, at last relented.[43] But these rare outbreaks had clearly discernible local causes and were easily controlled. They were far removed from the perpetual civil wars in the time of Edward's father.

* * *

The dawdling prospect of a lasting peace gained impetus in December 1352 when Pope Clement died and Cardinal Etienne Aubert became Pope

Innocent VI. Though no less French in sympathy than Clement, Innocent had a real determination to end the contumacious strife between his leading children-in-God, and as a jurist he gave tangible form to his resolve. He ordered a conference of all concerned to meet at once to work out a draft for his approval, on the footing that each side should give up its chief demand, King John his insistence on feudal homage for Guienne and Aquitaine, Edward his claimed hereditary title to the throne. Edward had doubts of the conference's impartiality, since it was to be conducted by the agile Cardinal Guy de Boulogne, who was uncle to the reigning queen of France. But he had to comply, and soon a powerful embassy was on its way to Guînes, led by Archbishop Simon Islip, Duke Henry of Lancaster, Bishop Bateman of Norwich, and Richard Arundel.

King John was no more ready than Edward to lay aside the sword. In his stolid way he saw it as his kingly duty to recover, truce or no, all that Edward had taken from his father. In truth his kingdom was in no better case than England to support the war. Though France was proportionately less hard hit numerically by the plague, John faced many of Edward's problems, with a government less concerted and more venal. John's equivalent of the statute of labourers was no more effective than its model. His *gabelle* and other taxes were uncollected and unpaid. His debasement of the issue of gold *moutons*, so called because they bore the Lamb of God on the reverse, produced inflation of 70 per cent within six years. Therefore his soldierly attempts to reform the army were valueless. Unable to pay their men, captains disbanded them with the result that they wandered mutinously, living off the already stricken country. Though John won back Saint-Jean-d'Angély in Poitou, that was the limit of his success; he was held off in Aquitaine by Ralph, the new earl of Stafford. John's scattered forays did more harm than good since his smarter opponent, Edward, could point to his flagrant contraventions of the truce and plead the right of self-defence for his retaliations.

Yet John's campaigning did only minor damage to his cause. More damaging was the fault of temperament which drove him to over-reward his favourites and destroy those against whom he nursed a grudge. As soon as possible after his accession he had given the two high offices of state to personal friends. Geoffrey de Charny, failed hero of the Calais coup, became Chamberlain; and on the execution of Raoul, comte d'Eu, his place as Constable was taken by Charles de la Cerda, the Spanish pensioner at the court of France. Indeed, it was said that the unfortunate comte d'Eu's abrupt demise was in part explained by John's desire to make room for la Cerda, and that their intimacy was too close for propriety. The defeat of his Castilian fleet at Winchester did nothing to reduce la Cerda's favour. Early in 1352 John married him to Margaret daughter of Charles of Blois, as part of the plan worked out with Jeanne de Penthièvre to win back her husband from the persuasive Edward by paying off

Blois's ransom as collateral. Though the scheme fell to pieces when the supporting French invasion of Brittany was routed at Mauron by Sir Walter Bentley with the loss of so many gallant knights of the Star, la Cerda's marriage drew him even closer into the royal orbit. To provide for him in his new station, John gave him the county of Angoulême. It was to prove a disastrous error, for it brought John into conflict with the man who in the end would drive him to captivity and ruin. Angoulême was not John's to give; it was bespoken to Charles of Navarre.

Charles of Navarre has not been popular with historians of whatever allegiance, and though he was not so called by his contemporaries, he is commonly known as Charles the Bad. It has had to be conceded that he was handsome and delicate in person, melodiously well-spoken, debonair, quick, daring, a competent soldier, and every inch the royal scion that he was. But it is also said that his fine appearance, like his whole life, was a lie, and that he was ambitious, greedy, sly and unprincipled – a 'perpetual conspirator', murderously expert in his chosen art of poisoning. The catalogue of contrasting qualities, a kaleidoscope of good and evil in a single person, fairy tale prince one moment, villain of melodrama the next, is bewildering. It is only grudgingly, if at all, conceded that his unamiable propensities were forced on him by circumstance, and that there was justice in his claim to be the true king of France, Prince of the Lilies on all sides, robbed of his high destiny. Against the might of established monarchy, his only resort was guile. There could be no question of keeping his word.

When Louis X died in 1316, his rightful successor had been his only daughter, Jeanne, Charles's mother-to-be. But France had never been ruled by a queen, and Jeanne was not even a woman, merely a little girl. Her mother, Margaret of Burgundy, had died a prisoner in Château-Gaillard after the scandal of the Tour de Nesle, and Jeanne's legitimacy could be questioned. Moreover, her father had died leaving his second wife, Clemence, pregnant with a possible son. Naturally, the late king's brother, Jeanne's uncle, Philip the Long, took charge; and when the awaited child, John the Posthumous, for one reason or another lived for only a few days, it was easy for him to declare Jeanne unacceptable in all respects, and become king himself as Philip V. He fobbed her off with her lesser title as queen of Navarre. He married her well to Count Philip of Evreux, an obliging prince of the royal blood. And he promised her the fat lands of Champagne and Brie, though, as his coronation went unchallenged, he never quite brought himself to give them up.

When Philip died, Jeanne was again passed over by her younger uncle, Charles IV. In 1328, when all other Capets had left the stage, Jeanne was a third time set aside, this time by her cousin, Philip of Valois. Her husband died at the siege of Algeciras in 1343, and she was left a forgotten widow who never even saw her queendom of Navarre. But Philip of Valois now had another, less patient rival in Edward of England, and he, having a solicitous regard for French royalty in distress, found sanctuary for her and her several children in Aquitaine. A year later, Jeanne died there, of the plague.

Jeanne's eldest son, Charles, born in 1332 when Philip had already been four years on the throne, came on the scene too late to defend his mother's cause, though as a boy he may have heard his parents mulling over their shabby lot sometimes on winter evenings. Nearly of age at her death, he took up his crown of Navarre, and determined to right her wrongs on his own behalf, not yet thinking as high as the crown of France but of the compensatory provinces long promised and still withheld. King Philip, embroiled with Edward, was well aware of the threat Charles posed. His little kingdom of Navarre lay far away beyond the Pyrenees, but his patrimony, the county of Evreux, was in the heart of France. It embraced large tracts of Normandy, parts easily accessible to Edward, with Caen and Pontoise; and his fortress of Nantes and Meulan commanded the Seine almost up to the gates of Paris. To improve family feeling, for at his age there can have been no other reason, Philip, in the last months of his life married Charles's seventeen-year-old sister, Blanche; also, in place of Champagne and Brie, he promised him Angoulême, more quickly available though less valuable.

King John carried on his father's efforts at appeasement. He made Charles his lieutenant in Languedoc, and included him with the other princes of the blood and his favourites, la Cerda and de Charny, among the first knights of the Star. Charles fawned at court, apparently content; but by 1351 he was already in touch with Edward about a dismemberment of France. In 1352, John, unsuspecting, gave him the hand of his little daughter Princess Jeanne; but the dowry, probably of more interest to Charles than his child bride, was not paid up. Rich gifts wax poor when givers prove unkind. At this tactless moment John gave Angoulême to la Cerda, and the fat was in the fire.

Edward watched the mounting tension closely. He knew that he had no lasting affinity with Charles of Navarre. Essentially, they were rivals for John's crown. Charles's claim through his mother was exactly like his own, except that, annoyingly, it was superior, stemming from the senior branch. But unlike most pretenders Charles had to face not one, but two, powerfully entrenched opponents. He could not make his way alone. For the moment John was their common enemy. Charles could become a convenient replacement for Edward's long list of earlier cat's-paws, Baliol in Scotland, Robert of Artois, John de Montfort, Godfrey de Harcourt. Perhaps they could come to some arrangement later. Edward told Lancaster, for all practical purposes his foreign minister, to sound Charles out.

Henry of Lancaster found an ingenious opportunity. In that same year of 1352, passing through Cologne after a frustrating trip to the crusade in Prussia, he told how he had been waylaid and robbed, and dropped the name of Otto of Brunswick, King John's fiery retainer. Otto's challenge swiftly followed him back to London, and soon Henry was on his way to Paris for a judicial combat. The famous soldier was given a rapturous ovation; so rapturous that when the usually flamboyant Otto came into the lists at Saint-Germain-des-Prés, either from unease because the home crowd was against him, or possibly drugged, he reeled in his saddle, dropped his shield, and was unable to couch his lance. King John hastily flung down his warder, dismissed the quarrel as a nullity without awarding costs, and after many consultations, Henry went home with the chaste token he had chosen from the king's carte-blanche, a single thorn from the sacred crown in the Sainte-Chapelle for his Newark at Leicester.

The thorn was not his only trophy from the pantomime at Paris. While there, he had met Charles of Navarre, present for his wedding to the young Jeanne. They shared a distant ancestress in Blanche of Artois, niece of St Louis: she had married, first, Henry III of Navarre and, second, Edmund Crouchback, first earl of Lancaster. This led to Charles being Henry's sponsor for the duel. Their preparations allowed them long, intimate discussions. Perhaps Charles was to blame for Otto's strange malaise; he certainly expressed his resentment about la Cerda and Angoulême.

The peace conference met at Guînes in the new year, and rumbled on inconclusively through most of 1353. In his capacity as Constable of France, la Cerda was always in attendance. When it broke up for Christmas he retired to his chateau at L'Aigle in Normandy, part of the dowry of Margaret of Blois, his wife, and hard by territories of Charles of Navarre. On 8 January 1354, Charles surprised the hated Constable at dawn, and had him murdered in his bed.

He did not attempt to hide his guilt from the outraged King John. He shut himself up at Evreux and prepared for war. 'Know that it was I who had the Constable killed', he bragged in a letter to Lancaster – he dealt through Lancaster as his personal relative in order to preserve the fiction of Edward's supposed neutrality. As though the signal had been prearranged, Edward, hoping to gain better terms at Guînes, told Lancaster to press on with an invasion of Normandy in support of Charles's rebellion. But before it was ready, John gave way, aghast at the implications and still weak from the defeat at Mauron. On the advice of Cardinal Guy de Boulogne, who did not wish his now promising peace conference to be upset, John met Charles at Nantes in February 1354. At the intercession of two queens dowager, his aunt, Jeanne of Evreux, the widow of Charles IV, and his sister Blanche, widow of Philip VI, Charles begged pardon for the murder in return for a huge cash payment and a large part of the Cotentin peninsula, with lordship over Edward's Norman allies, the de Harcourts. He then wrote again to Lancaster saying that his quarrel with King John was over. Lancaster had to put off his invasion and take in professional good part the diplomatic quip of Guy de Boulogne that his hole had been stopped for slipping into France. At no cost to himself Charles had outwitted both the rival powers. He had foxed the redoubtable Lancaster, and extorted panic concessions from King John at an imaginary sword-point.

Guy de Boulogne also was pleased at the reconciliation. By April 1354 his draft treaty of Guînes, safe from last-minute distortions, was ready for ratification by Pope Innocent at Avignon. On the whole it was favourable to France, but Edward could not now fail to abide by it. In May he asked Parliament whether they wanted a lasting peace, and was answered with a resounding shout of 'Aye! Aye!' During the autumn, the English embassy set off piecemeal for Avignon; among them one who was to die there, William Bateman, bishop of Norwich and founder of Trinity Hall, the affluent lawyers' college at Cambridge. Last to leave were the leaders, Richard of Arundel and Henry of Lancaster, who carried a secret schedule of extra provinces such as Normandy, that Edward was to lay claim to, together with the order that he could give them up for a 'bonne fees'. In spite of safe-conducts, Henry had a small army of five hundred in his company, and when they arrived on Christmas Eve it took all day for them to press through the welcoming dignitaries to the great Palais des Papes.

Henry was lodged with the chief French delegate, Duke Pierre of Bourbon, in the rooms of the pope's own brother, splendidly fitted with crimson carpets in place of the usual rushes. Though he and Arundel had been given large allowances to match the polished magnificence of the occasion, his private outlay during his two months' stay more than doubled that for all his other diplomatic missions put together. Twenty-five thousand gallons of the best Bordeaux were crammed into his cellars. Wherever he went, all declared 'how he had not his fellow in the world'. Everything was geared towards success. And yet, the gorgeous ceremony mysteriously ended in utter failure.

The reason was Charles of Navarre. His case was included for consideration in the general settlement, and in November he too left Normandy for Avignon, where a bishop's lodgings were made ready for him. But even as he set out, King John, suspecting he was plotting to betray their new agreement, descended like a whirlwind upon Normandy and seized his castles. Charles arrived not in headlong flight as he made out, but with a fresh grievance to add to the set purpose John suspected. The effect was catastrophic. The French were having second thoughts about surrendering the homage for Aquitaine. As architect of the peace, Guy de Boulogne, trying to bring them to their senses by an obvious threat, allowed Henry of Lancaster and Charles to use his rooms for ostentatious secret meetings. But far from driving the French to endorse the terms of Guînes as Guy intended, the two agreed to ditch the peace on grounds of French intransigence, and revived their scheme to partition France by force.

At the end of February 1355 the conference dissolved, merely prolonging the truce from April to the end of June. The war was then to be resumed. King David of Scotland, having got so far towards release that he was at Newcastle awaiting only the surrender of his hostages, had to return to his captivity. Charles went on down to Navarre beyond John's reach and began to raise an army. Henry of Lancaster, avoiding an attempt to arrest him on the way, went home to England.

Edward's plans for his new campaign were already laid. In general they were to follow the successful Crécy pattern of ten years earlier. The Black Prince would go to Aquitaine, as Lancaster had done in 1345. After driving south and east to eradicate French encroachments towards Bordeaux, he would stand poised to march north towards Lancaster, who by that time would have landed in Normandy in support of operations already launched by Charles of Navarre. Even before the peace conference at Avignon had finally broken down, approaches had been made to the Emperor Charles IV to fill the role previously designed for Jacob van Artevelde of Flanders, of leading a third probe from the eastern frontier into France.

At first sight such a proposal sounds a forlorn hope, for the Emperor Charles had hitherto had strong French connections. He had spent seven formative years at the court of France, where he had been tutored by Cardinal Pierre Roger, who later as Pope Clement VI, notoriously French-minded, had secured the Empire for him. He had close marriage ties with the French royal family, and he had fought for France at Crécy, where his blind father had died heroically. Yet the idea was not by now impossible. Since he became emperor, differences of interest had developed with King John about their border provinces, the Dauphiné for one. Edward had obliged him by not thwarting his election. Furthermore, not only Pope Clement, but his family connections with France, his elderly first wife, King Philip's sister Blanche, and his own sister Bonne, mother of King John's numerous family, had been removed by death.

The scheme, however, came to nothing. Charles IV was an oddity for his time and unconventional. Unknightly in appearance, he is described as a round-shouldered man with black hair and beard and sallow cheeks; he was an austere ascetic whose five marriages were certainly more dynastic than sensual in impetus. Like King Robert the Wise of Naples in the previous generation, he was a scholar, a friend of the intellectual Petrarch, a savant and something of a necromancer. As emperor he had turned his back on the rest of Europe, had busied himself with his kingdom of Bohemia, and his great foundation of the University of Prague. The most Edward could wring from him was a cautious promise of neutrality.

Edward resolved to carry on without him. After all, the Flemish advance from the east had in the end contributed nothing to the victory of Crécy, and as he knew very well, imperial allies could be more of a disappointment than an asset. This time the scene of action would be strictly in the west, and he would have, in addition to Godfrey de Harcourt of the Crécy landings, the far more powerful Charles of Navarre, overlord of most of Normandy.

During the spring of 1355 the fleets were busy forming. For once, Edward seems to have reserved no place for himself in the adventure. His fear of censure by the pope for breaking the truce, even in the last months of its existence, is evident. The Black Prince's expedition lying in the southern parts needed no disguise, for there was no reason why he should not reinforce his own duchy of Aquitaine; but Lancaster's vessels, preparing less obviously in the port of London, flew Lancastrian flags and streamers, not the arms of England, to indicate that not Edward, but the duke as a private person, was going to help his kinsman Charles of Navarre regain his rights in Normandy. As war approached, the replacement of arms and armour long disused and rusty became a difficulty. Prices soared, and Edward took stringent measures to break down the armourers' black market prices. When Parliament next met, he caused Sir Walter Manny to explain the disappointment of their hopes for peace by blaming the failure of the conference at Avignon on the French. Since the wool trade was now prospering, he received a ready grant of fifty shillings a sack on wool for the next six years, subject only to the now routine condition that he would not impose any extra-parliamentary levies in the meantime. Their generous provision for a war they did not want allowed him an expenditure, apart from his other resources, of over a thousand marks a day.

When the truce ended at the end of June, events followed promptly and on schedule. On 10 July Lancaster sailed from the Thames, rounded the North Foreland, heading west by south towards Normandy. A little later Charles of Navarre, with Navarrese reinforcements to aid his Norman vassals, arrived at Cherbourg from Bayonne and joined the Black Prince, who sailed in his turn for Aquitaine on 9 September. But as in 1345, the weather once more took a hand. Lancaster could make no progress in the Channel against south-westerly winds, and ended up at Portsmouth in September. Meanwhile, Charles of Navarre had started his offensive, but owing to King John's prescience in seizing Normandy the previous winter, he was too hard pressed to wait for Lancaster to try a landing on beaches now heavily defended. For once, it was not another mercurial change of allegiance but the lack of an alternative that forced him to accept a further reconciliation with King John on 10 September at Valognes.

A Normandy landing was now impossible. Lancaster's expedition was diverted to Brittany, but it did not sail. Instead, since the truce was officially ended, Edward himself took it across to Calais in November, where he ravaged about in the swampy pale on the only apparently purposeless exploit of his life. Presumably he intended to distract King John from Charles of Navarre and Normandy; certainly, John came east towards him, but refused all provocation to give battle. After a fortnight, short of food, Edward returned to Calais, and to the unwelcome news that the Scots, supplied with French arms and money, had once more erupted, stormed Berwick, and taken many prisoners, including Sir Thomas Gray of Heton, veteran of Neville's Cross, who philosophically spent his two years in Edinburgh jail writing the first part of his *Scalacronica*. (See page 240.)

This time Edward did not, as he had so surprisingly done previously when at Calais in 1346, leave the North to fend for itself. He hurried back to England in a rage, blaming all on the captain of Berwick for deserting his post, until Queen Philippa reasonably pointed out that the wretched man had only accompanied him to Calais at his own express command. Once more he set out for the hated Border; once more his supply fleet was storm-shattered on the way; once more the Scots melted away, burning as they went. This time there was no maiden to beguile him. He took from the hopeless Baliol his title King of Scotland, recaptured Berwick, and under the standards of both kingdoms ravaged his way to Edinburgh. But though he expended his anger in the bitter winter darkness, he gained nothing except further Scottish resentment at their 'Burnt Candlemas'.

It was late March 1356 before he was back in the South and able to pick up the threads of his dislocated French campaign. The Black Prince had duly reached Bordeaux in the autumn, carrying his terror south-eastward to the Mediterranean at Narbonne and back again. His men were all in good heart except, as Sir John Wingfield reported, for a shortage of fresh fish and vegetables. He now waited at Libourne, ready to drive north as planned towards the expected invasion in Normandy. Only the invasion had not yet taken place. As in 1345, the main project had been put back for a year.

So far the credits all lay with King John, but not for long. Seeking to raise money for the war, John had gained a grudging grant from the three Estates towards the end of 1355, and had reimposed the hated *gabelle*, or royal salt tax, the equivalent of Edward's *maltôtes* on wool. At the same time, to safeguard Normandy, he invested his son Charles the dauphin as its duke. To reduce discontent at the *gabelle*, the new duke made it his business to consult closely with his leading Norman vassals, Charles of Navarre, for the moment once again in obedience, and the de Harcourt family. Only eighteen and weakly looking, the dauphin showed craft beyond his years. He was able to penetrate the Norman lords' incessant plotting with the English, and he kept his father well informed. On 6 April 1356 King John, riding at full speed from Paris with a powerful guard, appeared suddenly in the great hall of the castle at Rouen where the dauphin was entertaining his new friends to dinner. Charles of Navarre's brother, Philip, and Godfrey, head of the de Harcourts, had wisely stayed away, but Charles himself and the others were arrested. While a scaffold was prepared in the euphemistically named Field of Pardons, John polished off their interrupted feast. Then, after seeing Godfrey's three nephews beheaded without trial, together with a squire called Doublet who had offered violence, he carried Charles of Navarre off to prison in the Louvre, as a hostage too valuable to be disposed of so condignly.

Philip of Navarre and Godfrey de Harcourt rebelled, and raised the Norman countryside to avenge their kinsmen. As soon as possible they crossed to England, and Philip, in his brother's name, did homage to Edward as king of France. The homage was an important condition of Edward's armed assistance, since Charles of Navarre's title to the throne was superior to his own, and only by formally subordinating it could their dealings become satisfactory from Edward's point of view. Godfrey de Harcourt also did homage and, bereft by John's violence of heirs of his own blood, bequeathed to Edward all his lands in the Cotentin peninsula, in particular the valuable estate of Saint Sauveur-le-Vicomte.

The way was now clear for Lancaster's long-deferred invasion. He landed unopposed at La Hogue in June and concentrated at Montebourg near the safe Navarrese territory of Saint-Sauveur, with Philip, Godfrey and Sir Robert Knollys, who brought up a small force from Brittany to join him. In a lightning raid deep into Normandy, Knollys rescued Breteuil and other Navarrese towns that were under siege, and slipped safely back to Montebourg before King John, who was pursuing with his main army, could catch up with him. He then moved down into Brittany, ready to go south to meet the Black Prince when he started his strike northward from Bordeaux. Lancaster had some 3,000 men in all, and the prince perhaps 8,000. Neither could dare to face John separately, though together they might do so, given their high quality and leadership.

King John assessed the situation perfectly. They would try to meet in the valley of the Loire, and there, with the friendly Breton havens at their backs, combine against the enemy. He avoided the error his father had made in 1346, when the force was split and he himself had been sent south only to get tied down at Aiguillon. Instead, he made all towns on the prince's route secure, and sent a force nominally under his third son, the sixteen-year-old John, count of Poitou, afterwards duke of Berry, as far as Bourges, south of the Loire, to watch the prince's progress. Meanwhile he mustered his own great army intact at Chartres, well placed to drive a wedge between his enemies. Though he had failed to destroy Lancaster in Normandy, he could still contain him in the north, and then might catch an isolated Black Prince far from his base in Aquitaine.

Leaving Bernard d'Albret to defend Aquitaine against the count of Armagnac, the prince, with the Captal de Buch and his other Gascon allies, crossed the Dordogne at Bergerac on 4 August 1356 and started his long march north. Probably he had sent word home by a returning ship of his impending departure in response to the landing in Normandy; but that was the last that would be heard of him until he reached Lancaster three hundred miles away, with whom he clearly had no direct contact, since Lancaster only learned the eventual outcome when the astounding news was relayed to him by Edward from England. King John was better informed of the prince's movements than were his friends, through his outpost down at Bourges; and John was waiting for him.

The prince was travelling fast and light. He would be well supplied at his destination but until then he must live off the land passed through. He wasted and plundered as he went, partly to satisfy his men, who had been told they could keep what they could get, partly to tempt the clam-like fortresses on his way to open and give battle. But they obeyed their orders: rather than risk defeat in detail they would let him through into the trap that was prepared for him. Covering a steady ten miles a day, three weeks after he set out from Bergerac he came near Bourges, where he expected to encounter the count of Poitou's holding force. A probe, however, showed that at his approach King John's son had retired towards Tours, so the prince headed north-west in that direction.

By this time both his friends and his enemies were hurrying towards him, making for the Loire, Lancaster south-east from Brittany for Angers, King John due south from Chartres for Blois. Thinking to avoid King John until he had met Lancaster and also, he may have been hoping, his father north of the river, the prince hit the Loire at Amboise, midway between Tours and Blois, on 7 September, and tried to slip across. He could not do so. Amboise was strongly held, the bridge was broken down, and the wide river was in flood. For four days he waited for news of his friends, but no news came. He was short of fodder, short of food, and his extensive train of booty, so dear to his men, was an encumbrance. The French were growing dangerously numerous on the northern bank, and on 10 September King John crossed the Loire at Blois. To avoid encirclement, the prince pulled back from the river to Montbazan twelve miles south, and there at last had word of Lancaster.

The duke had reached the Loire south of Angers. He had not yet crossed, since the bridges were all wrecked, but he evidently hoped to do so, because the prince waited two vital days for him. Indeed, throughout the next fateful week the prince seemed unable to believe that his famous and elusive cousin would not somehow manage to spurt through and join him further south. In fact Lancaster could not do so. For the only time in his life, and at this most crucial moment, the great soldier failed. King John, remembering the English escape by the ford at Blanchetaque on the Somme, had taken steps to make the Loire impassable to his enemies in either direction over all its relevant length, while he could cross it where he chose. He also sent a strong detachment along the north bank to Saumur only thirty miles from Angers, and not only stopped Lancaster, but forced him to retire slowly and disconsolately towards Brittany, abandoning his heartfelt pledge to rescue the heir apparent 'in one way or another'.

On that same 10 September King John passed through Blois, and bore down on Amboise, so lately deserted by the prince. At the same time, following elements of his enormous army swarmed over the Loire on a hundred-mile front between Orleans and Saumur, with orders to pass round the prince and concentrate behind him at Poitiers on his only line of retreat. The country south of the river was alive with the enemy pouring down towards Poitiers. All hope of meeting Lancaster was gone, and in front, only a day's march away, the king of France was methodically preparing to strike. The prince showed his breeding. His retreat, though precipitate, was cool. Before he left Montbazan on the 12th he found time to explain to the papal cardinals, importunate as usual, that it was not in his power to make the truce they craved, as certainly it was not. In all, he covered nearly eighty miles in five days with large French columns skirting him on his western side and King John pursuing him in the east. In all the circumstances, his later claim that his withdrawal towards Poitiers had been no retreat, but a deliberate plan to entice John to his doom, must seem too broad of hindsight.

At Châtellerault, fifty miles south of the Loire, he halted for two days, either from sheer exhaustion or to allow his baggage waggons to catch up; Colonel Burne's suggestion that he had a lingering hope that Lancaster would still join him must be discarded. Possibly he thought he had shaken off King John, for close to each other though they were, the armies were moving on parallel routes and were completely out of touch. At all events the prince's halt at Châtellerault enabled John, all unawares, to outstrip him on the east, and when the prince resumed his southward march past Poitiers, his vanguard was just in time to brush with the French king's rear as it turned westward from Chauvigny across his path to concentrate in the city with the mighty host now clattering in from all directions. The prince stumbled on a few miles to Chabotrice, but could go no further and halted in the woods.

By every rule of tactics, King John had won hands down. It remained only for him, with ponderous and formal ritual, to engulf his helpless prey. The prince was trapped. Even though he proved able to feed and water his parched horses, rest his men, who had covered four hundred miles in little more than forty weary days, and pass his impedimenta over the river Miosson at Novaille in order to make a start towards the south, all of which he managed, he still could not disengage his army from the overwhelming enemy hourly increasing in size only five miles away at 'Peyters' as he called it, and closely watchful of his every move. Even if, as he also tried, he could have slipped away by night, he was still separated from the safety of the Dordogne by the two hundred miles of hostile desert he had stripped on his way north, while the garrisons he had left intact behind him would certainly come out to bar his retreat across the Vienne or the Charente until King John's pursuit brought him to book. Such awesome thoughts as these must have passed through the prosaic though military mind of the Black Prince as he stood at bay by his smoky camp fire on that damp evening of Saturday 17 October 1356.

It was fortunate for Edward back in England that he had no clear idea what was happening in France. Lancaster would certainly have reported his failure to relieve the prince, and Edward must have known the position was very grave. If his son and heir were lost, with him would go not only senior commanders, Beauchamp of Warwick, Ufford of Suffolk, but most of the younger English chivalry, William Montagu of Salisbury, John Chandos, Bartholomew Burghersh, young Edward Despenser, nephew of the hero of the Somme crossing before Crécy, Ralph Stafford, Reginald Cobham, James Audley, and the Gascon Captal de Buch – nearly half of the knights of the Garter. What a hideous revenge for John, for the destruction of his order of the Star at Mauron in Brittany! But Edward cannot have known the even worse implications until the first dispatches arrived after all was over.

King John had put everything into his grand offensive. He had called out a levy nation-wide. The Estates had voted him an army of 30,000 men. Everyone who was anyone in France was with him. All four of his sons were there – the dauphin Charles, the eldest, not yet twenty, the youngest, Philip, a mere fourteen – John's brother, Philip of Orleans; and Pierre, duke of Bourbon. There were twenty-six dukes and counts; the Chamberlain, James de la Marche, Bourbon's brother; Walter de Brienne, Constable in succession to Charles de la Cerda, murdered by Charles of Navarre; Sir Eustace de Ribemont, who had won Edward's chaplet of pearls at Calais; and Geoffrey de Charny, who carried the sacred Oriflamme of France. Once he had overpowered the prince, John would be free to sweep on through Aquitaine as far south as Bayonne and the Pyrenees, conquer the old English duchy, and win the war at a single blow. Yet there is no sign that the third expedition the prince expected his father to lead was ever mounted. Most uncharacteristically, Edward waited fretfully at home while the fate of his dream empire was decided by others far away, unaware of what was happening in the front.

The next day, Sunday, was a day of quiet. The papal cardinals, Talleyrand of Périgord and his colleague, bustled between the camps and arranged a conference. The prince was willing to offer much to go in peace. He offered his prisoners' plunder, all he had gained since he left Bordeaux, and to swear not to fight again in France for seven years. King John, however, insisted on complete surrender, as well he might. Had he attacked then and there, all was ready for his taking. But though rashness was his usual failing, at this supreme moment he resorted to a fatal caution. The English had the rest of the day to make further arrangements for withdrawal and, if that should fail, to stand and fight. Though hopelessly outnumbered, they believed themselves the better soldiers. Flexible, and wary, they would hide behind hedges and use other stratagems unworthy of knights. They were sternly disciplined – at Mauron, Sir Walter Bentley, although he had won the battle, hanged thirty archers for having given ground – and they had a personal stake in victory, for they were to have the ransom of any prisoners they took. They also had the longbow.

That night they held a council of war, at which nothing was decided. The whole initiative was with the enemy, and they lay down to rest with the opposing patrols within bowshot of each other. Their dread was that, instead of attacking, John would surround and starve them into surrender without a blow being struck. They need not have worried. At dawn the enemy outpost was stirring like a swarm of bees, and the cardinals sorrowfully departed. The pomp of France was on the march from Poitiers.

> He either fears his fate too much,
> Or his deserts are small,
> That puts it not unto the touch,
> To win or lose it all.[44]

King John, a studious soldier, was determined not to lose it all by repeating past mistakes. Remembering the havoc done to massed knights on horseback by the English archers at Crécy, he readily agreed with Sir William Douglas who, having survived the 'Burnt Candlemas' in Scotland the previous winter, had lately joined him, that they should fight dismounted, except for a screen of cavalry, mostly Germans, to take the place of the Genoese crossbowmen, so badly disgraced ten years before, as vanguard. To avoid the former overcrowding and disastrous trampling, he had his battles follow each other in prescribed sequence at considerable intervals. He also took care this time to advance when his men were fresh and at a proper time of day. So they trudged uncomfortably on, that autumn morning of 19 October 1356, less than superb, their flourish dulled, their knightly spurs discarded, their long steel-pointed sabatons removed for ease of marching, their lances shortened into common spears, towards the English half-hidden behind their hedge, to whom the prince had just delivered a gloomy harangue about the privilege of dying all together for their country.

A movement of waggons back towards the river Miosson convinced the two French marshals commanding the cavalry that the prince was continuing his withdrawal, begun during the night, when a stream of traffic had blocked the bridge at Novaille. They charged the hedge, but were shot to pieces by the archers, and those that got through were dispatched by Salisbury. Marshal Clermont was killed, Marshal d'Endreghen made prisoner.

The first main battle, or body of soldiers, called the Dauphin's Battle, came on steadily through the riderless horses plunging about the field, though its real leader was not Charles the dauphin, who was too young and in any case not cut out to be a soldier, reluctantly enduring here the one and only battle of his life. Probably it was the Constable, de Brienne, the highest ranking officer after the king, since his division contained three of the four royal princes and he is known to have lost his life that day. The columns of Warwick and Salisbury broke through the hedge towards him, picked their way over the dead and wounded, and fought on foot in open ground. It was now that the English lost most of their casualties; the prince had to commit a good part of his reserve, and it was long before the first French battle crumbled. A body of knights led the dauphin and his brothers Louis and John away to safety in the direction of Chauvigny before returning to the fight. As they went, they met the second battle moving up under the king's brother, the inexperienced Philip of Orleans, only a few months older than his nephew Charles the dauphin. Seeing defeat all round them and the princes leaving the field, the second battle broke and fled without engaging.

King John, imperturbably adhering to his schedule, had remained well back behind a ridge to the north, so far away that he had no idea of what was happening in the front. After the rout of the second battle, therefore, there was a long delay – a delay precious indeed for the exhausted English, who were able to staunch their wounds, fetch water from the river, retrieve their arrows and straighten their battered weapons. Even so, when at last he breasted the rise with his great host, the effect was devastating. John had with him the whole army that had so decisively chased Lancaster out of Normandy, a force that by itself was larger than the one with which his enemy had begun the day, far larger than the weary remnant less than a mile away, facing his ponderous advance with hours still to go before darkness fell. 'The great number of the enemy frightened our men', said the chronicler Geoffrey le Baker frankly. Some of them began to drift away, though that point is not stressed in English sources.

With or without the advice of Chandos, who never left his side all day, the Black Prince took the momentary decision that won him everlasting fame. To prevent panic, he would attack. He would gain complete surprise. Since Bannockburn forty-odd years before, the English had seldom attacked, certainly not in his present predicament; and King John did not grapple easily with the unexpected. Furthermore, the prince would attack on horseback. Heavy cavalry still held a general advantage over foot. The French were dismounted only out of respect for his archers, but the same did not apply the other way round because the enemy had no bowmen. Nor could they follow suit to meet his charge, since the prince had kept his horses handy in the wood behind him, while they had left theirs far away beyond the ridge.

He ordered his reserve to mount, and divided it into two. One part he gave to the Captal de Buch, to ride round under a low hill on the right and fall upon the enemy's flank. The other he led himself in a vigorous frontal charge, starting at a good round trot and ending in full gallop with Anglo-Gascon yells of 'St George!' and 'Guienne!' The solid French phalanx bent under the double impact. Then Warwick and Salisbury came at them on foot with the men-at-arms and archers. The mass broke into small pockets. One by one, the famous banners of France were submerged. Pierre, duke of Bourbon, Eustace de Ribemont and Lord Beauyeu fell. James of Bourbon, the duke's brother, John and Charles of Artois, and the less royal soldier of fortune Arnold de Cervole, the redoubtable archpriest, were taken prisoner. The Gascon Guiscard d'Angle was given up for lost but recovered in captivity. The Scot Sir William Douglas, wounded in the groin, escaped the field, anxious about his fate if found among the prince's enemies; and not without reason, since that irritable nobleman was only with difficulty restrained by Chandos from killing the chief bodyguard of the papal cardinal Talleyrand, whose flagrant French inclination was at last found proved.

As the banners dwindled, attention focused on the stark figure of King John, the centre of every man's endeavour on one side or the other. He fought manfully beneath the Oriflamme (until Geoffrey de Charny who bore it was cut down),[45] slogging away glazedly with his battle-axe, his face streaming with blood from two head wounds. Giving encouragement to him was his youngest son, Philip of Burgundy, crying out, 'Defend yourself, father! To the right, father! No, now to the left!' At last, face to face with a certain Denis Morbèque, an outlawed knight from Artois whom the English had recruited into their ranks, King John, seeing none of noble blood to whom he could speak in the French language, gave up his right gauntlet and the battle of Poitiers was over.

The prince took off his helmet, and while his pavilion of red silk was being pitched, drank wine among his officers. At Chandos's suggestion his standard was set high in a bush to recall his men who were pursuing their personal fortunes as far as Poitiers, where the governor Lord Roye wisely closed the gates. In addition to the jewelled baldrics and other ornaments the French had confidently brought into the field, the soldiers secured four or five prisoners apiece. The rule was that those worth 10,000 crowns or more went to the crown, who would reward their captors later, but those of less degree could make their own arrangements. The victors too had suffered heavy losses, and when the count was taken it was found that there were far more prisoners than there were guards to watch them on the long journey home. Many ransoms were settled cheaply for cash; others were made payable at Bordeaux before Christmas, an engagement that astoundingly was mostly kept.

The prince's method of paying his soldiers explains why the carnage was proportionately less heavy at Poitiers than at Crécy, where his father had not allowed personal ransoms. Morbèque, a poor man, was given 2,000 nobles down for King John, and eventually 12,000 gold crowns more, his value to the state being later settled at 3 million. The prince paid 25,000 gold crowns for James of Bourbon, and handsomely rewarded Chandos and James Audley, badly wounded, though they had made no prisoners. On the other hand, the lord of Narbonne bought himself out privately for only 5,000 gold florins. The soldiers spent their money during a riotous Christmas at Bordeaux, where prices soared.

Meanwhile, King John had become a bone of brisk contention. Denis Morbèque, to be sure, clung on to his gauntlet grimly, but there were dozens ready to relieve him of his invaluable royal captive. Scrapping began. The king, dragged this way and that, bluffly protested. 'Gentlemen! Pray conduct me and my son to my cousin the Prince, and do not make such a riot about my capture. For I am so great a lord that I can make you all rich.' Marshals sent hurriedly to find him fulfilled his wish. The prince had the king's wounds dressed, and that evening served him dinner in his tent. Next morning the army set out on a rapid march for Bordeaux. No one tried to rescue King John though, on his arrival, the count of Armagnac sent a service of plate for his use in the abbey of Saint-André where he was honourably lodged. His helmet, with the gold coronet encircling it, the prince sent off at once to his father in England, as earnest of his victory.

* * *

The defeat of Poitiers stunned France. The king was a prisoner, a disaster almost impossible to believe. A hundred years before, St Louis had been captured by the paynims at Mansura, but that had been a noble misfortune sustained in the cause of Christ and he had been quickly ransomed. It was very different from falling ineptly into the hands of a petty, incursive Anglo-Gascon army that everyone had thought was doomed. In the south, Languedoc went into mourning. The colourful Provençal head-dresses were put away, all minstrelsy and dancing were forbidden. All government, all society, depended on the king. It was accepted that he must be redeemed however huge the cost.

A month after the battle, the Estates met in Paris to review the situation. While sharing the generous public reaction to the king's mishap, their tolerance did not extend to his advisers who had brought things to such a pass. There was a growing revulsion against his ministers, and against the popinjay nobility who had once more failed their people in the field and now expected to have their ransoms paid. The nation had endured crippling taxation and debasement of the currency to raise money for a victory which had turned into a humiliating defeat. As usual after a campaign, disbanded soldiers of all nations leagued themselves into Free Companies and plundered the already desolate countryside unimpeded by the usual guardians of law and order, the great lords of the castles, who were mostly dead or in capitvity. Roving bands joined forces with the rebellious adherents of the imprisoned Charles of Navarre, who did what they liked in Normandy. Though Godfrey de Harcourt, one of the Navarrese leaders, was caught and killed in the Cotentin, there were plenty of others to take his place.

King John's substitute in his absence, Charles the dauphin, did not seem a likely instrument for restoring order. Only nineteen years old, he was unprepossessing in appearance, bookish rather than knightly, and apparently unable to beget children upon his charming wife and cousin, Jeanne de Bourbon, to whom he had been married for seven years. He had run away from this first battle, his Dauphiné was ruled for him by others, and as duke of Normandy he had been doubtfully intimate with Charles of Navarre.

The provost of the merchants of Paris, Etienne Marcel, a rich demagogue reminiscent of Jacob van Artevelde of Flanders, was determined that no power should be given to the seedy youth, and that he should not fall under the influence of his father's ministers. He demanded thorough reform of the royal finances, and a council appointed by the Estates whom the dauphin must obey. Another faction, more extreme, even felt that Charles of Navarre would be preferable to the inadequate Valois kings, and his crony Robert le Coq, bishop of Laon, demanded Charles's release.

Sensing rebellion, the dauphin dismissed the Estates and went unsuccessfully to Metz to seek help from the emperor Charles IV, his uncle. In March 1357 the Estates repeated their demands as the condition of their now essential financial grant. The dauphin, a mere lieutenant for his father, referred the matter to King John, who from his stately prison at Bordeaux rejected the whole transaction, so that the taxes were never collected and the reforms did not take place. The Estates were powerless to cajole the absent king. Anarchy increased, and sedition rumbled.

Etienne Marcel and Robert le Coq between them stage-managed an 'escape' by Charles of Navarre, who was most ready to oblige by offering himself in the role of a reformer-king. They brought him to Paris in a fanfare of acclaim and forced the dauphin to receive and pardon him. In March 1358 Marcel invaded the dauphin's palaçe of Saint-Pol, murdered his friends and marshals in his presence, and forced him to put on the vulgar civic cap, half red, half blue, in place of his own discreet brownblack gold-embroidered beaver, which Marcel then insolently wore himself. Thinking the dauphin altogether in his power, Marcel, who now saw himself as king of Paris, had him made regent in order to circumvent the distant though still authoritative interference of King John. But the dauphin unexpectedly used his new dignity to escape from Paris – and ignored all enjoinders to return. He deposited his royal womenfolk in the fortress of Meaux, called his own independent Estates, raised an army and attacked the marauding Navarrese, preparatory to marching on his capital. Defiantly, Marcel began rewalling the right bank of the city, whose ancient ramparts had long since been engulfed by later building.

The disaffection of the Paris burgesses spread wider afield and to a lower level of the people. On 28 May 1358 in the Beauvais district, misery flared into a violent insurrection of the peasants, known as the Jacquerie from the homespun tunics that they wore. They had no weapons, no leaders, no aims except hatred of privilege and a famished lust for pillage. They multiplied with terrifying speed, whole districts joining in simply because others were doing so, and their sudden eruption without specific cause achieved complete surprise. They specialized in sacking castles, in killing and in raping. 'Among other infamous acts,' says Froissart, protesting that delicacy prevented him from detailing their worst atrocities, 'they captured a knight, and having fastened him to a spit, roasted him before the eyes of his wife and children; and, after ten or twelve had violated her, they forced her to eat some of her husband's flesh, and then knocked her brains out.'

The Jacquerie was a rising of despair, of the lowest of the low, whether in town or country, and it found no sympathy with the respectable. People lived too close to barbarism to indulge sentimental fancies about the noble savage. Rebellion in the servile orders of society was blasphemy against God and man, as unnatural as rebellion in the farmyard. Charles of Navarre saw his opportunity to turn the general terror and revulsion to his advantage. Setting his professional squadrons upon the undrilled rabble masses he extirpated them remorselessly, hacking them down in their thousands, and the more he slew the more of a public hero he became. When finally he trapped and killed their rustic leader William Cale, alias Jacques Bonhomme, he was worshipped as the saviour of mankind.

Not so Etienne Marcel, who sided with the rebels – not from any demotic favour for their insensate fury, but to exploit their potential for embarrassing the dauphin. When Meaux was attacked, and the townspeople, rising in support, opened the gates to the mob, the dauphine and the many other royal ladies sheltering there came into deadly peril, herded together in the castle behind the market place and only scantily protected by the dauphin's uncle, young Philip of Orleans, whose duchess was among their number. So far from going to the rescue, Marcel sent part of his civic guard from Paris to consolidate the rebel hold on the place while the blood-crazed rioters finished off their carnage. However, two Gascon noblemen of a more proper disposition happened to be passing through the neighbourhood, Gaston Phoebus, count of Foix, and Jean de Grailly, Captal de Buch. Though of opposed allegiance, for Gaston Phoebus was of the French persuasion and the Captal was a resounding hero of the English side at Poitiers, they were cousins, and to relieve the tedium of the present truce had gone off together on crusade to Prussia, whence they were now returning with their retinues. Hearing of the defenders' despair, they gained access to Meaux ahead of the invaders and, when the murderous attack began, stormed out upon them from the market place, slaughtering thousands and throwing them in droves into the Marne. They saved the ladies, hanged the mayor, shut up the remaining citizens in the town and burnt them alive.

The revolution ended as suddenly as it had begun, with peasants dangling in clusters from the trees. Marcel's part in it had a ruinous effect on his prestige, and the dauphin was able to advance with his army to the gates of Paris. In panic, Marcel offered the city to Charles of Navarre in return for help, but Charles, the realist, left for the suburbs at Saint-Denis, where he basked in his new-found fame at the head of an expanding mixed army of hopeful fellow-travellers, and proceeded to play both sides. Through his sister Jeanne d'Evreux, the queen-dowager, he promised the dauphin to deliver up Marcel to justice. At the same time, he quietly accepted from Marcel a twice-weekly delivery of bullion by the horse-load to keep the dauphin out of Paris. Threatened on all sides and afraid of his own citizens, Marcel secretly called in roving English companies to take over the city, and when his civic guard went out to challenge these most hated of all enemies, he betrayed them to an English ambush in the Bois de Boulogne. That was too much for the Parisians. One night while Marcel was going the rounds of his new walls, he was struck down, like van Artevelde at Ghent before him, by his own supporters.

On 3 August 1358 Charles the dauphin, now accorded his due esteem as regent, re-entered his capital and rode to the palace of the Louvre. Quietly, in the way that was to prove habitual to him, he had won the first great diplomatic victory of his reign. He had outwitted and divided his two wily and apparently all-powerful enemies, Etienne Marcel and Charles of Navarre. Without reproach to himself, the revolutionary Jacquerie had been put down, and he had evaded the dangerous urbanist attempt to make constitutional encroachments on the authority of the throne. For the first time there was a glimmer of hope for the recovery of France and of the Valois monarchy, where so recently there had been none.

Paris, where he had stubbornly refused to show his presence until it had returned freely to its loyalty, from now on became his royal home. Secure within, once he had completed the walls so hurriedly raised by Marcel to keep him out, he set to work to make Paris, once and for all time, the seat of majesty, the centre of government, the cradle of learning and the arts. As time went by he added noble embellishments to the old fabric of the city. In the west, he transformed the gaunt old Louvre into a comfortable modern palace, though he preferred to live at the other side of the town, in his new personal mansion, the Hôtel de Saint-Pol in the Saint-Antoine quarter, soon to be overshadowed by the defiant Bastille, the most massive of six grim barbicans punctuating the new walled encirclement of which it was the eastern anchor backing on the Seine. Between the Bastille and his palace, in the formerly open spaces now brought within the city confines, he founded his graceful convent of the Célestins, the portal of whose fashionable church displayed his statue and that of his queen, Jeanne. He created the Hôtel de Saint-Pol, and further down towards the river bank were public pleasure grounds for playing *boule*. The left bank remained, as always, the domain of the university. And outside the walls, a few miles to the east, St Louis's pleasant retreat in the woods of Vincennes was converted into an impregnable fortress.

Henceforth Paris was a sure refuge for the hitherto helpless, wandering regent. But though Paris was much, it was not France. To the north and west, Charles of Navarre, robbed of the crown he had seen within his grasp, together with his brother Philip, did as they pleased almost up to the city walls from their Seine fortresses of Mantes and Melun. Paris was besieged. No one could go in or out, and the destruction of its natural garner, the surrounding market gardens, sent prices soaring in Les Halles, so that actual starvation followed. An army the regent contrived to raise from Tournai and other distant loyal provinces was routed in a fog on the Oise near Noyon in that same August 1358. Thereafter there was no holding the Navarrese. They rode about from place to place, squeezing all and sundry, compelling those who could not pay to periods of service in their army, holding towns to tribute by the threat of famine, selling safe-conducts for supply convoys after first plundering them of all that took their fancy, in particular 'good hats, ostrich feathers, and spear heads'. At this moment of satanic triumph, when he had reduced the north of his putative kingdom to ruin and prostration, Charles of Navarre proposed to King Edward of England a resumption of their plan to dismember France.

It is a problem to know why Edward left it for Charles of Navarre to point out his obvious opportunity, and had not already taken advantage of it. If he ever really intended to become king of France, he could easily have done so at any time during the two years since Poitiers. There was no effective government in France to stop him, and every month he allowed to pass, while the regent was achieving the first faint stirrings of recovery, made the project fractionally less simple.

At home, everything was geared towards further venture. Though his latest devastating victory belonged strictly to his son, the Black Prince, Edward had no cause to cavil at it. There was glory enough for both, and his prestige was now enormous. In contrast to the misery of France, his land was full of peace and plenty. Trade was prosperous. Exports and customs duties both stood high; while Edward's personal credit, once so shaky, was now excellent, for no real property was more attractive than a couple of captive kings. His parliaments, though they stood upon their rights in controlling his private dealings with financiers, and insisted on the power of consenting to his manipulation of the wool supply, were respectful and far from ungenerous in their grants. Bishop Edington, who became Chancellor in 1356, maintained and improved the smoothly efficient civil service he inherited from John Thavesby, and trained up his astute protégé, William of Wykeham, to be an indispensable Keeper of the King's Works and Forests, and eventually his own successor, of whom Froissart was to write, 'all things were done by him and without him nothing was done'. As for the provinces, if they were not exactly law-abiding, they had nothing to match the ravening companies in France. The sheriffs and justices of the peace, more closely watched than formerly, became gradually less flagitious. Sound, professional government contrived to keep the king's administrative worries to a minimum.

In foreign affairs, the destruction of France had left a void in Edward's favour. Flanders was silent. The Empire kept to itself. The collapse of the 'Auld Alliance' had drawn the teeth of the Scots, and Edward's dismissal of the pretender Baliol had removed the chief irritant of their clannish life. On 3 October 1357 the Scots accepted a ten-year truce. On promise of a ransom of 100,000 marks, with hostages to guarantee its regular payment, their King David was restored to them, leaving memorials to his long captivity scratched on the walls of Nottingham castle. With him went his neglected queen, Edward's sister Joan, who after seven years in France and eleven in England, returned to spend the brief remainder of her childless and unfortunate life in the rude highland exile ordained for her in infancy by her mother, Isabella; beside whom, nevertheless, she chose to be buried, when the time came, in the Greyfriars church in London. David's was not a happy homecoming. Always profligate, he had become a stranger to Scotland and wholly English in his ways and motives. He blamed his heir and nephew, Robert Stuart, whom he had always resented, for his capture at Neville's Cross, and asked the Scottish lords to accept the Black Prince in his place as their future king, which they indignantly refused to do. He then named his other nephew, Alexander, as his heir, though, since Alexander died in the second plague while serving as one of the hostages in London, Robert Stuart was eventually restored to his proper place in the succession. From Edward's point of view the truce held despite these family ructions, and that was what he cared about.

The military outlook was no less promising than the domestic or the diplomatic. Since the battle of Winchelsea, and his peace with Castile, Edward had held command of the seas. His successful war, with its prospect of easy gain, was popular; at home, there would be no shortage of knightly contractors eager to take up his indentures. In France, his English-led companies, though for the moment he shrewdly disowned them, swarmed ready waiting for him to arrive. And, as he found when he finally made the bid, there would be an embarrassing number of foreign allies hoping to join his banners for what seemed certain to be for better not for worse. He had the ships, he had the men, he had the money too. There was nothing in these years to prevent him seizing the crown of France. The tactical dispositions were already perfect. After Poitiers, the prince's army, flushed with victory, was still afoot in Aquitaine, as was Lancaster's army, unscathed in Brittany. In 1357 they could well have repeated their manoeuvre of the previous year, and met on the Loire, this time without opposition. Edward could have joined them from de Harcourt's estates, now his own property by will, in the Cotentin peninsula. Then, augmented on his way by the Navarrese and the Free Companies, he could have marched on Paris, not yet completely walled and in the grip of civil riot, and taken possession of the helpless dauphin.

Yet Edward attempted no such thing. On the contrary, in March 1357, six months after the crushing victory at Poitiers, he had his son agree a truce with King John in Bordeaux, pending an intended general settlement on the lines recently abandoned at Avignon – in the new circumstances an astonishingly generous proposal for the French. Then, in May, having bought out at great expense his Gascon allies' interest in their unexpected and illustrious royal prisoners (as Froissart says, 'he promised them great rewards and profits, which is all that a Gascon loves or desires') the prince sailed with them for home, to make a Roman holiday in London. Lancaster followed from Brittany not long after, so that both offensive expeditions were withdrawn from France and disbanded. Throughout the vital period while the dauphin was precariously building up his authority, Edward was careful to observe the truce and did nothing to embarrass him. Whatever his private dealings with Robert Knollys and the other freebooters, in public he loudly disclaimed their depredations, and he did not respond to Charles of Navarre's major proposal in the autumn of 1358 except to send the Captal de Buch to aid him, who as Navarre's distant relative could claim to be acting in his private capacity without infringement of the truce.

In short, the two years after Poitiers, when Edward could so easily have seized all that he said he wanted, were among the most peaceful and least spectacular years of his entire reign; so quiet, indeed, that the records find room for glimpses of his day-to-day affairs, casting a rare and welcome light upon his personal whims and fancies. In April 1357, hearing of the miraculous fortitude of a woman who, condemned for the murder of her husband, had survived forty days in prison without eating or drinking, he pardoned her. In July 1358 he presented Westminster Abbey with a notable relic, the head of St Benedict, abbot and confessor. (St Benedict is said to have died in Italy in A.D. 453, and how his head came into Edward's hands we are not told.) In October he provided, no doubt at a suitable fee, a testimonial for a Hungarian gentleman, confirming that he had achieved the remarkable feat of passing a whole day and night in St Patrick's Purgatory on the island of Lough Derg in Ireland. In November he ordered the streets of London to be cleaned for the funeral of his mother, Isabella, who had lately died at her retreat in Hertford castle at the ripe age of sixty-six.

Why did Edward let slip his golden opportunity? It would seem that if he ever really had a design of becoming king of France, he had by now abandoned it. For this there may have been a variety of reasons. One of the purposes of his war in the first place had been to satisfy the animal spirits of both himself and his magnates in lucrative foreign ventures full of glamour and excitement, and so put an end to the unrest at home which had brought down his father. That purpose had long since been achieved. His authority was unquestioned. The more unruly of his subjects were rampaging in France with his tacit consent, ostensibly in the service of Charles of Navarre, unreliable ally though he was. The nobility, welded into a brotherhood of arms, were unflinching in their loyalty. He must have realized, now that giddy youth was past, that France in its present state was no country in which to be king. He had already learnt the cost of garrisoning his conquests in Brittany, of administering Aquitaine. To hold down the whole country was not a practical proposition.

What he had been aiming at, at least since the negotiations at Guînes in 1353, was to resurrect the old Anglo-Angevin empire as it had been in the time of Henry II, comprising the western half of France, or as much of it as he could get, depending how his bargaining status stood at any given moment. Poitiers had set it very high, indeed, but he does not appear to have increased his demands excessively, at least at first. He also insisted that all the cessions should be made over to him in full sovereignty without any debt of homage to the overlord of France. Edward's obsession with homage was something of a personal quirk, for by this late date in feudalism it was little more than a picturesque formality, but he regarded it as shameful vassalage. The memory lingered deep of the double humiliation inflicted on him by King Philip in the dark days at the beginning of his reign. He had been forced to do homage twice then. He would never do it again, and certainly not to Philip's son John, who was now his prisoner.

The other thing he demanded from any settlement was money. He expected, like any commercial entrepreneur, a solid return from his successful enterprises. Most of his life he had been pinched for cash. Now he looked for his captured enemies to make him rich – not only to support his sumptuous state, but to enable him to resist the encroachments of his parliaments, which were forever attaching conditions to their grants, and interfering with his practice of making over the customs to rich monopolists in return for large-scale loans of ready money.

The lure of gold may be the explanation for Edward's otherwise baffling dealings at this time with Charles of Blois, the captive claimant to the duchy of Brittany, whom he twice allowed to return to France for the purpose of collecting his enormous ransom, in exchange for his freedom and Edward's recognition of his claim to Brittany. In 1353, while on parole at Calais, Blois had arranged that King John, who was anxious to win him back, should pay his ransom, and that his daughter Margaret should marry John's Constable and favourite, Charles de la Cerda. But the murder of la Cerda soon afterwards by Charles of Navarre ended the scheme, and the upright Blois returned to his captivity. In August 1356, just before Poitiers, he was released again, this time permanently and in Brittany itself, on promise of 700,000 gold florins. This has been seen as a 'most opportune' device on Edward's part to distract John's attention from the effort Henry of Lancaster was about to make to meet the Black Prince on the Loire. But in the end it gained him nothing except the money, and not all of that, since he had to forgo half of it to secure the regular payment of the rest.

Edward's mercenary transactions with the French candidate for Brittany, his own former stubborn enemy, were a shabby betrayal of his long commitment to the rival claimant, young John de Montfort, whom he had brought up in England as his ward, and who became his son-in-law by marrying Princess Mary. And it was bound to lead to a new outbreak of the war of succession, as in due course it did. So at least thought Edward's governors-general, who were trying to run the duchy as a pacified English province at a minimum of cost to the home government. On the first occasion, Sir Walter Bentley, the wounded victor of Mauron and an able ruler, protested so violently that he was dismissed from his appointment and imprisoned for two years in the Tower. On the second, Henry of Lancaster, who had de Montfort in his care and had been commissioned to establish him in his inheritance, was informed by the Black Prince that he must raise his lengthy and unimportant siege of Rennes since it was contrary to the truce he had just concluded at Bordeaux in March 1357. He took no notice, on the grounds that as Lieutenant of Brittany he took orders not from the prince in Aquitaine but from the king in England. When a direct order to raise the siege followed from Edward in person he ignored that too, saying that he was fighting the quarrel of the duke de Montfort, not that of the king his sovereign. It was not until a second and peremptory command was on its way that he reluctantly complied – and then not until he had enforced a token surrender, flying his banner for a few hours from the walls, and entering briefly to take wine with Bertrand du Guesclin, whose bold defence of Rennes was the start of his brilliant though illiterate career.

Lancaster's Nelson touch, the only time in his life he is known to have been at cross-purposes with his royal master, like Bentley's defiance, was a strong statement of his disapproval of Edward's double-dealing at the expense of his youthful ward and of the English interest in Brittany. Conversely, it indicated the lengths Edward was prepared to go to in pursuit of money. When eventually he released David of Scotland in October 1357, he took advantage of his improved position to increase the ransom previously agreed by 10 per cent to a staggering total of 100,000 marks. Now he had the king of France to bargain for, and could expect to

gain an incomparably greater reward. Because of his huge superiority by
land and sea, Edward would not have to go to war to serve his territorial
and financial aims. The unspoken threat would be sufficient argument. But
with whom should he negotiate? With reason, he did not trust Charles of
Navarre, and realized that there could not for long be room for both of
them in France. And though he dismissed too lightly the pitiful young
regent, by turns driven out of his capital by the riff-raff and then shut up in
it in conditions of mounting famine, he would have been exceptionally
prescient to take the regent seriously at this stage. There was no real
government in France, only a confusion of intriguing factions, rampant
brigandry and hungry rebellion.

On the other hand, far removed from such ignoble strife, in the genial
calm of England, Edward had at his elbow, in the person of its king, the
fountain of all authority in France, the captive arbiter of policy. With all
the time in the world, with daily opportunity for earnest discussions or
cosy chat, why should they not between themselves, cousin to cousin, king
to king, resolve what was generally regarded as their personal quarrel? The
reasoning was sound, and there was more to it than that. It is evident from
all his personal dealings that Edward mixed with his awe-inspiring dignity
a twinkling and compelling charm. Add to that the emotional bond of
victor with vanquished, kindly captor with despondent exile, and he was
well-nigh irresistible. Already three other such notable prisoners, men of
different kinds and nations – the pleasure-loving comte d'Eu, late Constable of France; the lickerous David of Scotland; the pious Breton, Charles
of Blois – had all been affably persuaded to adopt wholeheartedly his view
of their various situations. There was no reason why stout John should not
succumb as well.

John did succumb, quite painlessly. His own view of his predicament
was simple and subjective. He genuinely deplored the misfortunes of his
people, but as he saw it those misfortunes arose purely from the loss of his
fatherly controlling hand. It was their first duty, as it was also his, to win
him back his liberty at any cost. He also delighted in the easy atmosphere
of the English court, so different from the mistrust and bickering of his
own. He admired the fiery Prince of Wales, whom he had got to know well
during the winter at Bordeaux, and on the eleven-day voyage home. So
different from his pallid son the dauphin. As for the king of England, he
was the last word in royal grace and chivalry.

Edward made the most of his captive's impressionable character.
Whether from natural courtesy or from policy, from the moment of his
capture John was treated with the greatest veneration. On the voyage to
England he was given a vessel to himself to protect him from annoyance,
and his entry into London on 24 May 1357 was more like a welcome for a
visiting potentate than the bringing home of a defeated enemy. As he rode
across London Bridge and through the teeming streets he was the focus of

the gaze of thousands who had flocked to see him. He was dressed in his full panoply of state, lacking only one jewel, later discovered on the battlefield of Poitiers. He was mounted on a great white charger as token of his majesty, while at his side in plain soldier's garb the prince rode a small black hobby. The official mood was one of thanksgiving and prayer rather than of victory, except that the citizens, not to be done pawkily out of their just show of triumph, defiantly stacked all their arms and armour outside their doors and in their windows, so that the procession could hardly make its way for the mounds of bows and arrows, hauberks, breastplates, gauntlets, vambraces, swords, spears and battle-axes laid out for the king of France to see. The prince presented his charge to his father enthroned in Westminster Hall. The king, coming forward to embrace his royal prisoner, led him, his son Philip and the other French notables to dinner in the palace.

Until the papal legates, chief of whom was Cardinal Talleyrand de Périgord, had duly appeared and confirmed the two years of truce, John lodged with Edward in his own apartments. After that, the French king and his son were sent off to Windsor, where they had liberty to hawk and hunt. As soon as it had been made ready for them they moved into the Savoy, the most magnificent mansion in England, only recently completed in the latest style, out of his spoils from Bergerac, by Henry of Lancaster, who was still abroad in Brittany. The Savoy was conveniently placed in the fields near Charing Cross, midway between the government offices at Westminster and the busy but insalubrious City; and its pleasant gardens ran down to the Thames. Here John lived in great state, with a French household of about a hundred, including a king of minstrels and Monsieur Jean le Fol. He saw much of the royal family. After all, they were his kith and kin, and cultivated people. Though they chatted between themselves in their rude newfangled idiom, they were still able to speak to him in tolerable French. He seems to have been especially fond of the kindly Queen Philippa, and in 1358, like the rest of her family, he sent messages by John of Paris to Isabella, the French Queen Mother, now nearing her end at Hertford castle, receiving in return two volumes of *Lancelot et le Sang Réal*, since it was known that novel-reading, like music, chess and backgammon, were the solaces of his tedium.

Grand festivities were arranged for his diversion. Edward decided that the St George's Day celebrations at Windsor in April 1358, the first since John's arrival, should be unusually elaborate for the benefit of him and his French companions. Safe-conducts were issued to knightly competitors far and wide. Isabella, making her last public appearance, attended with her daughter, Joan of Scotland, now once again at liberty and living with her at Hertford, and splashed out £421 on jewels for the occasion. King John, who knew that the cost of the tournaments would eventually be offset against his ransom, remarked with soldierlike drollery that they would cost a pretty penny. In December of that year, when David of Scotland on one of his frequent visits to London was staying at the Greyfriars and attempting to persuade Edward to some moderation of his terms of ransom, Edward sat down between him and John to a lavish Christmas dinner. At Reading on 19 May 1359 there was a very splendid wedding when Edward's son John of Gaunt, now aged nineteen, married Henry of Lancaster's younger daughter, Blanche. In London a week later, as part of the celebrations, the mayor, sheriffs and corporation, twenty-four in all, challenged all comers to a three-day joust. There was surprise at first that the royal family was not present at so popular an event, and also at the unexpected skill of the merchant challengers, until the delighted roars of the crowd revealed that the king himself, happily disguised as the mayor, was fighting in his long-familiar way in the simple livery of John Lovekin, fishmonger; that his sons were the sheriffs, and his knightly friends the remaining aldermen, all honouring the colours of the city. King John, who was looking on, could scarcely credit such madcap condescension.

All this time Edward was steering his impressionable visitor towards a settlement on the terms he wanted. By May 1358 they had advanced so far towards a treaty that the papal commissioners went home satisfied that their task had been satisfactorily achieved. Territorially, Edward's demands were very modest, rather less than he had been ready to accept in the negotiations at Guînes five years before. It is true that the treaty concerned only the liberation of King John, and that no question was raised of Edward renouncing his claim to the crown of France. Even so, considering the transformation brought about since then by the Poitiers campaign, and the hard fact of John's captivity, this reversion to the terms of Guînes seemed very moderate. So at any rate thought the dauphin in Paris, who had expected worse and, had these terms stood alone, would have been ready to accept them. The financial requirement, on the other hand, was staggering. John's ransom was fixed at four million golden crowns, well over half a million pounds. So vast a sum can only be represented in contemporary terms by remembering that Edward's average annual expectation from his parliament was about one-sixteenth of the amount. France in its ruined state just did not have that kind of money. The first 600,000 were to be paid within six months, and when John started to collect it, though the less damaged southern provinces of Languedoc responded nobly, little or nothing was forthcoming from the north. In the meantime there had been the further deterioration in the state of France. There had been the swift apocalyptic terror of the Jacquerie with its horrifying savageries on either side. Etienne Marcel, the leader of the Paris merchants, had been murdered; and though the dauphin had managed to regain his capital, it was a city of chaos and starvation, closely besieged by Charles of Navarre, who was master everywhere outside the walls, and had now made to Edward his proposal of partition.

Navarre was right: France was defenceless. But that did not mean that Edward would follow his suggestion; it meant that leaving Navarre aside, he could get far more out of John than he had supposed. Soon after their jovial Christmas dinner at the end of 1358, his friendly charm gave way to haughty, posturing threatening. He used John's failure to collect the first part of his ransom as an excuse to renounce their treaty, and began to mobilize against the time when the truce would end in April, only a few months ahead. He encouraged his captains of irregulars, the Captal de Buch, Robert Knollys, Peter Audley and Sir Eustace d'Ambréticourt, to intensify their supposedly private warfare deep into France at the side of the Navarrese. Most telling of all, he threatened John with a harsher regimen than the princely life he had been leading at the Savoy, and to cut his entourage by half, since John had no funds to keep up so much state.

Seeing his hopes of freedom dwindle, John hastily promised to agree to whatever was asked of him. He did not for a moment think that Edward's estimate of his value to his people was a crown too much. On the contrary he took the Pétainist view that they were in honour bound to pay it, since their calamity in losing him had been due to their own perversity and folly. Only by tribulation could they be redeemed. Edward allowed himself to be persuaded to prolong the truce until Midsummer Day. By 24 March 1359 they had devised a second, private treaty, more comprehensive and far more exacting than the first. This time Edward was to have the whole western half of France, with the homage of Brittany; the whole of the ancient Angevin empire, though not as in former times owing feudal duty to a French overlord, but in full sovereignty as an English palatinate detached from France; with, in addition, the important accretions on the Straits of Dover since Angevin days, Calais, Guînes, Boulogne and Ponthieu. The money, the stumbling-block before, would remain the same, four million crowns, except that far more of it was to be paid in a shorter time. In return, Edward would withdraw his obtrusive claim to the crown of the other half of France. The terms were so preposterous that it is probable Edward never expected or intended John to stomach them, but had merely thrown them out impatiently in answer to John's pleading for a second chance. He realized now that he had delayed longer than he should in letting three years slip away since Poitiers, lotus years spent in visiting shrines, in maudlin predication of his own burial place in Westminster Abbey, in refusing Pope Innocent's inconvenient demand for payment of the thousand marks annuity promised by King John with all arrears for 140 years, in dragooning all young men worth £2 a year to accept the honour of knighthood on pain of a £10 fine, in entertaining himself and John. He wished to get on with his preparations for a resumption of the war, already well in hand, before the autumn rains glued down his army, and before Charles the dauphin, who was showing unexpected signs of authority in Paris, grew any stronger.

King John was unaccountably undermined by Edward's pressures and readily accepted this worst of surrenders, but his son and the Estates of France in May refused to ratify it, declaring it neither tolerable nor practical. They added that King John might remain in England if his liberty depended on such terms and, with a new patriotic temper, voted supplies for war. John was deeply affronted at his rejection by his people, and attributed it to the infernal influence of Charles of Navarre, who certainly did not wish to see a friendly settlement between his rivals. 'Son Charles, Son Charles!' he gloomed. 'You are led by the King of Navarre, who is too cunning for you.' He confessed to Edward bitterly that only by the arms of his conqueror could he oblige his subjects to do their duty. His effective prestige had gone. For the rest of his life he was a chessboard king, moved about by others according to strategies in which he had no part.

In August 1359, John, who in April had already been moved out of London to take the place at Hertford left vacant by the late Queen Isabella, was banished for greater security during the coming campaign to Somerton castle, a run-down fortress in the fens of Lincolnshire, with William, Lord Deyncourt, as his bland custodian. Though remote, his captivity was not uncomfortable. His retinue had been halved, but he still had a skeleton staff of fifty for whom he had to furnish the whole place with trestles, forms, and tables, as well as providing luxurious hangings, cushions, coffers and sconces for the private apartments of himself, his son Philip, and his jester Jean le Fol, in such quantity that, at the end of his eight-month sojourn at Somerton, three waggons were required to carry them away. Presents of wine from France were brought in by the port of Boston, 140 tuns at a time, working out at the intoxicating figure of 700 gallons a head, though doubtless some of it was sold off on the side to pay for other necessaries. To judge from his generous gifts to shrines, priories and parish churches round about, he had liberty for riding out, while Philip, now seventeen, kept greyhounds, falcons, and at least one pricey jouster.

Like most nobles in captivity, John spent much time in exhortative correspondence, and he sent frequently to Lincoln for parchments, papers, and ink at fourpence the bottle. His king of ministrels made not only musical instruments, but clocks as well. His passion for fine clothes was stirred by the present of a suit from Joan of Boulogne, his second queen, her kindly though distant consolation for his exile. He ordered eight others in five months; for Easter, a marbled violet velvet trimmed with miniver from Brussels; for Whitsun, a rosy scarlet lined with blue taffeta. The country was scoured as far as London for the 2,550 skins of miniver and 'goes' required for a single outfit, and to keep his household dressed in matching style he arranged for a special tailoring business to be set up in Lincoln. He had a very sweet tooth for sugar plums, and a large silver-gilt *bonbonnière*, specially made, and full of costly *sucre rosé vermeil*, was always at his elbow. So he whiled away his trivial, and apparently bachelor, existence.

Obstinate, stupid, vain, vengeful, haughty, compendium of medieval princely failings that he was, King John, though honourable and pious, could still deny the charge most generally levelled at him by the voice of history, that his dealings with Edward during his four years of captivity were inept and selfish, and damaging to his country. From the moment his son Charles the dauphin re-entered Paris in August 1358, there was a chance that he might reassert the authority of the monarchy as the central government of France. To do so he needed a prolongation of the two-year respite already gained, goodness knows how, from Edward's crushing intervention. That respite John obtained for him. Discussion of his first and moderate treaty occupied the whole of 1358. When at last Edward rejected it as insufficient, and began to mobilize, it was essential to distract him from his purpose once again, and that could only be done on terms so vastly appeasing as to make it obviously worth while. It is possible that the extravagance of the second treaty of March 1359 was deliberately proposed by John in the certainty that it would be refused by his son and the Estates of France. In any case, it worked. The truce was prolonged, and one way and another it was not until the end of 1359 that Edward was ready to unleash his offensive. By that time it was too late. John had gained two vital years, and could comfortably reflect in his durance vile at Somerton that it was the supposed biter who had been bit.

The precious months of 1359 were used to good advantage by the regent in restoring some sort of order around Paris, with such makeshift forces as he had. In March his new Constable, Robert de Fiennes, and Guy de Châtillon, count of Saint-Pol, who at Amiens had already stopped the eastern probe by Philip of Navarre and his Norman and English allies towards the English base at Calais, drove them back from Saint-Valéry on the Somme all the way to their starting point in the Cotentin. Then a mixture of accidents befell Edward's allegedly unsponsored free-lance leaders. Sir Peter Audley, having failed in an attempt on Châlons, died suddenly at Beaufort, whose hereditary lordship he was supposed to be holding peacefully for the duke of Lancaster. Sir John Segar, trying to sell his captured castle of Nogent-sur-Seine to the bishop of Troyes, was hacked to pieces by the mob. In Champagne, the energetic Hainaulter Sir Eustace d'Ambréticourt had three teeth knocked out by Sir Broquart de Fenestrages and was taken prisoner. Emerging from Brittany to chance his arm in the fat papal territories in the south, Sir Robert Knollys, most terrible of *condottieri*, at whose approach citizens drowned themselves in the Loire or broke their necks jumping from the walls and the charred gables which, after his departure, were known as 'Knollys' mitres', was driven back by royal forces. Sir John de Pecquing, who had arranged the escape of Charles of Navarre from prison and was his right-hand man, was strangled in his bed by his own chamberlain. Such small successes against hated *routiers* had an immense effect in restoring shattered French morale. Little by little, the localities took courage to defend themselves.

More significant diplomatic victories followed. By working upon Count Louis de Malines, the regent destroyed the English interest in Flanders and secured the arrest of English agents among the merchants. Then he laid frontal attack to Melun,[46] part of the Navarrese encirclement of Paris, on the Seine, only thirty miles south of the city, then defended by two other English leaders, Sir James Pipe and Hugh de Calveley. The siege of Melun was hampered by the presence of the three tame queens whom Charles of Navarre had lodged there: his aunt, Jeanne d'Evreux, dowager of Charles the Fair; his sister Blanche, second wife of Philip VI; and his own wife, Jeanne, daughter of King John. All three complained very vigorously about the springalls and other engines of war that the regent Charles, respectively their great-nephew, step-grandson, and brother, had sent out from Paris to plague them, and demanded surrender, so that Pipe and Calveley had their work cut out to keep them quiet. However, Charles of Navarre grew tired of waiting for Edward to take up the alliance he had offered, gave up Melun, and in August came to another settlement with the regent, who extended it to include the young earl of Harcourt by marrying him to a daughter of the duke of Bourbon, his own wife's sister. By the autumn of 1359 the regent had pacified his own duchy of Normandy, had neutralized Edward's obvious allies, and had severely clipped the wings of Edward's stool-pigeons already at the scene of action. He was now free to make such provision as he could against the invasion so fortunately long delayed.

Edward's plan, apparently of his personal designing, was simple, over-confident, and based on a major misconception. He believed that in King John he had in his power the only authoritative voice in France. What he had heard of the dauphin did not appeal to him. He did not understand bookish, quiet young men, and, a frequent blind spot of the strong, he disregarded what he did not understand. He was justly proud of his army, unquestionably the finest in Europe. He thought that its mere military display would inspire such terror as to topple the fumbling puppet, and lay France prostrate at his feet. Because it was based on false premises, what was to be his last campaign, a masterpiece of military technique in organization and control, was politically barren, the worst miscalculation of his career.

It was very carefully planned. As Colonel Burne has pointed out, the parade-ground precision of his marches indicates that they had been worked out in detail well beforehand, with the aid of maps, a hitherto unheard-of aid in warfare: the Gough map of 1325, based on a general survey of England ordered by Edward I, is the only one known to have existed. Edward knew that he was faced with a long itinerary into the heart of France far removed from his base at Calais, at the dead of winter, and through country he knew to have been systematically pillaged. Therefore his provision for the commissariat was the most elaborate ever seen. Not only food, clothing and shelter but every conceivable necessary had been thought of. There were forges for arms and horse-shoes, and hand-mills and ovens for making bread. For the king's amusement and for his larder there were a pack of sixty hounds with their huntsmen and thirty falconers, and collapsible leather boats which would come in handy either for fording rivers or for fishing during Lent; also no doubt the royal band, which had marched with him to Crécy. There were hundreds of clerks and household servants, artificers of every trade, pioneers with picks and shovels to dig mines or make up bridges and the rutted winter roads. It is usual to quote a baggage train of six thousand wagons, though this may be an exaggeration. On only one item had a chance been taken: forage for the great number of draught horses and cavalry – no doubt because its bulk by weight would have taken up too much shipping. But its omission would be much regretted.

Non-combatants may almost have exceeded fighting men, for it is possible that Edward did not embark as large an army as is generally supposed. True, the echelon of the nobility was there in force, everyone of any moment who was anyone, down from the king's four sons (young Thomas, now about five, was left as custodian of the realm) and the great Lancaster, so that the roll-call of famous captains from Sluys and Crécy, Winchelsea and Poitiers, read like the grand finale of an opera. But, for the rank and file, Edward had no need of unwieldy numbers, and though all able-bodied men had been called up, they were mainly for home defence. No navy would intercept his Calais landing, there was no French army able to oppose his in the field. He could land where he liked, he could go where he liked. What he needed for his purpose was not numbers but a compact force expert in drill and perfect in discipline, since his main purpose was processional.

What was that purpose? He told his army before they sailed that they would not return until he brought back peace with honour, a rousing but inconclusive formula. He appears to have persuaded himself of the extraordinary idea that the French were ready to accept him for their king. If he offered, with force and majesty enough, to bring peace and order to their shattered land, they would discard the discredited and expensive prisoner they had not seen for the last three years, and flock to him instead. Consent to a medieval monarch presupposed three things: a hereditary title, a show of effective power, and the mystical aura conferred by the crowning of the Lord's anointed. The first two, Edward had all ready. The last, and most essential, he would now obtain. Rheims, the sacred city of Champagne, guarded the bones of Saint-Remy and the Sainte Ampoule of holy chrism brought down to him by a white dove from heaven, with which all the kings of France had been anointed since the time of Clovis.

From Calais, his hard-won port of entry to his new kingdom, he would descend in awesome though peaceable pomp on Rheims, where the walls would admit him like the walls of Jericho, and the archbishop, Jean de Croon, would willingly complete the ceremony.

How far Edward really believed in his self-imposed romantic mission remains doubtful. What, for example, did he plan to do with the unfortunate King John, whose restoration he had so lately been discussing? There certainly could not be two anointed kings of France, and the fate of a rejected sovereign was never happy. But however improbable of achievement, the scheme had practical possibilities, and Edward was ever an opportunist. Faced with the threat, the dauphin would be obliged to lead his little army out of Paris to defend his heritage. If he failed to do so he would lose it by default. If he did so, he would be defeated, and Edward would be able to dictate what terms he liked.

Edward wanted to create dread, and since anticipation is the soul of dread, he made no effort to keep his preparations secret. There were none of the false trails and sealed orders to be opened at sea as in the Normandy expedition. On the contrary, he let his intentions be known far and wide. In consequence, not only did the dauphin know as early as July that Edward would head for Rheims, but, during the summer, swarms of adventurers from his formerly allied provinces and from the Empire crowded into Calais. So eager were they, this time, not to miss their chance of following Edward's always victorious army in search of plunder that they arrived months too early. Calais was soon full to bursting, and as the date of the king's arrival, supposed to be 8 September, was steadily put off, they became the gravest nuisance. They could find no lodgings. They ate and drank everything. As prices soared and they ran out of money, they had to sell their arms and harnesses. Fighting broke out between the nations. Worse, their horses champed up the reserves of fodder laid in for the expedition, and in any case Edward, who was keen to impress his new French subjects, had no desire for his dignified progress to his coronation to include a rabble of uncouth plunderers. At the beginning of October, Lancaster and his contingent was sent off in advance to deal with them, a useful move which enabled his shipping to return in time to take part in the main lift. Lancaster persuaded them to pay their bills, shoe their horses and pack up, and led them, a good-natured, tactful Pied Piper, away from Calais towards the Somme where they could pillage to their hearts' content while he spied out the route the army was soon to take. He then turned back for Calais, where the king's army, having sailed at last from Sandwich on 28 October, had arrived that evening and marched into the billets vacated by the Germans.

Edward set out as soon as his ships had been discharged and on 4 November met Lancaster returning with the still dissatisfied allies, who at once began demanding money. Edward, whose low opinion of them had not altered since his early campaigns, now twenty years in the past, could not undertake to pay them. If they liked to take pot-luck in the booty they were welcome; alternatively he would give them enough money to get them home. Most chose the second course and, as they passed on their way to Calais to redeem belongings they had left in pledge, cast hungry professional eyes upon the prodigious baggage train, mouth-watering but impossibly well guarded by the Black Prince who followed close behind.

The army separated, to march in three equidistant columns converging short of Rheims, a manoeuvre they executed with remarkable precision. Progress was slow. Unusually bitter and incessant autumn rains damped the triumphant display, and the cumbrous waggons creaked and stuck helplessly in the boggy roads. Yet discipline was perfect. There was no straggling and 'they did not leave a bag behind them'. Edward's orders to be friendly to the inhabitants were strictly kept, for Knighton says they behaved as if they were at home. To the north, the king, with his two sons Lionel and Edmund, John de Montfort, his ward of Brittany, and most of his favourite old commanders, followed a line undeviatingly straight towards his goal. Twenty miles to the south, the Black Prince kept company with him by a less simple route requiring a crossing of the Somme. He had with him his favourite brother, John of Gaunt, his inseparable John Chandos, and also Sir Thomas Gray, whose *Scalacronica*, begun while he was a prisoner in Edinburgh jail before his release at the truce of 1357, is the only contemporary account of the campaign. Between them, the middle column under Roger Mortimer, the newly restored grandson of the tyrant earl of March, and now Constable of England, was taken over by Lancaster and added to his own retinue.

Each column had its own supply train, and its own frontage to explore for foodstuffs, particularly forage, though there was little to be found. The dauphin had made his choice of the black alternatives before him. Sooner than risk a fatal defeat, he had occupied the welcome time Edward had unexpectedly allowed him in provisioning and strengthening the towns on the line of march, and had ordered their captains on no account to venture out. Accordingly, at Amiens, his Constable, Robert de Fiennes, let the Black Prince pass the Somme unchallenged; neither did Guy de Châtillon, count of Saint-Pol, molest the king as he made his way round Arras. However, when Lancaster approached Péronne, the less obedient Galahad de Ribemont (cousin of Eustace de Ribemont who had earned Edward's chaplet of pearls at Calais and had died at Poitiers) could not resist accosting and nearly trapping an unsuspecting German knight by pretending to be his renowned but unknown English ally Bartholomew Burghersh. In sodden Artois, all comestibles had been taken into the towns, and the intervening country, already denuded by three years of pillage, was systematically laid waste, and anything left had been scooped up by the Germans in their recent raid. Further south, near Cambrai, devastation had not been carried out, since it was now become part of the Empire, and regarded itself as neutral. Edward paused gratefully to load up food and fodder, deaf to the complaints of the inhabitants. Since they were not to be his French subjects, there was no point in sparing them.

At the end of November the columns converged on Rheims and loosely surrounded it at a distance, taking shelter from the still pouring rain in the many deserted abbeys and châteaux round about. From the abbey of Saint-Basle, perched high on the edge of the Forêt de la Montagne to the south, Edward was in full view of his heart's desire, the twin western towers of the great cathedral; but after a month of desolate travel he was no nearer to its attainment. Archbishop Jean de Croon did not welcome him as the Lord's anointed, but resisted him to the utmost of his power. The gates of the city did not open at his amicable request. The new and solid walls of this Jericho did not fall down. Rheims was well prepared for the expected siege. With his elaborate equipment Edward could probably, though at a price, have taken the place by storm, but so rough an action would have exposed the sheep's clothing he was wearing. He made no attempt to do so. Diversions to exercise the troops took place thirty miles away to the east; in one of these, Chaucer, hauled off to war in the service of Prince Lionel, was briefly taken prisoner. Such diversions had no effect on the basic situation.

In the short wet days of winter, far from home, it was a sparse and dismal Christmas, relieved only by the excellent local wines supplied by the companionable free-lance Eustace d'Ambréticourt, who was making his fortune in the neighbourhood. Morale was failing. Horses were dying from exposure and starvation. After five weeks, Edward gave it up; and on 11 January 1360 moved off southwards towards Burgundy.

The House of Burgundy, whose duke was the greatest and most venerable of the twelve peers of France, was a cadet branch of the French royal house of Capet, which had long kept a close hold on Burgundy's allegiance through dynastic marriages – a policy intensified in the fourteenth century when the family ties between Capets, Valois and Burgundians became positively bewildering. Louis X, Philip V, Charles IV and Philip VI, kings of France, all married Burgundians. Duke Otto IV of Burgundy married the daughter of Philip V, and Duke Philip's widow became the second wife of King John II. But there were territorial disputes between France and Burgundy, and the French subjection of their dukes did not appeal to the Burgundian nobles. When Otto IV died in 1349, Burgundy, now also including the former French county of Franche-Comté, fell to his infant grandson, Philip de Rouvre, and during his minority the effective government was in the hands of his widowed mother, Jeanne de Boulogne, a Frenchwoman who promptly married, as his second wife, King John of France. While Edward was besieging Rheims with his great army, the Burgundians, thinking that he would soon be king of France, and that he was well poised to make them the first victims of his abasement of their Valois overlords, suggested a treaty of neutrality. Edward enthusiastically took them up, marched south in his intimidating triple columns, and by resuming the old argument of rape and plunder so heartening to his dispirited troops, showed that they had best make their offer good enough. On entering Burgundy he took Tonnerre by storm despite the presence at the nearby castle of Auxerre of the French Constable, de Fiennes, who made no attempt at a sortie. From Tonnerre, Edward went on down the Serein valley into the heart of the duchy at Guillon, where the Burgundian ambassadors soon arrived, among them Sir John de Vienne, the brave captain of Calais, and began negotiations.

It was now mid-February. The rains were slackening and the days getting longer. While the talks proceeded, the troops kept up the pressure with their raids, on one of which Roger Mortimer was killed, being replaced as Constable by John Beauchamp, younger son of the earl of Warwick. Meanwhile Edward spent a pleasant month going out every day with his hawks and hounds and no doubt scudding about the river in the collapsible leather boats in search of Lenten fish. Towards the end of March, a satisfactory treaty had been reached. In return for a three-year truce and the return of certain captured towns, the Burgundians undertook to revictual his army free of charge and to pay him 200,000 gold *moutons* to see him on his way. This was an excellent arrangement, in Edward's old hard-headed style. He extended it to the county of Nevers and other districts round about, and it was finally to prove the only solid achievement of the whole campaign. But he still had not foregone his fatuous design upon the throne of France, for it was a special condition of the truce that the duke of Burgundy and other nobles should, when the time came, support him at his coronation.

While at Guillon, Edward was joined by Robert Knollys and the Captal de Buch and their roving bands, whom he had now officially pardoned for their supposed disobedience in breaking the former truce. Reinforced, rested and replenished, and with his rear secured, he set off north for Paris to force conclusions with the dauphin, now more than ever isolated. Since his object was to provoke a battle, Edward dropped his mask of clemency as soon as he was out of Burgundy; he told his commanders to let their troops have their head and to revert to their normal code of frightfulness, a technique wherein the Black Prince once more showed himself an expert, as he had done before in Aquitaine. Their ferocity hardened when the news came in of a major French reprisal raid on Winchelsea. They had stormed the church during Mass, seized the best-looking maiden there and gang-raped her to death in front of the congregation. They were successfully driven off, but carried away great spoil and nine other shapely women whose fate was little better. For fear of a repetition, the home government called up all able-bodied men from sixteen to sixty, patrolled the coast, and in case of a rescue bid, moved King John from Somerton to the security of the Tower.

On Tuesday 31 March the army arrived at Longjumeau, twenty miles south of Paris, and for the second time in his career Edward was within comfortable striking range of the enemy capital. He paused to assess the situation over Easter. He may have hoped that the panic caused by his appearance would cause a civil insurrection in the city, remembering how the dauphin Charles had been driven out by Etienne Marcel in 1357. If so, he was disappointed. Soon after his landing in the autumn, the mercurial Charles of Navarre had once again changed sides and planned to assassinate the dauphin in his capital; but the plot had been discovered, and Charles had been forced to flee to his citadel at Nantes further down the Seine. Since then there had been no further sign of insubordination. On the contrary all the events of the next ten critical days were to show that Paris was strictly obedient to the orders of one cool, superior intellect. The great encircling walls of Etienne Marcel had been completed, a solid protection which had not been there when Edward last threatened the city in 1346, and they contained the whole army of France, since the fast-moving Constable, Robert de Fiennes, who had watchfully coasted him all the way from Amiens to Tonnerre in Burgundy, had now once again slipped past him into Paris.

For a few days no move was made by either side, though the indefatigable papal peacemakers soon appeared. The Master of the Friar Preachers and the abbot of Cluny arranged a conference on Good Friday, 3 April, in the leper-house at Longjumeau. They based their efforts on the first treaty of London, made between John and Edward in January 1358, which had been generally acceptable to the Estates of France. No progress was made; Edward in his later, inflated mood was demanding more and more. As soon as the conference was over, he stepped up his war of terror, slaughtering and burning so that the smoke and flames were clearly visible in the city, where pitiful droves of refugees were pouring in and receiving their Easter communion in the open. The dauphin retaliated by moving the main slaughterhouses within the walls, and burning further suburbs, emphasizing his already evident policy to stock up the capital and at the same time deny all possible assistance to the enemy outside. A week after the first peace conference a second, on 10 April, in the abbey of Cluny near the Sorbonne, likewise broke down. Edward moved forward to the gates of Montrouge and sent Walter Morny to exasperate the garrison with a squadron of specially created knights, an expensive honour evaded by young Colart d'Ambréticourt, brother of Sir Eustace, on the specious grounds that he could not find his helmet. Edward also sent Henry of Lancaster with a herald, to challenge the dauphin to come out and fight. Charles stood firmly by his decision to resist all provocation.

Edward was now in unexpected difficulties. He could neither get into Paris, nor persuade the dauphin to come out and take his beating like a man. Nor could he obtain anything like satisfactory terms of peace. Only one thing was clear. He could not stay where he was. The devastation had been so great that there was nothing for horses or men to eat and the besiegers were worse off than the besieged. On 12 April, under cover of a demonstration at the walls, the army moved off quietly and quickly, still in its orderly three formations, heading south-westward towards Chartres. There is much doubt as to Edward's motives. Froissart says he was headed down the Loire to Brittany to refresh his army for a renewed assault on Paris. Certainly, he had John de Montfort in his train, and may have seen a chance to set him up firmly in his defenceless duchy; at worst, he would find food and fodder on the way, for as Gray says in his *Scalacronica*, there was none to be had at Paris. Perhaps he hoped, by resorting to a favourite stratagem of feigned retreat, to induce the dauphin to attack him, as he had lured the dauphin's grandfather at Buironfosse and, fatally, at Crécy; and as his son the Black Prince had lured, though unintentionally, the dauphin's father to what had proved against all odds to be his doom at Poitiers.

If that was his aim, he was disappointed. Though there was pursuit, and though it was duly ambushed, it was a very limited one. On seeing Edward's strident banners, the dauphin knew the game was his; he only had to wait. Chance, or as some thought Heaven, helped the dauphin. As the English army neared Chartres next day, 13 April, known ever afterwards as Black Monday, it was hit by a freak convulsion of the weather. The sky went dark; and it turned bitter cold. Thunder cracked, the lightning forked and flickered, hailstones pelted down as big as pigeons' eggs. The storm was phenomenal enough to attract the notice of almost all the chroniclers. Horses and men were killed, among them at least two of the nobility, Lord Robert Morley and Guy Beauchamp, eldest son of the earl of Warwick, probably from thunderbolts striking their wet armour. Though, when the storm was over, the army continued its faultless southward march, in a superstitious age it would have taken a less impressionable man than Edward not to have seen in the onslaught the rebuke of God for his pride and obduracy. Indeed, Froissart says that he turned aside to Chartres cathedral, and vowed to the Virgin to accept terms of peace. His mind was further changed when the usually cool-headed duke of Lancaster, who had led the English mission at both the recent peace talks, and had probably been against the expedition from the start, spoke out boldly, calling it a waste of time and money. He said that the king now stood in peril of losing in one day more than he had gained in twenty years, and urged him to accept the best terms he could get lest worse befall. Edward took his advice. He was, in fact, in some potential danger, wandering about in the heart of a hostile country without supplies and miles away from ships to take his army home. He had already lost more than twelve hundred cavalry mounts, not to speak of drays, and Knighton says so many perished in the storm that he was no longer fully mobile. At Châteaudun he learned that the abbot of Cluny, anxious to rub in the lesson of God's wrath, was hurrying after him with new proposals.

He said that he would go back to Chartres. There, the dauphin's emissaries arrived on the 27th; and at the tiny hamlet of Brétigny between there and the king's residence at Sours, on May Day 1360, the momentous conference to end the war was begun. The French deputies, staid clerical councillors, must have gazed quizzically at their soldierly counterparts, Lancaster, Northampton, Warwick, Salisbury, Stafford, Cobham, Chandos, Morny, Sir Frank Halle (of Auberoche), the Captal de Buch – a veritable hall of fame whose names had become household words as they raged through France during the last twenty years.[47] In only eight days, by 8 May, an agreement was prepared dealing with matters so complex and important as to show that the terms had already been settled in previous discussions except for certain points where Edward had obstinately held out. Since King John was still a prisoner, the sealing of the draft was left to the Black Prince and the dauphin, and on the 9th a joint commission carried it to Paris, from which Charles, with the rest of the royal family, had exerted a daily control by courier on the course of the proceedings. They were received 'as messengers from Heaven, all the bells ringing, and the people thronging the streets as to see a triumph, all the streets being spread and tapestried with cloth of gold'.

Edward on the other hand had no cause for rejoicing. He had taken no open part in the negotiations, and his subsequent actions displayed an unbecoming haste and a surly temper. His great enterprise had been a costly failure. His lordly demand to be crowned at Rheims showed his misunderstanding of the hatred his actions had bred among the French. His failure to cow the dauphin Charles at Paris showed his fatal underestimation of the implacable enemy of his remaining years. Worst of all, his statesmanship, his invincible generals, his crack army, for all their tremendous preparation, had achieved little or nothing beyond the shekels wrung from the Burgundians. The terms he now had to accept were far lower than those he had rejected two years earlier, in 1358. In outline they were strictly realistic. He was to keep, free of all duty of homage to the French crown, a reconstructed duchy of Aquitaine that now included all the lands in France Edward had inherited, all his recent conquests, and Poitou, Limousin, Angoumois, Quercy, Rouergue and Saintonge. In northern France, as well as retaining Ponthieu, which he had also held at his accession, he retained Calais. All this was enough to satisfy his oath not to go home until he brought with him peace with honour. On the map, Edward was lord of half of all that part of France that lay south of the Loire. Yet it was a sovereignty the French crown could no more accept in perpetuity than it had the earlier lordship over French soil of Edward's Angevin predecessors. Indeed, historic sovereignty was yielded up: he gave up all right to Normandy and the other northern provinces of Touraine, Anjou and Maine that he had secured, and the overlordship of Brittany he had exercised for over twenty years. And he renounced his title to the crown of France. Sacrificed too was his alliance with the Flemings, the diplomatic beach-head from which he had first launched his wars. By comparison, the French abandonment of the 'Auld Alliance' with the Scots mattered little for the time being, given that David II was Edward's client anyway. Finally, to offset Edward's gain from the Burgundians, John's ransom was slashed by a quarter, from four to three million crowns, on unanswerable grounds of practicality. All in all, Edward had lost far more than he could have gained without ever setting out on his expedition. However much the Peace of Brétigny was cried up as a crowning victory, in his heart he knew it for a defeat.

Without waiting for news of the regent's swearing to the peace in Notre-Dame, Edward marched his whole army off due north for the nearest Channel port. He paused only long enough on his way for the Black Prince to complete his part of the formalities at Louviers on 16 May. Then, while Lancaster led the columns back to Calais to return home later in the month, he rode with a French escort straight to Honfleur, where he embarked on the 18th with his four sons, with John de Montfort and with the great earl of Northampton, now probably sickening for the fatal illness from which he died in the September. Edward arrived in Rye before the day was out and on the next was at Westminster, where he at once sent for King John to be brought from the Tower to meet him in the palace chapel. It is not clear why he was in such a hurry to see King John, who was in no position to refuse, and in fact must have been delighted at terms so much less severe than he could possibly have imagined for his tortured country, since, after going with the Black Prince to see Queen Philippa at Windsor, he made lavish oblations in St Paul's.

In July, John, escorted by the Black Prince, Lancaster and Chandos, was transported to Calais, together with Prince Philip and the other Poitiers prisoners, and housed in the castle. By the terms of Brétigny, the first 6,000 gold crowns were to be paid within four months and forty hostages were to arrive at Calais, whereupon John would be released. By October, Edward himself was in Calais, and, with the Black Prince and Lancaster, dined with King John in the castle. Then two of Edward's younger sons and two of John's rode off to Boulogne to fetch the dauphin who, together with his father, attended a return banquet in Edward's lodgings. On 24 October, the two kings confirmed the Treaty of Brétigny in the church of St Nicholas at Calais. Unable, from modesty, to decide which of them should kiss the pax first, the two kings settled the matter by kissing each other. Their two eldest sons likewise swore to keep the peace, as did Philip of Navarre on behalf of the king, his brother. The abbot, Androine of Cluny, who conducted the Mass, was commended to the pope and suitably rewarded by being made a cardinal. Formal letters patent ratifying the treaty were duly exchanged by the two parties and Edward accepted 400,000 crowns of John's ransom, with a pledge that the balance would be paid at Christmas. Raising the cash had led to desperate measures in France. Though on stiff terms, the Jews were allowed back in France for a period of twenty years; and John got 600,000 gold florins out of Galeazzo Visconti, the rich tyrant of Milan, by contracting a marriage between his eleven-year-old daughter, Isobel, and Visconti's nine-year-old son.

Significantly, two matters were left outstanding. The renunciations, of territory and fealty, though drawn up and sealed, were not exchanged at Calais; exchange was deferred until 30 November 1361. When that time came, however, Edward did not press the matter, doubtless preferring his concrete gains to what he felt were purely ceremonial extras. He stopped calling himself king of France; but on the French side, the fact that sovereignty over Aquitaine was never finally renounced in due form proved of immense propaganda value later on. The other matter left in suspense was the fate of Brittany: the truce of Rennes was extended until the summer of 1361.

The ceremonies concluded with a huge supper for John in the castle at Calais, at which Edward's four sons served bareheaded. The following day, Edward escorted John a mile out of Calais, whence, as foot pilgrims, three of Edward's sons – the Black Prince, Lionel and Edmund – accompanied the French king as far as Boulogne, where they dined with the dauphin.

A week later, Edward, his sons, and thirty hostages, left for England, reaching London on 9 November 1361.

BOOK IV

GLISTERING PHAETON

Down, down I come; like glistering Phaeton,
Wanting the manage of unruly jades.
King Richard II, Act III, scene iii

Shall the sword devour forever? Knowest thou not that it will be bitterness in the latter end?

2 Samuel 2, xxvi

GLISTERING PHAETON

For all the reservations about it born of hindsight, the treaty of Calais was the high point of King Edward's reign. If, owing to the cool doggedness of the dauphin its terms were not so sweeping as those he had hoped to wheedle from King John, they were broad enough to make Edward lord of a third of all France. The terms were guaranteed to the limit of possibility not by oaths alone but by a solid phalanx of important hostages, including four French princes of the blood who were there for all to see as they 'took their pleasure about the city and used hunting and hawking, and rode into the country to take the air, and went to masks and balls, and visited the ladies and gentlemen without any control'. A sound treaty with Pedro of Castile had neutralized that monarch's powerful fleet. Scotland was pacified at last. King David had been sent home on promise of a ransom of 100,000 marks and further hostages. More English than the English now, David returned frequently to London and was trying to disinherit his unpalatable successor, Robert Stuart, in favour of the Prince of Wales. The Avignon papacy was thoroughly discredited, and Parliament, otherwise respectful, loudly insisted on statutes to reduce papal interference. The once overmighty barons were now Edward's brothers in arms; the calm definitions of the law of treasons of 1352, still in force today, were a far cry from the treachery of the days of Mortimer at the beginning of the reign. A sense of national identity was emerging. The adoption in 1362 of English in the law courts was an eloquent comment on the old law of Englishry, only abolished in 1339, whereby a whole Hundred of native Englishmen had been punished for the death of a single Norman. The vernacular literature was emerging as well. Young Chaucer had been ransomed from brief captivity near Rheims during the recent campaign and the first text of *Piers Plowman* was in the making. In comparison with the agonized chaos of France there was peace and prosperity in England, where justices of the peace now kept order in the countryside. And, too, there was the knowledge of how much glory had been won. As Petrarch put it, once thought 'the most timid of the barbarians' and 'inferior to the wretched Scots', the English were now seen as 'the most warlike of peoples', whose 'numerous and unexpected victories' had 'overturned the ancient military glory of France'.

Financially, Edward was better off than ever before. If not rich, he was at least solvent. His accounts for 1363 show that he and his family continued in their free-handed not to say extravagant way. Apart from the upkeep of castles and the normal expenses of government, the royal Works accounted for over £14,000. His personal income was a round £15,000. His wine bill was £6,700 – common or garden Bordeaux was two to four pence a gallon, but Edward drank Rhenish as well. The Wardrobe cost £8,000. Silver vessels and jewels cost another £4,000 odd; there was also the purchase of horses, of hounds and of falcons, and the wages of huntsmen. The sum of £1,756. 19s. 2d. had to be repaid that 'ma dame la reigne' had borrowed from the Exchequer; and the debts of his sister Joan, Queen of Scots, who had died the previous year, were to be settled. The Prince of Wales required more than £2,500, while the allowances of £100 each for Prince Edmund and his two married daughters, Margaret of Pembroke and Mary of Brittany, had also to be provided for. But if all these expenses resulted in a deficit of over £50,000, about 50 per cent, there was all the same the comfort of knowing it could be met from the ransoms of France and of Burgundy and the revenues of Calais and Ponthieu.

Before he aged too much, a touch of autumn graced Edward's splendour. He treated his people with a mellow majesty very different from the inflexible discipline of his grandfather, the great Edward I, with whom he must inevitably be compared. Knighton records that in 1363, at Leicester, where the execution of a certain Walter Winkebourne had been bungled, appeal was made to the king, who happened to be passing through, whether the wretch should be hanged again, and that he heard the king say, 'Since God hath given him life, I'll give him my pardon.'

He had already chosen his place of burial in Westminster Abbey, and he may have felt that his active life was behind him – that he could retire like a prosperous man of business to his favourite sport of hawking, to pilgrimages and tournaments, to the supervision of his great buildings: of the college he had already founded, King's Hall, Cambridge, later swallowed up in Trinity; of the task, now resumed under William of Wykeham, of converting the old 'Domus Regis' of Windsor castle into a fit home for the Order of the Garter; of the gaunt fortress of Queenborough, named after Philippa (who had herself founded Queen's College, Oxford, attending, with womanly care for detail, to the composition of the college soup and the washing of the fellows' heads), which was being raised by Henry Yevele in the mouth of the Medway; and of the magnificent nave that same great mason was preparing to create at Westminster.

In the early 1360s, therefore, the outlook seemed bright. But even thus early not everything went well. Heralded by the usual reports of signs and portents and accompanied by a tremendous storm and southerly gale on 17 January 1362, the plague returned, having already reappeared in Italy and France. It was particularly severe on the young and those of the wealthier classes who had escaped earlier visitation, and it struck down more men than women. It made so many widows that it was alleged these unhappy women were 'without shame' in their search for new partners. For Edward it was a special misfortune that to the deaths from plague of two earls, nineteen barons and six bishops (of Armagh, Chichester, Ely, Lincoln, London and Worcester) was added that of Duke Henry of Lancaster in March 1362. For fifteen years, Lancaster had in effect been Edward's foreign minister, and his death left the king with no great diplomatist at a time when the tangled state of affairs across the Channel needed a good deal more diplomatic skill than Edward himself was master of. The consequences for John of Gaunt, however, were far from un-pleasant. Duke Henry was survived by two daughters. Maud, the elder, was herself a plague victim; in consequence, as husband of Maud's younger sister, Blanche, Gaunt acquired the whole of her father's great estates and became duke of Lancaster.

In that same year, 1362, Edward celebrated his fiftieth birthday not only by the first distribution of Maundy pence and the issue of a general pardon; he also signalized his singularly amiable relations with his several sons by making territorial magnates of them all. The Black Prince was made prince of Aquitaine, subject only to liege homage and peppercorn rent of an ounce of gold each Easter. Lionel of Antwerp became duke of Clarence; Edmund of Langley was made earl of Cambridge; and young Thomas of Wood-stock became earl of Buckingham and, eventually, duke of Gloucester. In this, too, Edward resembles a successful, middle-aged entrepreneur, con-fident enough in the future of the family business to delegate some of his powers to his dutiful sons while he himself turns aside to taste more of life's pleasures. It was unfortunate, therefore, that the Black Prince showed too little skill as prince of Aquitaine and John of Gaunt none at all when circumstances later made him England's effective ruler. More forgivably, the new duke of Clarence was not much of a success in his new role. Having married Elizabeth de Burgh, heiress of Ulster, he was sent out to govern Ireland. Though he defeated the rebel O'Brien he was never able to extend English control beyond a restricted area round Dublin; and the Irish once killed a hundred of his men 'while they lay in their quarters' and 'no man could tell how'. Moreover, it was as rich aristocratic land-lords as well as bitterly quarrelling members of one great family, all sprung from Edward's loins, that Gaunt's descendants became the Lancastrians of the so-called Wars of the Roses a century later, interminably con-testing control of the crown with the descendants of Edmund of Langley, labelled Yorkists because he, in due time, added the dukedom of York to his earldom of Cambridge.

* * *

Across the Channel, the war bequeathed chaos to all parts of France, whether nominally subject to King John or King Edward. The miseries of France included more than those caused directly by war and plague: the deserted houses, ruined fields, desecrated churches and depopulated towns, and the desperate efforts of the crown to squeeze money from individuals and communities to pay the ransoms due to England. The distress was intensified by the ravages of the so-called Free Companies. These soldiers turned bandits roamed the countryside as free-lance forces beholden to nobody except those who on occasion could employ them and promise them booty.

After Poitiers, many English and Gascon soldiers had preferred this marauding life at the expense of the defenceless French to returning to the hazards of normal life at home. They were veteran fighters, often led by able, if ruthless, captains. After the treaty of Calais their numbers were increased by late-comers ('*Tard-Venus*') similarly disinclined for the rigours of civilian life. They were constantly merging into larger hordes, capable, under experienced leadership, of exercising decisive influence over the operations of warfare and diplomacy in France, Spain and Italy. Petty rulers and great ones would pay them to fight their wars for them, or seek to get rid of them by paying them handsomely to go away. Although the rank and file might be cut-throats of any of the nationalities drawn into the Anglo-French struggle – Scots, Welsh, Germans and Flemings as well as English and French – their leaders were mostly such formidable characters that they and their companies were soon much in demand, notwithstanding their persistent ravaging of the towns and villages even of the princes who hired them. One of the most famous of the mercenary commanders was Sir John Hawkwood. The landless younger son of a small Essex landowner-cum-tanner, Hawkwood led a well-armed band known as the White Company and was eventually hired at various times by the warring city-states of Italy. He served Pisa, Florence, the pope, Milan – whichever at any time offered the best terms. Stipulating only that he would not fight against the king of England, he became the most feared, though not necessarily the most frightful, of all the *condottieri* in Italy. He married into the same wealthy Visconti family of Milan to whom King John had sold off his daughter Isobel; and after his long and profitable career he was commemorated by Uccello in the fresco to be seen in the Duomo at Florence.

Arnold de Cervole, another mercenary leader, was more nobly born and, because he had once been a beneficed cleric, was known as 'the Archpriest'. He formed his company after Poitiers and was formidable enough for Innocent IV to pay him protection money to stop him attacking Avignon. In 1364 the young Duke Philip of Burgundy paid the Archpriest a large sum to take his troops elsewhere, treating him with deep respect while negotiating the deal.

More typical than either, though no less colourful, was Sir Eustace d'Ambréticourt, a friend of Froissart, a grandson of the needy Sir Eustace who had helped Edward's mother Queen Isabella in Hainault before her invasion of England in 1326, and son of Sir Sanchio, a founder Knight of the Garter. At Poitiers, carried away by his gift for panache, Eustace charged the French single-handed before battle had been joined, and was overpowered by a posse of Germans and tied to a cart until his men rescued him later on in the victorious day. Afterwards he set up as a Companion chief, with Courageous Manny, nephew of the great Sir Walter, as his lieutenant, and was elected as their leader by the English and the Germans. During Edward's siege of Rheims in 1359, while operating in Champagne, where he lost three teeth and gained a fortune, Eustace supplied the king with wines looted from that splendid region.

The fame of his exploits stirred the sad heart of Elizabeth of Juliers, a niece of Queen Philippa and widow of John, earl of Kent, the Fair Maid's brother. Now a nun at Waverley near Winchester, Elizabeth wrote to Eustace in their common language, even though she had never seen him. She sent gages as well as love letters and gave him a splendid charger, of which Eustace was so proud that when his troop had to ransom him, he insisted they ransom the horse as well. Left at a loose end by the peace, in 1360 he returned to England, stole Elizabeth out of her convent, and induced a hedge-priest, John Ireland, to marry them before sunrise in the private chapel of a manor house in Kent on their way to elope from Sandwich. They were caught: and Elizabeth's breaking of her vows counted as a deadly sin. To keep this fact suitably in remembrance, in addition to her daily recitation of the seven penitential psalms, the fifteen gradual psalms, the Litany, *Placebo* and *Dirige*, Archbishop Islip also required both of them to give freely to the poor whenever they had carnal intercourse. Word quickly spread of the benefits attendant upon their matrimonial exertions, and most mornings Eustace found himself cheered on by clamorous villagers.

It was his involvement with one of the Free Companies that may well have precipitated King John into the strange course of action which he chose to follow during the rest of his life. The Companies were causing such anarchy in France when the king returned from captivity that he decided to employ the Archpriest, de Cervole, to assist a royal army to rout the other brigands. Against the Archpriest's advice, the royal force attacked some *Tard-Venus* entrenched on a height near Lyons called Brignais, and was quickly defeated. The Archpriest himself was taken prisoner, as were many rich nobles, all of them held to ransom. James of Bourbon and his son Peter, both descendants of St Louis, were mortally wounded. It was perhaps despair at yet one more defeat for men of chivalry, and this time by brigand professionals, that prompted King John to seek ways of relieving himself of the admittedly awesome burdens of bringing back order, prosperity and honour to his ruined country. After Brignais he went to Avignon and spent a year unsuccessfully trying to organize a crusade, first with Pope Innocent VI and then with Urban V. His only real support came from Peter of Lusignan, king of Cyprus, the nominal king of the now defunct Latin kingdom of Jerusalem. On Good Friday 1363, the Crusade was proclaimed and John designated its captain-general. The Crusade was to start in 1365; and, while Peter set off to the court of the emperor to solicit, unavailingly, military aid from Charles IV, John moved to Montpellier. He showed no anxiety to return to Paris to attend to the ills of his own kingdom; and now seems to have seized a golden chance to rid himself of them altogether.

By December 1363, Edward had allowed his four royal French prisoners to visit Calais to make arrangements about their ransoms. But in that month, the principal hostage, John's son Louis, prince of Anjou, out of love, it was said, for his young wife Mary of Blois, whom he had married only a short time before becoming one of Edward's prisoners, broke parole while on a pilgrimage to Boulogne and refused to return to captivity. At once, John announced that Anjou's action had so impugned his honour as king that he now had no choice but once more to surrender his royal person to Edward as a prisoner. Contemporaries seem to have been hardly less at a loss to explain John's supererogatory view of his chivalric duty than have subsequent historians. The more unkind suggested at the time that he rather enjoyed being fêted as a royal prisoner in convivial surroundings and that there was much enjoyable female company to be had in captivity among the English. He was not personally bound to answer for Anjou's escape; perhaps, therefore, he hoped to negotiate a financial deal with Edward about his ransom or even, though this is scarcely a rational excuse, to get Edward to join the proposed Crusade. It is tempting to ascribe to John the simple anxiety of an outstandingly unsuccessful monarch to be free of responsibilities he knew were beyond him. Crossing the Channel in the depths of winter he reached Dover on 3 January 1364, rode next day to Canterbury to offer a jewel at the shrine of Thomas Becket and thence to Edward's manor at Eltham. The two kings went on to London where, 'with great mynstrelsie', he was conducted to the Savoy. Clearly, John was behaving like the very soul of chivalry. His willing, ceremonial return to the custody of England's genial and martial king must have struck Londoners as being as much a tribute to Edward's own chivalric qualities as to John's. At the Savoy, he was frequently visited by Edward, and John made return visits to Edward's palace at Westminster. Henry Picard, the Gascon-born London vintner who had been mayor in 1357, gave a great feast soon after John's return at which were present, in addition to Edward and John, three other kings: David of Scotland, Peter of Cyprus and Waldemar of Denmark. The two latter were doubtless there to present their crusading plans. Edward declined to involve himself;

though his refusal was said to have been made 'graciously'.

And then, in March 1364, John fell suddenly ill, and died on 8 April. Barely forty-five, he had hitherto been in excellent health; and there was no plague about. It was all so unexpected, and the scoundrelly Charles of Navarre expressed so much delight at the news, that there was speculation that it might be the outcome of a plot by Charles to poison John for having thwarted Navarre's ambitions in Burgundy a year or so earlier.

With a proper sense of chivalric theatre, John bequeathed his bowels to St Paul's, his heart to Canterbury and his body to Saint-Denis in Paris. At each of these places there was a magnificent funeral service. The procession to St Paul's was graced by horses caparisoned with the arms and lilies of France and the number of torches and wax tapers used inside the cathedral ran into thousands.

The dauphin, shortly to be crowned King Charles V of France, had the last word. In a letter of thanks to Edward, he acknowledged 'how graciously and with what good cheer you received our dear lord and father again in your kingdom . . . we thank you to the fullest extent of our ability and will always hold ourselves beholden to do anything we can for your honour and pleasure'. Even more than customarily in the rituals of chivalry was this indeed form without substance. A semi-invalid of unknightly demeanour, Charles was to content himself with the roles of conscientious administrator and astutely thoughtful diplomatist, leaving the campaigning and heroics to others. He would make no major decision without consulting not only the renowned astrologer-scientist, Thomas of Pisano, whom he paid handsomely to come to his side at Paris, but also, if he felt the need, the lawyers of most European universities. This unchivalrous refusal to enter lightly into a quarrel was not always pleasing to his own subjects, and was a source of endless irritation to the straightforward-thinking Edward. 'There never was a King', Edward later remarked ruefully, 'who had less to do with arms yet never was there a king who gave me so much to do.'

In thanking Edward elaborately for the courtesies shown to his father, Charles was giving notice that he would always be punctilious. But it was soon clear that he could use chivalric gestures not merely to defer but also, subtly, to defy. At his coronation, Charles arranged for the principality of Aquitaine, bestowed by Edward upon the Black Prince, to be represented in the person of that Louis of Anjou who had breached the chivalric code by escaping when he was Edward's hostage.

Within months of John's death, Edward's hold over his French dominions began to look less secure. In three diplomatically sensitive areas, Burgundy, Brittany and Flanders, there were setbacks. In 1361, the young Philip de Rouvre, duke of Burgundy, died of the plague. Son of King John's second wife, Jeanne de Boulogne, by her previous marriage, Philip was the only grandson of Duke Otto IV of Burgundy and had been betrothed to

Margaret, the widowed countess of Flanders, whose dower also included Brabant and Artois. After Philip's death, the best title to Burgundy itself was that of Charles the Bad of Navarre; but King John, just before leaving for Avignon to make his abortive crusading plans, hastened to Dijon and took over the duchy as Philip de Rouvre's next-of-kin. He then assigned Burgundy to his youngest son, Philip (known to history as Philip the Bold), partly because the Burgundians were unwilling to be absorbed into the kingdom of France and partly because John was, as usual, unprepared to assume additional personal responsibilities. It was not until John's death in 1364 that it became publicly known that Burgundy had been assigned to Philip, and the gift was assumed to be a reward for his bravery as a fourteen-year-old in personally defending his father in the mêlée at Poitiers. Gossip, however, reported that his appellation of 'the Bold' had a different origin, and had been conferred on him jestingly by Edward III. At a banquet given by Edward for his prisoners after Poitiers, Philip had struck the butler for daring to serve the king of England before the king of France. In conformity with his role as good-natured and magnanimous victor, Edward had tolerantly commented, 'Verily, cousin, you are Philip the Bold.' Resolute he certainly was. Almost his first act in his duchy was to clear it of the ravaging Companies. His principal means to this end was to hang as traitors every Frenchman he found among them.

Edward's counter-measure to this obvious accession of strength to the French crown was to try to detach Burgundy from the proposed Flanders marriage by arranging for Margaret of Flanders to marry Edmund, earl of Cambridge, now that death had removed Philip de Rouvre. At the prompting of Charles V, Urban V vetoed the marriage on the grounds of the couple's consanguinity. It did not modify English suspicions about the pro-French posture of the Avignon popes when, in 1369, the same Urban V permitted Philip the Bold to marry Margaret, even though Philip was more closely related to her than Edmund was. The manoeuvrings of the French king had thus opened the way for the creation of the great duchy of Burgundy which, though later on a threat to the French crown, denied Edward a Burgundian or Flemish alliance for the rest of his reign.

Events in Normandy and Brittany in 1364 also tended to England's disadvantage. In April 1364 Charles V enlisted the services of the celebrated mercenary Bertrand du Guesclin to deal with the troublesome Charles of Navarre. Du Guesclin, a Breton of exceptional ugliness and great powers of leadership, was one of the earlier captains to have a Free Company of his own. He began his career in Charles's service auspiciously. In May he signally defeated a force led by the Captal de Buch on behalf of Charles of Navarre (who was his cousin) at the battle of Cocherel in Normandy. Not only was the Captal himself captured; the battle marked the end of Charles of Navarre as a serious threat either to Paris or to Charles V's crown. Charles rewarded du Guesclin by making him count of

Longueville. It was the start of a strange partnership. Between them, Charles, a kind of crowned lawyer, and du Guesclin, a professional adventurer whose Breton name the French could scarcely pronounce in its original form, would in the end rob Edward of all his conquests.

Cocherel was also something of a defeat for Edward's young godson, de Montfort, since in the still unresolved dispute over the succession to Brittany, Charles the Bad had supported de Montfort while Charles V supported the rival claimant, Charles de Blois. Accordingly, when, a few months later, Charles sent du Guesclin into Brittany against de Montfort, who was besieging the town of Auray on the Breton coast, the English took action. Edward's lieutenant in France, John Chandos, sent a force to de Montfort's aid. It was composed wholly of Free Companies, the most notable leaders being Olivier de Clisson, Eustace d'Ambréticourt and Hugh de Calveley. Fought mainly hand to hand with axes and five-foot lances it was something of a battle to the death. One of de Montfort's cousins was killed by de Blois, who mistook him for de Montfort himself, and Olivier de Clisson was blinded in his right eye by an axe. While making a last stand with his Breton lords, Charles de Blois was killed by an English dagger. It was claimed that the dead man had passed an uneasy night before the battle, being much perturbed to observe that his white greyhounds had deserted to the enemy. Also killed were his standard bearer and his son John. Chandos routed the main French contingent, who remounted and fled. Then, turning to his chief prize, Chandos personally took du Guesclin prisoner. Breton, Norman and French losses were severe and the pursuit of the defeated merciless. Much of the credit for the victory was due to Calveley. In command of the rearguard he several times extricated Robert Knollys, Olivier de Clisson and d'Ambréticourt from trouble when hard pressed.

On the face of it, it was a victory for England. The Breton issue was settled in favour of the English client, de Montfort. Not surprisingly, the pursuivant who brought the glad news to Edward at Dover was made Windsor Herald. Yet Charles was not unduly cast down. He accepted the verdict of Auray and persuaded the widow of de Blois to abandon her claim by granting her a large pension; and he retained the homage of the duchy for future use if need be. He was not sorry that the continuing demand on French resources of sponsoring a candidate in Brittany had now stopped.

With Navarre and Brittany neutralized and Burgundy and Flanders detached from England's influence, Charles was better placed to restore order in his own territories. Initially, however, the ending of the war in Brittany increased the number of Companions in France to something like 60,000. They included many Englishmen and Gascons led by Sir Nicholas Dagworth, who had not forgiven the French for killing his father in 1349. The Companions routed a strong French army sent against them and took both Philip of Orleans and Louis of Anjou prisoner. Charles complained to Edward; under the terms of peace Englishmen were forbidden to make war in France. Edward duly issued admonitory proclamations; but, for the Companions, war was their trade and collecting ransom money their livelihood, and they took no notice. Edward therefore suggested he might raise an army to suppress them. Charles at once begged him to desist. Edward, for once, seems to have taken offence, allegedly vowing by the Virgin that he would never stir again about aiding the king of France 'even though the Companions should endeavour to thrust him out of his realm'. Edward had, he thought, made a chivalrous gesture to the son of his old friend King John, and felt it had been churlishly rejected.

By the time the Black Prince became prince of Aquitaine he had acquired a wife celebrated by the chroniclers as an eminently suitable match for her valiant husband. Yet, such was her chequered past, the prince married her secretly and only after some delay was Edward prepared to accept his new daughter-in-law. For the prince had taken as his bride no less a woman than Joan, the Fair Maid of Kent. No doubt it helped that she had, quite apart from her personality, other valuable assets with which to compensate for the dubieties of her earlier history. She was, when the prince married her, the widowed Lady Holland, Holland having died in 1360. Since the death of her father in 1352, she was also countess of Kent in her own right and one of the richest ladies in all England. True, she was the grand-daughter, and he the grandson, of Edward I, and a papal dispensation had had to be procured; and the king had signified his displeasure by absenting himself from the solemnization of the marriage at Windsor. However, it was by now a long time since she had ceased to be the countess of Salisbury, Holland having successfully petitioned the pope to annul her undoubtedly bigamous marriage to William Montagu some twelve years earlier; and presumably Edward soon acquiesced in the general opinion that she was a sufficiently splendid creature to preside with her husband over the brilliant court they established at Bordeaux to dazzle and delight the lords of Aquitaine, only some of whom, such as the Captal de Buch, had been vassals of the English crown before Brétigny. Thirty-three at the time of her marriage and thus a year older than her husband, she was, according to the Chandos Herald, 'beautiful, pleasing and wise'; while Froissart wrote that she was the most beautiful woman in all England and 'la plus amoureuse'.

If her husband was the slim but strong man suggested by his famous bronze effigy at Canterbury, he must indeed have been handsome. But he was also formidable, with something of the severity of his grandfather, Edward I. It does indeed seem that the Black Prince, though admired as a commander in the field, had his share of the harshness, arrogance and unthinking extravagance to be found in other paragons of chivalry. He lacked the easy grace that seemed to come naturally to Edward III, and was apparently not very good at taking his exalted state for granted. As prince of Aquitaine he was thought to insist too much on his dignity, keeping suitors waiting too long on their knees, and, untrammelled by a cheeseparing parliament in Aquitaine like that which his father had to deal with in England, he fell quickly into the temptation of dispensing hospitality and largesse beyond his means. Lavish feasts and tournaments, the maintenance of a huge retinue of knights and esquires on the prince's part, and his lovely wife's indulgence in sumptuous clothes and gorgeous jewellery (for which the prince was always ready to pay astronomical prices) – these things cost so much that he lost badly needed support in Aquitaine through the harshness of the taxes he imposed in order to pay for all this visual display.

He had relatively few armed forces of his own in Aquitaine and, since there was an official peace with France, he had played a spectator's part during the struggle for Brittany in 1364; but he had ransomed the Captal de Buch after Cocherel and it was Chandos, whom he now made Constable of Aquitaine, who had captured du Guesclin at Auray. Henceforward, the prince depended more and more on the Free Companies and became something of a super-*condottiere* himself, using his gifts for military leadership in the pursuit of interests not all of them necessarily those of England or even of his father's crown.

The settlement of Brittany let loose the Companies, and they once more fell to pillaging France. Since war was their sole occupation the only way to stop them was to find work for them to do somewhere else. In 1365, Charles IV, the German emperor, arrived in Avignon, and in a rare demonstration of unanimity between popes and emperors he and Urban V proposed that the Companies should go off to drive the Turks out of Hungary. This Crusade, conveniently combining Christian objectives with the political interests of the Germans, had little appeal for the Companies. Though the emperor promised to assign to them all the revenues of Bohemia for three years, they reckoned it was too far to go when they were already doing fairly well for themselves in France. Some did move towards a rendezvous with imperial forces in Lorraine, but their mere appearance in Alsace so terrified the inhabitants that they forced the emperor to turn his intended allies back.

The Companies retreated the less reluctantly because more congenial employment had now been proposed to them. The way seemed to open up for the subtle Charles V to divert them against Edward's useful ally the king of Castile. The strategic importance of the Castilian fleet had been several times demonstrated: in 1338 and again in the 1340s it had, while its king, Pedro, was in alliance with France, done much damage to English ports on the south coast. The defeat of the Castilians off Winchelsea in 1350 was the prelude to a reversal of Castile's allegiance. Pedro had already shown himself as ready to change sides as Charles the Bad. In

1348, he had contracted to marry Edward's daughter, Princess Joan of the Tower; but after the princess's death from plague, he married instead Blanche of Bourbon, the sister of Charles V's queen. But in 1363, Blanche died at the age of only twenty-five because, it was alleged, Pedro had poisoned her, either to please his mistress, Maria de Padilla, or to free himself from the French connection. Certainly he immediately switched to the side of Edward and in 1362 he was present at St Paul's when an Anglo-Castilian alliance was solemnly contracted by which Pedro would put his fleet at Edward's disposal if need arose.

To counter this, however, Charles V already had a valuable ploy. Pedro had acquired his appellation of 'the Cruel' not only because of his alleged poisoning of his wife Blanche but because it was claimed also that he had poisoned his father's mistress, Leonora de Guzmán, after burning before her eyes a friar who had prophesied that Pedro would die at the hands of her eldest son. He was naturally assumed also to be bent on murdering Leonora's three sons, his half-brothers. Led by the eldest, Don Henry of Trastamara, they fled to France for safety and succour, and Charles was pleased enough to see them. This was the more understandable in that Pedro's cruel deeds included oppressing the clergy and invading the lands of his neighbour King Peter of Aragon. There were other lurid tales about him. Once, it was said, when Rufus, king of Granada, appealed to him for help, Pedro put him on a donkey and had his forty-one Moorish escorts trampled to death. On the other hand, Pedro had, as a ruler, been distinguished by a generally tolerant attitude towards his Moorish and Jewish subjects, and this may well have generated much of the church's hostility towards him and many of the tales of his cruelty. Nevertheless, policy and morality as well as religion would all seem to provide them with justification when both Charles V and Urban V proclaimed themselves sponsors of the rights of Henry of Trastamara to the throne of Castile in place of his cruel half-brother. Since Don Henry had been fighting on the side of the French crown for years, Charles was certainly advancing the interests of France in supporting him. In addition, he could point to the duty of avenging the cruel murder of his sister-in-law; and he could get some peace for France by sending the Free Companies off to eject Pedro on the other side of the Pyrenees. The undertaking had the blessing of the church and, win or lose, the campaign would inevitably cause a good number of the Companions to die of sickness or privation even if they did not get themselves killed in battle. And the Anglo-Castilian alliance would be nullified.

Du Guesclin, a prisoner since Auray, was therefore ransomed and put in charge of the expedition, though nominal command was in the hands of John de Bourbon, a cousin of the allegedly murdered Blanche. That du Guesclin was called on, despite the defeat at Auray, was in part for astrological reasons. Du Guesclin was as devoted to this art as Charles, and the two of them were convinced that the signs were all favourable towards him. Many mercenary captains of distinction, including Hugh de Calveley and Eustace d'Ambréticourt, served against Pedro, until Edward called back all English mercenaries to his own cause.

Du Guesclin and his men were not fools, however. They would not venture across the inhospitable Pyrenees until they saw the colour of somebody's money. They marched therefore towards Avignon, where they presented themselves unashamedly to the pope as an array of cut-throats who plundered churches and robbed peasants of their cattle and wine. The pope was to grant them absolution for all their crimes, and 200,000 francs as an advance; and the cash must come not, as the pope proposed, out of a tax on the citizens of Avignon, but from the coffers of the church. The Vicar of Christ, having no choice, did as he was asked; and du Guesclin's force marched on to Barcelona. There, they were entertained lavishly by King Peter of Aragon, eagerly looking forward to the downfall of Pedro, but aghast to observe that the mercenaries pillaged his own country as relentlessly as if they were at war with him rather than with Pedro.

After paying Charles the Bad to let them through Navarre, they then demanded that Pedro the Cruel allow them into Castile because, they said, they were going on a Crusade against the Moorish kingdom of Granada. Once he had received the offensive reply that this deliberately sardonic request was intended to produce, du Guesclin moved into Castile and marched on the capital, Burgos. Everyone seems to have deserted Pedro forthwith and, without difficulty, Don Henry of Trastamara was crowned king of Castile in his place. With Maria de Padilla (whom Pedro may, in fact, have married secretly before doing so publicly after the death of Blanche) and their daughters, Pedro fled first to Seville, where his personal fortune in jewels was stored, and thence to Corunna. Here, he had the archbishop of Compostela and the dean of Toledo put to death, to make clear that he and not Don Henry was king in Castile. That done, he took to the sea, and in due course arrived in Bordeaux to seek aid from the Black Prince. At once, the usual courtly balls and feasts and masks were organized, to demonstrate that Pedro was still a real king, and the prince of Aquitaine the soul of chivalry.

So far in all this, the prince had been very much the dog that had unaccountably failed to bark. He knew Charles V was behind du Guesclin and aiming to overthrow King Edward's Castilian ally, Pedro. No more than anyone else was he likely to have been deceived by Charles's public support of du Guesclin's claim that his men were marching on behalf of the Lord Jesus Christ against the Muslim infidels of Moorish Granada. Yet he had done nothing to help Pedro. Even his father had done no more than order, too late, that no Englishmen or Gascon vassals of England should join du Guesclin. It has been suggested that the prince took no action because he thought Pedro the Cruel personally unworthy of support; that he was anyway too hard up and short of troops; or that, if Pedro was allowed to get into really deep trouble, he would be likely to pay the prince the more handsomely for securing his restoration. The most the prince had so far done had been to agree with Chandos to send ships to rescue Pedro from Corunna, just as, in fact, Pedro had reached Bayonne without such aid.

On the face of it the prince was in a strong position. For the second time in less than ten years he had the destiny of a king in his hands. After Poitiers it had been King John; now it was Pedro. Then it had been a question of how much to extract from John as the price of his liberty; now it was how much to charge Pedro for his crown. And, alluringly, Pedro was prodigal in promises of titles, territories and pensions. On the strength of such promises, the prince agreed to pay the expenses of a rescue expedition, on the understanding that the bill would be met by Pedro once victory had been won. Pedro promised the prince precedence over himself when marching through Spain; and even when the prince himself was not present the arms of England were to be carried in the vanguard. He would pay the prince 550,000 gold florins and bestow on him the castle of Ordiales and the title of lord of Biscay. He would leave his three daughters in Aquitaine as hostages. And as a mark of his good intentions he gave the prince a richly jewelled table. In imitation of the legendary Round Table of King Arthur, it nevertheless failed to impress the Princess Joan. 'I fear', she is supposed to have said, 'lest ill come of it. The present is beautiful but it will yet cost us dear.' She was right to have doubts. In the end the prince had to sell the table at the knockdown price of 300 marks to Thomas Arundel, bishop of Ely. Similarly, Chandos had doubts, advising the prince against championing so dubious a cause as that of Pedro. But the prince reminded Chandos that there had once been a time when he would have given the advice to march off to battle whether the cause were good or bad. When King Edward's council had the matter referred to them, they agreed with Chandos: Pedro's reputation was altogether too dubious. But Edward took his stand on the principle that usurpation was a sin and that the rights of legitimate sovereigns ought to be upheld – as regards France, of course, the theory had been that Edward was its legitimate king and not the Valois rulers. Edward also considered himself committed to aid Pedro by the treaty of mutual assistance of 1362. Nor could Edward ignore the fact that Don Henry was a client of Charles V. John of Lancaster was sent to Bordeaux to convey Edward's approval of the proposal that the prince should restore Pedro to Castile.

The prince's Gascon lords also had to be considered. They loyally accepted Edward's decision, they said; but who, they asked, would pay them and their retinues? The prince, relying on future rewards from Pedro, promised that he would pay them until the day of victory. But they then insisted that Charles the Bad be brought into it. Their crusading experience in Spain dictated this demand: they could cross the Pyrenees only by the pass of Roncesvalles, which was in the kingdom of Navarre. In keeping with his character, Charles struck a hard bargain. Known turncoat though he was, his terms were accepted: all the lands Pedro had seized from neighbouring kingdoms were to be handed back to them and 56,000 gold florins were to be handed over by the prince for expenses, in advance of Pedro's final settlement. Through the Black Prince, therefore, Edward had, and somewhat casually, allowed the crown of England to be aligned with, and the wealth of Aquitaine to be in pawn to, Pedro of Castile and Charles of Navarre, two of the most scandalous European rulers of their day, both reputed to be poisoners and both known to be quite unreliable politically.

Collecting forces together for the expedition proved a long and costly task, not completed until early in 1367. Most of the prince's Gascon vassals sent contingents, notably Jean d'Armagnac, on the promise of high payment; though the haughty count of Foix declined to serve in person since he regarded himself as a sovereign prince and therefore free to declare himself neutral if he chose. The Black Prince called back all the English Companies who had served du Guesclin against Pedro, but they had some difficulty in reaching Bordeaux in the first place: Charles the Bad was paid by Don Henry to close the pass of Roncesvalles to them for a time, and those returning via Montauban had to fight their way past the French garrisons of Toulouse and Narbonne. Other Free Companies joined in, convinced that the French wars were about to start again. A picturesque supporter of the great cause was the young and destitute King James of Majorca, on the understanding that he would be restored to the island throne from which Peter of Aragon had driven his father.

The prince ended up with a larger army of Companions than he could afford and had to break up some of his plate to raise funds. He also prevailed upon King Edward to part with 100,000 francs due to him out of King John's ransom. Edward also sent about a thousand men under Lancaster, and there were also many volunteers from England. The prince decided there would have to be cuts. Having agreed that the redoubtable lord of Albret should raise, and be paid for, a thousand spearmen, the prince wrote to him in December 1366 reducing the figure to two hundred. D'Albret protested that he was now being forced to make men redundant who might otherwise have advanced their honour abroad, 'as most knights do in time of peace at home', by going off to fight the heathen in East Prussia or the Muslims in Jerusalem. His uncle, Armagnac, and Chandos had to work hard to mollify d'Albret. Evidently, the prince did not have the right touch in his dealings with his Gascon lords and this incident was considered the foundation of d'Albret's later opposition to him.

Four days before the expedition set off, the Princess Joan gave birth to a second son, Richard of Bordeaux. Froissart, who was at Bordeaux at the time, claims that a Sir Richard Pontchardon, who seems to have had some reputation as an astrologer, predicted that, second son to a king's son though the infant was, he would be England's next king. His grounds for the prophecy were that Richard was born on 6 January, the feast of the Epiphany, commemorating the coming of the Three Kings to the infant Christ at Bethlehem; and that on that particular day there were three kings in Bordeaux to attend this latest newborn child. The kings of Castile, Navarre and Majorca seem a somewhat unlikely trio of Magi; but it does not alter the fact that the prophecy Froissart reports certainly came true. The mother's mind, however, was on more immediate possibilities. According to the Chandos Herald, the Princess Joan feared she might lose, as a result of this Castilian expedition, 'him who has no peer for valiance on earth'. Certainly, Englishmen in such numbers had never fought so far afield before; but neither had two such great men as Edward and the Black Prince allowed the preservation of a remote kingdom like Castile against such an indefatigable hidden enemy as Charles V to be undertaken by proxy, by paid armies of mercenary adventurers, and in the hope that neither king nor prince nor England would have to foot the bill. Significantly, Charles V had attended personally to the financing of Don Henry, whom the expedition was designed to overthrow.

On Sunday 10 January 1367, the prince left Bordeaux for Dax, on the frontier between Gascony and Navarre, where he was joined by King Pedro, Lancaster with his English contingent, d'Albret – grumpily – with his two hundred spears, the Captal de Buch and his Gascons, and Olivier de Clisson with his Bretons. Matters were then delayed by Charles the Bad. In spite of his recent agreements with Pedro and the prince, it was known that he was now in negotiation with Don Henry. Chandos and Lancaster sought an interview with him, and the mercenary leader Hugh de Calveley seized a couple of strongpoints in Navarrese territory. Charles took the hint only when, for once, Pedro actually put cash on the table – some 20,000 francs.

At the end of January, the army reached Saint-Jean-Pied-de-Port at the entry to the pass of Roncesvalles. In mid-February, the nearly twenty-mile ascent, followed by the steep descent to the village of Roncevaux itself, was begun. There was a bitter wind and the horses found the going narrow, stony and slippery. The army, perhaps some 30,000 strong, therefore had to proceed in three divisions at two-day intervals. Though his only active service previously had been to accompany King Edward from Rheims to Paris, Lancaster led the van, though the Constable, Chandos, was there also, to nurse the inexperienced Lancaster as he had nursed the Black Prince at Poitiers and de Montfort at Auray. Chandos led the mercenaries secured from the Companies; also in the van were the two marshals of the army, the Gascon Guiscard d'Angle, and Sir Stephen Cossington, as well as the celebrated mercenary captains, Sir Hugh de Calveley and Sir Matthew Gurney. The centre, cold and hungry because it seems to have had the worst of the weather, was led by the prince himself and the two villains in the drama, Pedro the Cruel and Charles the Bad. Accompanying them were the seventeen-year-old Thomas Holland, Princess Joan's son by the first of her husbands, and the famous if laconic mercenary Sir Robert Knollys. The rearguard contained the exiled King James of Majorca; Armagnac, the prince's wealthiest vassal; the Captal de Buch; and the lord of Albret. In addition there were the archers, mounted for the journey and destined, as in the past, to be decisive on the day.

By the end of February 1367 and – a tribute to their toughness and to good organization – with few losses from the rigours of the journey, the army reached Charles's Navarrese capital, Pamplona, where, to his rage, the mercenaries looted in customary fashion. The prince's objective now was to get to the Castilian capital of Burgos as soon as possible; but, seeking to approach it by way of Vittoria, he found Don Henry's forces strongly occupying the heights that overlooked the lower ground along which the prince was marching. Henry's forces were considerable. Apart from the Castilians themselves, who had rallied enthusiastically to his side, du Guesclin had gathered one army for him in France and Charles V himself had sent a second. In an unfavourable strategic position, and with his provisions running out, the prince decided to press on no further, but to turn aside to approach Burgos by a more favourable route. Seeing in this something of an adverse portent, Charles the Bad, weighing the odds in his usual self-regarding fashion, decided he might have been backing the wrong side. He marched off and arranged to get himself captured. The rival armies had in fact been sufficiently close for two of Don Henry's brothers to make a lightning assault on Lancaster's division that took him completely by surprise. He rallied his force, however, and it hung on until reinforcements arrived and the attackers withdrew.

As the prince now led his army along the north bank of the Ebro, Henry moved in parallel on the south side of the river towards Nájera. The prince offered Henry a peace formula. If he would hand Castile back to Pedro, he himself would act as mediator between the rival half-brothers. Du Guesclin and d'Audrehem, Henry's two experienced mercenary marshals, were in favour of negotiation. Obviously, Pedro would make a generous cash payment as part of any negotiated settlement and the mercenaries would equally certainly get a goodly share of it. But Henry was obdurate, taking his stand on an interesting combination of chivalric heroism with the principle of popular election. 'The people of this country', he told du Guesclin, 'have crowned me king and king I will remain and will live and die in my right.' Du Guesclin's reply was that of the warrior who fought for pay and not for principle. 'So be it,' he warned, 'but be ready for battle, for in the army of the prince are the best generals and the most fierce warriors in this world.' Henry's marshals realized, as the armies moved towards each other once more to contest the path to Burgos, that the Castilians did not, as previously, have mountain defences behind them, but only the open plain. Once again faced with a dearth of supplies, the prince had the choice of either battle or retreat. Indeed, the same was true of Don Henry: not to fight would be to lose his crown.

Henry's hope of victory at Nájera was like that which had encouraged the French at Crécy: that his cavalry could overwhelm the enemy archers by sheer weight of numbers and ride down their opponents while they were dismounted. The flanks of his army were protected by hosts of cavalry, making a most impressive array. Unfortunately, his heavy cavalry, composed of Spanish knights and members of the Hospitallers of St John and other military religious orders, had experience only of fighting the Moors and none of coping with English archers. The numerous light cavalry were but indifferently mounted, on small horses or mules, and had inadequate armour. The rank and file were ill-disciplined peasant spearmen or men hurling stones from slings. Only the mercenaries had much hope of dealing with the kind of forces the prince led; but, though they gave a good account of themselves, there were fewer of them on Henry's side than on the prince's.

His blood stirred by the spectacle of the huge and brightly coloured array of Henry's army as the two contesting powers drew near to each other, Chandos asked permission to lead his division under his own personal banner. The prince having solemnly acceded to his Constable's request, Chandos's banner was unfurled and, thus displaying it to his followers, he declaimed, 'Gentlemen, behold my banner and yours. Let us guard it to the death.' The prince dismounted his men for the attack, encouraging them by reference first to their stomachs ('There are your enemies, in possession of the utmost plenty while we are starving') and then to the Almighty, who, as God of battles, was besought to grant them victory.

The clash between the two centres, led on one side by Lancaster and Chandos and on the other by du Guesclin and d'Audrehem, was long and murderous. Chandos himself was felled by a large Catalan and saved himself from death only by drawing his dagger and killing the man by plunging it into his side as he lay on top of him. The Castilian centre eventually began to break under the hail of arrows and the fury with which Chandos now led his attack. Both the Castilian left and right flanks were broken by the deadly arrows of the archers. The disintegration of the left was accelerated by the flight of Don Henry's brother, Don Tello, which left du Guesclin's own flank horribly exposed. As the English and Gascons hacked their way into the Castilian centre, Henry found it impossible to rally his knights effectively for all that he declared, 'As long as you fight I will never flee.' He was reduced to calling loudly for 'that whore's son, Pedro of Castile' to do battle with him; but as his rank and file of terrified peasants fled for their lives he too was reduced to leading his retinue in flight from the field, in the hope of fighting again on a better day. The

Companions in his service therefore sought suitable opponents to whom to surrender in the expectation of being ransomed; Du Guesclin (for a second time) and d'Audrehem were especially prompt to do so. King James of Majorca gave chase to the fleeing foot-soldiers. The pursuit was merciless and bloody. Pedro was anxious that any Castilian lords and knights he captured should not be ransomed, but imprisoned so that they could plot no more against him. The prince prevented him doing this, refusing Pedro's promise to buy such prisoners in lieu of their ransom money. The prince also compelled Pedro to deal justly with the many Frenchmen and Scots who fell into his hands.

The prince's victory at Nájera against greatly superior numbers was better planned and better executed than those of Crécy and Poitiers, and for that reason was one of the most remarkable and celebrated English victories of the Middle Ages. All the same, it had some resemblance to Crécy and Poitiers, for it, too, had disappointing results: its ultimate beneficiaries turned out to be the defeated Henry and his patient backer, Charles V.

* * *

The battle won, Pedro congratulated the prince in fulsome terms: 'I owe you much gratitude for the glorious day which you have won for me.' The reported reply of the prince was 'Render thanks to God, for victory cometh from Him and not from me.' It soon became apparent, however, that there was as much irony in Pedro's words as in the prince's. Once they arrived in Burgos, Pedro showed no great eagerness to pay the prince's expenses, and the prince for his part seems to have suppressed his thoughts about Pedro's debt to the Almighty by presenting a bill several times larger than the 550,000 gold florins originally promised him. True, the prince was prepared to accept a score or so of Castilian castles or the province of Biscay in part payment, even though this made him seem rather more like the captain of a mercenary company than a sovereign prince who, acting as God's righteous instrument, had restored a legitimate king to his rightful inheritance. Yet the prince was neither ruthless nor reckless enough to press Pedro too hard. He contented himself with getting Pedro to swear an oath in the cathedral at Burgos that he would in due course fulfil his obligations.

In the summer of 1367 Pedro went south to Seville, where his wealth was stored; but there was still no sign of his paying up. With splendid effrontery, he announced that the Spanish nobility would agree to pay nothing to a foreign army standing on Spanish soil. If the prince took himself and his forces back to Aquitaine he would then be paid without fail. The prince, too late, angrily revised his opinion as to the nature of the power which had led him to Nájera and declared that it was 'the devil' who had dragged him into Pedro's affairs. He thought about looting the

Castilian cities; but his armies were hungry and borne down by the heat, and he himself was beginning to suffer from a fever. He was the more disturbed because Don Henry, with Charles's support, had hired fresh mercenaries in France and was threatening the borders of Aquitaine. The Princess Joan sent a force under Sir James Audley (of Poitiers fame) to head Henry off; and she protested to Charles that in harbouring Henry he was in breach of the Anglo-French peace. Charles carefully rebuked Henry, but nobody doubted that he would again uphold Henry as soon as it was politic to do so. Henry was also negotiating with King Peter of Aragon to let him once again march on Castile through Aragon. The prince's response was a scheme for the joint dismemberment of Castile in alliance with Aragon, Navarre and Portugal. In August 1367 the prince and King Peter agreed to attack Pedro in 1368 if he had not by then paid his debts; the complicity of Navarre and Portugal would be sought; and as his own reward the prince would acquire Biscay and other Castilian territories and the title king of Castile. With this agreement to console him, the prince returned to Aquitaine in that same month of August 1367.

He returned therefore as a bankrupt who nevertheless had great expectations. Yet he had put himself in a position not unlike that of Pedro before Nájera. He too was now calling on others to win the kingdom of Castile for him; but whereas, though he had avoided parting with much of it, Pedro actually had the money with which to pay his friends, the prince had only debts. No less equivocal was his position as a prince who had set out to restore his father's ally and was now proposing to overthrow him. Had he proclaimed himself king of Castile on the morrow of Nájera he might have got away with it. To plan for the title when he was taking a disease-ridden army back from Castile to Aquitaine was scarcely realistic. Henry was still Charles's protégé and still a legitimated son of the previous king of Castile. As a result of Pedro's bad faith and the prince's lack of realism the victory of Nájera led to the downfall of both of them.

Back in Aquitaine, the prince dismissed his mercenaries, regretfully telling them that for the time being he could not pay them for the eight months they had campaigned with him. Fortunately, their leaders mostly being English, they were prevailed upon to try to recoup their losses by pillaging beyond the borders of Aquitaine. John of Lancaster also led his contingent back to England: Parliament could ask awkward questions about the expense if it stayed where it was. And the prince was so short of money that he decided to let du Guesclin be ransomed. Chandos had objected to this for fear du Guesclin might attack Pedro, thus giving him an excuse for not paying his debts. Du Guesclin accused the prince of being too frightened to ransom so redoubtable an opponent; nonchalantly, the prince replied by naming the most exorbitant figure he could think of – 100,000 francs. Du Guesclin called his captor's bluff; within a month, Henry, Louis of Anjou and Charles V had paid up.

So it was that within a matter of months, all that had been won at Nájera was lost again. With the prince bereft of men and money, and faced with growing discontent among his Gascon vassals over the taxes he sought to extract from them to pay for his adventures, Henry was let into Spain once more, by Peter of Aragon, who had developed new quarrels of his own with Pedro. Supported by funds and mercenaries from Louis of Anjou, Henry had captured Burgos by November 1368 and was advancing on Toledo in February 1369. There, at Charles V's instigation, he was reinforced by a strong mercenary force under du Guesclin. As Pedro marched north from Toledo to confront Henry, his army, composed mainly of Moors and Portuguese, was surprised and overwhelmed. With twelve followers, Pedro took refuge in a castle near Montiel. Trying to escape, he was captured and brought to Henry. According to Froissart, the two rival kings fought it out with knives and daggers, each calling the other the son of a whore, with Henry eventually killing Pedro with a thrust from his dagger.

Pedro's death did not merely nullify the great victory of Nájera. It also ended the Anglo-Castilian alliance that King Edward had so prudently cemented. Henceforward, under its new king, Castile's fleet was at the service of Charles V. The inhabitants of England's south coast ports would suffer much in the years ahead for the prince's ill-judged Spanish adventure.

The year 1368 was in other ways a bad one for King Edward and his family. In April of that year, Lionel, duke of Clarence, the king's second son, went off to Milan to marry Violante Visconti, the thirteen-year-old daughter of Galeazzo Visconti, the rich Milanese tyrant who was then celebrating a recent victory over the rival state of Montferrat. He had already expressed his exultant feelings by giving Hawkwood a million florins for his contribution to the victory, as well as another of his numerous daughters as a bride. Having succeeded in getting King John's daughter Isabella into his family just after the Peace of Brétigny, he now offered two million florins and several towns as bait to entice into the clan Lionel, brother of the now famous Black Prince.

A widower since 1363, Lionel, now aged twenty-nine, was tall and handsome, and fairly capable. He journeyed to Italy for the marriage ceremony with a retinue of almost five hundred and well over a thousand horses, pausing to be feasted at the Louvre in splendid manner in April 1368 by Charles V and his royal brothers, who loaded the prospective bridegroom with costly gifts. There was, after all, peace between Edward and Charles. Both had kept themselves, officially at any rate, aloof from the Castilian imbroglio; and if Charles was aware that events in Aquitaine were making a breach in the peace ever more likely, it is unlikely that Lionel, his father Edward, or even the Black Prince, gilded by the glory of Nájera, supposed that anything much was amiss, with Pedro as yet still king in Burgos. At Milan, Lionel's retinue was augmented by fifteen hundred soldiers of Hawkwood's White Company. The wedding banquet in June consisted of thirty courses interspersed with the distribution of gifts to the bridal couple. They included over seventy caparisoned horses; silver vessels; pictures framed in gold decorated with jewels; falcons; coats of mail; jewelled surcoats; and choice wines in enamelled bottles. Present at this sensational affair were Petrarch, Chaucer and Froissart.

It all came to nothing. After four months more of Lombard heat and hospitality, Lionel succumbed to a mysterious fever and died on 17 October 1368. Yet he fared more quietly in death than his young widow during the remainder of her own short life. Lionel was buried at the side of his first wife, Elizabeth de Burgh, at Clare in Suffolk. By the time she died at thirty-six, Violante had been married first to an adolescent sadist, the marquis de Montferrat, whom an ostler stabbed to death in the mountains near Parma, and then to one of her Visconti cousins, who was killed by her brother.

Meanwhile it was becoming clear that its Iberian consequences were among the lesser troubles to result from the Black Prince's Castilian adventure. Its chief consequence was to crack the thin veneer of the ceremonial peace between Edward and Charles V. For most of the years since the treaty of Calais, Charles had had too many problems within his own unoccupied area of France to want to provoke an open quarrel with Edward. The fact that everything that happened on the Continent in the 1360s worked to his advantage does not necessarily mean that Charles engineered it all. But whereas Edward, never again quite the man he was after the dreadful winter campaign of 1359–60, had by and large grown inattentively self-confident, Charles was forever on the watch to make the most of whatever advantage offered itself, provided it involved no risk. Though he had not so far made much capital out of the recent increase of French influence in Burgundy, Navarre and now Castile, he had done much to strengthen France both militarily and financially. The need to pay for his father's ransom had led to increased taxes, and these were thereafter levied continuously. For their collection a strong network of administrative officials dependent on the crown was created. Charles was thus able to pay his army more regularly and thereby to improve its discipline. He destroyed castles that were too difficult to defend and ensured the better maintenance and garrisoning of those that could be defended. This policy would enable defensive forces to remain in being even if, should the English come again, they pursued their usual policy of pillaging the countryside. In addition, he charged John de Vienne of Calais with the rebuilding of his fleet.

Yet it was not Charles who lit the fuse of a renewed war but the disaffection the prince now occasioned among his vassals in Aquitaine. They were already displeased at having returned from the rigours of the

Castilian campaign without getting their expenses, let alone the titles and territories they had hoped for. This aggravated their basic dislike of the prince's haughty manner, the interference in their affairs of his English officials, and his attempts to centralize the administration, and therefore the profits, of justice. They felt less independent than they had been as vassals of France. The prince made matters worse by continuing to suppose that a magnificent court providing a splendid succession of costly festivities was the essence of sound government even when that government was to all intents and purposes bankrupt. To maintain his state, his officials had to exercise the prince's rights of purveyance unrestrainedly. This caused trouble enough in England; applied in Aquitaine, by what was coming more and more to be seen as an alien and tyrannical government, it caused deep resentment. Cattle, corn, wine and hay were seized by the prince's officials without payment and as a matter of routine. Accordingly, when it was decided to revive the ancient and unpopular hearth tax, the *fouage*, there was a crisis, particularly in the old English Gascony. There, alleging that their vassals could not be taxed without the consent of their lords, John of Armagnac and Arnaud, lord of Albret, two of the greatest nobles in Guienne, refused to allow the *fouage* to be levied in their lands. The prince replied that since the Estates of Aquitaine had agreed to the tax, it must apply to everybody. Whereupon, in August and September 1368, two of the prince's most powerful subjects, Armagnac and Arnaud d'Albret, appealed to Charles, as suzerain of Aquitaine, to grant them the justice that their immediate lord, the prince of Aquitaine, was denying them.

The appeal came while Charles was busily winning over to his side the notable Breton captain Olivier de Clisson. Clisson's father having been beheaded by Philip VI, his mother had taken him to Edward's court. There, he had been brought up with de Montfort and had fought furiously against the French at Cocherel, at Auray and at Nájera. Perhaps feeling that he should have been better rewarded after losing his eye while fighting for de Montfort's cause at Auray, Clisson developed a savage dislike of de Montfort and of Chandos, of whose successes he was evidently jealous. Charles, by restoring his father's lands to him, wooed Clisson back to the side of France. He was shortly to be as ferocious against the English as he had earlier been against the French, slaughtering his opponents with violent brutality. Henceforth, though Edward still had a friend in de Montfort as duke of Brittany, one of the most feared of Breton lords was now committed to Charles. And the appeal of the Gascon lords, when it came, was made almost simultaneously with another of Charles's quiet diplomatic coups. In May 1368, Arnaud d'Albret married Queen Jeanne's youngest sister, Isabella de Bourbon. Such a marriage was a potential alliance between Charles and the most disaffected of the prince's Gascon vassals; though it could, of course, be represented as nothing of the sort.

Indeed, Charles was at pains up to this point to do nothing to suggest to Edward that the terms of the treaty of Calais would be breached by France; and for his part Edward was amiably, perhaps smugly, content not to be too pressing. By 1367, Charles had paid substantial instalments of John's ransom, and all the more important hostages held by Edward had left their captivity. As part of the marriage treaty which transformed Coucy the hostage into Coucy the husband of Edward's daughter Isabella, Guy of Blois was allowed his freedom too. Alençon broke his parole while in France; Louis de Bourbon gained his liberty by using his influence to persuade Urban V to appoint William of Wykeham to the see of Winchester. The duke of Berry was paroled and never returned. Clearly, Edward thought he could afford to be chivalrously magnanimous.

Edward may indeed be accused of a lack of political insight in all this; but the military reputation of his English opponents, only recently enhanced by the prince's victory at Nájera, compelled Charles to move with the utmost deliberation when the Gascon lords appealed to him in 1368. Just as Edward had never ratified his renunciation of the title of king of France as required by the treaty of Calais, so Charles had never ratified his renunciation of his suzerainty over Edward's French possessions. As was his custom, therefore, he consulted the lawyers. From Montpellier, Toulouse, Orleans and Bologna, the answer was the same. There having been no formal renunciation, he still had suzerainty over Aquitaine and he would do wrong to the Gascon lords if he failed to give them the justice their prince denied them. Quietly and carefully, as many of the prince's lordly vassals as possible were cajoled into making further appeals to Charles. Every pulpit in the land was made into a propaganda centre from which the rightness of Charles's cause was broadcast. Legal digests of Charles's case were circulated to all the courts of Europe, and Charles and his queen reinforced the homilies of the clergy by a series of carefully stage-managed acts of public piety and by frequent processions to churches, abbeys and cathedrals. The upshot was that Edward was declared guilty of treason for having laid hands on King John, his liege lord; and in January 1369 a summons reached the prince at Bordeaux calling on him to appear before the Parlement in Paris.

The prince's reply was in character, at least according to Froissart. He would, he said, indeed come to Paris but with 'helmet on head' and with 60,000 men. To make his feelings clearer still he arrested Charles's messengers, alleging they had stolen a horse from the innkeeper at Bordeaux at whose premises they had lodged. The prince's answer, however, amounted to fighting words but nothing more; and when the prince warned King Edward that Charles was a real threat to them Edward reproved his son for being too hasty and belligerent. Edward was, indeed, notably conciliatory during the manoeuvrings that followed the first Gascon appeals to Paris. He besought Charles not to receive the appellants, though he did at the same time ask for a further instalment of John's ransom. Charles's answer was that this was not possible because of the devastation of France by the mercenaries returning in disillusionment from their unrewarding victory at Nájera. Edward persisted, suggesting that instead of receiving the appellants, Charles should act as arbitrator between them and the prince.

These placatory gestures were inappropriate for dealing with an opponent pedantically convinced that he had the law on his side and conscious that he could defend his country a good deal better than his father had. The truth was that steadily, all through the 1360s, Edward relaxed his hold on public affairs. Though his glorious image was undimmed, it was less and less publicly displayed. He began to shun both Windsor and Westminster and to spend most of his time at his more secluded residences at Eltham and Sheen. Though he was not yet in his dotage, his interest in administrative matters became intermittent; though never merely sedentary, activity now usually meant indulgence in his passion for hawking and hunting. The geniality had become over-complacent, the cordiality a self-indulgent faith that all would be as well in the future as it had been in the past.

The prince was in a worse plight. From the moment of his triumph of Nájera his health began to decline rapidly. He seems to have fallen victim to attacks of dysentery, or dropsy, or malaria. His limbs became so swollen that, so far from mounting his horse, he could hardly get up from his bed. Suddenly, at the age of thirty-eight, he had come to the end of his active career. And so, to meet the calculated threat that Charles was mounting against their power in France, the English had at their head a faltering king and an invalid prince.

While du Guesclin destroyed the prince's ambitions and England's Castilian alliance by putting Don Henry back on his throne in Spain early in 1369, Charles declared the prince a contumacious vassal and Aquitaine forfeit to the French crown. While an embassy from Paris appeared before Edward bearing gifts of wine, Charles suddenly seized Abbeville, the chief city of Ponthieu, ceded to Edward at Brétigny. Edward at once sent the embassy packing, together with the wine (fifty pipes of it), which was seized on the way by the authorities at Calais. Charles then sent a formal defiance to Edward, amounting to a declaration of war. According to Froissart, it was delivered to Edward sitting in Parliament at Westminster. On hearing the defiant contents of the menial fellow's message, 'the English lords were very surprised and looked at each other, unable to utter a word'. William of Wykeham, as chancellor, found it fairly simple after such an affront to get Parliament to grant the king a generous subsidy on wool and leather, to fix prices for horses and armour and to order the setting up of poles and other obstacles to invasion along the south coast and the confiscation of the wealth of alien priories. They were also persuaded to request the king to resume the title of king of France;

whereupon Edward was graciously pleased to allot all lands in France other than those of church or crown to whoever could conquer them – an obvious attempt to attract the services of the Free Companies. In reply, Charles declared that all territory held by the English was confiscated to the crown of France, that Aquitaine was still subject to his allegiance and that since Edward had not fulfilled some of the minor territorial terms of the treaty of Calais, that treaty was null and void.

Charles's elaborate diplomacy worked well. He neutralized pro-English Flanders by marrying his youngest brother, Philip, to the daughter of the duke of Flanders. He got the safely restored Henry of Castile to offer him his fleet and he was soon persuading the unreliable Charles the Bad of Navarre to remain neutral. All over Aquitaine, nobles were defecting to Charles and forming small forces to try to capture such castles as they could. Armagnac and d'Albret were followed on to the French side by the lords of Poitou, Périgord, Quercy, Rouerge and Agenais, and by towns such as Cahors, Millau and Agen. Louis of Anjou was the driving force behind this movement, using threats, promises and privileges as the means to win back their allegiance to his royal brother. Once the French lords were won over, their castles did not have to be attacked; and with the castles in their control they could defend, if not dominate, the countryside. While Anjou operated in this way from Toulouse, his brother, the duke of Berry, attacked from the Auvergne. And even within his family circle, Edward had evidence that shrewd men were increasingly doubtful about England's prospects. His illustrious son-in-law Enguerrand de Coucy, earl of Bedford and Knight of the Garter, former hostage in the French cause though he was, did not, it is true return to his French allegiance, since he did not want after all to lose his English lands. But he did not fight for England either. He went off instead to fight for the new pope, Gregory XI, against the Visconti in Italy. With a similar exercise of caution, the prince's own close friend, Edmund de Pamiers, chose this moment to go off on crusade.

The almost bedridden prince called back Chandos from his retirement and the available English leaders of the Companies, notably Robert Knollys from his rich estates in Brittany and Hugh de Calveley from Spain. He sent his captains off to make spoiling raids on French lands, so that 1369 was spent in a succession of skirmishes in which, on the whole, the English came off best, without thereby solving many problems. But English morale suffered a severe blow when Chandos was killed at Lussac, while leading three hundred men to regain from the French the abbey of Saint-Savin, near Chauvigny in Poitou. Coming upon a dismounted French force of superior numbers to his own, he responded to the initial French attack by advancing, sword in hand, only to slip on the dew-wet grass. As he lay, he received a fatal sword thrust beneath his eye that pierced his brain. The blow had come from his blind side, since he had lost the sight of one eye in battle already, and he had failed to close his visor. This last circumstance gave some the impression that this seasoned warrior felt in his heart that the English cause was a lost one. Though his tactical skill at Crécy, Poitiers and Nájera had contributed much to England's victories, he had learned sagacity along with the more obvious arts of his trade: he had opposed the Castilian expedition before Nájera and the imposition of the *fouage* after it. His death was extravagantly mourned. 'There was', Froissart wrote, 'for these three hundred years past, no knight in all England more courteous, more gentle, or more distinguished by every noble virtue.'

Those who thought the death of Chandos at the very beginning of 1370 an omen appeared to be proved right by events. A large force led by Lancaster and the earl of Warwick was sent to Calais by Edward to recover Ponthieu. It drew away from Rouen and Harfleur forces assembled for an attack on England's southern coasts but, though the French land forces were superior to the English, Charles avoided battle and the English returned to Calais frustrated. And on the march the earl of Warwick died of the pestilence, thus depriving the English of yet another valuable commander.

Next, Edward sent Sir Robert Knollys from Calais on a campaign of provocative pillage in the hope of bringing the French to battle, or at the very least to divert French forces from Aquitaine. Though still only a mere knight, Knollys, now a man of fifty, was almost the most notable leader of mercenaries still active. He had been Master of the Household to the prince and had estates in both Brittany and Norfolk. There was little to be gained in glory from this campaign. Knollys found the gates of all the cities closed to him, so that though perforce the countryside was pillaged for supplies, there were no towns to sack or even to take shelter in. He continued to the gates of Paris itself, but Charles preferred the pillaging of the countryside to the risk of military defeat. Knollys burned the suburbs of the capital and then withdrew. The frustration this bred in his knights was demonstrated when one of them, for a wager, rode up, just before the retreat began, and knocked on one of the city gates. The French commanders merely laughed at the jester; but, on his way back to the main force through the suburbs he and his companions had burned, he was killed by a butcher wielding a cleaver. By allowing Charles to condemn them to a futile policy of devastating the countryside, the English were making themselves conspicuous enemies not just of the French king and his nobles but of the French people as a whole.

As Knollys made off towards Chartres he was pursued by du Guesclin, whom Charles had summoned up from Limousin (where he had been Louis of Anjou's lieutenant) and appointed Constable of France. It was a shrewd move. For all du Guesclin's lowly birth, his exploits had given him an extraordinary reputation that did much to overcome the conviction that Charles was somewhat inactive in the defence of his country against the marauding English under Knollys. Luckily for du Guesclin he caught up with Knollys at a time when his captains were in a low state of morale, complaining at how little gain or glory they had got for their efforts. When Knollys proposed a general retreat to his estates in Brittany, the more restless of his subordinates took this as a sign that this low-born knight was neither noble enough nor gallant enough to command them. The leading malcontent, Sir John Menstreworth, seems to have tipped off du Guesclin, enabling him to ambush the English rearguard under Thomas de Grandison and cut it to pieces. Olivier de Clisson was with du Guesclin, and doubtless enjoyed inflicting this defeat on his former comrades. It marked the end of the expedition, which went back to Brittany. Knollys was in disgrace; back in England, Menstreworth charged Knollys with improperly conducting the campaign and then fled to France. Later, Menstreworth was captured in Navarre and brought back to London, to be tried in the Guildhall and hanged, drawn and quartered as a traitor at Tyburn, on 12 April 1377.

Meanwhile, as Louis of Anjou was advancing up the Garonne, almost as far as Bergerac, where the Captal de Buch was in command, the duke of Berry marched through Limousin to Limoges, where the bishop opened the gates to him. The news that the bishop of Limoges had betrayed the city enraged the prince. Now based at new headquarters at Cognac, and strengthened by reinforcements brought up by Lancaster and Cambridge, the prince organized a full-scale assault by his whole force, swearing 'by the soul of his father' to exact revenge for the city's treachery. It took until October to mine the walls, since the prince himself had constructed its defences and Berry had left a stubborn garrison behind; it was a tribute to the prince's corps of engineers that the defences were eventually breached at all. When they were, the English swarmed in. With some eighty knights, the three captains of the garrison rallied against an old wall and resisted fiercely as Lancaster, Cambridge and the earl of Pembroke took them on in single combat. The prince, watching the proceedings from a litter, was sufficiently mollified by this chivalric spectacle to spare the three captains' lives and to allow Lancaster to make the bishop of Limoges his personal prisoner.

Despite the fact that Froissart did not persist with it after the very first version of his chronicle, the figure he quotes of 'three thousand' men, women and children slaughtered on the day the city fell has survived to be a stain on the prince's memory. No local contemporary evidence seems to support the idea of a massacre. The local figure given is 'three hundred' and even this, like most medieval statistics, may well exaggerate. Nor is there any evidence that the prince's conduct of the operations that day excited adverse comment anywhere. Nevertheless it is at least ironical that the bishop of Limoges, the one person most responsible for the city's 'betrayal' to the French, was let off more or less scot free. Lancaster allowed him to go in peace to Avignon.

The failure of the Knollys campaign, a dismal postscript to the recapture of Limoges, marked the end of an era. Now too enfeebled to carry on, the prince decided to seek his father's permission to hand over his duties to Lancaster. Almost at the same time came further misfortune. His own elder son, Edward, died at the age of six on 6 January 1371; so that it was with the Princess Joan and their younger son, the future Richard II, that he left for England. Thereafter, deeply disappointed, greatly in debt and a permanent semi-invalid, he played only a minor role in the turbulent years that remained to him. The extent of the prince's failure was as yet little understood. He was still the hero of Poitiers and Nájera, the 'unconquerable prince' who had worn himself out in his father's service. The City Fathers marked his return by presenting handsome gifts both to him and to the princess.

The prince's departure merely accelerated the general collapse of English authority in Aquitaine, despite the continued loyalty of a few Gascon notables, particularly the Captal and Guiscard d'Angle. Du Guesclin's successful resistance movement to English rule owed more to diplomacy and to money than to chivalrous heroics. Many opposing captains whom it might have been hard to dislodge by force yielded to the blandishments of cash. Yet neither Edward nor his sons had lost much of their confidence. They had had setbacks; but, having beaten the French before, they were sure they could beat them again. This, which seems from hindsight to have been a refusal to face facts, was perhaps due to Edward's own personality. He had the knack of choosing good leaders and the even more unusual gift of preserving their loyalty throughout. He and his commanders remained brothers-in-arms to the end, convinced, in their superlatively martial way, that if they continued to perform as a team they would be sure to come out on top. They wept copious tears over the death of Chandos, and whatever the Gascons or the citizens of Limoges may have thought of him, the Black Prince, to the end of his life, was looked on as the finest soldier of his age. They mourned excessively at the death in January 1372 of Sir Walter Manny, that brilliant Flemish soldier whom Queen Philippa had brought to England in her retinue, whom Edward had made Knight of the Garter in 1359 and who had been Lancaster's second-in-command in 1369. Remembered principally for his part in the foundation of Charterhouse, he was given the splendid funeral due to a great soldier and the proud possessor of lands in Hainault, in Calais, and, through his wife, Margaret Brotherton (sister of the ill-fated Alice), of many manors in England. The spirit of men who had served leaders such as these and who had, after all, still not once been defeated by the French in a set-piece battle, could not easily or for long be daunted. It added to the conviction of brotherly invincibility among the English leaders that Edward, as well as not provoking quarrels among his commanders, was one of the very few English kings not to quarrel with his sons. He had confidently delegated Aquitaine to the Black Prince and, though offering now and again cautionary advice, seems not to have blamed him for what was regarded as its merely temporary loss. And now that the prince was stricken down so prematurely, Lancaster, as the king's second son, was moved effortlessly into his elder brother's place. There seemed no reason to doubt that he was anything other than a seasoned campaigner after his experiences from Poitiers onwards.

Unfortunately, Edward's self-confidence had gradually become indistinguishable from lassitude, and Lancaster was only a moderate soldier and an indifferent politician. By the 1370s, age had removed rather too many of the old guard of Edward's captains from the scene and Edward, the greatest of the captains, was now only intermittently his old vigorous self. Lancaster therefore found himself saddled with too personal a responsibility for the situation both at home and abroad, and had altogether too much ambition. He began his independent career as custodian of his father's reputation by jumping in at the deep end – and the wrong end – immediately. A widower since the death of Blanche of Lancaster in 1369, he married himself in September 1371 to Constance, one of the daughters of Pedro the Cruel. With her sisters, she had been kept at Bordeaux, first as hostage until Pedro paid up, and then in case she became queen of Castile in her own right, which would have obstructed the Black Prince's plan to acquire the Castilian throne for himself. Now, as the husband of Pedro's daughter, Lancaster could claim to be the legitimate king of Castile and thus secure the support of those Castilians who were opposed to Don Henry. In case Constance might inconveniently die young, Edmund of Cambridge was married to Constance's sister, to make sure of keeping Castile in the family. Returning to England with his bride, having left Aquitaine in the hands of the Captal de Buch and Thomas Percy, Lancaster was officially recognized as king of Castile by Edward's Council in January 1372. He began signing his letters in Castilian royal style, *Nos el Roy*.

It was, however, urgent to try and stop the rot in Aquitaine. Not without difficulty, reinforcements, including archers and horses, were got together under John Hastings, the twenty-six-year-old earl of Pembroke, and Guiscard d'Angle. The latter advising that, if sufficient funds were made available, many Poitevins would return to their English allegiance, the expedition was supplied with £20,000 to that end. But Charles, who had spies and agents not only in Aquitaine but at Westminster, outbid the English in advance and, more important, at last reaped the reward of his years of patient support of Henry of Castile and secured the cooperation of the Castilian fleet. When the English reached La Rochelle, the port in Aquitaine where they proposed to land, they found the Castilians waiting for them. The 200-ton galleons were more manoeuvrable than the square-rigged English sailing ships, which could only sail before the wind. The oarsmen (180 to each galleon) were well paid, and not the criminal galley slaves of legend, and the officers were professional fighting sailors, unlike their English counterparts who were soldiers who happened for the time being to be at sea. The encounter, on 23 June 1372, was a disaster for the English. The Castilians rammed the English ships, poured flaming, oil-soaked arrows in their rigging and from their high poops hurled down stones on the English archers. The entire English naval force was destroyed, and the ship containing the £20,000 fell into Castilian hands as well, as did many prisoners, including both Pembroke and Guiscard d'Angle. Within the next few months, with no reinforcements to threaten him, du Guesclin gained a firm hold not only on La Rochelle but on most of Poitou and Angoulême.

La Rochelle's fortress was so strong that it ought to have been hard to take, and it commanded the harbour of the town. The unlucky squire in charge, Philip Mansel, was fooled into handing over the fortress by the mayor, who showed him a letter with King Edward's seal on it. Mansel being illiterate, it was no problem for the mayor to inform him that it contained his royal master's instructions to give the fortress up. The citizenry of La Rochelle made the most of this civilian contribution to their return to French allegiance. They demanded – and got – a royal charter granting them a mint and permission to destroy the castle that so menacingly dominated their town. That Charles and du Guesclin accepted these terms indicates the difference that success can make to men's tempers when it is compared with the way the prince had dealt with the people of Limoges.

Not that the customs and usages of noble chivalry were much in evidence after La Rochelle. Like their German contemporaries, the Castilians were not good at being chivalrous to prisoners. Pembroke, d'Angle and their fellow lords and knights were taken back to Spain and kept under lock and key in castle cells or dungeons. It took a year to get them out and du Guesclin it was who saw to it that the proprieties were eventually observed. He exchanged the chief prisoners for some of his Castilian estates and thus acquired the right to their ransom money. Weakened by his imprisonment or, as rumour alleged, as a result of having been poisoned by the Castilians, Pembroke died at Arras in a horse litter on his way home. Du Guesclin sent the young earl's heirs the bill for his ransom money – 130,000 gold francs – but Charles V restrained du Guesclin from persisting with his demand, and compensated him out of the royal purse.

The French king showed no such charity when dealing with the Captal de Buch. The Captal had been captured in the land fighting after the fiasco at La Rochelle by a Franco-Castilian force led by Owen of Wales. Charles had characteristically cultivated this young man because he claimed, as grandson of Llewelyn ap Gruffydd, to be the true Prince of Wales. Charles refused to ransom the Captal on the grounds that, having switched to the French side after Cocherel, he had then renewed his allegiance to the Black Prince in 1369. King Edward offered large sums for the Captal's release, and Charles's own lords pleaded that this distinguished soldier should not be left to rot in prison. Charles's reply was that it was dangerous to allow so famous a soldier to resume his role as a commander of the forces of the enemy. He could go free, he said, if he would swear allegiance to France. The Captal refused; he even refused to swear not to take up arms against the French. Rather than make such a promise, he said, he would die in prison; and this, after four years of melancholia, he duly did in 1376, allegedly of despair on learning of the death of the Black Prince.

Edward was still resolved that Charles must be dealt with. It hardly seemed possible that what had cost him so much to win had been almost entirely lost merely through the absence of large English forces from France, as the result of back door diplomacy and what amounted to a flurry of minor skirmishes. If, by two great battles, France had earlier been defeated and Aquitaine won, one more great battle would surely put all to rights again. In August 1372, therefore, the elderly warrior-king himself, the invalid prince, the not particularly gifted Lancaster, and Edmund of Cambridge, set sail from Sandwich together with all their surviving great captains. They had a considerable fleet and were resolved to descend upon Aquitaine. Not surprisingly, given the hazards of the adventure and his own precarious health, the prince sought to assure the future: before they left he had his infant son, Richard of Bordeaux, declared King Edward's rightful heir. Unrelenting gales prevented them ever getting to Aquitaine, however, and after something like two months wretchedly at sea, they gave up. Had they managed to reach their objective, the Castilian fleet was waiting for them. This further fiasco was the prelude to renewed, uninterrupted triumphs by du Guesclin. He overran Brittany, forcing de Montfort to fly to England. Nantes and Brest fell to the French, and Charles planned an invasion of the south coast of England, being assured by Owen of Wales that he could guarantee a simultaneous rising in Wales, thus anticipating in fantasy events by which Owen Tudor's grandson, Henry, overthrew Richard III some one hundred years later. Though there was no Welsh rising, Charles did in fact begin to rebuild the French navy; and after Edward's death the Franco-Castilian fleet did much damage to the south coast.

The long sea route to Aquitaine was now seen to be blocked by the Castilian navy. Accordingly, in 1373, another expeditionary force was dispatched, this time to Calais. Led by Lancaster, its object was not simply to relieve Aquitaine, but to go on across the Pyrenees again and overthrow Henry of Castile. This would eliminate the Franco-Castilian naval alliance by placing Lancaster on the throne he had claimed ever since his marriage to Pedro's daughter Constance. A realistic policy would have been to recognize Henry as king of Castile and to set about building up England's navy. Unhappily, Edward and his family were prisoners of their own glamour. By heroic feats of arms, they believed, the lost French conquests could all be won back; and, by a second Nájera, Lancaster would do better even than his brother, the Black Prince, by himself reigning in Burgos, and have all his expenses in getting there paid out of English taxes.

The force with which Lancaster set out from Calais in the August of 1373 was one of the largest England had ever loosed upon the French. But it did not march south towards Aquitaine. Instead, Lancaster led it through Champagne and Burgundy. Perhaps the idea was that the great battle the English wanted to fight was not one against the hired, low-born mercenary du Guesclin, who barred their way to Aquitaine, but against the king of France himself, skulking unchivalrously in his capital. As a result, Lancaster involved his forces in a five-month, thousand-mile march before it eventually reached Aquitaine. There was another campaign of pillage and devastation, such as Robert Knollys had conducted, with the idea of doing as much damage as possible to the enemy's resources and of provoking his forces to come out of their strongholds and fight like men and true knights. This, as when Knollys was at work, they refused to do. Charles forbade direct confrontations and encouraged people to flee the countryside and take refuge in the fortified towns. Olivier de Clisson was at hand with the advice of a hardened professional: 'The English are confident they can never lose a battle . . . the more bloodshed they see, whether on their own side or on that of the enemy, the more furious and unyielding they become. I advise you not to fight unless you can take them at an advantage.' Du Guesclin fully cooperated too. As the English force turned towards Aquitaine he, like the duke of Burgundy, subjected it to continuous hit-and-run raids and ambushes.

Achieving no martial response and gaining no great cities, Lancaster's men found themselves, as autumn was followed by winter, awash with rain, and adrift in the inhospitable Auvergne, mountainous and scarcely inhabited. Here there was little to devastate, little even to beg for, let alone steal, and nowhere to shelter. Almost all the horses died of cold or hunger, and the men were in little better condition than their mounts as they stumbled on, on foot, their armour useless and rusting. Half the soldiery were dead by the time the army, almost to the end still harassed by du Guesclin's raids and ambushes, staggered into Bordeaux. In January 1374, having also run out of money, Lancaster agreed to a truce with du Guesclin at Périgueux. Du Guesclin and his men can have been hardly less wearied by the struggle than their demoralized English opponents, for, though a total strategic failure, Lancaster's campaign had brought great hardship and misery to the French.

Little more now remained in English hands in Aquitaine than Bordeaux and Bayonne and the districts immediately around them. In the north they still had garrisons in Calais and Boulogne and, in Normandy, Saint-Sauveur-le-Vicomte, stubbornly defended until the signing of a general truce. That came in June 1375, cutting short one more effort by de Montfort to regain Brittany.

Already, in August 1374, Edward indicated that he was ready for this general truce. Since ravaged France, despite having effectively reversed the treaty of Brétigny, was itself exhausted, Charles agreed to the urgings of the legates of Gregory XI, and a peace conference opened at Bruges in March 1375. Louis de Male acted as mediator, England being represented by Lancaster, and France by Philip the Bold. By the end of June 1375 a year's general truce was agreed, though in the event it was renewed annually until 1377. The English were at last prepared to admit that they could no longer hope to control and defend the large area of France they had acquired in 1360; and Charles, for his part, was ready to hand back some of the territories he had regained. But the sticking point was the issue of sovereignty. Whatever the size, large or small, of any lands they retained in France, the English refused absolutely to hold them as vassals of the French king. The legal wrangle went on all through the last two years of Edward's reign, the expense and inconclusiveness of these luxuriously conducted debates about the small print of feudal contractual under-takings augmenting civil discontent in both England and France. But Charles was as obdurate as the English. He had gone to war to establish his sovereignty through all his kingdom. To give way would be to admit that his cause had not been just; and he was determined to be rigidly legalistic to the end. And the English, despite all their recent costly reverses, had no intention of giving up their dream of holding sovereign dominion over as much of France as they could take and keep.

* * *

England was on the whole reasonably content in the earlier 1360s. The ransoms extracted from the high-born prisoners captured in the wars represented a substantial transfer of real wealth from France to England. The fact that it was extravagantly spent by king and court and aristocracy meant that at least some of it passed into the hands of lesser folk who did not, at first at any rate, wonder whether it might not have been better employed than in conspicuous display. After all, to spend generously, to distribute largesse, was one of the chivalric virtues. And, anyway, more sober minds could take comfort from the fact that the peace after Brétigny led to a healthy revival of wool exports to Flanders through English Calais.

The coming of peace enabled Parliament to take up a more critical stance, now that it could do so without being told it was impeding the king's wars. In this decade it gained additional powers which Edward yielded without much fuss. His amiable, sanguine temperament and his jolly, uncomplicated view of life made him easy to deal with. He did not storm, like Henry II, or look terribly, like Edward I. His reputation as a warrior put him so far above personal criticism that he had no need to appeal to the principles of sanctified kingship or to justify himself by reference to the powers exercised by his illustrious predecessors – if only because few of them had ever been as illustrious as he was. In the parliament of 1361 he graciously consented to mitigate the evils of purveyance: items bought for his royal use would be paid for at the current going price. He would not in future levy special taxes on merchants without the consent of the Commons. He agreed, though for long it had little effect, that trials in the courts of law should be conducted in English and not Norman French. It was not very logical for Edward, claiming to be king of both England and France, to encourage the use of two quite different languages in his two realms; but logic was not Edward's strong point.

On one matter he did make an initiative, requesting Parliament yet again to forbid matters within the jurisdiction of the royal courts to be referred to the papal court at Avignon. In 1366 he aroused more anti-papal feeling by telling Parliament that the pope was proposing to demand large arrears of tax. This arose out of the fact that, as the price of getting Innocent III to lift the interdict he had placed on England, King John had promised in 1214 to pay the pope 10,000 marks a year as a symbol of England's fealty to Rome. In 1366, king and Parliament gave the sort of answer appropriate to the greatest fighting people in Europe. Neither John nor any other king had the right to put the kingdom or its people under subjection 'without their assent and accord'. Naturally, since the Avignon popes were considered (not always justly) as mere lackeys of France, Edward encouraged such fighting words. He did not bother that the language appeared to exalt Parliament (as representative of 'the people') as much as it rebuffed the pope. Like its sponsorship of the English language, Parliament's insistence on English independence was a matter of national prestige, not one of establishing a parliamentary constitution.

Unhappily for Edward it was not simply that affairs across the Channel took such a turn for the worse after 1368. In August 1369, Queen Philippa died. Edward was there at her end but, of their children, only Thomas of Woodstock; all his brothers were at the wars. Universally admired and respected, she was suitably eulogized by Froissart. 'In all her life,' he wrote, 'she did neither in thought or deed anything whereby to lose her soul, as far as any creature could know.' She may well have been the last wise counsellor Edward ever had. For the rest of his life Edward's private hours were dominated by his much-maligned mistress Alice Perrers. Their liaison seems to have begun in 1364, and she attained a quasi-official status through her appointment as a maid of Queen Philippa's bedchamber in 1366. Alleged to be ugly and greedy for money, she was also evidently litigious, though in this respect she did not differ greatly from many propertied persons in the fourteenth and fifteenth centuries. Inevitably she was described as having come from nothing, the child of a domestic servant who later became a tailor. It appears more likely that she was the child of a prominent Hertfordshire landowner, Sir Richard Perrers, parentage that would make her coming to court in no way a breach of protocol. Most of what is recorded of Alice comes from the chronicler of St Albans abbey, who was not likely to take a kindly view of her because the abbey was involved in a long and bitter legal dispute with her father. Uncertainty exists as to whether she married once, or twice, or not at all. Some form of marriage contract does seem to have been arranged between her and a Sir William of Windsor, a castle official, and the king on one occasion gave Alice over £1,500 on William of Windsor's behalf. But in 1376, when the Commons insisted that she was William's wife, Edward denied on oath all knowledge of her being married. She seems to have been an intelligent woman, though the chronicler chose rather to say that she influenced the king by her 'clever tongue'. She was obviously good at accumulating money, at going energetically to law to defend her right to it and at negotiating financial deals with the leading men in government in Edward's later years, such as Lancaster, Lord Latimer and William of Wykeham. Shortly before his death, Edward bestowed a knighthood on John, 'the son of Dame Alice Perrers'. It was believed that Edward was his father.

Alice's ascendancy seems to have been complete after Queen Philippa's death. Edward felt his wife's death keenly, for the two of them had remained on good terms, if somewhat distant ones, to the end of her life. Thereafter he does appear to have gone fairly quickly to pieces. Though he was sixty by 1372, and to have survived so long was unusual in that age of plague and battle, there would seem to have been reasons other than mere longevity for this fairly steady descent into what looks like senile dementia. Probably, he had one or more strokes. One chronicler alleged that for more than a year before he died in 1377 he had a mind not much stronger than 'a boy of eight'. He tended in his last years to agree with whatever those around him suggested. On the whole his martial reputation protected both his person and his crown. From more quarters than one, certainly, there were complaints that he had indulged overmuch in the pleasures of the flesh. The attack on him in the so-called prophecy of John of Bridlington, circulated in the mid-1370s, back-dated his misdemeanours to the high noon of his career, at Calais in 1347. But the political thrust of this piece of propaganda was less against the ageing king than against Lancaster, who ruled on his behalf, perhaps linking the king's sexual weakness with the similar fault in Gaunt, so as to contrast them with the nobility and untarnished fame of the Black Prince. Certainly, if a once so splendid king, however ruined in mind and body, was safe from the contempt visited on his father at the close of his reign, on his successor, Richard II, and on the feeblest of his descendants, Henry VI, his reputation protected nobody but himself. In consequence, though he was not personally blamed for all that went wrong, everyone around him was. Since, too, those who needed to make their deeds official needed the king's consent, they can have had no choice but to approach him through the lively and acquisitive Alice. She therefore became not only powerful but rich, intensely unpopular and the subject of every kind of rumour. In the record of the monkish chronicler she is written down as a probable witch: she was in league with a magician, a friar skilled in the black arts, who had fashioned wax images of Alice and the king, depicting the once great warrior as a mere puppet in his mistress's hands. Then, by devilish incantations and other occult means, he had caused reality to conform to his waxen image of it. She was later accused of having gone to Westminster Hall when the Court of King's Bench was in session and to have instructed the judges as to the verdict she required them to return in a case in which she was personally involved. Parliament complained that she was costing the king, and therefore the country, up to £3,000 a year. The doting king encouraged these tales by handing over royal manors and jewels to her, including, in 1373, some of Queen Philippa's. In 1374, doubtless bedecked with these royal jewels, she paraded through London in a chariot to attend a tournament in the role of 'Lady of the Sun'. There seemed little doubt about it: the nation's hero-king had fallen victim to the wiles of a vulgar, extravagant strumpet. If the poor king was sickly and enfeebled, she was the obvious cause of it. Yet it is just as likely that she prolonged rather than shortened his life as his general health faded in the 1370s, perhaps by then less of a mistress and more of a favourite nurse and enlivening companion. Edward had fallen for her when his faculties were sound, and it is unlikely she was the harridan she was made out to be. In terms of hard cash she was probably less expensive than Queen Philippa, who had herself been notably extravagant. Unfortunately, extravagance, though acceptable in the worthy consort of a great king in his days of glory, was unforgivable in a low-born mistress who monopolized the favours of an ageing king at a time when all the glory seemed to have been stolen both from him and from his people.

The failure of Lancaster's campaign of 1373-4, the loss of almost all Aquitaine and the flat refusal of Charles to surrender his sovereignty over an inch of French soil brought to a head all the anger and frustration from which the English had been suffering since the mid-1360s. From 1369 onwards, Parliament had watched the Black Prince come sick and bankrupt home from his glorious victory at Nájera; had been asked for money to mount a naval expedition that hardly sailed out of sight of land; and then for the huge force that Lancaster had dissipated in unprofitable marches which had failed even to fight, let alone defeat, the French, and which, far from saving Aquitaine, had made certain the loss of it. The money that had flooded in during the 1360s from all those enormous ransoms had ceased and the flow was not renewed. Castilian and not English ships commanded the Channel. On the northern borders, Scotland, once so compliant under the collaborationist David II, was now, under its first Stuart king, Robert II, once more in alliance with France and as troublesome as it had ever been. Exacerbating the discontent was a return of the Black Death in 1374–5, itself doubtless taken as a sign of divine disapproval. There was, too, a general growth of lawlessness among soldiers back from the wars, encouraged by the corruption of justice by those who could bribe or bully judges and juries. Labourers and landowners were in continuous conflict, the former determined to make the most of the current scarcity of labour by demanding high wages, the landowners trying to enforce the wage freeze proposed by the largely ineffective Statute of Labourers of 1349. A groundswell of anger at the feckless extravagance of the chivalric wealthy and against the pretensions of worldly churchmen was also obvious at this time.

Philippa's death left Edward relatively isolated. Lancaster and the Black Prince were usually abroad fighting their wars, Lionel of Clarence was dead, Edmund of Cambridge something of a nonentity, Thomas of Woodstock still too young. Government passed largely into the hands of William of Wykeham, bishop of Winchester, as Chancellor, and Brantingham, bishop of Exeter, who was Treasurer. Most bishops got their appointments in the fourteenth century as a form of payment for services rendered to the crown, and Wykeham's preferment was owed entirely to his services to Edward in the rebuilding of Windsor. His confident administration of his rich diocese helped to make him the wealthiest commoner in England, and thereby to stir up the general dislike of churchmen.

The first sign of serious trouble had come in the parliament of 1371, with the failure of the prince's Castilian adventure and the defeat of the redoubtable Robert Knollys in the previous year. The young earl of Pembroke who, a year later was to be captured by the Castilians at La Rochelle, succeeded in getting a motion accepted in Parliament that the highest offices of state ought to be held by laymen and not clerics. This attractively disguised a condemnation of the king's government under the form of a protest against the excessive power of the church, and avoided the slightest criticism of either the king or the Black Prince. If things had gone wrong, it must have been the fault of crafty, over-rich clerics, feathering their own nests and obstructing the war effort. Edward I had had a similar situation at the end of his reign and had hit back hard. Edward III, though at first curtly rejecting the proposal, then agreed to it. He did not have much fight left in him now, showing something of the lassitude that had afflicted his father in his last years. Accordingly, Wykeham was replaced as Chancellor, first by Robert Thorpe and then by Sir John Knyvett, both of them lawyers. Sir Richard Scrope replaced

Brantingham as Treasurer. Significantly, Scrope was a close friend of Lancaster, suggesting that, with Edward and the Black Prince both well past their prime, Lancaster was already manoeuvring himself into power. This was neither surprising nor even particularly sinister on the face of it, and the only person to show much nervousness was the prince, already concerned about the prospects of his son, Richard.

The parliament of 1371 provided two further signs of the dissatisfaction of the country's notables with the unfavourable turn of events abroad. Complaints were made about the decay of the navy: so many vessels had been requisitioned for the crown that there was a great lack of work for the country's seamen and watermen. With more lasting consequences, Parliament laid down that in future their consent would be required before the king could impose any tax on the wool trade. Clearly, Parliament – and already from the point of view of taxations the Commons was its most important constituent – was prepared to let the king have money while he was winning the war and bringing home the booty and the ransoms. But now they wanted to keep a closer watch on how he got his money and what he did with it.

Once back in England in 1371, Lancaster himself presided over the new lay Council that Parliament had called into being. The new men were glad of the support of the one active member of the king's family and found nothing amiss in his scheme to make himself king of Castile. He welcomed their dependence on him, and clearly looked on them as financial backers for his cross-Channel adventures. But when he came back from his disastrous military failures of 1373–4, and again from the abortive peace negotiations at Bruges in 1375, he, in his turn, was blamed for all that had gone wrong since 1371, and not unreasonably. Enormous sums had been wasted on fruitless campaigning and the court itself had become a centre of scandal and corruption. It was Lancaster who had produced failure abroad; and it was his stooges at Westminster, Knyvett and Scrope, who had failed to make any impression on the ailing king or the money-making court clique that was battening on him. For their part, the disgraced clerics, not least Wykeham himself, let it be known that the scandals were the inevitable result of their own dismissal from power in 1371. For the first time, too, there appeared a small crack in the hitherto unusual harmony within King Edward's family. Philippa, only daughter of Lionel, duke of Clarence, dead since the excess of enjoyment attendant upon his wedding to Violante Visconti, had married Edmund Mortimer, earl of March and Marshal of England. An ambitious twenty-five-year-old, Mortimer was conscious of the fact that he was the husband of the lady who stood next in succession to the crown after Richard of Bordeaux, in the event of the death of the Black Prince; for Lionel had been born well before John of Lancaster. Richard, in view of his extreme youth, might well die of the plague should it return; and it seems to have been taken for granted that

Lancaster might try to displace Richard or at the very least control him. Mortimer therefore set himself up as an ally of the clerics against Lancaster and the king's detested court. Since the Commons were now thoroughly opposed to Lancaster and his friends, the scene was set for a confrontation. It added to the general air of scandal that Lancaster, as well as manipulating the king through the unpopular Alice Perrers, was regarded as a confirmed womanizer. By this time he was making no secret of the fact that, like his father, he had a mistress, Katherine Swynford, whose husband had died fighting in Aquitaine. (After the death of Blanche of Castile in 1394, Lancaster married Katherine; and Henry VII's mother was descended from their eldest son, John Beaufort, earl of Somerset.)

An additional ground of discontent was the allegation that the protracted peace negotiations at Bruges had been deliberately prolonged in order that the high-born princes, nobles and prelates there assembled could indulge in extravagant festivities and dancing. An angry and certainly biased chronicler of the time declared that Lancaster's spending while at Bruges had been 'horrible and incredible'. More serious still were allegations that Edward's Chamberlain, Lord Latimer, and Richard Lyons, a London merchant-financier, abetted by Alice Perrers, had conspired to cheat and rob the revenue.

Latimer was Chamberlain by virtue of his status as a long-established boon companion of the king. He had been at Crécy and at Auray and was a Knight of the Garter. He and his confederates were now said to have defrauded the customs by exporting wool direct to Continental buyers instead of by way of Calais, through which all wool exports were supposed to be channelled in order to be taxed. They had negotiated loans for the king and charged him up to 50 per cent interest for their pains. They had bought up the king's debts at a discount and then reclaimed the full amount from the Treasury. And Alice Perrers, so it was insisted, was up to her neck in all this, quite apart from the gifts the king lavished on her.

Purveyance, as ever, featured prominently as a grievance. The king had the right to commandeer supplies from the immediate neighbourhood both for himself and for his army whenever they were on the move. This could easily be abused. Purveyors acting (so they always said) in the king's name would seize whatever took their fancy without payment. There was no redress. A less general but no less deeply felt grievance arising out of the recent warlike expeditions against France was that of the inhabitants of the south coast, on whom troops were billeted willy-nilly before they were all fully assembled in readiness for embarkation. Inconveniences just about bearable during a victorious war, they were hard to endure at a time when everything was going wrong and when the king's servants were robbing him and his subjects right and left.

When Parliament met at the end of April 1376, Sir John Knyvett, as Chancellor, asked them, in view of the grave danger from France and

Castile, for a grant to enable the king to continue the war. There followed an attack on the king's government so sustained that it was, in effect, dismissed. The Commons had not acted with such effect before – which is why this was remembered as 'The Good Parliament'. Several factors explain the Commons' exceptional success on this occasion. One was the knowledge of these relatively insignificant knights and burgesses that they had the support of the up-and-coming Edmund Mortimer. The other was that for the first time in their history they found a resolute spokesman (there was as yet no official Speaker) in Sir Peter de la Mare. His firmness in concerting a formidable indictment of the king's advisers was only in part explained by the fact that he was a member of Mortimer's house-hold; it was evident that he spoke for, and was supported by, a solid body of members.

One other circumstance, though basically quite irrelevant, also encouraged them. The excitement was heightened by the appearance, at the formal opening of Parliament on 28 April 1376, of the Black Prince. His dropsy was now severe. He had been carried to Westminster from his manor at Berkhamsted, his purpose that of showing himself on behalf of his heir, the nine-year-old Richard. He had come to show himself graciously to both Lords and Commons, as it were to call in aid his own tremendous reputation as a form of guarantee that the child of such a father was indeed the rightful heir to the throne of England. But it was widely assumed that, in seeking assurances that his son would indeed be accepted as his successor, the prince must be against both Lancaster and the detested ministers over whom Lancaster had presided. Certainly Lyons thought it worth trying to win the prince's support by sending him a barrel, ostensibly full of fish, but in fact containing £1,000. The prince returned the gift; but King Edward jocularly accepted a similar gift, on the grounds that it was his own money he was getting back anyway. There is no evidence that the prince suspected Lancaster, or that Lancaster wanted the throne. After all, at that particular date he still fancied he was king of Castile. He may well have thought it more dashingly chivalric to win a crown in foreign fields than to conspire to usurp one at home.

Sir Peter proceeded with a careful mixture of firmness and caution. Summoned to speak for the Commons in the presence of the Lords over whom Lancaster, as effective head of the government, was presiding in the king's absence, he insisted on not doing so until all the rest of the Commons were summoned too. They had previously been told, according to custom, to disperse once their formal business was concluded, and it took a couple of hours to collect them all together again. Once they were reassembled, de la Mare insisted they would grant no taxes until they had the assistance of twelve peers to draw up plans to put right the evils of the king's present government. They chose four bishops, one of whom, William Courtenay, bishop of London, was particularly anxious to restore church control of government, together with four earls and four barons, all with recent campaigning experience in France. The king's views were sought. The reply came that he had no objections. After all, he needed the money the Commons were withholding from him.

The twelve lords agreed with the Commons that Latimer, Lyons, Alice Perrers and others should be charged with various financial mis-demeanours, and that Latimer be further charged with having, while in command in Brittany, sold Saint-Sauveur to the enemy, and with having prevented the relief of Bécherel. But it was Peter de la Mare who presented to the Lords the joint committee's verdict that the king would not now be asking for money if he had not had dishonest and extravagant advisers. Sir Peter's charges were then further enlarged upon by others of the Com-mons. When Latimer demanded to be told on what authority he was being accused, de La Mare replied that the Commons were charging him as one body. Thus, the device of impeachment and the institution of Speaker of the Commons were both at once foreshadowed.

Lancaster was openly furious at this unprecedented interference by such low-born persons with the crown's right to govern. He referred to them privately as 'hedge knights' – a typically military gibe at men whose status as knights derived from their position as landowners in the shires and not from the performance of brave feats on the battlefield. But for the moment he had too few friends among the Lords to do anything except give in. Latimer and Lyons, therefore, were deprived of office and imprisoned. Alice was ordered to leave the court; the best the king could do for her was to plead that she be treated not too harshly. Minor offenders who suffered also included a Lollard knight, Sir Richard Sturry. Alice's removal from his presence was probably the only element in the situation that Edward could really take in. He had meekly concurred in the fall of Wykeham; now it was Latimer's turn. It was thought on all sides that Edward was now senile of mind; it made men's suspicions all the greater. But at all points the leaders of the Good Parliament were careful to consult their sovereign, and never to treat him as of no account. His mind having failed, he had fallen among thieves. They were Good Samaritans to a poor, unfortunate old man.

The anti-clericals being thrown out, the new Council which the Com-mittee of the Good Parliament imposed on the king had a strong ecclesias-tical flavour. The former Chancellor, William of Wykeham, was recalled, and among the other councillors was Simon Sudbury, who had been archbishop of Canterbury since 1375.

* * *

On 17 May 1376, the condition of the Black Prince took a turn for the worse. On Trinity Sunday (8 June 1376) he died. He was forty-six years of age, the fifth adult child of the king's to die before him. Edward was at the deathbed, along with Lancaster, Edmund, Thomas of Woodstock, and their eldest sister, Isabella, and her husband, de Coucy. The doors of his room were, at the prince's own command, kept open so that former brothers-in-arms, as well as other notable lords and Londoners, might kneel by his bed to take their sorrowful farewell of their once great captain. The dying man besought all who came, from the king and Lancaster downwards, to swear to support Richard of Bordeaux. All did as they were bid and, if the chroniclers are to be believed, the place was full of lamentation. Yet they also record that he showed one last flash of his old harsh temper, needing much persuasion from the attendant clerics before he would ask to be forgiven by all those he had harmed during his life. This customary formula was almost more than he could bring himself to utter even now. And when Sir Richard Sturry, the disgraced Lollard knight who had been one of Latimer's clique, appeared, the prince, on account of some unknown past quarrel, refused to make his peace with him. He did so just before the end, but with evident bad grace.

Grief at his passing was expressed internationally as well as nationally. Charles V and his French nobles attended a Requiem Mass for the prince in Paris. The French chroniclers no less than the English wrote solemn eulogies. The prince had been 'a gallant and noble prince' than whom not even Alexander the Great had borne himself more proudly. He had been 'one of the greatest knights on earth'. To Froissart he was 'the Flower of Chivalry of all the world.' Theatricality being an essential element in chivalry, the prince had left an elaborate will and detailed instructions about his funeral and memorial. To his son, Richard, he left a great bed embroidered with angels. Among his bequests were 'a cross of wood of the Holy Cross' and hangings of arras displaying the deeds of Saladin, as well as 'chamber hangings of ostrich feathers of black tapestry with a red border and swans with the heads of ladies'. He gave instructions that the effigy on his tomb at Canterbury was to show him 'fully armed in plate of war and half the face exposed with our leopard helm set beneath the head of the image'. He also ordered that there be inscribed on his tomb 'where one may be able most clearly to read it at sight' lines of verse that are the more striking for their apparent inappropriateness to a monument other-wise designed to make the prince look as splendid in death as he had been in life. The sense of the French words is that whoever passed by the tomb should take note:

> Such as thou art, some time was I
> Such as I am, such shalt thou be.
> I little thought on the hour of death
> So long as I enjoyed breath.
>
> Great riches here I did possess
> Whereof I made great nobleness.

I had gold, silver, wardrobes and
Great treasure, horses, houses, land

But now a caitiff poor am I,
Deep in the ground, lo here I lie.
My beauty great is all quite gone,
My flesh is wasted to the bone.

. . . .

And if ye should see me this day
I do not think but ye would say
That I had never been a man;
So much altered now I am.

For God's sake pray to the heavenly King
That he my soul to heaven would bring.
All they that pray and make accord
For me unto my God and Lord,
God place them in his Paradise,
Wherein no wretched caitiff lies.[48]

The verse derived from a thirteenth-century French translation from the Latin made by Petrus Alphonso, one-time physician to Henry I. The prince's choice of it illustrates the paradoxes of the chivalric state of mind. Almost the only obvious false note is at the start. By the end of his life, it is most unlikely that the prince had 'little thought on the hour of death'. Plague had made death horribly familiar to all; war had made it his own constant attendant; and sickness had for years past marked him as its imminent victim. Those who were earliest 'able most clearly to read it at sight' would have been impressed by its solemn intimation of mortality, its reminder that riches and 'nobleness', like beauty of body, were indeed ephemeral. It was these ideas that, in their reflective moments – and it is evident that the prince, like his cousin, Henry of Lancaster, thought seriously about life – could make lusty fighting men humble as well as aggressive. Much chivalric extravagance, whether in the reckless distribution of largesse or the fury with which they fought in the heat of battle, derived from a deep realization of how short a time a man had in which to be either generous or brave. The quite exceptional respect in which the prince was held, despite all his faults, suggests that for all his unregenerate haughtiness he was seen to represent more than did most of his peers the combination of courage and courtesy, pride and magnanimity, which chivalry was supposed to instil even though in practice it frequently failed to do so.

* * *

Immediately after the Black Prince's funeral, and as a last warning to Lancaster, the Good Parliament petitioned the king to allow 'the noble boy Richard' to appear before them 'so that the lords and commons of the realm might see and honour him as the very heir apparent'. On 25 June 1376, Richard was presented to Parliament by Archbishop Sudbury, who declared him 'the right image and very likeness' of the departed Black Prince. The point was obvious. Parliament was loyal to the warrior-king, to the warrior-prince, and to Richard, their one true heir. Lancaster was out in the cold. He was not even a member of the new royal Council that Parliament had set up.

That much achieved, the Good Parliament dispersed early in July. The shire knights gave a great banquet at Westminster for the other members of the Lords and Commons, Lancaster being the only notable absentee. Edward, from his sickroom in the palace of Eltham, genially courteous to the end, contributed two barrels of wine to the feast.

Though cited as a precedent for the later pretensions of the Commons to have the final word in matters of government, the Good Parliament's work was bodged, and soon undone. Their Council of Nine, set up to advise the king, could not stop Lancaster from also advising the king, or prevent the king taking that advice. Once Parliament was dissolved, its members, commoners and lords alike, dispersed to their estates in the country, thereby ceasing to influence the day-to-day conduct of business. Moreover, the Good Parliament had done nothing about the state of the country or its defence, and had not even voted the crown any money. Their line was simply that once the king was rescued from Latimer and his clique, his financial troubles were over. And since government was not Parliament's business anyway, all Lancaster now needed to do was to carry on as the effective head of government with the king's consent. And that consent was easy to obtain. Edward had only one wish left: to be as comfortable and unworried in his fuddled and lonely old age as possible. And that meant he wanted Alice. So, at the king's command, he said, Lancaster got Alice back. After all, the king's health had been much worsened by her removal from his side. And while Alice looked after Edward as he lay sick at Havering Bower over Michaelmas in 1376, Lancaster ordered his rival, Edmund Mortimer, earl of March, as Marshal, to leave the country to go and inspect the garrisons at Calais and Bordeaux. Objecting to thus being sent into exile, Mortimer resigned his post. Lancaster at once gained the support of Lord Henry Percy, the second most important member of the Council of Nine, by making him Marshal instead. Lancaster then had Latimer released and restored to his place, got the Lords to declare the Council of Nine dissolved and had Peter de la Mare put in prison. Next, he had Wykeham arraigned before a Great Council of the Lords at Westminster in October 1376, on charges parodying those made against Latimer. Wykeham was held personally responsible for the fact that, despite all the revenues and subsidies that had been collected, and despite, too, the ransoms received for King John, King David of Scotland and the duke of Burgundy, the Treasury was, by 1369, found to be empty. It was further alleged that he had released French hostages so as to curry favour with the papacy at Avignon and to get himself the see of Winchester. Like Latimer before him, he was charged with fiddling the treasury accounts to his own profit. Strongly defended by William Courtenay, bishop of London, and other clerics, Wykeham managed to come out of the affair with nothing more drastic than the confiscation of all his temporal wealth and with being ordered to leave London.

With the opposition thus silenced, Lancaster summoned a new parliament in January 1377, arranging this time that the Commons elected his own steward, Sir Thomas Hungerford, as the first official Speaker. The Commons were warned that Charles intended a seaborne invasion as soon as the existing truce expired in the coming June. Extra large sums of money were needed, and it was decided to introduce a poll tax: everybody over fourteen, irrespective of wealth, rank or sex, was to pay fourpence. Unpopular though he already was, Lancaster was now suddenly imposing taxation, hitherto levied only on the propertied classes, upon those with little or no property. It was a departure from custom typical of Lancaster's political insensitivity, for even before Parliament had been persuaded finally to approve the poll tax, he faced unmistakable evidence of the temper of a populace already deeply resentful to him.

Lancaster was in fact undone by his sponsorship of the turbulent John Wyclif, Master of Balliol and the leading exponent of an already well-established, though unofficial, theological doctrine which in effect exalted the authority of the state over that of the church. It denied to priests of any kind not only the special status usually ascribed to them in the medieval church but also the wealth and privileges which that status had enabled the more influential of them so conspicuously to acquire. In 1376 Wyclif had published a learned dissertation proposing that all church property be returned to its original secular owners and that all clerics be excluded from government office. Already favoured by government in the 1370s for his attacks on the power of the pope and the payment of taxes to the papacy, Wyclif was just the high-powered propagandist Lancaster needed to support his own campaign to get more taxes from the church and his feud against wealthy churchmen such as Wykeham. Accordingly, the bishops thought it time to call Wyclif to account for his attacks on his spiritual superiors. Archbishop Sudbury and Courtenay, bishop of London, summoned Wyclif to Convocation at St Paul's on 19 February 1377.

Lancaster might well have been turning his attention at this time to preparing the country's defences in readiness for what now seemed an inevitable resumption of the war by the French. Instead, with his usual shortsightedness, he chose to take up the cudgels (almost literally) on

Wyclif's behalf. He turned up at the hearing at St Paul's accompanied by Sir Henry Percy, his new Marshal, and a large body of armed retainers. His idea seems to have been not merely to frighten the bishops out of their attempt to silence Wyclif but also to rouse popular feelings against them. At almost any other time, in almost any circumstance, and under any less disliked a ruler, this could have been achieved with almost no trouble. Anti-clericalism was widespread, as may be observed in the passionate anger of Langland's *Piers Plowman* and the more worldly writing of Chaucer. Wyclif's own highly intellectual attacks on worldly churchmen and on the pomp, extravagance and elaborate rituals of the church were paralleled among the laity by the so-called Lollards, many of whom enjoyed the patronage of men of influence. Anti-clerical legislation had been frequent during Edward's reign, and the Good Parliament had attacked the alien papacy and its clerics as energetically as it had demanded the expulsion of Lombard, Jewish and Saracen bankers (who, they insisted, were all spies). The Commons pointed out that papal cardinals at Avignon held the offices of deans of York, Salisbury and Norwich and of archdeacon of Canterbury, drawing all the revenues and emoluments of these offices, but without ever once setting foot on English soil. Church property, the Commons said, should be diverted to the worship of God and to acts of charity and no longer be used to maintain a foreign (and pro-French) power like the papacy that took five times more from the country than the king's own revenues.

In supporting Wyclif, Lancaster ought, therefore, to have had wide popular support. But his arrival at St Paul's with what Londoners took to be some sort of heavy mob was interpreted as an attempt to destroy the cherished independence of the City and to do violence to Courtenay, who was popular in London. What was the Marshal of England doing in the City with an armed force? As his men shoved people around, first outside and then inside the cathedral, tempers flared. Courtenay himself was enraged and drew sharp words from Percy by informing him, 'You have no authority in my church.' When that altercation ended, another began. Lancaster and Percy demanded that Wyclif be allowed to sit during the proceedings. Courtenay replied by demanding of Lancaster whether he was a supporter of Wyclif's attacks on the church. Courtenay was a son of the earl of Devon, a direct descendant of Edward I, and a great lord in his own right, and exactly the sort of prelate Wyclif preached against; and Lancaster tried to make capital out of this. He accused Courtenay of relying on his noble birth in being thus argumentative and said, 'Your relatives will have enough to do to save their own skins.' Lancaster's words and manner greatly annoyed the crowd nearby. After all, Courtenay had been a friend of the Good Parliament; but Lancaster made matters worse by shouting, 'I will make you bend, you and all the rest of the bishops.' Courtenay retorted by declaring that any attempt by the Marshal or his men to arrest those in the crowd who were by now demonstrating their disapproval of Lancaster would be met by instant excommunication. Lancaster was then thought to have made some reference to dragging the bishop out of the cathedral by his hair; whereupon the crowd turned so ugly that, with Percy and Wyclif, he thought it wisest to push his way out of the cathedral.

London seethed. Next day, learning that Percy had put a London citizen into Newgate for uttering words hostile to Lancaster, numbers of his friends started a riot. They forcibly released the prisoner and then burst into Percy's house in Aldersgate. Not finding him at home they surged towards Lancaster's Savoy Palace. Neither Lancaster nor Percy was there either for, warned while dining on oysters with a rich Flemish wool merchant that the mob was looking for them, they had made their escape. They hurried to the river, Lancaster badly barking his shins in his haste, and taking a boat, took refuge with the Princess Joan of Kent and her son, Richard, at Kennington.

Courtenay hurried to the Savoy and calmed the mob by assuring them that Lancaster had not, as some believed, beheaded him. The demonstrations still went on. A too noisy critic of Peter de la Mare, hero of the Good Parliament, was beaten up and died of his injuries. Only the intervention of the mayor stopped the crowd strangling a Scottish knight, Sir Thomas Swinton, who tactlessly flaunted the badge of Lancaster in the street. Placards were displayed proclaiming that Lancaster was not the king's son and that his real father was a butcher in Ghent. The Princess Joan herself sent messengers to the Londoners, to beg them not to rage so furiously against Lancaster.

The City Fathers thought it best after all this to eat some politic humble pie. After all, their failure to restrain the London mob could well provide the excuse Lancaster wanted to put the independent-minded City under the control of the Marshal. A deputation waited upon the king at Sheen. For the moment he was a little better, thanks, it was said, to the use of 'restoratives and good meats and fresh broth' and 'sops of wheat bread' apparently steeped in goat's milk. Other food, it seems, 'he could neither eat nor taste'. Amiably mild, the king told the Londoners he did not want to limit their independence but recommended them to come to some accommodation with Lancaster. When they were next summoned to the king in early March he could hardly speak, communicating with them through the Chamberlain. The City aldermen agreed to dismiss the mayor for failing to quell the riots and to make a kind of penitent procession to offer a wax taper to the statue of the Virgin at St Paul's. The procession was boycotted by the populace. One thing gave Londoners pleasure: Sir Peter de la Mare was released from prison.

In May and June 1377 the Anglo-French peace negotiations at last petered out. Charles was still ready to leave the English with some territory; but on the issue of sovereignty he still refused to budge. And he wanted Calais back. The English representatives returned, so they said, to seek further instructions from their king. By the time they reached England he was dead. His improved health in March had lasted long enough to enable him to celebrate St George's Day on 23 April at Windsor. Here, his final act as head of his own family was to bestow knighthoods on Richard of Bordeaux and on Lancaster's son, Henry, thus simultaneously honouring his own successor as king and that successor's eventual supplanter, the future Henry IV. In the official sphere, Edward's last task was to come to the aid of his old friend William of Wykeham. Lancaster had assigned all the bishop's confiscated secular wealth to Prince Richard. Edward was persuaded, no doubt fairly easily, to restore Wykeham's properties to him on payment of a fine of 10,000 marks. Unkind chroniclers say Wykeham paid Alice Perrers to put in a good word for him as well. The contemporary view of her as a sharp financial operator is reflected by those who reported that the confiscation of Wykeham's temporalities in the first place was as much her idea as Lancaster's. For the allegation that she snatched the king's rings from his fingers, and made off with them the moment he was dead, there seems no corroborative evidence.

The ups and downs of Edward's physical condition in his last years, combined as they were with what seems to have been a strong disinclination to attend to anything of a mentally taxing nature, suggests a strong constitution broken, but until the end only intermittently, by a series of strokes. Whenever he felt better he was always capable of a little hunting or hawking. At the worst of times he seems to have been feeble but not irritable, maintaining the cheerful affability whose absence from their demeanour contributed so much to the less favourable impression made by the Black Prince and Lancaster. Nor could he be solemn to order. The story goes that the shocked clerics around his deathbed found it all but impossible to get him to attend to the appropriate rituals of confessing his sins and preparing his soul for the world to come. He insisted on talking about his hawks and his hounds instead. He thus made a less mawkish end than his eldest son, and it is tempting to say that he was the sort of man who enjoyed life and preferred to go into eternity with past pleasures still lively in his remembrance.

The Victorian biographer who described him as dying the bedridden slave of an infamous adventuress was over censorious. His loneliness in his latter years could have been enough in itself to explain the pleasure Edward took in the company of the spirited Alice Perrers. By 1377, Queen Philippa had been dead for almost ten years. Of their twelve children, only Lancaster, the most quarrelsome, and Edmund and Thomas, the least effectual, survived him, along with Isabella de Coucy, who herself died the following year. Almost all the companions of the time forty years before, when he had begun his adventures against the French were long since dead:

his cousin Henry of Lancaster (1361), and five of the six earls he had created, Montagu of Salisbury (1344), William de Clinton of Huntingdon (1354), Hugh Audley of Gloucester (1347), William de Bohun of Northampton (1360) and Robert Ufford of Suffolk (1369). Only Hugh Courtenay, earl of Devon survived, a rare fourteenth-century octogenarian. The old soldiers, Thomas Beauchamp, Manny and Arundel, and the newer generals, Chandos, the Captal de Buch and John Hastings, were also dead. Edward had outlasted six archbishops of Canterbury, five popes, and his two great adversaries, Philip and John of France. When he died at Sheen on 21 June 1377 he was not, however, wholly alone. Alice was certainly there, even though she made off at once, with or without his rings. The Princess Joan and her court were no great distance away at Kennington, Edmund and Thomas were both at hand, as was his son-in-law, de Montfort. All of these accompanied his funeral procession from Sheen to Westminster where, as she had requested on her deathbed, he was buried next to Queen Philippa. Across the Channel, Charles V ordered a Requiem Mass. Also attendant on him in death on the south side of his tomb are memorials of the Black Prince, Joan of the Tower, Lionel, Edmund, Mary of Brittany, and the infant William of Hatfield. The figures on the north side, of John of Lancaster, Blanche of the Tower, Margaret of Pembroke and Thomas, have gone. His great sword stands by the Coronation Chair in the Abbey, a reminder of his great height of six feet, so unusual in those times.

There is indeed appropriateness in the well-known contrast between the effigy of the king that surmounts this tomb and the funeral effigy displayed in the museum. The latter, taken to be from a death mask, shows a mouth slackened by age or perhaps twisted by a stroke. The stylized king, less haughtily aggressive than the representation of the Black Prince at Canterbury, has a long face and a long straight nose. He has the carefully flowing mane and beard of a man grand and majestic, a venerable sage whose character has been shaped and annealed by the ordeal of battles fought and won. And so, on the one level, Edward died a foolish, fond old man, unable to take serious things seriously. The death mask may hint at this; the formal tomb asserts, correctly, that this was the lesser part of the story. The accident of his longevity led to an underestimation of his significance. Fifty years after his death, Lancaster's grandson, Henry V, achieved a success in France that paralleled Edward's; but he died at thirty-five, the age at which Edward became the victor at Crécy. Had Edward died as soon after Crécy as Henry V died after Agincourt he would have been spared the long shadows cast over his fame by the disasters of his final decade and the submergence of his personality by the dominating Alice and the ill-tempered Lancaster. And Henry V could hardly have become an English hero had he not had the precedent of Edward III to act upon. To a greater extent and for a longer period than any other English monarch during the medieval period and beyond it, Edward united the ranks of the aristocracy in a common loyalty to the crown. This willing loyalty on the part of the great men of his time was achieved without the force and the fear that were the stock-in-trade of William I. He was not their scourge, as Henry II and Edward I had so often been. And, as bringer of victory and the spoils of war, he fulfilled more nearly than any other what had been, since earliest times, the role that men expected their king to fulfil. He had done so, however, as much by the chivalrous generosity of his character as by his employment of the military arts. It is hard to find a parallel to the long-lasting abstention from envy and self-seeking that marked the leading men of Edward's reign. The hostility of Menstreworth towards Knollys is virtually the only example of its kind until the feuding between the followers of Latimer and those of Wykeham, and between the Mortimer and Lancaster connections, that set off the tumults of 1376–7 as Edward neared death. The capacity to lead men as inherently self-assertive and combative as the aristocracy of any medieval kingdom, to give them unity of purpose and keep that unity even during the years of frustration that followed Brétigny, argues that Edward had exceptional qualities. His extravagance and his hearty geniality were prescribed chivalric virtues; but few chivalric figures displayed them in so civilized a fashion and few succeeded as well as Edward in extending the chivalric courtesies to include men of less than aristocratic rank without detracting from his dignity.

His military campaigns did more than provide congenial employment for a belligerent and potentially contumacious nobility. If by the end of the reign the chivalric modes were already wearing thin, that was perhaps because after all it was not the panoplied tearaways in knightly armour who had played the decisive role at Crécy, Poitiers and Nájera. That had been the work of the archers, men of the common sort wielding the longbow, a weapon originating in the countryside and, as a weapon of war, copied from the Welsh. Edward united the aristocracy for almost all his long life; but the decisive contribution of common men to his and his eldest son's victories gave a new confidence to men of low degree who, ever since William's Normans came, had played only a passive role in England's affairs. Their share in the glory, though not much celebrated by the lordly ones who commanded them, made it that much easier to look on what had happened as essentially great English victories. Since 1066 the aristocracy in England had been more French than English. The wars fought since that date had been to a large extent private wars between one group of international aristocrats, based for the most part in England, Normandy and Gascony, and another group of aristocrats, scarcely distinguishable from them in race, culture or customs but loyal to the king of France. Scores of them were vassals of England in respect of some of their lands and of France in respect of others. But the bowmen of England were wholly English and, because of their victories, proud of it. And Edward and the

Black Prince were so much better than the French as commanders that both common men and those of the knightly class experienced the same sense of elation at serving an English sovereign and his son instead of failures like Philip and John, or an unknightly king like Charles who forbade pitched battles like a coward and conducted his campaigns like a lawyer.

Two small pieces of evidence seem to symbolize the difference Edward's years as king had wrought. The inscription on his tomb read *Pugna Pro Patria*. It was perhaps the first time since the Saxons had marched south to defeat at the hands of William of Normandy that the subjects of England's king had been told they had a fatherland to fight for, or even a king who regarded England as his fatherland. It would be the grossest exaggeration to say that Edward had 'made a nation'. But he had brought the ingredients of nationhood together and fired men's ideas with the idea of the nation. For this reason it is possible to suggest that in the long run Edward's real success as a king was not military but political.

The second hint comes from the evidence that there was a Frenchman who thought as much at the time. Ever since he had ceased to be one of John's hostages in London and become the husband of Edward's daughter Isabella, Enguerrand de Coucy had a double allegiance to the kings of England and of France that had hitherto been by no means unusual. He was Edward's son-in-law, earl of Bedford and a member of the Garter. But he was also one of the greatest of French lords. With the resumption of war after Edward died, he renounced his English allegiance, returned his English lands and parted from his royal English wife. It was more than a gesture. It expressed the shrewd judgment of a seasoned soldier and diplomatist that his bread would be better buttered on its French side than its English side. But such men had not previously thought it necessary so formally and publicly to choose, and with such finality, whether to be French or English, or thought that loyalty to one sovereign lord and king was incompatible with loyalty to another.

The final measure of Edward's contribution as a king is the contrasting failure of the incompetent Lancaster. Edward, true, had run both Wykeham and, in the first instance, Latimer; but Lancaster stirred up the faction fight between Wykeham and Latimer. Edward had let Alice run him; but Lancaster used Alice as a political pawn. Edward had quarrelled with popes. But Lancaster had quarrelled so vulgarly with English bishops that he had turned the London citizenry into rampaging defenders of their bishop at a time when only by the exercise of the most conspicuous stupidity could anybody persuade ordinary people to say a good word for clerics of any sort. After all, poor Sudbury, who had been at Courtenay's side when Lancaster insulted him in St Paul's, was dragged to a brutal death by another London mob only four years later.

Whereas Edward had found proud employment for England's common men, Lancaster, supreme during the first years of Richard II's reign, gave them, and more than once, the poll tax, and left the inhabitants of southern England a prey to plundering raids by Frenchmen and Spaniards. Their fury boiled up into the so-called Peasants' Revolt of 1381, of which Sudbury was the most distinguished victim. But for the courage of the young Richard at a critical moment there would indeed have been a bloodbath. Yet, if Edward had not done what he had in the years of his prime to make men of lesser degree proud of their country, they might not have had the courage to protest as violently as they did in 1381 against misgovernment at home, disaster abroad and against the galling contrast between the gaudy extravagances of the chivalric classes and the relative poverty of the humbler sort of men. There was a lot more to the making of a nation than inspiring patriotism among the rich. Most certainly without realizing it, Edward had added something new to the political mix: a new spirit of self-respect among men whose status had hitherto required them to be altogether mute about the shortcomings of those who had lordship over them. The rebels of 1381 were, naturally, duly hanged. But afterwards, in times of crisis, the clamorous voices of the yeomen, craftsmen and shopkeepers of the land would be heard again, as they had not been heard before. In Edward's reign, some of them had at last begun to feel themselves members, like their betters, of a proud and victorious nation.

NOTES

1 Aquitaine, Gascony and Guyenne were for practical purposes synonymous terms.
2 Maurice Druon, *The She-Wolf of France*, London, 1960, pp. 55,59,159,275.
3 The affair of Isabella and Mortimer is well described, in the light of the known facts, by Margaret Campbell Barnes in *Isabel the Fair*, London, 1957.
4 'Scituri, quod si (quod absit) propter absentiam vestram dicta negotia contigerit retardari; ad vos, prout convenit, graviter capiemus.'
5 John Uttley, *The Story of the Channel Islands*, London, 1966, pp. 64–5.
6 T. Wright, *Political Poems and Songs*, I, Rolls Series, 1859, p. 72.
7 In different accounts the place is variously named as Berwick, York, or even Warwick. But Newcastle is the last known location of Edward.
8 *Chronique de Jean le Bel*, ed. J. Viard and E. Déprez, 2 vols, Paris, 1904–5; vol. II, J. Viard's introduction.
9 *Oeuvres de Froissart*, ed. Kervyn de Lettenhove, 25 vols, Brussels, 1867–77.
10 Le Bel, I, p. 284n. But see Barnes, *The History of King Edward III*, Cambridge, 1688, p. 251, who says it was on the Tweed near Berwick.
11 G. F. Beltz, *Memorials of the Order of the Garter*, London, 1841, p. xlv; Barnes, *Edward III*, p. 251.
12 Le Bel, II, p.2.
13 Margaret Galway, 'Joan of Kent and the Order of the Garter', *University of Birmingham Historical Journal*, I (1947–8), pp.13–50.
14 The earl's mother, the dowager Lady Elizabeth Montagu, can safely be excluded. She had long since been remarried to Sir Thomas Furnivall, and she had never been a countess. Excluded also is Alice de Lacy, scandalous wife of Thomas of Lancaster, and personal heiress to the earldoms of Lincoln and Salisbury. In 1341 they were both too old.
15 She was found to be 'under age' at Easter 1344 (*Year Books, Edward. III*, XVIII, p.4). In March 1345 Edward Montagu was excused £50 due to the king on her inheritance, apparently on her coming of age (G. E. Cockayne, *Complete Peerage*).
16 *Cal. Patent Rolls*, 1330–4, p. 402.
17 *Cal. Close Rolls*, 1349–54, p. 411.
18 Le Bel, II, p. 2.
19 Ibid., p. 26.
20 Ibid., pp. 30–4.
21 '*Comment le roy Edowart forfist grandement quand il efforcha la comtesse de Salbry.*'
22 *Chronique Normande du XIVème Siècle*, ed. Molinier, Société de l'Histoire le France, 1882, pp. 54, 59; *Chronographia Regum Francorum*, ed. H.

Moranville, Société de l'Histoire de France, 1891–7. pp. 197, 204–5; *Istoire et Croniques de Flanders*, ed. Kervyn de Lettenhove, Brussels, 1879–80, II, pp. 6, 9.

23 He was afterwards known as lord of Bungay (Cockayne, *Complete Peerage*).

24 See p. 174 below and Appendix, pp. 175–8, for Edward Montagu's later history.

25 'Though this is by no means certain' (Kenneth Fowler, *The King's Lieutenant*, London, 1969, p. 160).

26 Thomas Okey, *Avignon*, London, 1911, pp. 140–53.

27 Adam Murimuth, *Continuatio Chronicorum*, quoted in W. H. St John Hope, *Windsor Castle*, I, p. 112.

28 Edith Rickert, *Chaucer's World*, London, 1948, p. 208.

29 Maltravers afterwards returned to England, where his pardon was confirmed on the grounds that he had been condemned unheard. He was employed on several duties in the Low Countries, and in 1351 became Governor of the Channel Islands where he refounded the hospital of Bowes in St Peter Port, Guernsey. He died in 1365.

30 *Le Livre de Seyntz Medicines*, ed. E. J. Arnould, Anglo-Norman Text Society, Oxford, 1940, II, p. 72: 'This book was begun and finished in the year of our Lord Jesus Christ 1354. And it was made by a poor miserable sinner called Henry Duc de Lancastre. May God pardon his sins.'

31 By contrast, Chaucer, who somehow managed to get taken prisoner during the triumphant 1359 campaign, was redeemed for only £10.

32 Joan had no children by William Montagu in their eight years of marriage, though she had seven in all by her two subsequent husbands, the eldest, Thomas Holland, being born within a year of her divorce. Elizabeth Mohun was no more than seven when Montagu married her. Their only son, William, was killed tilting with his father at Windsor in 1382.

33 General Zeitzer, *The Fatal Decisions*, ed. W. Richardson and S. Freidin, London, 1956, p. 190.

34 Lance – a mounted knight with his necessary attendants. A section of about half a dozen men.

35 Knighton says, 'There fell one esquire before the fight, and three knights in battle. God Almighty preserved the rest.' Quoted Barnes *Edward III*, p. 357.

36 *de pennes*. Froissart means, 'or furred as soft as feathers'.

37 T. Wright, *Political Poems and Songs*, I.

38 Several officers afterwards received general pardons as rewards for valour, 'by testimony of Edward de Monte Acuto' (*Cal. Patent Rolls*, 4 September 1346, at Calais).

39 Barnes, *Edward III*, p. 377, locates him in garrison at Roxburgh in September or October 1346.

40 See John Arderne, *Treatises of Fistula*, etc., ed. for the Early English Text Society from a fifteenth-century translation by Sir D'Arcy Power, Kegan Paul, London, 1910; *De Arte Phisicali et de Ciruria of Master John Arderne* (1412), trans. and ed. by Sir D'Arcy Power, London, 1922; Sir D'Arcy Power, 'A System of Surgery, by Master John Arderne' *British Journal of Surgery*, vol. XV no. 57 July 1927; and G. G. Coulton, *Social Life in Britain from the Conquest to the Reformation*, Cambridge, 5th edn., 1956, pp. 496–501, 526.

41 Both Robert of Avesbury and Froissart give full and mainly consistent accounts of this action.

42 G. H. Moberley, *Life of William of Wykeham*, London, 1887, pp. 5–25.

43 Hastings Rashdall, *The Universities of Europe in the Middle Ages*, London,

1936, II, pp. 96–102; Barnes, *Edward III*, pp. 475–7. Cambridge too was to suffer severely in its turn during the peasant risings of 1381.

44 Lines written by James Graham, marquis of Montrose, on the night before his execution in 1650.

45 Presumably the Oriflamme was captured, for we hear no more of it.

46 Not to be confused with Meulan, also a Navarrese stronghold, a similar distance to the north-west.

47 Robert de Vere, earl of Oxford, had died at Rheims in January.

48 A version done in English by John Weever, in *Ancient Funerall Monuments*, 1631.

BIBLIOGRAPHY

OFFICIAL SOURCES

Calendars of Close Rolls, Edward III, HMSO, London, 1892–1927.
Calendars of Fine Rolls, Edward III, HMSO, London, 1912–29.
Calendars of Inquisitions Post Mortem, Edward III, HMSO, London, 1908–52.
Calendars of Papal Letters, ed. W. H. Bliss and C. Johnson, HMSO, London, 1895–7.
Calendars of Patent Rolls, Edward III, HMSO, London, 1894–1916.
Foedara, etc., *Acta Publica*, etc., ed. T. Rymer, 20 vols, London, 1704–35; new edition, to 1383, ed. Clarke, Caley and Holbrooke, 4 vols, Record Commission, London, 1916–69.
Rotuli Parliamentorum, Index, Records Commission, London, 1832.
Select Documents of English Constitutional History, 1307–1485, ed. S. B. Chrimes and A. L. Brown, London, 1961.
Year Books, Edward III, ed. A. J. Horwood and L. O. Pike, Rolls Series, 1883–1911.

CHRONICLES

AVESBURY, ROBERT OF, *De Gestis Mirabilis Regis Edwardi Tertii*, ed. E. M. Thompson, Rolls Series, 1889.
BAKER, GEOFFREY LE, *Chronicon*, ed. E. M. Thompson, Oxford, 1889.
BEL, JEAN LE: *Chronique de Jean le Bel*, ed. J. Viard and E. Déprez, 2 vols, Société de l'Histoire de France, Paris, 1904–5.
Chronique Normande du XIVème Siècle, ed. Molinier, Société de l'Histoire de France, 1882.
Chronographia Regum Francorum, ed. H. Moranville, Société de l'Histoire de France, 1891–7.
FROISSART, JEAN: *Oeuvres de Froissart*, ed. Kervyn de Lettenhove, 25 vols, Brussels, 1867–77.
—— *The Chronicles of Froissart*, trans. John Bourchier, Lord Berners (1523–5), ed. W. P. Ker, 6 vols, London, 1901–3.
HIGDEN, RANULPH, *Polychronicon*, VIII, ed. J. R. Lumby, Rolls Series, 1882.
Istoire et Croniques de Flandres, ed. Kervyn de Lettenhove, Brussels, 1879–80.
KNIGHTON, HENRY, *Chronicon*, ed. J. R. Lumby, 2 vols, Rolls Series, 1889–95.
MURIMUTH, ADAM, *Continuatio Chronicorum*, ed. E. M. Thompson, Rolls Series, 1889.
WALSINGHAM, THOMAS, *Historia Anglicana*, ed. H. Riley, 2 vols, Rolls Series, 1863–4.

OTHER CONTEMPORARY WRITINGS

ARDERNE, JOHN, *Treatise on the Fistula* (1376), ed. Sir D'Arcy Power, Early
English Text Society, London, 1910.
LANCASTER, HENRY DUKE OF, *Le Livre de Seyntz Medicines* (1354), ed. E. J.
Arnould, 2 vols, Anglo-Norman Text Society, Oxford, 1940.

BIOGRAPHIES

King Edward III
BARNES, JOSHUA, *The History of King Edward III*, Cambridge, 1688.
LONGMAN, WILLIAM, *Life and Times of Edward the Third*, 2 vols, London, 1869.
MACKINNON, JAMES, *History of Edward III*, London, 1900; reprinted Ipswich,
1974.

King Edward II
HUTCHINSON, HAROLD F., *Edward II*, London, 1971.

Queen Isabella
BARNES, MARGARET CAMPBELL, *Isabel the Fair*, London, 1957.
DRUON, MAURICE, *The She-Wolf of France*, London, 1960.
JOHNSTONE, HILDA, 'Isabella, the She-Wolf of France', *History*, new series, XXI,
December 1936, p. 208.

The Black Prince
DUNN-PATTISON, R. P., *The Black Prince*, London, 1910.
HARVEY, JOHN, *The Black Prince and His Age*, London, 1976.

Others
CHUTE, MARCHETTE, *Geoffrey Chaucer of England*, New York, 1946.
DAVIS, I. M., *The Black Douglas*, London, 1974.
DOBSON, SUSANNA, *The Life of Petrarch*, 2 vols, London, 1803.
FOWLER, KENNETH, *The King's Lieutenant, Henry of Grosmont, First Duke of
Lancaster*, London, 1969.
HARVEY, JOHN, *Henry Yevele*, London, 1944.

GENERAL POLITICAL WORKS

GREEN, V. H. H., *The Later Plantagenets*, London, 1955.
HARVEY, JOHN, *The Plantagenets*, London, 1948.
MCKISACK, MAY, *The Fourteenth Century*, Oxford, 1959.
MYERS, A. R., *England in the Later Middle Ages* (Pelican History, vol. 4), London,
1952.
RAMSAY, Sir J. H., *The Genesis of Lancaster, or the Reigns of Edward II, Edward
III and Richard II*, 2 vols, Oxford, 1913.
RENOUARD, YVES (ed.), *Bordeaux sous les rois d'Angleterre*, Bordeaux, 1965.
VICKERS, KENNETH H., *England in the Later Middle Ages*, London, 1930.

BROADER SURVEYS

BRYANT, ARTHUR, *The Age of Chivalry*, London, 1963.
CLARKE, MAUDE V., *Fourteenth Century Studies*, ed. L. S. Sutherland and M.
McKisack, Oxford, 1937.

COULTON, G. G., *Mediaeval Panorama*, 2 vols, London, 1938.
———, *The Mediaeval Scene*, Cambridge, 1930.
———, *Social Life in Britain*, Cambridge, 1956 edn.
DAVIS, H. W. C. (ed.), *Mediaeval England*, Oxford, 1924.
DEFOURNEAUX, MARCELIN, *Le Vie quotidienne au temps de Jeanne d'Arc*, Paris, 1952. de la Roncière, Contamine, Delort (eds), *L'Europe au moyen age*, vol. III in Série Histoire Médiévale, Collection University of Paris, 1971.
EVANS, JOAN, *Life in Mediaeval France*, London, 1957 edn.
FOSS, MICHAEL, *Chivalry*, London, 1975.
HARVEY, JOHN, *Gothic England*, London, 1947.
HUIZINGA, JOHN, *The Waning of the Middle Ages*, London, 1924.
JUSSERAND, J. J., *English Wayfaring Life in the Middle Ages*, trans. Lucy T. Smith, New York, 1925.
POOLE, A. LANE (ed.), *Medieval England*, 2 vols, Oxford, 1958.
POWER, EILEEN, *Mediaeval People*, London, 1924 (reprinted).

WARFARE

BLAIR, CLAUDE, *European Armour*, London, 1958.
BURNE, LT-COL ALFRED H., *The Crécy War*, London, 1955.
HARGREAVES, REGINALD, *The Narrow Seas*, London, 1959.
OAKESHOTT, R. EWART, *The Archaeology of Weapons*, London, 1960.
PERROY, EDOUARD, *The Hundred Years War*, London, 1959.
WILLIAMSON, J. A., *The English Channel*, London, 1959.
ZEITZLER, GENERAL, *The Fatal Decisions*, ed. W. Richardson and S. Freidin, London, 1956.

PARTICULAR TOPICS

BELTZ, G. F., *Memorials of the Order of the Garter*, London, 1841.
BENNETT, H. S., *Life on the English Manor, 1150–1400*, Cambridge, 1960 edn.
CHAMBERS, E. K., *The Mediaeval Stage*, 2 vols, Oxford, 1963.
COCKAYNE, G. E., *The Complete Peerage*, 13 vols, London, 1910–59.
COULTON, G. G., *Chaucer and His England*, London, 1952 edn.
DIXON, W. HEPWORTH, *Her Majesty's Tower*, I, London, 1869.
DUGDALE, Sir WILLIAM, *Summons to Parliament and Great Councils from 1264 A.D.*, London, 1685.
EVANS, JOAN, *English Art, 1307–1461*, Oxford, 1949.
——— (ed.), *The Flowering of the Middle Ages*, London, 1966.
GALWAY, MARGARET, 'Joan of Kent and the Order of the Garter', *University of Birmingham Historical Journal*, I (1947–8), pp. 13–50.
HOLMES, G. A., *The Estates of the Higher Nobility in Fourteenth Century England*, Cambridge, 1957.
HOLMYARD, E. J., *Alchemy*, London, 1957.
HOPE, W. H. ST JOHN, *Windsor Castle*, 2 vols, London, 1913.
HOUSTON, MARY G., *Mediaeval Costume in England and France*, London, 1939.
KEEN, MAURICE, *The Outlaws of Medieval England*, London, 1961.
LLOYD, NATHANIEL, *A History of the English House*, London, 1931.
NATANSON, JOSEPH, *Gothic Ivories*, London, 1951.
NICHOLS, J., *The History and Antiquities of Leicester*, 4 vols, London, 1795–1811.
OKEY, THOMAS, *Avignon*, London, 1911.
OWST, G. R., *Literature and Pulpit in Mediaeval England*, Oxford, 1961 edn.

RASHDALL, HASTINGS, *The Universities of Europe in the Middle Ages*, 3 vols, London (OUP), 1936 edn.

RICKERT, EDITH, *Chaucer's World*, London (OUP), 1948.

RICKERT, MARGARET, *Painting in Britain: The Middle Ages*, London, 1954.

SALZMAN, L. F., *English Industries in the Middle Ages*, Oxford, 1923 edn.

STANLEY, DEAN A. P., *Historical Memorials of Westminster Abbey*, London, 1882.

STONE, LAWRENCE, *Sculpture in Britain: The Middle Ages*, London, 1955.

TOMLINSON, AMANDA, *The Medieval Face*, National Portrait Gallery, London, 1974.

Transactions of the Leicestershire Archaeological Society, 1925.

UTTLEY, JOHN, *The story of the Channel Islands*, London, 1966.

WAGNER, ANTHONY RICHARD, *Heralds and Heraldry in the Middle Ages*, Oxford, 1956 edn.

WRIGHT, T. (ed.), *Political Poems and Songs*, I, Rolls Series, 1859.

INDEX

Entries in italics refer to genealogical tables